D1601620

SUPREME COURT STATECRAFT
The Rule of Law *and* Men

Supreme Court Statecraft

The Rule of Law *and* Men

by WALLACE MENDELSON

The Iowa State University Press / A M E S

The following publishers have generously given permission to reprint the following articles from copyrighted works.

Vanderbilt Law Review: "The Influence of James B. Thayer upon the Work of Holmes, Brandeis, and Frankfurter," 31:71–87, © 1978; "The First Amendment and the Judicial Process: A Reply to Mr. Frantz," 17:479–85, © 1964; "A Missing Link in the Evolution of Due Process," 10:125–35, © 1956

Harvard Law Review Association: "Judge Learned Land," 76 *Harv. Law Rev.* 322–35, © 1962

The Academy of Political Science: "Hugo Black and Judicial Discretion," 85 *Polit. Sci. Q.* 17–39, © 1970

The Journal of Politics: "Mr. Justice Douglas and Government by the Judiciary," 38:918–37, © 1976; "A Response to Professor Goldman," 39:159–65, © 1977; "A Note on the Cause and Cure of the Fourteenth Amendment," 43:152–58, © 1981; "The Untroubled World of Jurimetrics," 26:914–22, © 1964; "An Open Letter to Professor Spaeth on Jurimetrics," 28:429–32, © 1966; "Law and the Development of Nations," 32:223–38, © 1970

University of Pennsylvania Law Review and Fred B. Rothman & Co.: "The Judge's Art," 109 *Univ. Pa. Law Rev.* 524–38, © 1961

Michigan Law Review: "Clandestine Speech and the First Amendment — A Reappraisal of the Dennis Case," 51:553–59, © 1953

California Law Review, Inc., and Fred B. Rothman & Co.: "On the Meaning of the First Amendment: Absolutes in the Balance," 50 *Calif. Law Rev.* 821–28 (1962), © 1978 California Law Review, Inc.

The University of Chicago Law Review: Mr. Justice Black, the Supreme Court, and the Bill of Rights, 28:583–85, © 1961; Jefferson on Judicial Review: Consistency through Change, 29:327–37, © 1962

Virginia Law Review and Fred B. Rothman & Co.: Foreign Reactions to American Experience with "Due Process of Law," 41:493–503, © 1955

American Political Science Association: Democracy and the Divine Right of Judges — A Review of E. Rostow, The Sovereign Prerogative (1962), 57 *Am. Polit. Sci. Rev.* 161–62, © 1963; The Neo-Behavioral Approach to the Judicial Process: A Critique, 57 *Am. Polit. Sci. Rev.* 593–603, © 1963

Texas Law Review: Professor Cahn on Jefferson, Commager, and Learned Hand, published originally in 37 *Tex. Law Rev.* 721–24, copyright © 1959 by *Tex. Law Rev.*

Emory Law Journal, Emory School of Law, Atlanta, GA 30322: The Politics of Judicial Activism, 24:43–66, © 1975

Minnesota Law Review: Dred Scott's Case — Reconsidered, 38:16–28, © 1953

The Yale Law Journal Co. and Fred B. Rothman & Co.: New Light on *Fletcher* v. *Peck* and *Gibbons* v. *Ogden,* reprinted from 58 *Yale Law J.* 567–73, © 1949

University of Missouri: ERA, the Supreme Court, and Allegations of Gender Bias, 44 *Mo. Law Rev.* 1–10, © 1979, for one edition

Notre Dame Law Review: The Iron Ring of Discrimination, 37 *Notre Dame Lawyer* 344–45, © 1962

Trustees of Indiana University and Fred B. Rothman & Co.: Separation, Politics, and Judicial Activism, 52 *Indiana Law J.* 313–22, © 1977

Was Chief Justice Marshall an Activist? reprinted by permission of the publisher, from *Supreme Court Activism and Restraint,* edited by Stephen C. Halpern and Charles M. Lamb, pp. 57–76 (Lexington, Mass.: Lexington Books, D. C. Heath and Co., © 1982, D. C. Heath and Co.), in English only, for one edition

© 1985 The Iowa State University Press. All rights reserved
Printed by The Iowa State University Press, Ames, Iowa 50010

First edition, 1985

Library of Congress Cataloging in Publication Data

Mendelson, Wallace.
    Supreme Court statecraft.

    Includes index.
    1. United States — Constitutional law. 2. United States. Supreme Court. I. Title.
KF4550.M37   1985   342.73   85–2489
ISBN 0–8138–1047–7   347.302

DEDICATION

M

In the endless flow of time and space
We shared a moment or two of grace.

CONTENTS

INTRODUCTION

IN a daring confrontation with his monarch, Chief Justice Coke repudiated government under man in favor of government under law. *Non sub homine sed sub Deo et lege.* Eventually the Rule of Law—a precept at least as old as the works of Aristotle—became a prime principle in the Anglo-American way of life. Legal rules, however, are not self-executing, and judges too are terrigenous creatures. If most of them are more law-abiding than were kings, perhaps that is because the appellate process achieves what it is supposed to achieve. But what of those at the judicial summit whose decisions are not subject to appellate review? As Mr. Justice Jackson put it, "We are not final because we are infallible, but we are infallible because we are final."

There are difficulties also in the law itself. Even the most gifted law-makers cannot foresee and provide explicitly for all the combinations of circumstance or all the vagaries and varieties of human conduct. Our Constitution does not escape this problem. It comes to us out of the eighteenth century—the work of men too wise to think they could prescribe the details of policy for an "undefined and expanding future." They were not in complete accord on vital issues, just as we are not. So for the most part they, like the amenders, wrote not only in generalities, but sometimes with calculated ambiguity. Their forte was the open-ended hint. In many contexts, then, even our highest law leaves room for, and so invites, government by judges—especially by those who (somewhat like kings) are free not only of appellate review, but of elections as well—and hold office for life.

In this imperfect legal setting we expect judges to clear their endless dockets, uphold the Rule of Law, and yet not utterly disregard our need for the discretionary justice of Plato's philosopher king. Judges must be sometimes cautious and sometimes bold. Judges must respect both the traditions of the past and the convenience of the present. Judges must reconcile liberty and authority; the whole and its parts; the letter and the spirit. It follows, as Felix Frankfurter observed, "Constitutional law . . . is not at all a science, but applied politics, using the word in its noble sense." While each of the following essays explores one or more of the abiding problems of American constitutional law, collectively they may be found to support Frankfurter's observation.

The problem may be put in the form of a fable. Far away in a great ocean there is an island untouched by modern civilization. Its government is simple. When community problems cannot be solved informally, high priests consult the skull of the tribal founding father. There they find answers for all issues. If this seems crude, it works. For consciously or otherwise, what the priests "find" in the skull they extrapolate from the deeply held values of their society. The priesthood is not representative and responsible in any modern political sense. Indeed it might well be called autocratic, though its only force is the force of a myth. Yet its power is great, because in a long view its pronouncements reflect more than whim or merely private preference. The symbolic skull satisfies the humanly urgent need for stable authority based on some extraordinary sanction, while the priests accommodate the inevitable need for change without loss of continuity.

The myth of the skull no doubt will live as long as the priests read with reasonable accuracy, and respect, the true values of their society. When they do that, the "consent of the governed" prevails. The ruled in fact rule. If the priests held stubbornly to outworn traditions, or widely unwanted "progress," they would soon be in trouble. The myth would lose its force. The governed would come to see they were being ruled not by something transcendent, but by mere men. This, Plato suggested, humanity cannot long abide. Hence the need for "noble fiction" in government — even in its judicial branches.

I

The Judge's Art

1 ✣ The Influence of James B. Thayer upon the Work of Holmes, Brandeis, and Frankfurter

James Bradley Thayer was one of the major figures in American constitutional law if only because of his influence upon Holmes, Brandeis, and Frankfurter (to say nothing of Learned and Augustus Hand). Now almost forgotten, Thayer, along with Christopher Columbus Langdell, John Chipman Gray, and James Barr Ames, was one of the giants at the Harvard Law School during its "golden age" at the close of the nineteenth century.[1] His legal career began only after serious flirtation with divinity and the Greek and Latin classics.[2] That his interest in such matters was never suppressed entirely is evident in his *A Western Journey with Mr. Emerson* (1884).[3] Yet Thayer was not a cloistered scholar. Graduated from Harvard Law School in 1856, he became a leading practitioner at the Boston bar before becoming Royall Professor of Law at Harvard in 1874, having previously turned down a Harvard professorship in English. His tongue and pen, moreover, were always ready to promote such "good causes" as tariff reform, better treatment of Indians, and reform in the granting of corporate charters.[4] His great study, *A Preliminary Treatise on Evidence at the Common Law*, published in 1898, led in due course to Wigmore's masterpiece—Wigmore having been one of his students. Thayer also compiled the first casebook on American constitutional law, *Cases on Constitutional Law*, in 1895. Apart from his technical work, he is now known—by the few who remember—for his insistence upon judicial respect for the political branches of government. In his classic essay, "The Origin and Scope of the American Doctrine of Constitutional Law,"[5] he in-

---

1. *See* THE HARVARD LAW SCHOOL 1817-1917, at 30-33 (1917); Beale, *Langdell, Gray, Thayer and Ames—Their Contribution to the Study and Teaching of Law*, 8 N.Y.U. L.Q. REV. 385, 390 (1931); *James Bradley Thayer*, 15 HARV. L. REV. 599 (1902); *The Late James Bradley Thayer*, 36 AM. L. REV. 248 (1902).
2. *See* Hall, *James Bradley Thayer*, in 8 GREAT AMERICAN LAWYERS 345, 347, 350, 373-75 (W. Lewis ed. 1909).
3. The volume is the chronicle of Thayer's journey with the aged essayist Ralph Waldo Emerson, his wife's cousin.
4. *See* Hall, *supra* note 2, at 379.
5. Thayer, *The Origin and Scope of the American Doctrine of Constitutional Law*, 7 HARV. L. REV. 129 (1893).

sisted that judicial review is strictly judicial and thus quite different from the policy-making functions of the executive and legislative branches. In performing their duties, he said, judges must take care not to intrude upon the domain of the other branches of government. Full and free play must be permitted to "that wide margin of considerations which address themselves only to the practical judgment of a legislative body."[6] Thus for Thayer, legislation could be held unconstitutional only "when those who have the right to make laws have not merely made a mistake, but have made a very clear one,—so clear that it is not open to rational question."[7] Above all, Thayer believed, the Constitution, as Chief Justice Marshall had observed, is not a tightly drawn legal document like a title deed to be technically construed; it is rather a matter of "great outlines" broadly drawn for an unknowable future.[8] Often men of reason may differ about its meaning and application; in short, the written Constitution offers a wide range for legislative discretion and choice. The judicial veto, then, is to be exercised *only in cases that leave no room for reasonable doubt.*

> This rule recognizes that, having regard to the great, complex everunfolding exigencies of government, much which will seem unconstitutional to one man, or body of men, may reasonably not seem so to another; that the constitution often admits of different interpretations; that there is often a range of choice and judgment; that in such cases the constitution does not impose upon the legislature any one specific opinion, but leaves open this range of choice; and that whatever choice is rational is constitutional.[9]

---

6.   *Id.* at 135.
7.   *Id.* at 144.
8.   McCulloch v. Maryland, 17 U.S. (4 Wheat.) 315, 407 (1819).
9.   Thayer, *supra* note 5, at 144. When such a "range of choice and judgment" is available to the legislature, the choice is, in Thayer's view, "a part of that mass of legislative functions which belong to it and not to the court." Thayer, *Contitutionality of Legislation: The Precise Question for a Court,* 38 THE NATION 314, 314-15 (1884). Thayer did not extend the same deference to the exercise of state legislative power vis-à-vis congressional authority:

> [w]hen [in this context] the question is whether State action be or be not conformable to the paramount constitution, the supreme law of the land, we have a different matter in hand. Fundamentally, it involves the allotment of power between the two governments,—where the line is to be drawn. True, the judiciary is still debating whether a legislature has transgressed its limit; but the departments are not co-ordinate, and the limit is at a different point. The judiciary now speaks as representing a paramount constitution and government, whose duty it is, in *all* its departments, to allow to that constitution nothing less than its just and true interpretation; and having fixed this, to guard it against any inroads from without.

Thayer, *supra* note 5, at 154-55 (emphasis supplied). In Thayer's view, however, when Congress has exercised its power to regulate a particular aspect of interstate commerce and when the state also has exercised its regulatory power in the same area,

> it would appear to be the office of the Federal legislature, and not of the Federal courts, to supervise and moderate the action of the local legislatures, where it touches these parts of commerce.

Thayer traced these views far back in American history, finding, for example, that as early as 1811 the chief justice of Pennsylvania had concluded:

> For weighty reasons, it has been assumed as a principle in constitutional construction by the Supreme Court of the United States, by this court, and every other court of reputation in the United States, that an Act of the legislature is not to be declared void unless the violation of the constitution is so manifest as to leave no room for reasonable doubt.[10]

This view of the judicial function, of course, was the bedrock upon which Holmes, Brandeis, and Frankfurter built their judicial philosophies. Holmes had been Thayer's young friend and colleague on the Harvard faculty. Later, referring to Thayer's famous essay, Holmes wrote:

> I agree with it heartily and it makes explicit the point of view from which implicitly I have approached the constitutional questions upon which I have differed from some of the other judges.[11]

The young Brandeis had studied constitutional law under Thayer; thereafter they became close personal friends.[12] Much later Frankfurter referred to Thayer as "the great master of constitutional law" and in a lecture at the Harvard Law School observed that

> [o]ne brought up in the traditions of James Bradley Thayer, echoes of whom were still resounding in this very building in my student days, is committed to Thayer's statesmanlike conception of the limits within which the Supreme Court should move, and I shall try to be loyal to his admonition.[13]

> [I]f I were to name one piece of writing on American Constitutional Law . . . I would pick [Thayer's once famous essay] . . . [b]ecause . . . it's the

---

. . . [T]he question whether or not a given subject admits of only one uniform system or plan of regulation is primarily a [national] legislative question, not a judicial one. For it involves a consideration of what, on practical grounds, is expedient, or possible, or desirable . . . .
J. Thayer, Legal Essays 36 n.1 (1927). When Congress has not exercised its power, the question whether the subject of the state regulation requires uniformity "is for Congress, and the State regulation 'must stand until Congress shall see fit to alter it,' " Id.; see Gabin, Judicial Review, James Bradley Thayer, and the "Reasonable Doubt" Test, 3 Hastings Const. L.Q. 961, 977-83 (1976).

10. Thayer, supra note 5, at 140. The case to which Thayer made reference is Commonwealth ex rel. O'Hara v. Smith, 4 Binn. 117 (Pa. 1811).

11. Quoted in Mark De Wolfe Howe, Introduction, in James Bradley Thayer, Oliver Wendell Holmes, & Felix Frankfurter on John Marshall, at xi (1967).

12. Felix Frankfurter on the Supreme Court 252 (P. Kurland ed. 1970) [hereinafter cited as Frankfurter on the Supreme Court]; see Letter from Louis D. Brandeis to Alice Goldmark (Oct. 13, 1890), reprinted in 1 Letters of Louis D. Brandeis 92-93 (M. Urofsky & D. Levy eds. 1971); Letter from James B. Thayer to Louis D. Brandeis (1878), reprinted in A. Mason, Brandeis: A Free Man's Life 43 (1946). When Thayer went abroad in 1882-1883, the young Brandeis assumed his former professor's course in evidence at Thayer's request.

13. Frankfurter on the Supreme Court, supra note 12, at 542.

great guide for judges and therefore, the great guide for understanding by non-judges of what the place of the judiciary is in relation to constitutional questions.[14]

To hold that Thayer's views were fundamental in the work of the three justices is not to suggest that they stopped where he stopped. Each of them indeed built upon his insights to develop what may be called the classic Harvard approach to constitutional adjudication. The Thayer touch is obvious in Holmes and Brandeis dissents in numerous substantive due process cases. In *Coppage v. Kansas*,[15] for example, in which the Court invalidated a state statute prohibiting employers from requiring employees to agree not to become or remain members of labor unions, Holmes observed in dissent:

> In present conditions a workman not unnaturally may believe that only by belonging to a union can he secure a contract that shall be fair to him. . . . If that belief, whether right or wrong, may be held by a reasonable man, it seems to me that it may be enforced by law . . . . Whether in the long run it is wise for the workingmen to enact legislation of this sort is not my concern, but I am strongly of [the] opinion that there is nothing in the Constitution of the United States to prevent it . . . .[16]

Similar views appear in Holmes' dissent in *Adkins v. Children's Hospital*,[17] in which the Court struck down a congressional minimum wage statute for women in the District of Columbia:

> The criterion of constitutionality is not whether we believe the law to be for the public good. We certainly cannot . . . deny that a reasonable man reasonably might have that belief. . . .
> [Therefore,] I am of the opinion that the statute is valid . . . .[18]

Holmes' dissent from the Court's invalidation in *Bartels v. Iowa*[19] of a state statute requiring the use of English as the medium of instruction in the public schools provides another example of Thayer's teaching:

> I think I appreciate the objection to the law but it appears to me to present a question upon which men reasonably might differ and therefore I am unable to say that the Constitution of the United States prevents the experiment being tried.[20]

In Brandeis' opinions Thayerism was generally fleshed out by extended "real life" analysis of the circumstances that had produced the challenged legislation, by the history of similar measures

---

14.   H. PHILLIPS, FELIX FRANKFURTER REMINISCES 299-300 (1960).
15.   236 U.S. 1 (1915).
16.   *Id.* at 26-27.
17.   261 U.S. 525, 567 (1923) (Holmes, J., dissenting).
18.   *Id.* at 570-71.
19.   262 U.S. 404, 412 (1923) (Holmes, J., dissenting in part).
20.   *Id.*

in other jurisdictions, and by resumés of relevant statistical and other studies—all this to establish the reasonableness of the legislation in question.[21] Brandeis had perfected this innovating emphasis upon the "facts" in his highly successful Brandeis Brief in *Muller v. Oregon*.[22] Prior thereto,

> [s]ocial legislation was supported before the courts largely *in vacuo*—as an abstract dialectic between "liberty" and "police power," unrelated to the world of trusts and unions, of large-scale industry and all its implications. In the [Brandeis approach] the facts of modern industry which provoke regulatory legislation were, for the first time, adequately marshalled before the Court. It marks an epoch . . . .[23]

The Brandeis technique was more studied than Holmes'. Indeed Holmes reported to his friend Pollock that his colleague had chided him for indifference to extensive factual research:

> Brandeis the other day drove a harpoon into my midriff with reference to my summer occupations. He said you talk about improving your mind, you only exercise it on the subjects with which you are familiar. Why don't you try something new, study some domain of fact. Take up the textile industries in Massachusetts and after reading the reports sufficiently you can go to Lawrence and get a human notion of how it really is. I hate facts. I always say the chief end of man is to form general propositions—adding that no general proposition is worth a damn. Of course a general proposition is simply a string for the facts and I have little doubt that it would be good for my immortal soul to plunge into them, good also for the performance of my duties, but I shrink from the bore—or rather I hate to give up the chance to read this and that, that a gentleman should have read before he dies.[24]

In contrast to Brandeis' massively researched opinions, Holmes' efforts generally were expressed—as from Olympus—in a few epigrammatic sallies resting heavily upon Thayer and upon a deepseated skepticism that led him to question even the foundations of his own most basic beliefs.

> When I say that a thing is true, I mean that I cannot help believing it. I am stating an experience as to which there is no choice. But as there are many things that I cannot help doing that the universe can, I do not venture to assume that my inabilities in the way of thought are inabilities of the universe. I therefore define the truth as the system of my limitations, and leave absolute truth for those who are better equipped. . . .
>
> . . . .
>   . . . To have doubted one's own first principles is the mark of a civilized man.[25]

---

21. *See, e.g.*, the Brandeis opinions in New State Ice Co. v. Liebmann, 285 U.S. 262, 280 (1932); Jay Burns Baking Co. v. Bryan, 264 U.S. 504, 517 (1924); and Adams v. Tanner, 244 U.S. 590, 597 (1917).

22. 208 U.S. 412 (1908).

23. FRANKFURTER ON THE SUPREME COURT, *supra* note 12, at 251-52.

24. Letter from Oliver W. Holmes to Frederick Pollock (May 26, 1919), *reprinted in* 2 HOLMES-POLLOCK LETTERS 13 (M. Howe ed. 1961).

25. Holmes, *Ideals and Doubts*, 10 ILL. L. REV. 1, 2-3 (1915).

I used to say, when I was young, that truth was the majority vote of that nation that could lick all others. . . . I think that the statement was correct in so far as it implied that our test of truth is a reference to either a present or an imagined future majority in favor of our view. If, as I have suggested elsewhere, the truth may be defined as the system of my (intellectual) limitations, what gives it objectivity is the fact that I find my fellow man to a greater or less extent (never wholly) subject to the same *Can't Helps.*[26]

I see no meaning in the rights of man except what the crowd will fight for.[27]

In sharp contrast, Brandeis was a hopeful progressive. Indeed he had been a major leader of the Progressive Movement.[28] His elaborate judicial opinions upholding regulations of business often must have been labors of love. Yet, he like Holmes was quite capable of vigorous judicial support for economic measures that he privately disliked. This is obvious, for example, in his dissent in *New State Ice Co. v. Liebmann,*[29] perhaps Brandeis' most brilliant statement of the principle of judicial restraint. There he makes quite clear his own distaste for the measure in question, a state statute prohibiting the manufacture, sale, or distribution of ice without a license:

The objections to the proposal are obvious and grave. The remedy might bring evils worse than the present disease. The obstacles to success seem insuperable. The economic and social sciences are largely uncharted seas. We have been none too successful in the modest essays in economic control already entered upon. The new proposal involves a vast extension of the area of control. Merely to acquire the knowledge essential as a basis for the exercise of this multitude of judgments would be a formidable task; and each of the thousands of these judgments would call for some measure of prophecy. Even more serious are the obstacles to success inherent in the demands which execution of the project would make upon human intelligence and upon the character of men. Man is weak and his judgment is at best fallible.

Yet the advances in the exact sciences and the achievements in invention remind us that the seemingly impossible sometimes happens.[30]

In such cases, then, Brandeis, the inspired Progressive, and Holmes, the thorough-going skeptic, found common ground in Thayer's mandate of hospitality for legislative experimentation. As Brandeis observed in various ways over and over again:

The discoveries in physical science, the triumphs in invention, attest the value of the process of trial and error. In large measure, these advances have been due to experimentation. . . . There must be power in the States and the Nation to remould, through experimentation, our economic practices and in-

---

26. Holmes, *Natural Law,* 32 HARV. L. REV. 40, 40 (1918).

27. Letter from Oliver W. Holmes to Harold J. Laski (July 28, 1916), *reprinted in* 1 HOLMES-LASKI LETTERS 8 (M. Howe ed. 1953).

28. *See* MASON, *supra* note 12, at 99-441.

29. 285 U.S. 262, 280 (1932) (Brandeis, J., dissenting).

30. *Id.* at 309-10.

stitutions to meet changing social and economic needs. . . .

To stay experimentation in things social and economic is a grave responsibility. Denial of the right to experiment may be fraught with serious consequences to the Nation. It is one of the happy incidents of the federal system that a single courageous State may, if its citizens choose, serve as a laboratory; and try novel social and economic experiments without risk to the rest of the country. This Court has the power to prevent an experiment. We may strike down the statute which embodies it on the ground that, in our opinion, the measure is arbitrary, capricious or unreasonable. We have power to do this, because the due process clause has been held by the Court applicable to matters of substantive law as well as to matters of procedure. But in the exercise of this high power, we must be ever on our guard, lest we erect our prejudices into legal principles. If we would guide by the light of reason, we must let our minds be bold.[31]

Holmes' response reveals a striking difference between the two jurists; it also suggests that although Holmes was a skeptic, he was not a cynic:

Generally speaking, I agree with you in liking to see social experiments tried but I do so without enthusiasm because I believe it is merely shifting the pressure and that so long as we have free propagation Malthus is right in his general view.[32]

It is noteworthy that in Thayer's day no significant free speech or press litigation had reached the Supreme Court. Thus he had no empirical grounds for considering a judge's role in that context. Holmes and Brandeis did. Their tacit conclusion was that for purposes of the first amendment a lenient rational basis test was inadequate. Accordingly, they devised the stricter "clear and present danger" test for first amendment utterance cases,[33] an approach calculated to give legislatures less leeway than in other contexts. Speaking of Holmes, the then Professor Frankfurter provided for the first time an explicit rationale for this double standard:

The Justice deferred so abundantly to legislative judgment on economic policy because he was profoundly aware of the extent to which social arrangements are conditioned by time and circumstances, and of how fragile, in scientific proof, is the ultimate validity of a particular economic adjustment. He knew that there was no authoritative fund of social wisdom to be drawn upon for answers to the perplexities which vast new material resources had brought. And so he was hesitant to oppose his own opinion to the economic views of the legislature. But history had also taught him that, since social development is a process of trial and error, the fullest possible opportunity for the free play of the human mind was an indispensable prerequisite. Since the history of civilization is in considerable measure the displacement of error which once

---

31. *Id.* at 310-11.

32. *Quoted in* A. BICKEL, THE UNPUBLISHED OPINIONS OF MR. JUSTICE BRANDEIS 221 (1957).

33. Whitney v. California, 274 U.S. 357 (1927); Schenck v. United States, 249 U.S. 47 (1919).

held sway as official truth by beliefs which in turn have yielded to other truths, the liberty of man to search for truth was of a different order than some economic dogma defined as a sacred right because the temporal nature of its origin had been forgotten. And without freedom of expression, liberty of thought is a mockery. Nor can truth be pursued in an atmosphere hostile to the endeavor or under dangers which only heroes hazard.

Naturally, therefore, Mr. Justice Holmes attributed very different legal significance to those liberties of the individual which history has attested as the indispensable conditions of a free society from that which he attached to liberties which derived merely from shifting economic arrangements.[34]

Another major supplement to Thayer's reasonable doubt principle was Brandeis' emphasis upon avoidance of unnecessary constitutional decisions by strict adherence to jurisdictional limitations such as those embodied in the standing, ripeness, mootness, and political question doctrines. This tactic, stressing what Bickel called the "passive virtues,"[35] found classic expression in Brandeis' concurring opinion in *Ashwander v. TVA*.[36] Concluding that the plaintiff in *Ashwander* had not sustained any past or potential injury and therefore had no standing, Brandeis reminded his colleagues that

> The Court has frequently called attention to the "great gravity and delicacy" of its function in passing upon the validity of an act of Congress; and has restricted exercise of this function by rigid insistence that the jurisdiction of federal courts is limited to actual cases and controversies; and that they have no power to give advisory opinions. . . .
>
> The Court developed, for its own governance in the cases confessedly within its jurisdiction, a series of rules under which it has avoided passing upon a large part of all the constitutional questions pressed upon it for decision.[37]

He proceeded to "codify" at some length the rules in question. As Brandeis put it off the bench, "[t]he most important thing we do is not doing."[38] The thought, of course, was that the fewer social issues preempted by courts, the greater the latitude for legislative experimentation—for progress by a pragmatic system of trial and error. This plainly is an extension of Thayerism.

It was the fate of Holmes and Brandeis to sit with activist, conservative colleagues in an era of relatively progressive legislation. In this special setting, Thayer's principle of judicial restraint generally led to liberal results. Thus Holmes and Brandeis were praised (or criticized) for liberalism. The fact is that, whatever the tenor of his decisions, Holmes was an old-fashioned, aristocratic

---

34. F. FRANKFURTER, MR. JUSTICE HOLMES AND THE SUPREME COURT 50-51 (1938).

35. *See* A. BICKEL, THE LEAST DANGEROUS BRANCH: THE SUPREME COURT AT THE BAR OF POLITICS 111-98 (1962).

36. 297 U.S. 288, 341 (1936).

37. *Id.* at 345-46 (Brandeis, J., concurring).

38. BICKEL, *supra* note 35, at 17.

social Darwinian—although for him Darwinism was an explanation, not an excuse. Moreover, his deep-dyed skepticism put him far above mundane struggles and partisanship. All his life Holmes held to the survivial of the competent:

> I don't disguise my belief that the Sherman Act is a humbug based on economic ignorance and incompetence [nor] my disbelief that the Interstate Commerce Commission is a fit body to be entrusted with rate-making . . . . However I am so sceptical as to our kr.owledge about the goodness or badness of laws that I have no practical criticism [criterion] except what the crowd wants. Personally I bet that the crowd if it knew more wouldn't want what it does—but that is immaterial.[39]

> The social reformers of today seem to me so far to forget that we no more can get something for nothing by legislation than we can by mechanics as to be satisfied if the bill to be paid for their improvements is not presented in a lump sum. Interstitial detriments that may far outweigh the benefit promised are not bothered about. Probably I am too skeptical as to our ability to do more than shift disagreeable burdens from the shoulders of the stronger to those of the weaker. . . . I believe that the wholesale social regeneration which so many now seem to expect . . . cannot be affected appreciably by tinkering with the institution of property, but only by taking in hand life and trying to build a race.[40]

> Malthus pleased me immensely—and left me sad. A hundred years ago he busted fallacies that politicians and labor leaders still live on.[41]

Holmes' dear friends Brandeis and Frankfurter in private life were "social reformers" who supported the very "fallacies"—wage and hour laws, for example—that in Holmes' view Malthus had "busted."[42] Professor Frankfurter had a hand in virtually every major liberal effort of the day. He was a founder of the American Civil Liberties Union and of the *New Republic,* a bible of liberalism in the 1920's and 1930's. He was counsel for the NAACP long before

---

39.   Letter from Oliver W. Holmes to Frederick Pollock (Apr. 25, 1910), *reprinted in* 1 HOLMES-POLLOCK LETTERS, *supra* note 24, at 163.

40.   Holmes, *supra* note 25, at 2-3. Holmes expanded upon this theme in his opinion for the Court in Buck v. Bell, 274 U.S. 200 (1927), in which the Court upheld a state statute providing for the sterilization of inmates afflicted with hereditary insanity or imbecility:

> In view of the general declarations of the legislature and the specific findings of the Court, obviously we cannot say as matter of law that the grounds do not exist, and if they exist they justify the result. . . . It is better for all the world, if instead of waiting to execute degenerate offspring for crime, or to let them starve for their imbecility, society can prevent those who are manifestly unfit from continuing their kind. The principle that sustains compulsory vaccination is broad enough to cover cutting the Fallopian tubes. . . . Three generations of imbeciles are enough.

Id. at 207.

41.   Letter from Oliver W. Holmes to Frederick Pollock (Aug. 30, 1914), *reprinted in* 2 HOLMES-POLLOCK LETTERS, *supra* note 24, at 219.

42.   *See, e.g.,* F. FRANKFURTER, *The Eight-Hour Day,* in LAW AND POLITICS: OCCASIONAL PAPERS OF FELIX FRANKFURTER, 1913-1918, at 203 (A. MacLeish & E. Prichard eds. 1939); THE SOCIAL AND ECONOMIC VIEWS OF MR. JUSTICE BRANDEIS (A. Lief ed. 1930).

that was fashionable and for the National Consumers' League as well. He fought the good fight for Tom Mooney,[43] for the Bisbee deportees,[44] for the victims of the Palmer Raids of 1920,[45] and for Sacco and Vanzetti[46] and played a (perhaps the) primary role in abolishing the labor injunction.[47] Frankfurter, of course, also was a major contributor to the New Deal.[48] Not only did he help found the *New Republic,* he wrote for it repeatedly until his appointment to the Supreme Court. One mentions this by way of emphasizing the off-the-bench liberalism of Frankfurter and the conservatism of Holmes. The latter, writing to Pollock, mentions the enchanting spring—"the air full of the smell of box and roses and . . . the yelling of birds," and then adds, "Really if a glance at the *New Republic* had not thrown the customary gloom over life it would seem fair once more."[49] Conversely, a brief passage in Frankfurter's highly eulogistic biography of Holmes reveals a sharp difference between the two on matters economic: Justice Holmes, Frankfurter wrote, "came dangerously close to believing in the simplicities of the wage-fund theory."[50]

If one accepts and slightly amends Arthur Sutherland's definition of a liberal as the sort of person who enjoyed the *New Republic* in the 1920's and 1930's, obviously Frankfurter, unlike Holmes, was a thoroughgoing liberal in his personal life.[51] His fate, however, was to sit on the Court with a number of liberal activists in an era when legislation was often quite illiberal. In that context the Thayer-Holmes-Brandeis principle of judicial restraint often led to less than liberal results. Accordingly, as a judge, Frankfurter was widely criticized—erroneously, of course—for conservatism, just as Holmes, operating in a different age and context, was widely praised—erroneously, of course—for liberalism. The point is that in their view—and in Brandeis' view—Thayer's conception of the relative roles of courts and legislatures was a principle for all seasons, not a tool to be used or ignored in the service of a judge's private

---

43. *See* L. BAKER, FELIX FRANKFURTER 68-73 (1969).

44. *See id.* at 66-68, 73.

45. *See id.* at 92-96.

46. *See id.* at 117-30.

47. *See id.* at 132-35.

48. *See id.* at 149, 153-79; PHILLIPS, *supra* note 14, at 235-50; ROOSEVELT AND FRANK-FURTER: THEIR CORRESPONDENCE 1928-1945, at 93-442 (M. Freedman ed. 1968).

49. Letter from Oliver W. Holmes to Frederick Pollock (May 26, 1919), *reprinted in* 2 HOLMES-POLLOCK LETTERS, *supra* note 24, at 14.

50. FRANKFURTER, *supra* note 34, at 44. Frankfurter's comment is in reference to Holmes' opinion in Plant v. Woods, 176 Mass. 492 (1900).

51. A. SUTHERLAND, CONSTITUTIONALISM IN AMERICA 470 (1965).

preferences, which Holmes called his *"Can't Helps."* This was the great lesson that Frankfurter learned from Holmes.

We have already seen that Frankfurter had the highest regard for Thayer. He also was a close friend of both Holmes and Brandeis for many years, long before he went to the Supreme Court. His numerous laudatory essays on each of them indicate his discipleship.[52] If respect for legislative experimentation as a tool for social progress characterized the work of Brandeis and skepticism the work of Holmes, dedication to democracy was the major theme of Frankfurter's jurisprudence. Perhaps only an immigrant, only one who had lived his first years under an emperor, could have been so dedicated to government by the people and to the diffusion of power. His judicial and other writings are filled with allusions to judicial review as a "limitation on popular government" and thus an "undemocratic aspect" of our system. He recognized, however, that "[o]ur right to pass on the validity of legislation is now too much part of our constitutional system to be brought into question."[53] Yet because this right is "inherently oligarchic" and practically uncontrollable and because it prevents "the full play of the democratic process,"[54] it is "vital that [this] power of the non-democratic organ of our Government be exercised with rigorous self-restraint."[55] For Frankfurter, the abuses of the "nine old men" were not ancient history. Nor could he pretend that activism on the left was any less "oligarchic" or any less an impediment to popular government than activism on the right. Accordingly, with Holmes and Brandeis he was deeply indebted to Thayer's rule of reasonable doubt—as is obvious, for example, in his *cri de coeur* in *West Virginia State Board of Education v. Barnette*,[56] the so-called second *Flag Salute Case*. There Frankfurter pointed out in dissent that on five previous occasions the Court had found no constitutional infirmity in a mandatory flag salute and that every one of the thirteen justices involved—including such heroic figures as Stone, Brandeis, Cardozo, Black, and Douglas—had so voted on one or more occasions. Indeed, of the forty-five votes cast in those five cases, forty-four had found the challenged measure to be within the ambit of

---

52. Several of Frankfurter's essays on Holmes and Brandeis are collected in FRANKFURTER ON THE SUPREME COURT, *supra* note 12.

53. American Fed'n of Labor v. American Sash & Door Co., 335 U.S. 538, 556-57 (1949) (Frankfurter, J., concurring).

54. West Virginia State Bd. of Educ. v. Barnette, 319 U.S. 624, 650 (1943) (Frankfurter, J., dissenting).

55. 335 U.S. at 555 (Frankfurter, J., concurring).

56. 319 U.S. at 646 (Frankfurter, J., dissenting).

democratic self-government. In view of this history, Frankfurter thought it clear that legislators could not be deemed unreasonable in enacting what thirteen justices had found to be within a state's constitutional authority.

> Only if there be no doubt that any reasonable mind could entertain can we deny to the states the right to resolve doubts their way and not ours.
>   . . . .
>   . . . I think I appreciate fully the objections to the law before us. But to deny that it presents a question upon which men might reasonably differ appears to me to be intolerance. And since men may so reasonably differ, I deem it beyond my constitutional power to assert my view of the wisdom of this law against the view of the State . . . .[57]

This obviously is pure Thayerism. On the same occasion, Frankfurter again expressed—as in his eulogy to Holmes quoted above—his dedication to the special Holmes-Brandeis concern for free speech and press:

> All channels of affirmative free expression are open to both children and parents. Had we before us any act of the state putting the slightest curbs upon such free expression, I should not lag behind any member of this Court in striking down such an invasion of the right to freedom of thought and freedom of speech protected by the Constitution.[58]

---

57. *Id.* at 661-62, 666-67.

58. *Id.* at 664. Frankfurter later observed again that such freedoms "come to this Court with a momentum for respect lacking when appeal is made to liberties which derive merely from shifting economic arrangements." Kovacs v. Cooper, 336 U.S. 77, 95 (1949) (Frankfurter, J., concurring). Here, too, Frankfurter objected to what he deemed his colleagues' doctrinaire, perverting use of the Holmes-Brandeis clear and present danger test.

If in Dennis v. United States, 341 U.S. 494 (1951), Mr. Justice Frankfurter was not very respectful of the discourse there in issue, surely the reason was that Dennis and his companions had spoken in secret and underground, *i.e.* conspiratorially. Their views had not been offered for what Holmes and Brandeis called "public discussion" as part of the "free trade in ideas" in the "competition of the market" where the public is offered exposure to conflicting views so that it can choose intelligently among them. Abrams v. United States, 250 U.S. 616, 630 (1919) (Holmes, J., dissenting). Recall Milton's famous line in *Areopagitica:* "[W]ho ever knew truth put to the worse, in a *free and open encounter?*" J. MILTON, *Areopagitica,* in 2 THE PROSE WORKS OF JOHN MILTON 96 (J. St. John ed. 1900) (emphasis supplied). Mill's *On Liberty* rests on what he called "the morality of public discussion." J. MILL, ON LIBERTY 99 (1887). Jefferson put it briefly: truth is "the proper and sufficient antagonist to error, and has nothing to fear from the conflict unless by human interposition [*e.g.,* secrecy] disarmed of her natural weapons, *free argument and debate* . . . ." 2 THE PAPERS OF THOMAS JEFFERSON 546 (J. Boyd ed. 1950) (emphasis supplied). Benjamin Franklin has it thus: "[W]hen Men differ in Opinion, both Sides ought equally to have the Advantage of being heard by the Publick . . . ." B. FRANKLIN, *An Apology for Printers* (1731), in 1 THE PAPERS OF BENJAMIN FRANKLIN 194-95 (L. Labaree ed. 1959). In Chafee's view, "the fundamental policy of the First Amendment [is] the *open discussion* of public affairs." Z. CHAFEE, FREEDOM OF SPEECH 30 (1920) (emphasis supplied). As Meiklejohn put it:

> What, then, does the First Amendment forbid? Here again the town meeting suggests an answer. That meeting is called to discuss and, on the basis of such discussion, to decide matters of public policy. . . . *The voters, therefore, must be made as wise as*

So, too, Frankfurter might well have gone even further than Brandeis in strict adherence to jurisdictional limitations, the "passive virtues," as devices for avoiding unnecessary constitutional decisions.[59] Indeed Frankfurter, as professor of federal jurisdiction at Harvard, may have led Brandeis to this ploy initially. In any event, Brandeis no doubt discussed such matters with his professorial friend and former associate in litigation, who was then the nation's leading academic specialist in the problems of federal court jurisdiction.

Finally, just as Holmes and Brandeis added something to Thayerism, so did Frankfurter in the *McNabb-Mallory* doctrine,[60] which permits the Court to avoid constitutional judgment by turning decisions upon its supervisory control over the lower federal courts. Such decisions, because they do not rest upon the Constitution, are subject to congressional control. They thus escape the anti-democratic element that Frankfurter found in constitutional review. Free of this element, the Justice had no difficulty in reaching a highly liberal and thus personally gratifying result in *McNabb* and in *Mallory*. Finally, in his opinion for the Court in *Railroad Commission v. Pullman Co.*,[61] Frankfurter launched the modern history of judicially developed federal district court abstention in cases in which state law may be dispositive[62]—another device for avoiding unnecessary constitutional adjudication.

If Holmes' methodological forte was skepticism (and the sprightly epigram) and if Brandeis specialized in mining the facts, Frankfurter's specialty was precedent. What these three approaches have in common is plain: each provides a considerable barrier against subjectivity in the judicial process. To that end, in crucial

---

possible. . . . And this, in turn, requires that . . . all facts and interests relevant to the problem shall be fully and fairly presented *to the meeting.*
. . . .
. . . [The fifth amendment's] limited guarantee of the freedom . . . to speak is radically different in intent from the unlimited guarantee of the freedom of *public discussion,* which is given by the First Amendment.
A. MEIKLEJOHN, FREE SPEECH AND ITS RELATION TO SELF-GOVERNMENT 24-25, 39 (1948) (emphasis supplied). Thus all of these great founts of our free-speech ideal seem to have anticipated Mr. Justice Frankfurter's stand in *Dennis;* namely, that freedom of speech means open, public discussion, not underground activity designed to achieve its goals by circumventing, rather than winning, community consent.

59. For pertinent examples, see the long line of his opinions from Coleman v. Miller, 307 U.S. 433 (1939), through Baker v. Carr, 369 U.S. 186 (1962).

60. *See* Mallory v. United States, 354 U.S. 449 (1957); McNabb v. United States, 318 U.S. 332 (1943).

61. 312 U.S. 496 (1941).

62. *See* C. WRIGHT, FEDERAL COURTS 170 (1963).

case after case Frankfurter's opinions carefully analyze *all* relevant decisions in search of what Holmes called an "external standard" for judgment. The scholarly effort that went into Frankfurter's opinions, for example, in *Harris v. United States,*[63] *Wolfe v. Colorado,*[64] *Culombe v. Connecticut,*[65] and the *Steel Seizure Case*[66] is astounding. Such painstaking toil, like that of Brandeis,[67] is the unspoken answer to a freewheeling justice who not long ago insisted that the Court is "vastly underworked."[68] How easy the job of activist judges—new or old—who do not find, but only make, the law! No great effort, intelligence, or integrity is required to read one's merely personal preferences into the Constitution; a great deal is required to keep them out. The point is not that anyone does this perfectly, but rather that some try and indeed, as in all phases of life, some are far more capable of objectivity and detachment than others. As Judge Hand observed,

> [W]e know that men do differ widely in this capacity [for detachment]; and the incredulity which seeks to discredit that knowledge is a part of the crusade against reason from which we have already so bitterly suffered. We may deny—and, if we are competent observers, we will deny—that no one can be aware of the danger [of his bias] and in large measure provide against it.[69]

For sixty years, from 1902 until 1962, at least one and for a time two of the "Harvard judges" were on the Supreme Court. In all those years their influence was far out of proportion to their numbers. With the coming of the hysterical 1960's—about the time of Frankfurter's retirement—almost all that they had stood for vanished. Perhaps not quite all, for no activist, modern or vintage, has ever admitted in public that he is an activist. Quite to the contrary, no matter how great the judicial leap, its authors always insist that it derives from some constitutionally appropriate (if previously invisible) source and that it really is not an innovation anyway.[70] Is

---

63.   331 U.S. 145 (1947).

64.   338 U.S. 25 (1949).

65.   367 U.S. 568 (1961).

66.   Youngstown Sheet & Tube Co. v. Sawyer, 343 U.S. 579 (1952).

67.   Brandeis' draft opinions "went through dozens, sometimes scores, of revisions." P. FREUND, ON LAW AND JUSTICE 127 (1968).

68.   Tidewater Oil Co. v. United States, 409 U.S. 151, 178 (1972) (Douglas, J., dissenting).

69.   L. HAND, THE SPIRIT OF LIBERTY 218 (1960).

70.   For example, the majority opinion in Miranda v. Arizona, 384 U.S. 436, 442 (1966), proclaims, "We start . . . with the premise that our holding is not an innovation in our jurisprudence . . . ." *See also* Israel, *Gideon v. Wainwright: The 'Art' of Overruling,* 1963 SUP. CT. REV. 211.

Need one say that in the Thayer view great policy leaps are for legislative bodies, not for courts, and that a flexible, living Constitution is one that makes reasonable accommodations to changing social needs *as perceived and enacted by legislatures*?

this not lip service to the Thayer tradition?

Since Frankfurter's retirement in 1962, courts have pushed beyond desegregation to integration via busing; they have undertaken to desegregate even private schools, to reapportion legislatures, to regulate private employment practices, to supervise municipal land-use planning, to provide a detailed abortion code, to oversee and redirect any number of welfare programs, to supervise police investigations, to outlaw capital punishment, in effect, and then to reinstate it with limitations, to direct credit policies of banks and credit card companies, to supervise the supervision of children in their schools, to monitor environmental quality, and even to manage prison and mental institutions.[71] Surely all of this (and more) constitutes a radical transformation of the role of judges in American life. Surely, too, judicial pretension no longer can be justified on the ground that it is only a negative, a veto, power.

If, then, the Thayer tradition of judicial modesty is outmoded—if judicial aggression is to be the rule in policy matters, as in the 1930's—some basic issues remain. First, how legitimate is government by judges? Is anything to be beyond the reach of their authority? Will anything be left for ultimate resolution by the democratic processes—for what Thayer called "that wide margin of considerations which address themselves only to the practical judgment of a legislative body"[72] representing (as courts do not) a wide range of mundane needs and aspirations? The legislative process, after all, is a major ingredient of freedom under government.

> Legislation is a process slow and cumbersome. It turns out a product—laws—that rarely are liked by everybody, and frequently little liked by anybody. . . . [W]hen seen from the shining cliffs of perfection the legislative process of compromise appears shoddy indeed. But when seen from some concentration camp of the only alternative way of life, the compromises of legislation appear but another name for what we call civilization and even revere as Christian forbearance.[73]

Let philosophy fret about ideal justice. Politics is our substitute for civil war in a constant struggle between different conceptions of good and bad. It is far too wise to gamble for Utopia or nothing—to be fooled by its own romantic verbiage. Above all, it knows that none of the numerous clashing social forces is apt to be completely without both vice and virtue. By give and take, the legislative process seeks not final truth, but an acceptable balance of community interests. In this view the harmonizing and educational function of

---

71. I am indebted here to Chayes, *The New Judiciary,* 28 HARV. L. SCH. BULL. 23 (1976).
72. Thayer, *supra* note 5, at 135.
73. T. SMITH, THE LEGISLATIVE WAY OF LIFE 91-92 (1940).

the process itself counts for more than any of its legislative products. To intrude upon its pragmatic adjustments by judicial fiat is to frustrate our chief instrument of social peace and political stability.

Second, if the Supreme Court is to be the ultimate policy-making body—without political accountability—how is it to avoid the corrupting effects of raw power? Can the Court avoid the self-inflicted wounds that have marked other episodes of judicial imperialism?[74] Can the Court indeed satisfy the expectations it has already aroused?

A third cluster of questions involves the competence of the Supreme Court as a legislative body. Can any nine men master the complexities of every phase of American life which, as the post-1961 cases suggest, is now the Court's province? Are any nine men wise enough and good enough to wield such power over the lives of millions? Are courts institutionally equipped for such burdens?[75] Unlike legislatures, they are not representative bodies reflecting a wide range of social interests. Lacking a professional staff of trained investigators, they must rely for data almost exclusively upon the partisan advocates who appear before them. Inadequate or misleading information invites unsound decisions.[76] If courts are to rely upon social science data as facts, they must recognize that such data are often tentative at best, subject to varying interpretations, and questionable on methodological grounds. Moreover, since social science findings and conclusions are likely to change with continuing research, they may require a system of ongoing policy reviews as new or better data become available.[77] Is the judiciary capable of performing this function of continuing supervision and adjustment traditionally provided by the legislative and administrative processes?[78]

Finally, what kind of citizens will such a system of judicial activism produce—a system that trains us to look not to ourselves

---

74. Consider, for example, the gross abuse of judicial power in the era of rampant economic activism that culminated in the Court-packing crisis of 1937. *See* R. McCloskey, The American Supreme Court 136-79 (1960). For other examples of judicially self-inflicted wounds, see L. Graglia, Disaster by Decree: The Supreme Court Decisions on Race and the Schools 129-31, 279-81 (1976); F. Graham, The Self-Inflicted Wound (1970); D. Horowitz, The Courts and Social Policy 171-254 (1977); C. Hughes, The Supreme Court of the United States 50 (1928).

75. *See* Johnson, *The Constitution and the Federal District Judge*, 54 Tex. L. Rev. 903, 905 (1976).

76. *See* Horowitz, *supra* note 74, at 274-84.

77. Glazer, *Toward an Imperial Judiciary,* in The American Commonwealth 104, 116-17 (N. Glazer & I. Kristol eds. 1976).

78. *See* Horowitz, *supra* note 74, at 264-66.

for the solution of our problems, but to the most elite among elites: nine lawyers governing our lives without political or judicial accountability? Surely this is neither democracy nor the rule of law. Such are the problems addressed by and—at least in the minds of jurists like Holmes, Brandeis, and Frankfurter—resolved by Thayer's doctrine of judicial restraint.

2 🦖 *Judge Learned Hand*

THE constitutionally assigned function of the federal courts is to decide "cases" and "controversies" — to settle conflicts between litigants.[1] Only in this context and to this end are they authorized to act at all. The rest is incidental. It goes without saying that a "case" or "controversy" has at least two sides, each of which is entitled to impartial consideration in the light of established rules. When the law plainly upholds one side and no other, litigation, if it arises at all, is not apt to go beyond a trial court. Cases that go further often present a dilemma, both sides of which have considerable, or little, support in law or morals.

One reason for this difficulty is that law is handicapped by the limitations of human foresight. Lawmakers, like the rest of us, cannot anticipate all the combinations and permutations of circumstance. They do well to provide for the obvious and leave some hints — inevitably vague and subject to differing interpretations — for the disposition of more difficult matters. Take, for example, Learned Hand's illustration — a collision between two motorcars: "There is no way of saying beforehand exactly what each driver should do or should not, until all the circumstances of the particular case are known. The law leaves this open with the vague command to each that he shall be careful. What being careful means, it does not try to say; it leaves that to the judge, who happens in this case to be a jury of twelve persons, untrained in the law."[2]

Holmes explained that "the meaning of leaving nice questions

---

[1] U.S. CONST. art. III, § 2.
[2] HAND, THE SPIRIT OF LIBERTY 105–06 (3d ed. Dilliard 1960).

to the jury is that while if a question of law is pretty clear we [judges] can decide it, as it is our duty to do, if it is difficult it can be decided better by twelve men at random from the street." [3] In short, a jury's verdict "is not the conclusion of a syllogism of which they are to find only the minor premiss, but really a small bit of legislation ad hoc . . . ." [4]

Like the legal standard of due care in the automobile collision case, such constitutional terms as "freedom of speech" and "due process of law" are not authoritatively explained, or self-explanatory. For Hand, this was not surprising:

[T]hese stately admonitions refuse to subject themselves to analysis. They are the precipitates of "old, unhappy, far-off things, and battles long ago," originally cast as universals to enlarge the scope of victory, to give it authority, to reassure the very victors themselves that they have been champions in something more momentous than a passing struggle. Thrown large upon the screen of the future as eternal verities, they are emptied of the vital occasions which gave them birth, and become moral adjurations, the more imperious because inscrutable, but with only that content which each generation must pour into them anew in the light of its own experience.[5]

Just as vagueness in the law of negligence is left for resolution by juries, so in Hand's view, vagueness in the Constitution was to be resolved by legislatures (and/or executives). What Hand said of Holmes in this context is self-revealing: "His decisions are not to be read as indicating his own views on public matters, but they do indicate his settled belief that in such matters the judges cannot safely intervene, that the Constitution did not create a tricameral system, that a law which can get itself enacted is almost sure to have behind it a support which is not wholly unreasonable." [6] And so only the most unusual circumstances could justify judicial veto of a legislative act — or a jury verdict. Hand's standard for intervention was essentially the same in both cases. It came simply to this: if there was room for doubt, legislation — like a verdict — must stand, however mistaken it might seem to judges. Ambivalence in the law was the province of jury and legislature — the two authentic voices of the people. Judicial in-

---

[3] HOLMES, *Law in Science and Science in Law*, in COLLECTED LEGAL PAPERS 210, 234 (1920).

[4] United States v. Levine, 83 F.2d 156, 157 (2d Cir. 1936).

[5] HAND, *op. cit. supra* note 2, at 155, 163.

[6] *Id.* at 28.

tervention was permissible only when a court was prepared to hold that *no* reasonable mind could have found as the legislature or jury did find.[7] In this (the orthodox) view, statute and verdict enjoy the same basic immunity from judicial interference, yet in extreme cases both are subject to a judicial check. As Hand put it with respect to constitutional issues:

> If a court be really candid, it can only say: "We find that this measure will have this result; it will injure this group in such and such ways, and benefit that group in these other ways. We declare it invalid, because after every conceivable allowance for differences of outlook, we cannot see how a fair person can honestly believe that the benefits balance the losses." [8]

In a democracy legislation is largely a matter of give-and-take — of striking a workable balance between conflicting social interests. Its essence is compromise — which is apt to find expression in terms that are more suggestive than exact, more calculated to avoid precise commitments than to embrace them. This, along with the imprecision of language and the limitations of human foresight, is the judge's burden. But far more is involved than a matter of legal technique. The legislative way of life is a major ingredient of freedom under government.

> Legislation is a process slow and cumbersome. It turns out a product — laws — that rarely are liked by everybody, and frequently little liked by anybody. . . . [W]hen seen from the shining cliffs of perfection the legislative process of compromise appears shoddy indeed. But when seen from some concentration camp of the only alternative way of life, the compromises of legislation appear but another name for what we call civilization and even revere as Christian forbearance.[9]

Let philosophy fret about ideal Justice. Politics is our substitute for civil war in a continuous struggle between different conceptions of right and wrong. It is far too wise to gamble for Utopia or nothing — to be fooled by its own romantic verbiage. Above all, it knows that among the myriad clashing social forces none is apt to be completely without vice or virtue. And so by give-and-take it seeks not final truth, but an acceptable balance of community

---

[7] This, the orthodox approach, has been questioned on the bench only with respect to the so-called "preferred-place" freedoms.

[8] HAND, *op. cit. supra* note 2, at 162.

[9] T. SMITH, THE LEGISLATIVE WAY OF LIFE 91–92 (1940).

interests. In this view the harmonizing and educational function of the process itself counts for more than any of its immediate legislative products. To override its pragmatic adjustments by moralistic fiats from the bench is to frustrate our chief instrument of social peace and political stability.

Given then the nature of compromise, the secrecy of the future, and the clogs upon communication, the burden of judging is to decide "cases" and "controversies" as to which the meaning of the law is often less than obvious. Nor is there an objective, extra-legal scale to weigh the conflicting interests that demand evaluation. In this impasse judgment entails discretion — or more crudely, lawmaking. But how can this be reconciled with the basic judicial function of settling disputes, as we insist, in accordance with a priori rules? Plainly both sides of this dilemma cannot be fully satisfied. Men must know what the law requires of them before they act, but society cannot risk stagnation in its judicial system. With respect to constitutional issues, as we have seen, Hand would leave the "interpretation" of the law largely to the politically responsible branches of government. But judicial review is only one means of judicial legislation. Statutory construction may be at least equally effective. Hand's solution is briefly put:

> [P]rovided that the opportunity always exists to supplant [laws] . . . when there is a new shift in political power, it is of critical consequence that they should be loyally enforced [by judges] until they are amended by the same process which made them. That is the presupposition on which the compromises were originally accepted; to disturb them by surreptitious, irresponsible [judicial] . . . intervention imperils the possibility of any future settlements and pro tanto upsets the whole system. *Such laws need but one canon of interpretation, to understand what the real accord was.* The duty of ascertaining its meaning is difficult enough at best, and one certain way of missing it is by reading it literally, for words are such temperamental beings that the surest way to lose their essence is to take them at their face. Courts must reconstruct the past solution imaginatively in its setting and project the purposes which inspired it upon the concrete occasions which arise for their decision.[10]

This view — like the reasonable-basis test — reflects the wisdom of the ages.[11] Recognizing the need for judicial discretion,

---

[10] HAND, *op. cit. supra* note 2, at 156–57. (Emphasis added.)
[11] See Heydon's Case, 3 Co. Rep. 7a, 76 Eng. Rep. 637 (Exch. 1584).

it confines the area of choice by an ancient and tested common law technique.[12] It treats the individual case as a minute continuation of the broad conflict that resulted in a legislative compromise. Accordingly it seeks decision not in the light of JUSTICE, but in the spirit of the legislative settlement — however slovenly and earthbound. In Hand's words, "If [the judge] . . . is in doubt, he must stop, for he cannot tell that the conflicting interests in the society for which he speaks would have come to a just result, even though he is sure that he knows what the just result should be. He is not to substitute even his juster will for [that of the lawmaking assembly] . . . otherwise it would not be the common will which prevails, and to that extent the people would not govern." [13]

Some modern "realists" (particularly those not trained in the law) reject the old approach — discretion confined by a technique — as a delusion, if not outright fraud. They insist that "political choice is inevitable and inherent in judging, and that judges should make no false pretense of objectivity. Rather . . . they should recognize that they are making policy, and . . . should consciously exercise their judicial power to achieve social justice" [14] — as *they* see it. In this view, apparently, the constitutional function of settling disputes impartially is incidental, or subordinate, to a court's discretionary "lawmaking" role. Judicial detachment is a false ideal. The great judge is an "activist," a legislator who uses the law's inevitable ambiguities to promote justice.

Surely this view reflects an unavowed, perhaps unconscious, disenchantment with the democratic process. At least that is what we said not so long ago of the "rugged individualists" who went to court to get the whole loaf when they could get only half via the democratic give-and-take of legislative bargaining. Modern libertarians insist that they have a better case because their values are "fundamental." But that was precisely the argument of their property-minded, activist predecessors.[15] Indeed, even Mr. Justice

---

[12] As the great Mansfield put it in Rex v. Wilkes, 4 Burr. 2527, 2539, 98 Eng. Rep. 327, 334 (K.B. 1770): "[D]iscretion, when applied to a Court of Justice, means *sound* discretion . . . . governed by rule, not by humour: it must not be arbitrary, vague, and fanciful; but legal and regular." (Emphasis added.)

[13] HAND, *op. cit. supra* note 2, at 109.

[14] BURNS & PELTASON, GOVERNMENT BY THE PEOPLE 541 (1957). The activist view is simply described, and not necessarily endorsed by the authors of this book.

[15] See, *e.g.,* the comment by Judge Orsdels in Children's Hosp. v. Adkins, 284

Douglas recognizes that "security of property . . . . is one of the preferred rights . . . ." [16] No doubt as abstract propositions both views are sound: free expression and private property *are* basic, indispensable elements of American culture. The difficulty is not the validity of either concept, but its application in a concrete case. Most of the evil of the world, after all, is committed in the name of some glowing abstraction, some eternal — and blinding — verity. In some contexts private property is a mask for exploitation, an instrument of legalized robbery. Sometimes speech is the equivalent of force, as Holmes suggested in the famous theater metaphor. Sometimes it is simply out of place, as, for example, the political harangue that disturbs the quiet of a hospital. Few would insist that the evils of obscenity, slander, incitement, or mere verbal noise could never be great enough to outweigh the social benefits of unfettered speech. The trouble in cases involving "limitations" on such fundamentals as property and utterance is that they require "the appraisal and balancing of human values which there are no scales to weigh. . . . The difficulty here does not come from ignorance, but from absence of any standard, for values are incommensurable." [17] Despite some glowing constitutional language, no past or present member of the Supreme Court, and no responsible commentator, has ever suggested that any of the great constitutional "rights" or "freedoms" are unlimited.[18] It is not merely that conservatives differ with liberals as to where the limits lie. Even such staunch libertarians as Justices Black and Douglas are far from agreement on the scope of "personal freedom" [19] — just as such thorough con-

Fed. 613, 622 (D.C. Cir. 1922), *aff'd*, 261 U.S. 525 (1923): "[O]f the three fundamental principles which underlie government and for which government exists, the protection of life, liberty, and property, the chief of these is property . . . ." This, of course, reflects an old American tradition. See FREUND, ON UNDERSTANDING THE SUPREME COURT 14–22 (1949).

[16] DOUGLAS, WE THE JUDGES 288–89 (1956).

[17] HAND, *op. cit. supra* note 2, at 161.

[18] Mr. Justice Black has insisted, though not from the bench, that *within* its "area" freedom of speech is absolute — but he recognizes that the "scope" of the "area" is not clear. Black, *The Bill of Rights*, 35 N.Y.U.L. REV. 865, 875 (1960). See Cohen, *Justice Black and First Amendment "Absolutes": A Public Interview*, 37 N.Y.U.L. REV. 549, 557–58 (1962).

[19] See, *e.g.*, Communist Party v. Subversive Activities Control Bd., 367 U.S. 1 (1961) (first amendment issue); McGowan v. Maryland, 366 U.S. 420 (1961); Reina v. United States, 364 U.S. 507 (1960); Barr v. Matteo, 360 U.S. 564 (1959); Zorach v. Clauson, 343 U.S. 306 (1952); Tenney v. Brandhove, 341 U.S. 367 (1951); United States v. Williams, 341 U.S. 70 (1951); Wolf v. Colorado, 338 U.S. 25 (1949); Frazier v. United States, 335 U.S. 497 (1948); Goesaert v. Cleary, 335 U.S.

servatives as Justices Sutherland and McReynolds could disagree
on the bounds of "private property" and "rugged individualism." [20] Indeed, even Mr. Justice Black has found the Bill of
Rights so lacking in clarity that he has shifted his position on
some of its most basic provisions.[21]

Nor is the difficulty of "interpretation" confined to those who
carry the merciless burden of adjudication. Professors Chafee
and Meiklejohn, the two great modern academic libertarians, are
deeply divided on the meaning of free speech — though both
agree that it is basic.[22] As John Marshall said long ago, our Constitution is "one of enumeration, and not of definition." [23] On most
crucial issues it leaves room for doubt and disagreement among
fairminded men.

What then is the Rule of Law, particularly in constitutional
litigation? For Hand it entailed avoidance of pretense that the
Constitution lays down unmistakable rules of decision for difficult
cases. It meant that in the adaptive process which permits the old
document to survive in a changing world, courts must play a secondary role lest society be confined by the limited outlook, the
"can't helps," [24] of a few "independent" judges. It meant that,
when judicial intervention was unavoidable, decision should turn
on fully disclosed, rational grounds within the accepted legal tradition — not on an emotional commitment to a "preferred" class
of proprietarian, or libertarian, interests. It meant that successive
decisions should be rationally coherent, that judges should respect

464 (1948); Louisiana *ex rel.* Francis v. Resweber, 329 U.S. 459 (1947). In the
Communist Party case, *supra* at 164, Mr. Justice Black rejects the "balancing"
approach, but he joined in the Court's opinion in *McGowan, supra*, which Mr.
Justice Douglas in dissent, 366 U.S. at 575, criticized because it used that approach.

[20] See, *e.g.*, Village of Euclid v. Ambler Realty Co., 272 U.S. 365 (1926); Buck
v. Kuykendall, 267 U.S. 307 (1925); Meyer v. Nebraska, 262 U.S. 390 (1923).

[21] See, *e.g.*, West Virginia Board of Education v. Barnette, 319 U.S. 624, 643
(1943) (concurring opinion); Mapp v. Ohio, 367 U.S. 643, 661–62 (1961) (concurring opinion). See also Palko v. Connecticut, 302 U.S. 319 (1937). *But cf.*
Adamson v. California, 332 U.S. 46, 68 (1947) (dissenting opinion); Chaplinsky
v. New Hampshire, 315 U.S. 568 (1942); Cohen, *supra* note 18, at 557. See also
FREUND, ON UNDERSTANDING THE SUPREME COURT 29–35 (1949). As to the "balancing" approach, see note 19 *supra*.

[22] Chafee, Book Review, 62 HARV. L. REV. 891 (1949). Even the two fountain-
heads of Anglo-American freedom — Milton's *Areopagitica* and Mill's essay *On
Liberty* — are hopelessly at odds on the philosophic foundation (and hence the
limits) of free speech.

[23] Gibbons v. Ogden, 22 U.S. (9 Wheat.) 1, 189 (1824).

[24] Holmes' term for things so familiar to a man that he can't help accepting
them as true.

their own precedents.[25] But coherence and respect did not require
blindness to changing social needs:

> A judge must manage to escape both horns of this dilemma: he
> must preserve his authority by cloaking himself in the majesty of
> an overshadowing past; but he must discover some composition
> with the dominant trends of his time — at all hazards he must
> maintain that tolerable continuity without which society dissolves,
> and men must begin again the weary path up from savagery.[26]

To reconcile old values and new needs Hand — like all great
judges — made changes in the law, but only within accepted presuppositions, only to vitalize existing rules. He did not invoke
new major premises. Rather he built inductively with existing
materials to provide continuity without rigidity, to preserve for
the people alone power to make major shifts in social policy. He
did not worship the past, but he knew that without respect for
past commitments judicial law is lawless, *i.e., ad hoc* and retroactive, providing no standard by which men can order their
affairs. After all, continuity is to judicial law what prospectivity
is to legislation: the means by which men know their legal obligations before they act. For a healthy society, both stability and
change are indispensable. Our separation of powers imposes
major responsibility for the one upon courts; for the other upon
legislatures. This was Hand's teaching. Plainly his is not the
activists' understanding of the Rule of Law and the role of courts
in American government. How differently some other judges see
their function is suggested in Mr. Justice Douglas' comment on
a recent book: "It makes a mockery of judges who insist that if
they were not imprisoned by the law they could do justice." [27]
This was precisely the context of Holmes' shocker, "I hate justice." [28] Or, as Holmes put it more moderately when the young
Hand teasingly bade him to "do justice," "That is not my job.
My job is to play the game according to the rules." [29]

Speaking of the great dissenters among the "nine old men,"
Hand observed:

---

[25] In a eulogy to his colleague Judge Swan, Hand observed: "He will not
overrule a precedent, unless he can be satisfied beyond peradventure that it was
untenable when made; and not even then, if it has gathered around it the
support of a substantial body of decisions based upon it." HAND, *op. cit. supra*
note 2, at 212.

[26] *Id.* at 130.

[27] N.Y. Times, Feb. 19, 1961, § 7 (Book Review), p. 3, col. 5.

[28] Quoted in HAND, *op. cit. supra* note 2, at 306.

[29] *Id.* at 307.

[They] believed that democracy was a political contrivance by which the group conflicts inevitable in all society should find a relatively harmless outlet in the give and take of legislative compromise after the contending groups had had a chance to measure their relative strength; and through which the bitterest animosities might at least be assuaged . . . . They had no illusion that the outcome would necessarily be the best obtainable . . . but the political stability of such a system, and the possible enlightenment which the battle itself might bring, were worth the price.[30]

Obviously Hand shared this view. He was as unpersuaded by the conservative activism of Justices Sutherland and McReynolds, as by the libertarian activism of Justices Black and Douglas. He could not "help thinking that it would have seemed a strange anomaly to those who penned the words in the Fifth [and fourteenth amendments] to learn that they constituted severer restrictions as to Liberty than Property . . . . [Hand could] see no more persuasive reason for supposing that a legislature is *a priori* less qualified to choose between 'personal' than between economic values; and there have been strong protests, to [him] . . . unanswerable, that there is no constitutional basis for asserting a larger measure of judicial supervision over the first than over the second." [31]

With the dominance of [the Holmes-Brandeis view as to "property rights" under the fourteenth amendment] . . . it might seem that the conflict was over. But the end was not yet; for, the latent equivocation involved reappeared as the field of combat changed. . . . [I]t began to seem as though, when "personal rights" were in issue, something akin to the discredited attitude . . . of the old apostles of . . . property, was regaining recognition. Just why property itself was not a "personal right" nobody took the time to explain . . . but the fact remained that in the name of the Bill of Rights [including the Civil War amendments] the courts were upsetting statutes which were plainly compromises between conflicting interests, each of which had more than a merely plausible support in reason.[32]

Should judges exercise the "sovereign prerogative of choice" that this entails? (In Hand's view, as we have seen, the majestic vagueness of the Constitution leaves room for doubt and disagreement.) To what extent should the nonaccountable branch supervise, or second-guess, the accountable branches — and in doing

---

[30] *Id.* at 204.

[31] HAND, THE BILL OF RIGHTS 50–51 (1958).

[32] HAND, *op. cit. supra* note 2, at 205–06.

so disturb the complex equations of a legislative settlement? Though he had less than bounding optimism with respect to popular assemblies, Hand's answer was clear: "[I]t certainly does not accord with the underlying presuppositions of popular government to vest in a chamber, unaccountable to anyone but itself, the power to suppress social experiments which it does not approve." [33] Freedom, after all, includes the freedom to make mistakes — to learn by the process of trial and error.

When Hand had been on the bench for almost half a century, a colleague wrote of him that he "has, I think, never except once[[34]] — and then only because he felt bound by Supreme Court decisions — held unconstitutional any federal statute not dealing with procedure." [35] His statutory constructions tell the same story — "he did not use himself as a measure of value." [36] How tightly he kept his personal preferences in check when performing his judicial duties is seen again and again, but nowhere more vividly than in the contrast between his *Dennis* opinion [37] and this contemporaneous personal view:

Risk for risk, for myself I had rather take my chance that some traitors will escape detection than spread abroad a spirit of general suspicion and distrust, which accepts rumor and gossip in place of undismayed and unintimidated inquiry. I believe that that community is already in process of dissolution where each man begins to eye his neighbor as a possible enemy, where nonconformity . . . is a mark of disaffection; where denunciation, without specification or backing, takes the place of evidence; where orthodoxy chokes freedom of dissent; where faith in the eventual supremacy of reason has become so timid that we dare not enter our convictions in the open lists, to win or lose. . . . The mutual confidence on which all else depends can be maintained only by an open mind and a brave reliance upon free discussion.[38]

---

[33] HAND, THE BILL OF RIGHTS 73 (1958).

[34] United States v. A.L.A. Schechter Poultry Corp., 76 F.2d 617, 624 (2d Cir.) (concurring opinion), *rev'd in part*, 295 U.S. 495 (1935).

[35] Frank, *Some Reflections on Judge Learned Hand*, 24 U. CHI. L. REV. 666, 690 (1957). As to the distinction between substance and procedure in this context, see Brandeis' comment:

"One can never be sure of ends — political, social, economic. There must always be doubt and difference of opinion; one can be 51 per cent sure." There is not the same margin of doubt as to means. Here "fundamentals do not change; centuries of thought have established standards. . . ."

MASON, BRANDEIS: A FREE MAN'S LIFE 569 (Anniversary ed. 1956).

[36] HAND, *op. cit. supra* note 2, at 132.

[37] United States v. Dennis, 183 F.2d 201 (2d Cir. 1950), *aff'd*, 341 U.S. 494 (1951).

[38] HAND, *op. cit. supra* note 2, at 284.

This private sentiment could easily have been made the nub of a decision in the *Dennis* case — but by what authority? Certainly not the historic purpose of the first amendment.[39] Certainly not judicial precedent.[40] Surely not on the ground that all reasonable men would necessarily reject the legislation in question. And so, as Mr. Justice Frankfurter said on review, Hand's opinion "fastidiously [confined] . . . the rhetoric of [precedents] . . . to the exact scope of what was decided by them." [41] In short, Hand obeyed the law — distinguishing between it and his own personal preferences. Plainly he was not what Professor Paul Freund calls a judicial opportunist using public office to promote his private libertarian bias.

Surely it is implicit in Hand's position that judges do not "legitimatize" a challenged measure by failing to find it unconstitutional; they merely find it not so clearly invalid as to justify judicial intervention. Thus *Dennis* does not absolve the people of their responsibility for the Smith Act. And more immediately important, it left a crucial problem of cold-war policy with the elected branches of government where, presumably, it belongs in

---

[39] See generally LEVY, LEGACY OF SUPPRESSION (1960). This book, I think, does not fully exploit the available evidence in support of the following thesis: the first amendment was not intended to abolish the Blackstonian precept that freedom of expression meant freedom from prior restraint, not from subsequent punishment. For example, see Cooley's statement that Blackstone's position "has been followed by American commentators of standard authority as embodying correctly the idea incorporated in the constitutional law of the country by the provisions in the American Bills of Rights." CONSTITUTIONAL LIMITATIONS 602 (7th ed. 1903). In support of this proposition Cooley justifiably cites Kent, Story, and Rawle. Though Dean Levy does not think so, I believe Cooley himself endorsed the proposition in question. *Compare* LEVY, *op. cit. supra* at 2 & n.6 *with* COOLEY, *op. cit. supra* at 602–15. Later treatises acknowledging the restricted purpose of the first amendment include 2 WILLOUGHBY, THE CONSTITUTIONAL LAW OF THE UNITED STATES 1186–1202 (1929), and Corwin, *The Constitution of the United States,* S. DOC. No. 170, 82d Cong., 2d Sess. 769 (1953).

Chafee, *Freedom of Speech in Wartime,* 32 HARV. L. REV. 932 (1919) seems to be a main foundation for a broader view of the historic purpose of the first amendment. *But cf.* Chafee's later observations:

Especially significant is the contemporaneous evidence that the phrase "freedom of the press" was viewed against a background of familiar legal limitations which men of 1791 did not regard as objectionable, such as damage suits for libel . . . [as well as] punishments for criminal libel and for contempt of court . . . . The truth is, I think, that the framers had no very clear idea as to what they meant by "the freedom of speech or of the press," but we can say . . . with reasonable assurance . . . [that] in thinking about it, they took for granted limitations which had been customarily applied in the day-to-day work of colonial courts. Book Review, 62 HARV. L. REV. 891, 897 (1949).

[40] Despite many challenges no act of Congress has been held invalid on first amendment grounds.

[41] Dennis v. United States, 341 U.S. 494, 527 (1951) (concurring opinion).

a democratic system (absent a constitutional mandate that leaves no room for doubt).[42]

> In such matters [of major policy] the odium of disappointing large numbers of persons must rest somewhere, and perhaps the most important question involved is at whose doors that odium shall lie. Shall the courts bear it, and can they while they keep an official irresponsibility to public opinion? [43]

Hand's answer was clear. Among other things it recognized that misplaced odium diverts criticism from the real culprits, dilutes responsibility, and thereby dulls the edge of the political process. Surely democracy were better served if the energy spent in criticizing the courts for not vetoing the Smith Act had been directed against Congress for enacting it — if the vituperation against the federal bench because of the right-to-counsel decisions [44] had been channelled more constructively against the "erring" states. (It is painful to speculate on how many college — and even law school — students are trained, however unwittingly, to think that in these and related cases the courts are the offenders; that the Constitution outlaws all that is unwise or unjust.)

To those who argue that courts can "light the way to a saner world," [45] Hand's answer was short:

> I should indeed be glad to believe it, and it may be that my failure hitherto to observe it is owing to some personal defect of vision; but at any rate judges have large areas left unoccupied by legislation within which to exercise this benign function. Besides, for a judge to serve as communal mentor appears to me a very dubious addition to his duties and one apt to interfere with their proper discharge.[46]

For Hand it was not merely that courts should not intrude upon the national political processes; he questioned whether in the long run they could do so successfully:

> [Few] would deny that government must be the compromise of conflicting interests, as Hamilton supposed. . . . For any times that can count in human endeavor, we must be content with compromises in which the more powerful combination will prevail. The

---

[42] See Mendelson, *Clandestine Speech and the First Amendment*, 51 MICH. L. REV. 553 (1953).

[43] HAND, *op. cit. supra* note 2, at 28.

[44] Betts v. Brady, 316 U.S. 455 (1942), and its progeny.

[45] HAND, THE BILL OF RIGHTS 70 (1958).

[46] *Id.* at 70–71.

most we can hope is that if the maladjustment becomes too obvious,
or the means too offensive to our conventions, the balance can be
re-established without dissolution, a cost greater than almost any
interests can justify. The method of Hamilton has had its way; so
far as we can see must always have its way; in government, as in
marriage . . . the more insistent will prevails.

Liberty is so much latitude as the powerful choose to accord to
the weak. So much perhaps must be admitted for abstract statement; anything short of it appears to lead to inconsistencies. At
least no other formula has been devised which will answer. If a
community decides that some conduct is prejudicial to itself, and
so decides by numbers sufficient to impose its will upon dissenters,
I know of no principle which can stay its hand. Perhaps indeed it
is no more than a truism to say so . . . .[47]

The "nine old men" could attest to the truth of that observation
(to say nothing of the *Dred Scott* fiasco and several other judicially self-inflicted wounds).

Of course, Hand recognized that in the short run courts can
frustrate the political processes, but not without damage to the
moral sanction on which their authority ultimately rests:

The degree to which [a judge] . . . will secure compliance with
his commands depends in large measure upon how far the community believes him to be the mouthpiece of a public will, conceived as the resultant of many conflicting strains that have come,
at least provisionally, to a consensus. This sanction disappears in
so far as it is supposed permissible for him covertly to smuggle
into his decisions his personal notions of what is desirable, however
disinterested personally those may be. Compliance will then much
more depend upon a resort to force, not a desirable expedient when
it can be avoided.[48]

When liberals replaced conservatives on the bench after 1936,
many (including some academicians) changed their minds about
the function of courts. Not a few who had been dedicated supporters of the judiciary became its enemies; while old enemies
became its friends. This suggests, of course, that something other
than "neutral principles" [49] were decisive. (Surely it is pertinent
to wonder how long today's academic activists would find judicial
review a fitting handmaiden to democracy, if the bench were again

---

[47] HAND, *op. cit. supra* note 2, at 71–72.

[48] HAND, THE BILL OF RIGHTS 71–72 (1958).

[49] See Wechsler, *Toward Neutral Principles of Constitutional Law*, 73 HARV.
L. REV. 1 (1959).

to be dominated by Sanfords and Sutherlands.) Hand's view of
the relative roles of statutes and decisions remained constant; he
strove for detachment whatever the relative liberalism of courts
and legislatures — whatever the nature of the interests at issue.
Some insist that such efforts are futile — that no one can escape
his own sense of justice. Yet, if neutrality is an illusion, if objectivity belongs only to the gods,

> [W]e know that men do differ widely in this capacity; and the
> incredulity which seeks to discredit that knowledge is a part of the
> crusade against reason from which we have already so bitterly
> suffered. We may deny — and, if we are competent observers, we
> will deny — that no one can be aware of the danger [of his bias]
> and in large measure provide against it.[50]

Hand's career on the bench, like Cardozo's and Holmes', is a
monument to the truth of this insight.

Plainly, Learned Hand had absorbed what Morris Cohen called
the great lesson of life: humility. His job, as he understood it,
was to decide "cases" and "controversies," not to create a brave
new world — the legislative function having been given to others.
He could neither pretend nor convince himself — like a Field or a
Murphy — that the Constitution was written in his image. He
recognized that in virtually all crucial cases it leaves room for
choice, and that in a democracy choice is the province of the political branches — i.e., of the people striving "however blindly and
inarticulately, toward their [own] conception of the Good Life." [51]
Unlike the ardent activists, he found the main significance of the
democratic process not in its immediate legislative product, but
in the tension-relieving and educational role of the process itself.
His hopeful skepticism was neither intolerant nor impatient with
the groping efforts of the democratic way of life. Indeed, unlike
some true believers, he was prepared to trust it even with fundamentals — whether proprietarian or libertarian.

---

[50] HAND, *op. cit. supra* note 2, at 218.
[51] *Ibid.*

3 ▨ *Hugo Black and Judicial Discretion*

That Hugo Black is one of the great men of his generation few would deny. That he is a master advocate seems equally clear. Few, perhaps not even Brandeis, can match him in the mounting of an argument. But is he a great judge? Many, of course, insist that he is. This view comes easily, if one is a liberal humanitarian—caring only for the policy outcome of a case (and willing to ignore many of Mr. Justice Black's recent results). Those, however—whether liberal or conservative—who care about method, who cannot dismiss law entirely as a myth, are not so easily persuaded.

If a great judge is one who leaves his mark upon the law, Mr. Justice Black no doubt is one of the elect. Yet largely because he is still so much with us, the essence of his impact is not entirely clear. Some see it in his quondam activism—his lionhearted insistence that we live up to our highest aspirations. Others find his efforts a monument to the emasculating effect of unworthy means upon great ends. Benevolent oligarchy after all is still oligarchy. But these are matters best left to our successors. The present purpose is simply to examine Mr. Justice Black's judicial techniques—the methods by which he reaches his striking results.

The foundation of his approach, it would seem, is distrust of judicial discretion and what he disdainfully calls "natural law." This may be his heritage from the "old Court" which taught so effectively that judges are not to be trusted with power to govern. Senator Hugo Black, it will be recalled, was a leader of the New-Deal Congress that found its main efforts gutted by judicial veto. In any event, Mr. Justice Black's major effort in constitutional law has been to eliminate from judicial cognizance some of the more troublesome problems, and to settle others by fixed, discretion-free "absolutes." The purpose is to minimize government by judges in favor of government by the people. Obviously the differences between Justices Black and Frankfurter—as the former has acknowledged[1]—is more a matter of method than of ultimate goals.

Yet for all his skepticism toward judges Mr. Justice Black is not after all a Learned Hand. Indeed he is (or was) obviously a dedicated social reformer. This may be a legacy from his formative years in impoverished, Populist, rural Alabama (see below). In any event, the paradox of a judicial reformer's zeal combined with a distrust of judges may be the crux of Mr. Justice Black's difficulties—particularly the ones that he resolves by finding "plain meanings" in at best dubious constitutional language and history.

I

Mr. Justice Black's votes suggest that he has little sympathy for the political-questions doctrine.[2] It is no doubt far too imprecise—too discretionary—for his taste. Yet he (and apparently he alone among his colleagues) is prepared to leave for the political processes two of the most litigated problems in American constitutional law: state intrusions upon interstate and local business. In both of these areas the "old Court" had exercised discretion with remarkable imprudence—or so it seems with hindsight.

The Articles of Confederation failed largely because they gave national trade no protection from parochialism. The Constitution makes good that failure. Ever since John Marshall's day

---

[1] Hugo L. Black, "Mr. Justice Frankfurter," *Harvard Law Review*, LXXVIII (1965), 1521.

[2] See, for example, *Colgrove* v. *Green*, 328 U.S. 549 (1946), and its successors; see also Hugo L. Black, *A Constitutional Faith* (New York, 1969), 14 ff.

it has been accepted constitutional doctrine that the commerce clause, without the aid of Congressional legislation, . . . affords some protection from state legislation inimical to the national commerce, and that in such cases, where Congress has not acted, this Court and not the state legislature, is under the commerce clause the final arbiter between the competing demands of state and national interests. . . .[3]

Some find the unique genius of our economy not in any special capacity of American businessmen, but in our vast common market, without which there would be no occasion or incentive for mass production and mass distribution. What freedom we have from local impediments upon the national market comes largely from the Court. In the long view this may be one of judicial review's more successful achievements:

It is easy to mock or minimize the significance of "free trade among the states" . . . which is the significance given by a century and a half of adjudication in this Court. With all doubts as to what lessons history teaches, few seem clearer than the beneficial consequences which have flowed from this conception of the Commerce Clause [as a negative upon the states].[4]

If we measure by the number of cases, this is probably the most important area of constitutional litigation. But the Court's effort need not rest entirely upon its accomplishments or upon history. When a state taxes or regulates interstate commerce, it generally burdens people in other states. Judicial intervention may be justified on the grounds of violation of one of the most basic democratic principles, no taxation (or regulation) without representation.

Yet there can be no denying—with the wisdom of retrospect—that from the eighteen-nineties to 1937 the Court too often misused its power under the commerce clause in the interest of laissez faire.[5] Apparently focusing on this abuse, Mr. Justice Black would repudiate the power itself, even though, like all judges, he knows there must be a national veto to protect the nation from

---

[3] *Southern Pacific Co. v. Arizona*, 325 U.S. 761, 769 (1945).

[4] *Panhandle Eastern Pipeline Co. v. Michigan Public Service Com.*, 341 U.S. 329, 340 (1951).

[5] See, for example, *Di Santo v. Pennsylvania*, 273 U.S. 34 (1927).

the myopic states. And so, insisting this is a legislative matter, he holds that the veto should be exercised by Congress rather than by the courts.[6] To substitute parliamentary supremacy for judicial review in this context is a fascinating thought, but it is not the system that we have adopted. Indeed it reflects in essence the old Virginia Plan which the Constitutional Convention rejected in favor of a court-enforced supremacy clause.[7]

Political realism, perhaps, has led the Justice to soften his position. He recognizes belatedly that in cases of "patent discrimination" against interstate trade the Court must act.[8] The term "patent" is revealing. If a court must intrude upon state commerce policy, it should do so only in obvious cases, that is, cases plain enough to foreclose the need of any significant judicial discretion. The difficulty, of course, is that what is obvious to one observer is not necessarily obvious to another.

Meanwhile a unanimous Court, while refusing to discard the ancient tradition of judicial review of state commerce policy, has "conceded" to Mr. Justice Black that these are matters on which Congress must have the last word.[9]

The commerce clause was not the only instrument of the "old Court's" commitment to Herbert Spencer; the Fourteenth Amendment suffered as well. The states, then, were hampered in the regulation of local as well as interstate business. Judicially imposed laissez faire has now gone with the wind, but the Court is still prepared to consider "substantive due process" claims on the Holmesian reasonable-man basis. Mr. Justice Black takes a more Spartan view, evidently finding in due process no substantive restrictions whatever upon state power to regulate the local economy.[10] In fact he has rejected as too "frivolous" for judicial re-

---

[6] See, for example, his dissenting opinion in *Southern Pacific Co.* v. *Arizona*, 784.

[7] A. C. McLaughlin, *A Constitutional History of the United States* (New York, 1936), 163 ff.

[8] *H. P. Hood* v. *Du Mond*, 336 U.S. 525, 545, 552, notes 2 and 3 (1949); see *Bibb* v. *Navajo Freight Lines, Inc.* 359 U.S. 520, 529 (1959), for a slight further softening.

[9] *Prudential Insurance Co.* v. *Benjamin*, 328 U.S. 408 (1946); see also the discussion of this point in *Southern Pacific Co.* v. *Arizona*, 769.

[10] *Polk* v. *Glover*, 305 U.S. 5, 10 (1938); *Ferguson* v. *Skrupa*, 372 U.S. 726

view business claims which every one of his colleagues has found worthy of adjudication.[11]

Just as disenchantment with judges prompts Mr. Justice Black to leave much to legislatures, so, too, he would expand the role of juries at the expense of judicial discretion. Dissenting in 1943, he insisted that for 150 years (no less!) judges have been eroding away "a major portion of the essential guarantee of the Seventh Amendment."[12] The chief evil, in his view, is the directed verdict. For generations state and federal judges have exercised such authority (subject to review on appeal) when, as they see it, the evidence in a case unmistakably points only in one direction. The thought is that a jury's function is to decide between competing factual claims when the evidence is in substantial conflict. If, however, a court is satisfied that rational men could find only one way, it may take a case from the jury. This is a safeguard against runaway verdicts. Experience suggests, for example, that in contests between unfortunate (injured) plaintiffs and rich corporate defendants, juries tend to follow their sympathies rather than the evidence. It costs them nothing, after all, to be generous with other people's money.

While Mr. Justice Black does not quite say every litigant has an absolute right to a jury verdict, his practice suggests that he is not far from that position. In sixty-odd Federal Employer's Liability Act cases that raised this problem over a period of twenty-one years, for example, the Justice voted only once to support a directed verdict.[13] In each instance a United States Court of Appeals or a state appellate court had agreed with the trial judge that the jury could not rationally find for the plaintiff.

The Justice, however, seems to distinguish between economic and other claims. In criminal proceedings he apparently finds

(1963), in which, retreating a bit, Mr. Justice Black may have all but carried the day; see also FPC v. *Natural Gas Pipeline Co.*, 315 U.S. 575, 599 (1942).

[11] *Cities Service Gas Co.* v. *Peerless Oil and Gas Co.*, 340 U.S. 179, 189 (1950); *Phillips Petroleum Co.* v. *Oklahoma*, 340 U.S. 190, 192 (1950).

[12] *Galloway* v. *United States*, 319 U.S. 372, 396 (1943); but see E. G. Henderson, "The Background of the Seventh Amendment," *Harvard Law Review*, LXXX (1966), 289.

[13] See W. Mendelson, *Justices Black and Frankfurter: Conflict in the Court* (Chicago, 1961), 24.

no erosion problem in a very recent innovation which permits the Supreme Court to override jury verdicts in cases involving alleged coerced confessions.[14] His moving opinion in *Chambers v. Florida*[15] may be the real beginning of the modern doctrine. We are told by one who should know that this decision, reached "after great internal struggles," was "not easy" for the Justice.[16] Perhaps the ancient "innovation" with respect to civil juries was equally difficult for those who made and followed it.

If Mr. Justice Black seems at odds with himself on the sanctity of trial by jury, the discrepancy is largely "nominal." In both situations he was, typically, on the generous side, here the side of the injured plaintiff workman and the criminal case defendant.

II

In due process and commerce clause litigation where only property is at stake, Mr. Justice Black would eliminate judicial discretion by all but eliminating the cases. He is not prepared to follow that heroic course with respect to "personal liberty." The problem then is to find a way to exclude judicial discretion in civil liberty cases without excluding judicial review. He found a solution in "absolutes," but this came only after an extended period of trial and error.

Most crucial constitutional litigation now arises under the Fourteenth Amendment. It guards liberty and property via the same terminology in the same clause: "nor shall any State deprive any person of life, liberty, or property without due process of law. . . ." Thus to distinguish between liberty and property for purposes of judicial cognizance presents some difficulty.

Mr. Justice Black's first effort—apparently influenced by Beard's "conspiracy theory"[17]—was to repudiate the long settled view that corporations are "persons" within the meaning of the

---

[14] *Brown* v. *Mississippi*, 297 U.S. 278 (1936).

[15] 309 U.S. 227 (1940).

[16] Charles Reich, "Mr. Justice Black and the Living Constitution," *Harvard Law Review*, LXXVI (1963), 679.

[17] See H. J. Graham, "The Conspiracy Theory of the Fourteenth Amendment," *Yale Law Journal*, XLVII (1938), 371.

due process clause.[18] Since most business is conducted by corporations, this would go a long way toward the Justice's apparent
goal. The difficulty was that corporations publish newspapers.
To deny them due process protection would jeopardize freedom
of the press—as the Justice "discovered" in *Times-Mirror*.[19] Another approach proved awkward when he sought to by-pass due
process in favor of the privileges and immunities clause as a shield
for free utterance.[20] This would circumvent the troublesome term
"property" in the due process clause, but, since the privileges
and immunities clause protects only citizens, it would also leave
aliens without civil-liberty protection—a difficulty which showed
up in the case of the alien Bridges.[21] Something more satisfactory
would have to be found.

To appreciate Mr. Justice Black's final solution one must recognize the dimensions of the problem. The Thirteenth Amendment
had abolished slavery, but the Black Codes soon demonstrated
that Negroes were far from free. As though recognizing the im-
possibility of enumerating all existing and future forms of human cruelty, the framers of the Fourteenth Amendment resorted
to the broad generalities of the privileges and immunities, due
process, and equal protection clauses. To avoid strait-jacketing
precision, they risked vagueness. The Radical Republican sponsors of this ploy also found ambiguity helpful in garnering
moderate support that would have been alienated by more outspoken terminology. And so the Fourteenth Amendment stands
as a trap to test the skill of judges and their respect for the
political processes.

After years of exegesis by the common law process of "inclusion and exclusion," it fell to Mr. Justice Cardozo to answer
counsel's argument that the Fourteenth Amendment imposed upon the states those restrictions which the Bill of Rights imposes
upon the national government.[22] Examining the relevant decisions,

---

[18] *Connecticut General Life Ins. Co.* v. *Johnson*, 303 U.S. 77, 85 (1938);
Wheeling Steel Corp. v. *Glander*, 337 U.S. 562, 576 (1949).
[19] *Times-Mirror* v. *Superior Court of California*, 314 U.S. 252 (1941).
[20] *Hague*, v. *C.I.O.*, 307 U.S. 496 (1939).
[21] *Bridges* v. *California*, 314 U.S. 252 (1941).
[22] *Palko* v. *Connecticut*, 302 U.S. 319 (1937).

he found that counsel's view had never been the law. Yet the Court had "absorbed" some Bill of Rights claims into the Civil War amendment, just as it had rejected others. With the creativity of a great common lawyer, Mr. Justice Cardozo found a rational pattern in the time-tested, piecemeal efforts of many judges over a long period of years. This pattern—the *Palko* rule—was adopted as a guide for decision In brief, the general provisions of the Fourteenth Amendment embrace only those principles "of justice so rooted in the traditions and conscience of our people as to be ranked as fundamental." Other less basic matters are within the province of local self-government. This approach sustained a legislative estimate of contemporary needs in the instant case. It was clear enough to yield a high degree of predictability, but still sufficiently flexible to accommodate an unknowable future. Above all, its growth potential was geared to the community's developing sense of values, not to the private preferences of a few independent judges.

Mr. Justice Black joined in Cardozo's *Palko* opinion. But he soon found it unacceptable (it is "imprecise," and does not exclude protection of property). In Mr. Justice Black's later view *Palko* must be the apotheosis of all the evils of "natural law."[23] And so after the false starts already mentioned he presented his ultimate solution in the *Adamson* dissent.[24] The privileges and immunities, due process, and equal protection clauses "separately, and as a whole"[25] mean *no more and no less* than the restraints enumerated in the Bill of Rights. This he insisted had been the historic purpose of the Fourteenth Amendment. The vagueness of the Civil War settlement would be cured by the "clearly marked . . . boundaries," the "specific" and "particular standards enumerated" in the Bill of Rights.[26]

---

[23] See his opinions in *Griswold* v. *Connecticut*, 381 U.S. 479, 507 (1965); *Adamson* v. *California*, 332 U.S. 46, 68 (1947); *FPC* v. *Natural Gas Pipeline Co.*, 599.

[24] *Adamson* v. *California*, 68.

[25] *Ibid.*, 71. This language was designed apparently to avoid the difficulties encountered in Mr. Justice Black's earlier efforts, mentioned above. The problem, however, remains. What clause or combination of clauses is broad enough to embrace the liberty of aliens, citizens, and corporations, but narrow enough to exclude their property?

[26] See note 23, above.

History—or was it instant history?[27]—"permitted" the Justice to do what he was not prepared to do via raw judicial discretion; namely, to incorporate the Bill of Rights into—and perhaps exclude substantive property interests from—the Fourteenth Amendment. Yet the Justice has found anti-historic meanings in the incorporated charter. The pristine purpose of the Sixth Amendment, for example, was to kill the common-law ban on legal counsel for criminal defendants; not to require government to furnish counsel for indigents.[28] How can the relatively mild separate-but-equal principle be outlawed by the (incorporated) Bill of Rights when slavery itself was not?[29] Surely there is nothing in history or in the "standards enumerated" in the great (incorporated) charter of 1791 which prohibits geographic representation in state legislatures (though not in Congress).[30] Surely neither history nor the long accepted meaning of words warrants the view that obscenity, libel, and slander are protected as freedom of speech and press.[31] Except for a recent reaffirmation,[32] one might have supposed Mr. Justice Black had long since abandoned his *Adamson* absolute for a more discretionary approach—which is what Mr. Justice Douglas explicitly has done.[33] This "switch in time" permitted Douglas to find meaning in the Fourteenth Amendment beyond the "specific" and "particular standards enumerated" in the Bill of Rights. He does not have to hold

---

[27] See C. Fairman and S. Morrison, "Does the Fourteenth Amendment Incorporate the Bill of Rights?" *Stanford Law Review*, II (1949), 5, 140.

[28] W. Beaney, *The Right to Counsel in American Courts* (Ann Arbor, 1955), 27-44.

[29] *Brown* v. *Bd. of Education*, 347 U.S. 483 (1954); see also *Dred Scott* v. *Sanford*, 19 Howard 393 (1857).

[30] *Lucas* v. *Forty-Fourth General Assembly*, 377 U.S. 713 (1964). Only Mr. Justice Douglas had concurred fully in his brother Black's dissent in *Adamson*. He bowed out in time for the reapportionment cases, however. See *Poe* v. *Ullman*, 367 U.S. 497, 516 (1961), in which Mr. Justice Douglas shifts from Black's *Adamson* position to the Rutledge-Murphy position in *Adamson*.

[31] *New York Times* v. *Sullivan*, 376 U.S. 254, 293 (1964); E. Cahn, "Justice Black and First Amendment 'Absolutes': A Public Interview," *New York University Law Review*, XXXVII (1962), 557-59; see note 35, below.

[32] *Griswold* v. *Connecticut*, 525.

[33] See note 30, above. It will not do to argue that Mr. Justice Black escapes his *Adamson* "straight jacket" via an expansive concept of "due process." See his very narrow view of that provision in *Application of Gault*, 87 S. Ct. 1428, 1462 (1967), and *Stovall* v. *Denno*, 87 S. Ct. 1967, 1974 (1967).

that the "incorporated" Bill of Rights forbids a geographic senate, but the Bill of Rights does not, that "trees or acres" may be represented in the Senate of the United States, but not in the Senates of Alabama and Colorado. So, too, he avoids his brother Black's implication that by "specific" and "particular standards" the Constitution distinguishes between geographic representation and poll taxes—to say nothing of contraceptives.[34]

A more determined absolute for Mr. Justice Black is freedom of expression. Massive evidence demonstrates that at best the purpose of the First Amendment's utterance clauses was to codify Blackstone,[35] to outlaw "previous restraints," but not subsequent punishment for words having a "pernicious tendency."[36] Until quite recently this view "has been followed by American commentators of standard authority as embodying correctly the idea incorporated in the constitutional law of the country by the provisions in the American Bills of Rights."[37] Henry Schofield's famous essay in 1914 probably initiated the modern libertarian view. It begins, however, by recognizing that the "nearly if not quite unanimous expressed view of our judges always has been, and is, that the constitutional declarations of liberty of the press are only declaratory of the English common-law right protected by the English courts at the time of the Revolution. . . ."[38]

III

After a long series of experiments—not unlike his search for meaning in the Fourteenth Amendment—Mr. Justice Black (bypassing history) found solace in the "plain meaning' of words. The "Bill of Rights means what it says"; " 'no law abridging' means *no law abridging*"; government cannot punish people for

---

[34] See *Reynolds* v. *Sims*, 377 U.S. 533, 562 (1964); *Harper* v. *Virginia Board of Elections*, 383 U.S. 663 (1966); *Griswold* v. *Connecticut*.

[35] See, for example, Leonard W. Levy, *Legacy of Suppression* (Cambridge, Mass., 1960); T. M. Cooley, Constitutional Limitations (7th. ed.; Boston, 1903); Henry Schofield, "Freedom of the Press in the United States," in *Essays on Constitutional Law and Equity*, II (Brookline, Mass., 1921).

[36] 4 *Commentaries* 151 (1769).

[37] Cooley, 602.

[38] Schofield, 510-11.

talking about public affairs "whether or not such discussion incites to action, legal or illegal."[39] In short, "the First Amendment with the Fourteenth 'absolutely' forbids laws punishing public discussion [here race libel] without any 'ifs' or 'buts' or 'whereases.' " In this view even the universally traditional limitations upon libel, slander, and obscenity are invalid.[40] Repudiating the "sophisticated" view that "you cannot have any absolute 'thou shalt nots,' " the Justice concludes: "I have an idea there are some absolutes. I do not think I am far in that respect from the Holy Scriptures."[41]

Semantics, like history, is not without difficulty. No doubt the First Amendment does mean what it says, but it says different things to different people, indeed to different libertarians. What it says to Mr. Justice Black is not always the same as what it says to Mr. Justice Douglas;[42] so, too, with Holmes and Brandeis.[43] Similarly, even such stout libertarians as Chafee and Meiklejohn find themselves at odds.[44] No wonder the latter chides those who insist that the words "abridging the freedom of speech or of the press" are "plain words, easily understood."[45] And in the end Chafee concluded:

> The truth is, I think, that the framers had no very clear idea as to what they meant by "the freedom of speech or of the press," but we can say . . . with reasonable assurance . . . that the freedom which Congress was forbidden to abridge was not, for them, some absolute concept which had never existed on earth.[46]

---

[39] The language quoted here and immediately following is found in *Koenigsberg* v. *California*, 366 U.S. 36 (1961); *Smith* v. *California*, 361 U.S. 147 (1959); *Barenblatt* v. *United States*, 360 U.S. 109 (1959); *Yates* v. *United States*, 354 U.S. 298 (1957); *Beauharnois* v. *Illinois*, 343 U.S. 250 (1952).

[40] See note 31, above.

[41] Cahn, 562.

[42] See, for example, *Communist Party* v. *SACB*, 367 U.S. 1 (1961); *Barr* v. *Mateo*, 360 U.S. 564 (1959); *Tenny* v. *Brandhove*, 341 U.S. 367 (1951).

[43] *Meyer* v. *Nebraska*, 262 U.S. 390 (1923); *Gilbert* v. *Minnesota*, 254 U.S. 325 (1920).

[44] See Zechariah Chafee's review of Alexander Meiklejohn, *Free Speech and Its Relation to Self-Government*, in *Harvard Law Review*, LXII (1949), 891.

[45] "The First Amendment Is an Absolute," *Supreme Court Review* (1961), 245, 247.

[46] Chafee, 897-98.

The difficulty with the First Amendment, of course, is not in its "thou shalt not" provision, but in the term "the freedom of speech or of the press." Is there any more equivocal term than "freedom"? What is freedom for the fox is death for the hen— a proposition strikingly relevant, for example, in incitement, defamation, and trial-by-newspaper cases. The framers might have spoken more clearly (and more expansively) if they had omitted the weasel word and had provided simply: "Congress shall make no law restricting communication."[47] Plainly they meant to say less than this. But how much less?

No justice has ever suggested that freedom of speech means freedom to say anything that one might choose at any time and any place. Precisely because the First Amendment provides no standards for distinguishing between the licit and the illicit, judges must exercise discretion. Since there are at least two sides in litigation, this is often—and oversimply—called "balancing." For Mr. Justice Black that approach is an anathema to be avoided by automation. Unwilling to abdicate in free-utterance cases (as he would in many property matters), he resorts to absolutism.[48] Yet this is no escape from discretion, if only because a judge must choose among absolutes. Shall it be liberty or property?[49] Even if we find that one of these alone is written in the stars (or in the Fourteenth Amendment), we are still plagued with choice. For both property and liberty have many facets.

John Marshall and his colleagues, for example, had a penchant for vested property rights.[50] In *Fletcher* v. *Peck*[51] they had to choose between property initially vested in a state (for its peo-

---

[47] This, plus the word "the" preceding the term "freedom of speech," suggests they intended to embrace the then liberal concept of free utterance as they found it in Blackstone. See notes 35-37, above, and related text.

[48] But see his recent opinions in *Brown* v. *Alabama*, 86 S. Ct. 719, 729 (1966), *Adderley* v. *Florida*, 87 S. Ct. 242 (1966), and *Cox* v. *Louisiana*, 85 S. Ct. 453 (1965), where free utterance seems to get balanced off against something else.

[49] See *Dred Scott* v. *Sandford*, in which the Court had an opportunity to choose between (a Negro's) "liberty" and (a slaveholder's) "property" as those terms are used in the Fifth Amendment.

[50] See E. S. Corwin, "The Basic Doctrine of American Constitutional Law," *Michigan Law Review*, XII (1914), 255.

[51] 6 Cranch 87 (1810).

ple) and the adverse property claims of allegedly innocent purchasers from a fraudulent land company. Later, in the *Charles
River Bridge* Case,[52] the Court had to weigh older against newer
forms of vested property—ultimately the claims of turnpike owners against those of canal and railroad companies.

We have heard much recently of "the right to privacy." Some
have forgotten that when Warren and Brandeis introduced that
concept, they did it to protect "inviolate personality" from freedom of the press. Years later Mr. Justice Brandeis—Holmes concurring—observed that "although the rights of free speech and
assembly are fundamental, they are not absolute."[53] Thus it is
long settled that verbal freedom ends where defamation of character begins. Obviously we place higher value in the sanctity of
reputation—though it is not mentioned in the Bill of Rights—
than in free talk. So, too, our concern for life is such that Holmes
did "not doubt for a moment" that government may punish verbal
"persuasion to murder."[54]

The point is obvious. Only some finite phase of liberty or
property is ever at stake in a law suit, and inevitably it is in
contest with another cherished but finite claim. The fraction,
claiming to be surrogate for the whole, pretends as such to be
an absolute. Then, for example, freedom of the press clashes with
the right to a fair trial. But nothing more is before the Court
than a few unfortunate editorials which, in their unique setting,
may or may not jeopardize a particular trial.[55]

We simply extract from a premise what we put into it, if we
decide such issues by labeling either fair trial or free press an
absolute. The label merely describes a result. Too often it achieves
decision by an a priori balancing of abstractions, with little regard for the peculiar circumstances before the Court. This evades
the real-world issue: Did these particular editorials substantially
threaten to pervert the outcome of this particular trial? That is

---

[52] 11 Peters 420 (1837).

[53] See *Griswold* v. *Connecticut;* "Privacy," *Law and Contemporary Problems,* XXXI (1966), 251-432; Samuel D. Warren and Louis D. Brandeis "The
Right To Privacy," *Harvard Law Review,* IV (1890), 193; *Whitney* v. *California,* 274 U.S. 357, 373 (1927).

[54] *Abrams* v. *United States,* 250 U.S. 616, 627 (1919).

[55] See *Craig* v. *Harney,* 331 U.S. 376 (1947).

largely a factual issue[56] in a zone of tension between two legal principles. Surely Platonic abstractions are not helpful here. That is why the Court rejects absolutism in favor of "balancing." This means, or should mean, simply that, caught in a clash of pretending absolutes, the Court balances the conflicting claims as best it can. More accurately, it reviews the balance struck by the primary deciding agency (here a trial judge or a jury, in other contexts a legislature). The issue on review is the traditional issue, as outlined by Learned Hand for cases involving the validity of statutes:

> If a court be really candid, it can only say: "We find that this measure will have this result; it will injure this group in such and such ways, and benefit that group in these other ways. We declare it invalid, because after every conceivable allowance for differences of outlook, we cannot see how a fair person can honestly believe that the benefits balance the losses.[57]

IV

Balancing puts the judge (and his discretion) in the decisional process, for good or ill. Unfortunately the absolute approach, whether in proprietarian or libertarian hands, does so, too. The "old Court" discredited for all time the pretense that the Constitution is so loud and clear that judges need not participate in the judicial process—or at least no more than to put statute beside Constitution to see whether they square.[58] Too many opinions hide the inevitable weighing process by pretending that judgments spring full-bloom from a document written generations ago by men who had not the slightest notion of the world in which we now live. Surely the choice is simply this: shall judicial discretion (balancing) be exercised openly and rationally or covertly and intuitively (behind the guise of absolutes)?

Open, rational balancing promises a particularized account of how a court arrives at its decision, instead of the familiar parade

---

[56] See the opinion of Mr. Justice Brandeis in *Burnet* v. *Coronado Oil and Gas Co.*, 285 U.S. 393, 405, 410-11 (1932).

[57] Learned Hand, *The Spirit of Liberty* (2d. ed.; New York, 1953), 179.

[58] *United States* v. *Butler*, 297 U.S. 1, 62-63 (1936).

of hallowed abstractions, elastic absolutes, and made-to-order history. Overt balancing makes it more difficult for a judge to rest on his biases without ever subjecting them to the test of reason. It should also provide a more rational basis for audits of judicial accounts. If in *Barenblatt*, for example, wrong things are balanced, the error can be exposed—with hope for improvement in technique through a continuing intellectual dialogue. But what chance is there for reason, for progress by trial and error, in the realm of a Platonic absolute, particularly one deemed comparable to "the Holy Scriptures"?

To avoid the tyranny of abstractions, Holmes admonished us the think things, not words; and Brandeis labored to shift the focus of judicial attention from wordplay to the facts of life. The "old Court" that goaded them into dissent was not cruel; it was blinded by "absolutes." Engrossed in heavenly preconceptions, it failed to see the earthy meaning of child labor, sweatshops, and yellow-dog contracts. The whole purpose of the Brandeis brief was to cure this blindness, to bring the decisional process down to earth. Walter Lippmann's words in another context are relevant here: "When men act on the principle of intelligence they go out to find the facts. . . . When they ignore it, they go inside themselves and find only what is there. They elaborate their prejudice instead of increasing their knowledge."

The crucial difference between balancing and absolutism is classically illustrated in *Southern Pacific Co.* v. *Arizona*. In what purported to be a safety measure, the state had limited the length of all trains operating within its borders. This was challenged on familiar *Cooley* grounds as a stricture on the national market. After stressing the Court's historic role in such cases, Chief Justice Stone, for the Court, examined the competing interests. On the one hand:

> Because of the Train Limit Law appellant is required to haul over 30% more trains in Arizona than would otherwise have been necessary. The record shows a definite relationship between operating costs and the length of trains, the increase in length resulting in a reduction of operating costs per car. The additional cost of operation of trains complying with the Train Limit Law in Arizona amounts for the two railroads traversing that state to about $1,000,-

ooo a year. The reduction in train lengths also impedes efficient operation. More locomotives and more manpower are required; the necessary conversion and reconversion of train lengths at terminals and the delay caused by breaking up and remaking long trains upon entering and leaving the state in order to comply with the law, delays the traffic and diminishes its volume moved in a given time, especially when traffic is heavy. . . .[59]

What, on the other hand, were the safety gains to offset these burdens upon shipper and consumer? The rationale of the law was that slack action increases in proportion to the length of a train and that slack action causes accidents. The record, however, indicated that any reduction in slack-action difficulties resulting from shorter trains was more than offset by increasing accidents from other causes (grade crossings, for example) due to the thirty per cent increase in the number of trains. In fact, the Court found, the "accident rate in Arizona is much higher than on comparable lines elsewhere, where there is no regulation of the length of trains." Finding substantial weight on the national side of the scale and nothing to counterbalance it, the court struck down the Arizona "safety" law. Surely, from beginning to end it was nothing but a "featherbedding" measure dressed up in safety terminology in an effort to get a favorable judicial response.[60]

Mr. Justice Black was highly critical. In his view the relative weight of the competing state and national interests was simply irrelevant to the judicial function in such cases. In his absolute view the judge's job is quite simple. There is little room for judgment. In the absence of what he calls "patent discrimination"[61] such state laws may not be questioned in court, regardless of their effect upon the national market (and despite the ancient tradition of judicial review in such cases). Conversely, it would seem, "patent discrimination," however harmless in a particular setting, absolutely invalidates a state measure. But why is "patent discrimination" necessarily more worthy of judicial attention than the kind of burden that was "patent" in *Southern Pacific*? If

---

[59] *Southern Pacific Co. v. Arizona*, 771-72.

[60] The Court has always gone far to sustain bona fide state safety regulations despite their impingement upon interstate commerce. A number of these cases are discussed in *Southern Pacific*.

[61] See note 8 and related text, above.

maintenance of an open national market justifies some descent from absolutes to realities in discrimination cases, why not in others? Had the Court in *Southern Pacific* ignored the relevant facts of life, would it not have been vulnerable to the kind of criticism that Stone, Holmes, and Brandeis leveled at the "absolutism" of the "old Court" in *Di Santo v. Pennsylvania*, for example? Indeed Stone's opinion in *Southern Pacific* is simply the positive side of his famous dissent in *Di Santo*.

Some may find an even more striking triumph of absolutism over reality in Mr. Justice Black's *Dean Milk* dissent.[62] There he saw nothing significant but health considerations in an ordinance prohibiting sale within a city of milk pasteurized more than five, or produced more than twenty-five, miles away, regardless of the quality or safety of the outside milk. The city, it may be noted, lay in the heart of a major Wisconsin dairy district. Without suggesting fraud, but perhaps with tongue in cheek, the court accepted the restricting ordinance as a bona fide health measure. Yet it found that legitimate local health interests could be secured without such draconian interference with the national (and local consumer) interest in an open competitive interstate market. Here as in *Southern Pacific* the Court, balancing legitimate local and national claims, chose a solution calculated to preserve the essence of both. Of course, for those who see nothing but a genuine health claim in *Dean Milk*, there is no problem and nothing to balance. Not so for those who see conflicting interests—none of which the Constitution gives a clear priority. It comes perhaps to this: if there is no reason to doubt one's premise, absolutism may be a sound approach where only one interest is at stake. But surely judgment, weighing, balancing, accommodation, must be the rule in litigation that entails a clash of rival interests— and competing constitutional principles (in *Southern Pacific* and *Dean Milk* the states' "police power" and the national commerce power).

V

All of Mr. Justice Black's detours around discretion—his abdications, absolutes, histories, and plain meanings—until recently

---

[62] 340 U.S. 349 (1951).

have led to a common "philosophic" destination.[63] Surely, then, they were themselves exercises in discretion. The Justice was not above the battle, he was in it. He was Martin Luther, not Erasmus. One "cannot raise the standard against oppression, or leap into the breach to relieve injustice, and still keep an open mind to every disconcerting fact or an open ear to the cold voice of doubt."[64] Mr. Justice Black was a committed man. If one liked his cause, well and good, except for conscience and the haunting thought that, but for chance piled on chance, there sat a different champion with a less congenial cause. It comes at last to this: Senators Sutherland and Black could be voted out of office, Justices Sutherland and Black (and their causes) could not.

Mr. Justice Black's votes were highly predictable in terms that have little to do with law.[65] His background may provide a clue. He was born in 1886 in rural Alabama, "a poverty-stricken and ignorant land" too barren even to afford extensive Negro labor.[66] This "poor white" country, torn by Populist upheaval, must have been his most impressing school. He "drew from the agitation in [his native] Clay County strong sympathy based on the most intimate acquaintance with the very poor, and he became absolutely saturated with the essential conception of the Populist philosophy . . . ," namely, that government should be used actively and aggressively to help the underdog. Later, as a young police-court judge and then as prosecutor in Birmingham, he saw what the "law" (the petty officialdom of jailers, bondsmen, police, and the like) means to the poor and the ignorant. And he did a great deal to protect them from it.

Thereafter, in private practice, he represented labor unions and

[63] See note 67, below, and related text. Mr. Justice Sutherland's devices—dual federalism, substantive due process, liberty of contract, etc.—were the instruments of another, quite different "philosophic" outlook.

[64] Hand, 138.

[65] Recent "surprises" mar the virtually perfect libertarian pattern of the Justice's words and votes. See, for example, *Bell* v. *Maryland*, 378 U.S. 226 (1964); *Hamm* v. *Rock Hill*, 379 U.S. 306 (1964); *Griswold* v. *Connecticut*; *Brown* v. *Louisiana*, 86 Sup. Ct. 719 (1966); *South Carolina* v. *Katzenbach*, 86 Sup. Ct. 803 (1966); *Harper* v. *Virginia Board of Elections*; *Fortson* v. *Morris*, 87 S. Ct. 446 (1967).

[66] Here I have drawn heavily upon John P. Frank, *Mr. Justice Black* (New York, 1948), chaps. 1, 2.

many personal injury victims, not a few of whom were injured workmen. This meant of course that he would have few major business clients. The shoe indeed was more apt to be on the other foot. He was fabulously successful in getting large jury awards— often so large that they were in danger of being reduced *by judicial intervention.*

Finally, when he entered politics as a Populist-inspired representative of the "little man," he could hardly fail to feel the pressures that the comfortable classes impose upon "agitators." Small wonder, then, if Mr. Justice Black should have had special concern for free utterance, jury trial, the one-man-one-vote principle, and the rights of the accused. Small wonder, too, that he should have had some doubts about laissez faire and "natural law."

If Hugo Black's heart seemed as big as the world, that may be because he knew the "short and simple annals of the poor" and the wrongs that feed on poverty. If he seemed more concerned with "justice" than with law, perhaps he remembered the old Populist teaching that law favors the fortunate. In any event, as his much-admiring biographer and former law clerk saw it a few years ago:

> In deciding cases Black is frequently a sentimentalist about people. A vivid and dramatic imagination fills in details that may or may not exist. If a case involves an injured veteran, for example, Black sees the veteran, and his family, and his children. If it should be an injured railroad worker, the man becomes as real to Black on an abstract record as if Black himself were making the address to the jury. In these and in the farmer foreclosure cases . . . Black's sympathies are so completely and automatically enlisted for the unfortunate that he is very nearly as much of a pleader as a judge. . . .
>
> He is a representative of that movement in American history which we have variously called the Grange, the Populists, the New Freedom, and the New Deal. . . . His significance as a Justice is that he knows what to do with the power thus given him.[67]

Using that power, Mr. Justice Black has seemed so unhampered by "rules"—so inspired by *ad hoc* or cadi justice—that one might have found him a dedicated practitioner of "American legal real-

---

[67] *Ibid.,* 134, 139.

ism."[68] A practitioner, that is, who found the unenlightened not yet prepared for "realism," and so spared their sensibilities by elaborate "legal" fictions.[69]

Realism-cum-fiction is not, of course, the only way to describe Mr. Justice Black's earlier approach. Professor Reich, speaking no doubt for a host of the judge's admirers, explained it more agreeably. Courts have the duty to enforce the Constitution and "to give it meaning in new settings as society changes. . . ." At least with respect to the Bill of Rights, "the framers' original balance of . . . power and . . . liberty cannot be disturbed unless the Constitution itself is amended." Consistency must be achieved through change. "There is no such thing as a constitutional provision with a static meaning."

> Does Black's concept of a dynamic Constitution square with the accepted notion of law? It can well be answered that no other concept is capable of maintaining the rule of law. . . .
>
> To obey the law, to preserve it in any true sense, surely can mean nothing less than to keep its spirit functioning. . . . This requires a Court that sees, understands, and creates—and then actively enforces the law in its current setting. . . . Only when given life by [an activist] Court can the law "rule."[70]

The "new" Mr. Justice Black dissents! Referring apparently to some of his ardent apologists, he rejects both judicial activism and legal realism:

> I realize that many good and able men have eloquently spoken and written, sometimes in rhapsodical strains, about the duty of this

---

[68] See E. Bodenheimer, *Jurisprudence* (Cambridge, Mass., 1962), 116 ff.

[69] So vulnerable are some of his devices that his greatest admirers on occasion find it necessary to offer "explanations." Professor Charles Black, for example, suggests that the Justice is too "long headed" to mean "absolute" when he says "absolute" in relation to the Bill of Rights. Talk of absolutes, it seems, is merely a device to stimulate a healthy attitude in judges when they exercise their inevitable balancing function. "Mr. Justice Black, the Supreme Court, and the Bill of Rights," *Harper's*, Feb. 1961, pp. 63 ff. After an elaborate and quite different "explanation" another all-out sympathizer concludes: "In its simplicity, the concept of 'absolutes' is perhaps an unsophisticated one. . . ." Reich, 744. Still another—who claims to have explored the history of the Fourteenth Amendment as thoroughly as anyone—admits privately that the *Adamson* incorporation theory is untenable. Yet he defends it and its author as being "closer" than *Palko* to the framers' intention.

[70] Reich, 703, 735, 752-53.

Court to keep the Constitution in tune with the times. The idea is that the Constitution must be changed from time to time and that this Court is charged with a duty to make those changes. For myself, I must with all deference reject that philosophy. The Constitution makers knew the need for change and provided for it. Amendments suggested by the people's representatives can be submitted to the people or their selected agents for ratification. That method of change was good enough for our Fathers, and being somewhat old-fashioned, I must add it is good enough for me.[71]

Putting it more bluntly on a later occasion, he observed:

The Court's justification for consulting its own notions rather than following the original meaning of the Constitution, as I would, apparently is based on the belief . . . that for this Court to be bound by the original meaning of the Constitution is an intolerable and debilitating evil; . . . and that to save the country from the original Constitution the Court must have constant power to renew it and keep it abreast with this Court's more enlightened theories of what is best for our society.[72]

An old proverb holds that the law is a jealous mistress—a beguiling Lorelei, one might add, who tempts each of us to find his own image in her bosom. No one escapes entirely. Some yield blindly, some with sophistication. A few more or less effectively resist. Mr. Justice Black, it would seem, until recently had so completely identified himself with his lady the law that he was unaware of the very thing his admirers once found most admirable, his creativity, his restructuring of the Constitution. In his view apparently he had merely followed the "plain meaning" of the "written" law; to do otherwise would be to indulge in "natural law" and judicial legislation.[73]

---

[71] *Griswold* v. *Connecticut*, 522. See Mr. Justice Roberts' famous squaring analogy in *United States* v. *Butler*, 62-63, and T. R. Powell's comment in *Vagaries and Varieties in Constitutional Interpretation* (New York, 1956), 43: "Try as I will, I cannot bring myself to admire both the candor and the capacity of the men who write such things to be forever embalmed in the official law reports. They must lack one or the other, or I must suffer from some such serious lack in me."

[72] *Harper* v. *Virginia Board of Elections*, 677.

[73] For a classic example of Mr. Justice Black's technique of overruling past decisions while purporting not to do so, see *Gideon* v. *Wainwright*, 372 U.S.

Here, then, was a man—creative, bold, courteous, compassion-ate—pursuing always a great ideal, government by law and not by men (his reaction to the abuses of the "old Court"?).[74] Yet he wanted other things, too, kindly and humane things not immedi-ately forthcoming from the legislative process. He was indeed an aggressive social reformer (his inheritance from the old days in impoverished, Populist-torn, Alabama?). But the ways of the activist reformer were not compatible with his "old fashioned" ideal, the rule of law—entailing as it does detachment in judges and more than heart's desire in their edicts.[75] If Mr. Justice Black seemed to practice, he could not accept in principle, the "realist" view that law is anything a judge may boldly assert and plausibly maintain. He knew what some of his most ardent apologists seem-ed unable to grasp: if law is indeed a myth, there is no demo-cratic justification whatsoever for a non-elected super-legislature that pretends to be a court.

Addendum

The above was conceived and for the most part written some years ago, when so accomplished a scholar as Professor Reich *inter alios* could still treat (and honor) Mr. Justice Black as a thoroughgoing libertarian activist.[76] Meanwhile there seems to have been a sea-change in the thrust of the judge's votes. This is reflected, for example, in the annual surveys of the Commission on Law and Social Action.[77] For years prior to 1963 Mr. Justice Black's "score" in favor of civil liberty was second only to that of Mr. Justice Douglas. In the 1963 and 1964 Terms he dropped to third place; in the two following Terms he fell to fifth place.

---

335 (1963); see also J. H. Israel, "*Gideon* v. *Wainwright*: The 'Art' of Over-ruling," *Supreme Court Review* (1963), 211.

[74] In *Kingsley International Pictures Corp.* v. *Regents of NYU*, 360 U.S. 684, 691 (1959), the Justice speaks of "the rule of law which our Constitution envisages." Elsewhere he tells us that "flexible" legal standards are not standards, they are "mush." See his "Public Interview," *New York University Law Review*, XXXVII (1962), 562.

[75] This ambivalence may be the seedbed of the difficulties that some of Mr. Justice Black's champions feel so compelled to "explain."

[76] Reich, *passim*.

[77] These surveys are issued annually in mimeograph form by the American Jewish Congress.

The 1967 Term found him in the seventh position. By the end of the latest 1968 Term he had fallen to place nine.

Comes now Professor Howard—like Mr. Reich an admiring former law clerk—suggesting that the Justice has never been an activist, that his recent stance is not a departure from, but a continuation of, a long time dedication to the rule of law.[78] In my view Mr. Howard's analysis is quite compatible with the judge's words—just as Mr. Reich's view is quite compatible with the judge's votes (prior to the early nineteen-sixties). Paul Freund no doubt is right in finding the *Griswold* dissent implicit in the *Adamson* dissent.[79] Yet surely, as suggested above, *Griswold* was hardly Mr. Justice Black's first opportunity for implementing his *Adamson* strictures had he seen fit to do so before 1965.

Mr. Howard, and indeed the Justice himself, quite properly insist that Hugo Black did, and does, believe deeply in the rule of law (however naive that may seem to many of the judge's most activist erstwhile followers). Yet surely in recent years Mr. Justice Black has not been as imaginative as he once was in discovering the "plain meaning" of the "written" law. Explanations for the change must await another day. In the meantime, these speculations: Is it mere coincidence that the seeming switch coincides with the departure of Mr. Justice Frankfurter, the apparent crisis in long smoldering relations between Justices Black and Douglas, and the advent of the "new" extreme activism of Mr. Justice Goldberg?

---

[78] A. E. D. Howard, "Mr. Justice Black: The Negro Protest Movement and the Rule of Law," *Virginia Law Review*, LIII (1967), 1030-1090.

[79] See Freund, "Mr. Justice Black and the Judicial Function," *U.C.L.A. Law Review*, XIV (1967), 467.

4 🍃 Mr. Justice Douglas and Government by the Judiciary

Not so long ago it was sound liberal doctrine that judges should avoid as much as possible adjudication of constitutional issues. This view found classic expression in the Brandeis minority opinion in *Ashwander*.[1] As the Justice put it off the bench, "The most important thing we do is not doing."[2] The thought of course was that the fewer social issues preempted by courts, the more that are left for resolution via the democratic process. With the advent of the Roosevelt Court the Brandeis view became majority doctrine in *Rescue Army* v. *Municipal Court*.[3] Old fashioned liberalism had won a major victory.

Deeply skeptical with respect to our political processes, today's "activists"—the new liberals?—seem markedly inclined to put their policy eggs in the judicial basket. Indeed their great victories have been won in court. And so it is not strange that a major element of modern activism is an effort to open more widely the gateway to the federal judiciary. Indeed it seems no more than caricature to suggest that the "neo-liberal" goal is to shunt as many policy issues as possible from the political processes to the federal courts, especially the Supreme Court. Mr. Justice Douglas was a leading spokesman for this approach. What follows seeks to demonstrate that proposition—and to indicate its implications in one major area of constitutional law.

---

[1] *Ashwander* v. *T.V.A.*, 297 U.S. 288 (1936).

[2] A. M. Bickel, *The Unpublished Opinions of Mr. Justice Brandeis*, 17 (1957).

[3] 331 U.S. 549 (1947). Justices Douglas and Murphy dissenting.

Certiorari

A major part of the history of the Supreme Court has been a struggle to keep up with its constantly increasing workload. This problem has been resolved from time to time by legislation.[4] But each remedial measure in time proves inadequate—as population explodes and social problems multiply. The last congressional relief came in the Judges' Bill of 1925. Again the reprieve seems to have been only temporary. As the Freund Committee Report saw it, "The statistics of the Court's current workload, both in absolute terms and in the mounting trend, are impressive evidence that the conditions essential for the performance of the Court's mission do not exist. ° ° ° [A]pproximately three times as many cases were filed in the 1971 Term as in the 1951 Term ° ° ° by 1971, 3,643 new cases were filed, an increase of 1,458 in ten years." Accordingly, "The percentage of petitions for certiorari granted has sharply dropped as the filings have increased. . . . In 1971, 5.8% were granted in contrast to 17.5%, 11.1% and 7.4% in 1941, 1951, and 1961 respectively." So too, "The number of cases . . . decided by opinion has not changed significantly despite the rising flood of petitions and appeals. ° ° ° At the 1971 Term 143 cases were so disposed of, with 129 opinions of the Court; during the preceding 15 years the average was 120 cases, with 100 opinions." The decline in the percentage of petitions granted "would seem to reflect, not a lessening of the proportion of cases worthy of review, but rather the need to keep the number of cases argued and decided on the merits within manageable limits as the docket increases." Thus "two consequences can be inferred. Issues that would have been decided on the merits a generation ago are passed over by the Court today; and second, the consideration given to the cases actually decided on the merits is compromised by the pressures of 'processing' the inflated docket of petitions and appeals."[5]

Last year the Supreme Court docketed over 4500 cases, the great majority of which did not merit any attention by the Court. Yet each Justice looked at each case to choose the few cases that should or even could be heard. The Chief Justice has predicted that, unless something is done, the filings will rise to 7000 cases by 1980. The inevitable result of this avalanche of cases is obvious; the time used in deciding not to decide will consume almost all of the time that should be devoted to hearing and deciding cases that fall within the Court's proper sphere.[6]

---

[4] For a history of this development, see F. Frankfurter and J. Landis, *The Business of the Supreme Court* (1927).

[5] Federal Judicial Center, "Report of the Study Group on the Caseload of Supreme Court" (1972).

[6] Judge S. M. Hufstedler, "Comity and the Constitution: The Changing Role of the

Mr. Justice Douglas saw no problem in such figures. Rejecting the "intimations" of *all* his colleagues that the Court was overburdened, he insisted: "The case for our 'overwork' is a myth. ° ° ° We are vastly underworked."[7] Perhaps so. Yet the fact is that the Court's carryover or backlog of cases has grown from 146 in 1951 to 428 in 1961, 864 in 1971 and 821 in 1975.[8]

The relief that Congress gave the Court in the Judges' Bill of 1925 made a large part of the Supreme Court's reviewing authority discretionary. By granting or denying writs of certiorari as a matter of grace the Court was authorized to pick and choose cases deemed worthy of review—and to refuse review of others. In five Terms (1967-71) the Court granted writs of certiorari in 594 cases for an average of about 118 cases per Term. In the same period Mr. Justice Douglas dissented from denials of certiorari in 1098 cases for an average of 219 per Term. In short, he would have increased the Court's decisional workload by 185 percent in this one, if major, category. In the last Term herein considered (1971-72) he achieved a total of 408 dissents in such cases. His nearest rival was Mr. Justice Brennan with 27.[9] The significance of these figures is revealed when one considers that during the Term in question there were 151 opinions of the Court and 281 per curiams.

The point is not simply that the Douglas appetite is great. The range of the social problems that he would solve by judicial edict seems unlimited—from the most trivial to the most desperate. He alone, for example, thought the highest court of the land should concern itself with the length of a school boy's hair.[10] And he alone persistently held it should concern itself with the validity of the Viet Nam war.[11] One re-

---

Federal Judiciary," 47 New York University Law Review, 841, 850 (1972). For other dimensions of this problem see H. Hart, "The Time Chart of the Justices," 73 Harvard Law Review 84 (1959); Chief Justice W. Burger, "Report on Problems of the Judiciary," 58 American Bar Association Journal 1049 (1972).

[7] *Tidewater Oil Co.* v. *U.S.*, 409 U.S. 151, 175-176, 178 (1972). After the shock of the Freund Committee Report two of the Justices seem to have discovered they were not as burdened as they had earlier "intimated." See A. Bickel, *The Caseload of the Supreme Court*, 15-19 (1972).

[8] These and other telling figures will be found in Federal Judicial Center, *loc. cit.*, and "The Supreme Court, 1974 Term," 89 Harvard Law Review 278 (1974).

[9] The figures presented in this paragraph were derived from an unpublished study on "Certiorari Policy and Mr. Justice Douglas" prepared for the author by T. O. Moore and G. Weinberg, students at the School of Law, University of Texas.

[10] *Olff* v. *East Side Union High School*, 404 U.S. 1042 (1972).

[11] The cases are cited in *Holtzman* v. *Schlesinger*, 414 U.S. 1316, 1319 (1973).

calls Maurice Finkelstein's comment on *Dred Scott* v. *Sanford:*[12] "A question which involved a Civil War can hardly be proper material for the wrangling of lawyers."[13]

Standing to Sue

It has long been settled that our federal courts do not give advisory opinions.[14] An adversary system, after all, presupposes real adversaries, i.e., litigants at loggerheads with more than hypothetical interests at stake. Without such status one lacks "standing" to sue in a federal court. Thus *Frothingham's* case[15] was dismissed because in challenging an early federal welfare measure, her only claim of interest *as a litigant* was that she was a taxpayer. But her tax share in the program in question was obviously infinitesimal. As an English judge once said, "A court will not stoop to pick up a pin." It has far more important business involving true injuries—and typically an overcrowded docket. Accordingly, Ms. Frothingham, whose real concern was simply a general, ideological dislike of the welfare program in question, was shunted over to the forum appropriate for such matters—the political arena. The standing doctrine thus rests on at least three legs: the adversary system; economic use of a scarce resource, i.e., the judiciary; and the separation of powers. What the last means in this context is that, while courts have a special role with respect to individuals and minorities who suffer particularized injury, it is the function of the political process to serve the Frothinghams, i.e., those who can claim no personal harm but only a general policy grievance. One may note incidentally that the Brandeisian avoidance route in *Frothingham* permitted the Court to escape commitment on a welfare measure which in that day most of the Justices seemed inclined to veto.

In his first year on the bench Mr. Justice Douglas, adhering to *Frothingham*, supported an opinion which held:[16]

No matter how seriously infringement of the Constitution may be called into question, this is not the tribunal for its challenge except by those who have some specialized interest of their own to vindicate, apart from a political concern which belongs to all. ° ° °

---

[12] 19 Howard 393 (1857).

[13] "Further Notes on Judicial Self-Limitation," 39 Harvard Law Review 221, 243 (1925).

[14] See *Hayburn's Case*, 2 Dall. 409 (1796) and discussion thereof in *Muskrat* v. *U.S.*, 219 U.S. 346 (1911).

[15] *Frothingham* v. *Mellon*, 262 U.S. 447 (1923).

[16] *Coleman* v. *Miller*, 307 U.S. 433, 464-467 (1939). See also *Tileston* v. *Ullman*, 318 U.S. 44 (1943).

One who is merely the self-constituted spokesman of a constitutional point of view can not ask us to pass upon it.

In later years Mr. Justice Douglas had no patience with the doctrine of standing. *Frothingham*, he said, was good enough "in the heyday of substantive due process when courts were sitting in judgment on the wisdom of reasonableness of legislation. ° ° ° But we no longer undertake to exercise that kind of power."[17] (This from the author of the new substantive due process in *Griswold* v. *Connecticut.*[18]) And so it developed that he alone among his colleagues held that tax payment *per se* gives standing to sue in the federal courts.[19] In *Flast* v. *Cohen*[20] the Court eased the ban on such suits just a bit—apparently to expedite Free-Exercise and Establishment-of-Religion cases which otherwise are often peculiarly difficult to initiate.[21] In a concurring opinion Mr. Justice Douglas rejected the Court's effort to limit its innovation. He endorsed those "few state decisions [which] are frankly based on the theory that [in this context] a taxpayer is a private attorney general seeking to vindicate a public interest."[22] (Or, he might have added, a private grudge!) The taxpayer interest as a limitation upon plaintiffs of course means nothing; for anyone who buys a pack of cigarettes is a federal taxpayer. It follows then in the Douglas view that a plaintiff need have no more at stake than a platonic interest—the kind of interest which in *Frothingham* was referred to the political processes. In short, the Justice would have the Court give advisory opinions.

Even more innovative was the Douglas dissent in *Sierra Club* v. *Morton*[23] involving the "civilization" of Mountain King Valley. There he urged a standing rule that would permit environmental issues to be litigated "in the name of the inanimate object [the valley] about to be despoiled." Those who have an "intimate relation with the inanimate object" should be recognized as "its legitimate spokesmen." While the Court has not accepted the Douglas approach, it has recognized

---

[17] *Flast* v. *Cohen*, 392 U.S. 83, 107 (1968).

[18] 381 U.S. 479 (1965).

[19] In *Schlesinger* v. *Reservists Committee*, 418 U.S. 208, 229 (1974), Mr. Justice Douglas argued for citizen standing.

[20] 392 U.S. 83 (1968).

[21] The limited nature of *Flast* is emphasized in *U.S.* v. *Richardson*, 418 U.S. 166 (1974) and *Schlesinger* v. *Reservists Committee*, 418 U.S. 208 (1974), Mr. Justice Douglas dissenting in both cases.

[22] Compare *Trafficante* v. *Metropolitan Life Ins. Co.*, 409 U.S. 205 (1972).

[23] 405 U.S. 727 (1972). This case was in fact a victory for environmentalists for it revealed that by a slight change in the pleadings such suits could be maintained.

what perhaps may be called environmentalist standing—at least when Congress can be said to have authorized it.[24]

It is easy to scoff at Mr. Justice Douglas' private attorneys general and his inanimate plaintiffs. To do so is to miss the point. They are important gambits to evade, i.e. abolish, the requirement of standing— to expedite the New Politics of judicial activism. The taxpayer suit means that any "public spirited citizen"—or crank—can trigger a judicial test on abstract, ideological grounds, i.e., in the absence of any injury or immediate threat to anyone, indeed perchance before any experience as to the actual operational effect of the challenged measure. This would be a substantial step back toward the old New York council of revision—a device rejected by the Constitutional Convention of 1787.[25] As we have seen, the Justice feels quite differently about standing in the context of the old activism of the 1920s and early 1930s. Yet, after all, Ms. Frothingham too was "seeking to vindicate a public interest"—she too was acting as a "private attorney general." The point is not that the Douglas approach is necessarily catastrophic, but that it would wrench our most basic notions as to the role of courts in a democracy.[26] As Mr. Justice Powell put it recently:[27]

Relaxation of standing requirements is directly related to the expansion of judicial power [at the expense of the elected branches]. The irreplaceable value of the power articulated by Chief Justice Marshall lies in the protection it has afforded the constitutional rights and liberties of individual citizens and minority groups [suing to protect their own unique, personal interests]. It is this role, not some amorphous general supervision of the operation of government [at the instance of ideological plaintiffs like Mrs. Frothingham] that has . . . permitted the peaceful coexistence of the countermajoritarian implications of judicial review and the democratic principles on which our Federal Government . . . rests.

Ripeness

Just as judges shun mooted issues, they avoid problems not yet ripe for adjudication. Why borrow trouble? Why make a "final" constitutional commitment on an issue that may never arise, or may arise in a context entirely different from that hypothesized in the unripe "case"?

Early in his judicial career Mr. Justice Douglas seems to have been

---

[24] *U.S. v. SCRAP*, 412 U.S. 669 (1973).

[25] See A. E. Sutherland, *Constitutionalism In America*, 172 (1965).

[26] Another important step in the development of the Douglas view on standing is *Association of Data Processing Service Organizations, Inc. v. Camp*, 397 U.S. 150 (1970).

[27] *U.S. v. Richardson*, 418 U.S. 166, (1974).

satisfied with the doctrine that precludes judgment on premature claims —even those involving free utterance.[28] A little later he was prepared to accommodate premature plaintiffs in hardship cases when otherwise their interests could be vindicated only at the risk of losing their jobs.[29] Finally, in his later years the Justice moved far beyond such pragmatic accommodations to what seems essentially an advisory opinion stance.

In *Poe* v. *Ullman*[30] a doctor and two of his patients—a husband and wife—sought declaratory relief from a Connecticut statute forbidding the use of contraceptives and the giving of medical advice on the use thereof. This law had been "in force" for some 80 years. During that time there must have been hundreds of state and local prosecutors in Connecticut. Yet, excepting one immediately aborted effort, nobody had ever been prosecuted for using, or advising on the use of, contraceptive devices.[31] Moreover the latter were as available in Connecticut drugstores as in those of any other state.[32] The Court refused to make what it considered an unnecessary constitutional commitment.

The fact that Connecticut has not chosen to press the enforcement of this statute deprives these controversies of the immediacy which is an indispensable condition of constitutional adjudication. This Court cannot be umpire to debates concerning harmless, empty shadows. To find it necessary to pass on these statutes now . . . would be to close our eyes to reality.

Mr. Justice Douglas (with two associates) dissented. For him the "law" in question presented a real threat to those in the plaintiffs' position.

Some four years later there was in fact a prosecution under Connecticut's birth control law (not in the *Poe* v. *Ullman* context, but against the operators of a birth control center). In *Griswold* v. *Connecticut*[33] Mr. Justice Douglas, for the Court, found the challenged law unconstitutional—in what seems an unnecessary, indeed reckless, judicial exertion. Surely the world's rampant birth rate is our most trying problem. From it derive, for example, the pollution problem, the environmental problem, the food and energy crisis—to mention only what is most obvious

---

[28] *Alabama State Federation of Labor* v. *McAdory*, 325 U.S. 450 (1945); *Watson* v. *Buck*, 313 U.S. 387 (1941).

[29] *International Longshoremen's . . . Union* v. *Boyd*, 347 U.S. 222 (1954); *United Public Workers* v. *Mitchell*, 330 U.S. 75 (1947). Cf. *Reserve Army* v. *Municipal Court*, 331 U.S. 549 (1947) involving another form of special hardship for the plaintiff.

[30] 367 U.S. 497 (1961).

[31] *Id.*, 501-502.

[32] *Id.*, 502.

[33] 381 U.S. 479 (1965).

and immediate. Yet *Griswold* holds that birth control is a *private* matter! It follows, then, that just as government may not forbid, so it may not compel (or encourage?) birth control. In a word *Griswold* removes from the ordinary political processes one of the world's most critical *public* problems, the birth rate.

What makes this crucial for present purposes is that the constitutional commitment might easily have been avoided without harm to anyone. By the time the case reached the Supreme Court one house of the Connecticut legislature had voted to repeal the offending statute.[34] A Brandeisian court would have withheld decision for a reasonable period to give the legislature an opportunity to complete its work. If indeed it did so, the case could have been dismissed as moot, and Mr. Griswold's conviction would have died by abatement.[35] More important the American people would not have been unnecessarily hamstrung in the context of a most perplexing public problem. Had the legislature not acted within a reasonable time, the Court could have responded appropriately—which at most would have been a decision confined to the matter at issue; namely, may a state forbid birth control (leaving untouched the broader issue of whether government may compel or encourage limits on population growth). It should be emphasized that perhaps the most important basis of Brandeisian restraint is that it leaves open as long as possible the opportunity for education by experience and such enlightenment as may come from the free play of the democratic processes.

Boyle v. *Landry*[36] was a broadgauged suit by groups of black residents of Chicago for declaratory and injunctive relief against enforcement of numerous state statutes and city ordinances. The trial court upheld all of these measures except one subsection of a mob action law and one provision of an intimidation statute. Only the latter ruling was appealed. The Court, per Mr. Justice Black, found it "obvious" that the allegations fall far short of showing any injury that would justify the remedy requested:

Not a single one of the citizens who brought this action had ever been prosecuted, charged, or even arrested under the . . . intimidation statute which the court below had

---

[34] *Id.*, 531, note 8.

[35] See *Hamm* v. *City of Rock Hill*, 379 U.S. 306 (1964).

[36] 401 U.S. 77 (1971). This was one of the companions of *Younger* v. *Harris*, 401 U.S. 37 (1971). In that group of cases Mr. Justice Douglas was prepared to go further than any of his colleagues in permitting federal district courts to injoin pending and future state prosecutions.

held unconstitutional. ° ° ° Rather, it appears . . . that those who originally brought this suit made a search of state statutes and city ordinances with a view to picking out certain ones that they thought might possibly be used . . . as devices for bad faith prosecutions against them. ° ° ° The policy of a century and a half against interference by the federal courts with state law enforcement is not to be set aside on such flimsy allegations as those relied upon here.

Only Mr. Justice Douglas dissented.   Without contradicting the Court's view that none of the petitioners had even been arrested under the intimidation statute, he pressed their general allegation (relating to numerous laws *en masse*) that "the appellants are arresting them without warrants or probable cause, and detaining them on excessive bail ° ° ° to harass them, not to prosecute in the normal manner."   Assuming these general allegations were in fact true with respect to the other (*validated*) measures, it is difficult to see how killing the intimidation statute would bring relief.   A policeman or prosecutor bent on improper harassment would hardly be discouraged by invalidation of the intimidation law *alone* under which admittedly there was no intention to prosecute—and under which, as the Court found, none of the petitioners had ever been arrested, charged, or prosecuted.

In *Laird* v. *Tatum*[37], involving Army surveillance of civilian activities, Mr. Justice Douglas made one of his last great dissenting efforts on behalf of anticipatory plaintiffs.   His argument began with a brilliant critique of military intrusions into civilian affairs.   None of his colleagues disagreed; for most of them the issue lay elsewhere.   Was the case ripe for adjudication?   The Court of Appeals (which had held in their favor) found, and the Supreme Court agreed, that the plaintiffs[38]

freely admit that they complain of no specific action of the Army against them. . . . There is no evidence of illegal or unlawful surveillance activities. ° ° ° So far as is yet shown, the information gathered is nothing more than a good newspaper reporter would be able to gather by attendance at public meetings and the clipping of articles from publications available on any newsstand.

Hoping then to convert an otherwise hypothetical case into something real, the plaintiffs argued that the *present existence of the surveillance system* had a *present inhibiting effect* on exercise of First Amendment rights.

Recognizing the tradition against advisory opinions, the Court held that "allegations of a subjective 'chill' are not an adequate substitute for a claim of specific present objective harm or a threat of specific fu-

---

[37] **408** U.S. 1 (1972).   See also *O'Shea* v. *Littleton*, 414 U.S. 488 (1974).

[38] **408** U.S. 1, 9 (1972).

ture harm." Here the essential claim was not present or future injury, but disagreement with executive use of Army data gathering. Such generality of objection is really an attack on the political expediency of legislative and executive measures, not a presentation of legal issues. Moreover, the Court observed, plaintiffs' counsel admitted at trial "that his clients were 'not people, obviously, who are cowed or chilled' "; instead they claimed to "represent millions of Americans not nearly as forward and courageous." It followed in the Court's view that, if plaintiffs themselves are not chilled but seek only to safeguard the "millions" who allegedly are, they clearly lack that "personal stake in the outcome of the controversy" which is essential to standing.

The major thrust of the Douglas-Marshall dissent (Justices Brennan and Stewart dissented separately) was the evil of military surveillance. The non-justiciability claim was "too transparent for serious argument" —accordingly little time was spent on that. "The present controversy is not a remote, imaginary conflict." And then this new point: "There is good reason to permit the strong to speak for the weak or the timid in First Amendment matters."

In its concluding remarks the Court observed that, carried to its logical end, plaintiffs' "approach would have the federal courts as virtually continuing monitors of the wisdom and soundness of Executive action; such a role is appropriate for the Congress [not for] the judiciary, absent actual present or immediately threatened injury resulting from unlawful governmental action." It is crucial that meanwhile Congress had in fact looked into the Army's surveillance program. Hearings were held by the Ervin Subcommittee on Constitutional Rights of the Senate Judiciary Committee. Thereafter the Army ordered a "significant reduction" in its challenged program.[39] As Mr. Justice Stone put it with respect to the old activists, "Courts are not the only agency of government that must be assumed to have capacity to govern."[40] It is worth passing notice that Mr. Justice Douglas did not object—nor did libertarians generally—when a former five-star general, as President, ordered military intrusion into civilian affairs at Little Rock in 1957. See *Cooper* v. *Aaron*, 358 US 1 (1958). That intrusion of course included surveillance.

MOOTNESS

The moot, like the unripe, case is untimely—the one coming too late,

---

[39] *Id.*, 7-8.
[40] *U.S.* v. *Butler*, 297 U.S. 1 (1936).

the other too soon.   Lateness in this context means simply that events have resolved the plaintiff's problem before judges have had an opportunity to do so.   Yet while prematurity, as we have seen, is still an effective barrier to judicial decision, much of the ancient doctrine of mootness recently has been cut away.   This disparity perhaps is explained by the view that moot issues may be a little less hypothetical than premature ones.   The former at least were once real controversies involving true adversaries and hard facts as a basis for adjudication.

In any event, beginning with an opinion by Mr. Justice Douglas,[41] the "collateral-consequences" exception has expanded "to the point where it may realistically be said that inroads have been made in the [mootness] principal itself."[42]   Beginning also in a Douglas opinion, an enlargement of the old "capable-of-repetition-yet-evading-review" exception has cut in the same direction.[43]   So too, we now know, class action status may save a case that with respect to the named plaintiff has become moot.[44]   Hints in some cases would go even further.[45]   Yet all this apparently is not enough for Mr. Justice Douglas as *De Funis* v. *Odegaard*[46] suggests.   There the plaintiff had challenged a law-school admissions program that favored minority applicants at his expense. Later he was admitted to the law school in question, and was a last quarter graduating senior when his case reached the Supreme Court for argument.   It was dismissed as moot—the Court thus avoiding the new and simmering problem of affirmative action.   Mr. Justice Douglas alone not only voted to take the case, but also proceeded to decide it by repudiating this kind of compensatory discrimination.   He would thereby have killed in the bud a new remedy for an old evil—a remedy the empirical meaning and implications of which we are just beginning to fathom.   All this was gratuitous—an advisory opinion—for it could hardly have helped De Funis.   He had already obtained the object of his suit.   Why, then, unnecessarily cut off the educational process of trial and error with respect to a difficult race relations problem?

---

[41] *Fiswick* v. *U.S.*, 329 U.S. 211 (1946).

[42] *Sibron* v. *New York*, 392 U.S. 40, 54 (1968).

[43] *Moore* v. *Ogilvie*, 394 U.S. 814 (1969).

[44] *Richardson* v. *Ramirez*, 418 U.S. 24, (1974).   Cf. *De Funis* v. *Odegaard*, 416 U.S. 412 (1974).

[45] *Sibron* v. *New York*, 392 U.S. 40, 51-52 (1968); *Carafas* v. *La Vallee*, 391 U.S. 234, 238 (1968).

[46] 416 U.S. 312 (1974).

POLITICAL QUESTIONS

The Supreme Court holds that some constitutional issues—"political questions"—are not to be resolved by federal courts. They are left accordingly for solution by the political processes. The rules for determining what constitutes a political question are easily stated,[47] but they are "soft." What seems really at stake is a prudential policy summarized as follows by Professor Bickel:[48]

> Such is the foundation, in both intellect and instinct, of the political-question doctrine: the Court's sense of lack of capacity, compounded in unequal parts of (a) the strangeness of the issue and its intractability to principled resolution; (b) the sheer momentousness of it, which tends to unbalance judicial judgment; (c) anxiety, not so much that the judicial judgment will be ignored, as perhaps it should but will not be; (d) finally ('in a mature democracy'), the inner vulnerability, the self-doubt of an institution which is electorally irresponsible and has no earth to draw strength from.

The Court's landmark opinion in *Baker* v. *Carr*[49] provided a lengthy résumé of the major political-question decisions. In a separate statement Mr. Justice Douglas expressed his "strongly" felt view that "many of the cases cited by the Court . . . were wrongly decided. In joining the opinion [he said] I do not approve those decisions." Again the great appetite! And again the Justice found himself alone in his views on an access-to-the-courts issue. But his solitude was confined to broad principle; he carried the day on the particular proposition that reapportionment is not a political question. For him this was the culmination of a long struggle. When the "original" reapportionment case—*Colegrove* v. *Green*[50]—was first considered in conference Chief Justice Stone (who was to die before a decision could be handed down) "made a long statement on why the courts should stay out. Only Mr. Justice Douglas was in opposition. Later he won [two] converts[51]—and eventually, in *Baker*, a majority. Yet his victory has turned somewhat sour. In *Whitcomb* v. *Chaviz*[52] the trial court had found an unconstitutional gerrymander at the expense of black ghetto residents in a multi-member district. The Supreme Court disagreed. Mr. Justice Douglas (joined by Justices Bren-

---

[47] See for example, C. A. Wright, *Federal Courts*, 45-48 (1970).

[48] A. M. Bickel, *The Least Dangerous Branch*, 184 (1962).

[49] 369 U.S. 186 (1962).

[50] 328 U.S. 549 (1946).

[51] Letter to the author, dated 17 November 1964, from A. T. Mason, the Stone biographer.

[52] 401 U.S. 124 (1971).

nan and Marshall) dissenting, recognized that "Gerrymandering is the other half of *Reynolds* v. *Sims.*" In short, one-man-one-vote (OMOV) alone means merely that all gerrymandered and other districts (in a given polity) must be equal in size. This of course is far from a guarantee against what the Warren Court called "diluted" votes.

In this setting Mr. Justice Douglas faced the majority's crucial problem which he stated and "resolved" in these terms:

> It is said that if we prevent racial gerrymandering today, we must prevent gerrymandering of any special interest group tomorrow, whether it be social, economic, or ideological. I do not agree. Our Constitution has a special thrust when it comes to voting; the Fifteenth Amendment says the right . . . to vote shall not be 'abridged' on account of 'race'. . . .

The Douglas solution, then, for what he called "the other half of *Reynolds*" was to permit all voting inequalities except those based on race. Thus non-racial gerrymandering against a slum or a college community, for example, would be permissible—the Justice having pegged his stand not on "equal protection" (the Fourteenth Amendment basis of *Sims*), but on the race-oriented Fifteenth Amendment. Permitting all but "colored" votes to be diluted by gerrymander, while forbidding dilution by malapportionment, is hardly a stand one would have expected of Mr. Justice Douglas. The explanation seems obvious. Equal political representation is a function of several factors, not just district size alone. OMOV *per se* might prevent diluted votes if all interests were uniform in strength and evenly spread throughout the polity. In the real world they are not thus homogenized. Some interest groups are large, some small; some are geographically compact, some widespread, and some spotty; some have advantages of prestige, some of organization, and some of dedication—others are correspondingly handicapped. All this and more in varying degrees. The result is layered, crazy-quilt patterns of changing interests. Equal sized voting districts imposed on such an uneven base are bound to produçe uneven results, i.e. diluted votes or what might be called inadvertent gerrymandering. Consider, for example, a polity divided into equal sized districts first by North-South boundary lines—and then alternatively by East-West lines. Because of the uneven interest base the former almost certainly will favor one set of voters; the latter another. Yet both satisfy the *Reynolds* test of size equality.

Against this background Mr. Justice Douglas in *Whitcomb* made three crucial points in what may be the most candid and illuminating opinion by an activist judge in a reapportionment case. First he recognized that OMOV alone is not an adequate solution to the problem of vote equality—it leaves unsolved "the other half of Reynolds." (Worse yet it gives a false impression of fairness and equality.) Then he recognized that the inadvertent gerrymander is none-the-less a gerrymander. This indeed, as he saw it, was *Whitcomb*, the plaintiffs having admitted "there was no basis for asserting the . . . districts [in question] were designed to dilute [their] votes. . . ."[53] Finally he recognized that, except with respect to race, the gerrymander problem is too unruly for handling by the judicial process. Briefly then, in the real world of non—homogenized interests we cannot have equal votes without facing the gerrymander problem, and most of the gerrymander problem is beyond the competence of courts. Surely this is a major reason why for years prior to *Baker* the Court treated districting as a political question. And this no doubt is also why—so far—it has avoided the gerrymander issue.[54] Surely the young Douglas of *Colegrove* had not anticipated his dilemma in *Whitcomb*. And so we are left with OMOV which by itself, the Justice seemed to suggest, is about as functional as half a pair of pliers.

Baker of course did more than make malapportionment justiciable. It was also a Warren Court effort to narrow the scope of the political question doctrine by treating it as no more than a rule to implement the Separation of Powers.[55] What remained after that limiting innovation was undermined in *Powell* v. *McCormack*,[56] which, by cavalierly dismissing five of *Baker*'s six rules for identifying political questions, seemingly discarded them. The one rule that was considered at length treats as "political" those issues which the Constitution commits "to a coordinate political department." The Court's conclusion was that the constitutional provision making each "House. . . . the Judge of the. . . . Qualifications of its own Members"[57] is at most a commitment "to Congress to judge only the qualifications expressly set forth in the Constitution." Since the House had excluded Powell on other grounds, the exclusion was held invalid.

---

[53] *Id.*, 149.

[54] *Gaffney* v. *Cummings*, 412 U.S. 735, 752-754 (1973) dampens any expectation that the Court will go deeply into the gerrymander problem.

[55] 369 U.S. 186, 217 (1962). Several pre-*Baker* cases apply the doctrine in situations entirely unrelated to the Separation of Powers. See F. W. Scharpf, "Judicial Review and the Political Question: A Functional Analysis," 75 *Yale Law Journal* 517, 538, 547 (1966).

[56] 395 U.S. 486 (1968).

[57] Article I, Section 5.

As some observers saw it, this makes the political question doctrine meaningless:[58]

All Constitutional questions turn on whether some organ of government exceeded its specified powers. Normally, the Court decides whether these powers were exceeded and rules accordingly. The political question doctrine supposedly interrupts that process by declaring a case nonjusticiable. But by the logic of *Powell*, the doctrine can be invoked only if the Constitution committed the power to an organ to act as it did. Thus a court must first inquire whether that organ exceeded its constitutional powers, and can dismiss the suit only if it did not. The same issues then will have been determined as if there were no political question doctrine at all, and the outcome will be the same for the parties.

It is not surprising that Mr. Justice Douglas concurred. What is surprising is his view that ". . . if this were an expulsion case I would think no justiciable controversy would be presented. . . ." Why exclusion is subject to court supervision when expulsion is not, was "explained" by the observation that the latter "may well raise different questions, different considerations." The puzzle is that in offering his view on exclusion the Justice had said, "At the root of all these cases . . . is the basic integrity of the electoral process. When . . . the electors choose a person who is repulsive to the Establishment in Congress, by what constitutional authority can that group of electors be disenfranchised?" We are not told why this consideration would not be equally relevant in an expulsion case. Later the Justice dissented when in *O'Brien* v. *Brown*,[59] the Burger Court apparently abandoned the *Baker* innovation which treated the political-question doctrine as merely a function of the Separation of Powers. The Democratic National Convention to which the Court relegated the *O'Brien* issue could hardly be considered a coordinate branch of the federal government.[60]

---

[58] "The Supreme Court: 1968 Term," 83 *Harvard Law Review* 62-68 (1969). See also Sandalow, *Symposium*, 17 *U.C.L.A. Law Review* 174 (1969).

[59] 409 U.S. 1 (1972). Cf. *Cousins* v. *Wigoda*, 95 Sup. Ct. 541 (1975).

[60] For later relevant Burger Court cases in which Mr. Justice Douglas participated, see *Roudenbush* v. *Hartke*, 405 U.S. 15 (1972) and *Gilligan* v. *Morgan*, 413 U.S. 1 (1973). The latter is particularly interesting because, (1) it "reinstates" those elements of the *Baker* political question test that *Powell* seemed to abandon (see text above); and (2) Mr. Justice Douglas, having to choose between mootness and the political-question approach, chose the former. It may be noteworthy that in *Powell* he avoided the term "political" in favor of non-"justiciable" vis-a-vis expulsion.

The Adequate State Ground

It has long been settled that a state court decision resting on an "adequate and independent" state-law ground will not be reviewed by the Supreme Court even though the case also involves federal law issues.[61] The reason is obvious. To review and correct the state court's views on federal law would not change the decision resting as it does on valid state law. In recent years the Court has been inclined to qualify the adequate-state-ground doctrine at least in habeas corpus cases.[62] The result, as *Fay* v. *Noia*[63] indicates, is that a federal district court may reverse a state conviction that would not be subject to direct review by the Supreme Court. This, along with the explosion of the scope of habeas corpus in *Brown* v. *Allen*,[64] was a tacit recognition by the Court that no longer could it adequately police the flood of state criminal cases by the conventional certiorari process.[65] And so in *Brown* and *Fay* it called upon the federal trial courts for assistance. These, then, become, so to speak, little supreme courts to "review" the decisions of even the highest state tribunals. Mr. Justice Douglas regularly supplied supporting votes in these cases, but no major opinions.

Substantive Law

To remove traditional limits on access to the courts is to multiply opportunities for judicial activism. As we have seen, Mr. Justice Douglas was not at first much interested in their removal. Later when he tried strenuously to open wide the judicial gates, he also initiated a hard push at the boundaries of substantive law. For him the one seems to have been a function of the other, or so at least the all-important Fourteenth Amendment cases indicate. As Archibald Cox put it, "The precepts restricting the occasions for constitutional adjudication are major elements in the distinction between determination by a Council of Wise Men and decision by a court."[66]

---

[61] See *Herb* v. *Pitcairn*, 324 U.S. 117 (1945) and *Williams* v. *Georgia*, 349 U.S. 375, 399 (1955).

[62] The turning point was *Fay* v. *Noia*, 372 U.S. 391 (1963) and cf. *Henry* v. *Mississippi*, 379 U.S. 443 (1965).

[63] 372 U.S. 391 (1963).

[64] 344 U.S. 443 (1953).

[65] See the discussion of certiorari above. For an excellent discussion of the explosion of habeas corpus, see H. Friendly, "Is Innocence Irrelevant: Collateral Attack on Criminal Judgments," 38 *University of Chicago Law Review* 142 (1970).

[66] *The Warren Court*, 20-21 (1968).

Substantive, i.e., economic, due process is the classic monument to judicial activism. It died, of course, with the advent of the Roosevelt Court. But what thereafter would the vague Due Process Clause mean? In an effort to confine, and yet not petrify it, *Palko* v. *Connecticut*[67] said it embraced only those principles of "justice so rooted in the traditions and conscience of our people as to be ranked as fundamental." Other less basic matters were left to the people and their elected representatives. For Justices Black and Douglas *Palko* left judges too much at large—too free to impose their value preferences. Scornful of an interpretation of due process which in their view took as its measure "to-day's fashion in civilized decency and fundamentals," they repudiated what they called the Court's "natural law" approach. This, they said, was[68] ". . . a violation of our Constitution in that it subtly conveys to courts at the expense of legislatures, ultimate power over our public policies in fields where no specific provision of the Constitution limits legislative power." To block this threat of activism Justices Black and Douglas insisted the Privileges and Immunities, Due Process, and Equal Protection Clauses "separately, and as a whole" mean *no more* and no less than the "specific" taboos in the Bill of Rights.[69] This, they claimed, had been a major historic purpose of the Fourteenth Amendment. Thus its linguistic vagueness would be cured by the "clearly marked . . . boundaries," the "specific" and "particular standards enumerated" in the Bill of Rights.[70] Plainly all this was a response to the abuses of the old Court—an effort to forestall judicial activism by confining judges to the written Constitution.

Mr. Justice Black remained faithful to these views—at least as a matter of doctrine.[71] Mr. Justice Douglas did not. By the time of the second birth control case,[72] when the reapportionment cases were already on the judicial horizon, he abandoned his anti-activist *Adamson* view:[73]

---

[67] 302 U.S. 319 (1937).

[68] *Adamson* v. *California*, 332 U.S. 46, 75 (1947).

[69] *Id.* 71. Justices Murphy and Rutledge, dissenting separately, agreed with their brothers Black and Douglas that "the Bill of Rights should be carried over intact into . . . the Fourteenth Amendment" but were not "prepared to say that the latter is entirely and necessarily limited by the Bill of Rights." *Id.* 124.

[70] This language will be found in the opinions of Mr. Justice Black—Mr. Justice Douglas concurring—in *Adamson* v. *California*, 332 U.S. 46, 82, 83, 91 (1947) and *FPC* v. *Natural Gas Pipeline Co.*, 315 U.S. 575, 600 note 4 (1942).

[71] See his opinions in *Griswold* v. *Connecticut*, 381 U.S. 479 (1965), and *Duncan* v. *Louisiana*, 391 U.S. 145 (1968).

[72] *Poe* v. *Ullman*, 367 U.S. 497 (1961).

[73] *Id.* 516-517.

Though I believe that "due process" as used in the Fourteenth Amendment includes all
of the first eight Amendments, I do not think it is restricted and confined to them. . . .
'Liberty' is a conception that sometimes gains content from . . . experience with the requirements of a free society.

Surely this is not unlike the view of "liberty" that supported the old
Court's abusive doctrine called "liberty of contract."[74]

What led Mr. Justice Douglas to change his mind so radically from a
modest to an activist outlook? Perhaps the New Left had something
to do with it. The Justice apparently came to see that after all the Bill
of Rights is quite old fashioned.[75] It does not cover many things deemed
crucial in our day: the environment, poverty, birth control, abortion,
and vote equality, for examples. Moreover it contemplates capital punishment. Having abandoned his *Adamson* stance, Mr. Justice Douglas
was doctrinely free to find, i.e., put, new meanings into the Fourteenth
Amendment—however far they might range beyond the "specific" and
"particular standards enumerated" in the Bill of Rights with its "clearly
marked . . . boundaries."[76] What this new freedom meant will be found
in its most striking form in the Douglas opinion for *Griswold* v. *Connecticut*[77]—a resurrection of rampant substantive due process. Mr.
Justice Black of course dissented, still rejecting—as in *Adamson*—what
he called the boundless "natural-law-due-process" approach to the
Fourteenth Amendment.[78] He was reminded of Holmes' quip apropos
the old activists: only the sky was the limit to what they could find in
due process.[79]

The Equal Protection Clause was one of those that Justices Black and
Douglas in *Adamson* found "separately, and as a whole" to have incorporated the Bill of Rights (and no more) into the Fourteenth Amendment. Again as in the new due process cases Mr. Justice Douglas

---

[74] See, for example, *Lochner* v. *New York*, 198 U.S. 45 (1905).

[75] See Mr. Justice Douglas' essay "The Bill of Rights Is Not Enough" in E. Cahn, *Great
Rights* (1963).

[76] See note 70, above, and related text.

[77] 381 U.S. 479 (1965).

[78] It is noteworthy that while Mr. Justice Douglas in *Poe* v. *Ullman*, above, insisted
that the Fourteenth Amendment was not "restricted and confined" to the Bill of Rights, in
Griswold he clings to its penumbral emanations. Was this a device for holding a necessary vote or, as he may have hoped, for winning Mr. Justice Black's support?

[79] *Baldwin* v. *Missouri*, 281 U.S. 586, 595 (1930). It is noteworthy that Justices Black
and Douglas quote Holmes' language in *FPC* v. *Natural Gas Pipeline Co.*, 315 U.S. 575,
600 (1942) and that Mr. Justice Black quotes it again in *Griswold*, this time against Mr.
Justice Douglas.

deemed that reading too restrictive. Of course the "specific" provisions of the Bill of Rights say nothing of poll taxes. The Justice, however, writing for the Court in a case involving election of state officials held them invalid: "Notions of what constitutes equal treatment for purposes of the Equal Protection Clause [he said] *do* change."[80] This case is especially interesting because only a few months earlier the American people had spoken on the poll tax issue. By constitutional amendment they had chosen to abolish such levies for federal elections and to leave them to local discretion in other elections.[81] A major argument for judicial activism (what used to be called government by the judiciary) is "failure" of the political processes to face up to our problems. "We the people" did face and act upon the poll tax problem. We resolved it in a way we deemed appropriate, and wrote our solution not in mere legislation but into the Constitution itself. That solution incidentally conformed completely with then existing Supreme Court law.[82] Yet the Justices repudiated what the people had done in their sovereign capacity as amenders of the Constitution!

Mr. Justice Black (and two others) in dissent again rejected judicial free-wheeling. He took the occasion to criticize the tendency of the Warren Court "to use the Equal Protection Clause, as it has today, to write into the Constitution its notions of what it thinks is good government policy." The Burger Court seems to agree. In *Dandridge* v. *Williams*[83] it rejected its predecessor's rule that any interest which the Court deems "fundamental" is entitled to the special protection of the strict-scrutiny rule under the Equal Protection Clause.[84] This unique safeguard, it held, could apply only to "constitutionally protected freedom," i.e., that grounded in the Constitution itself. Obviously this is *deja vu*. The Burger Court in *Dandridge* sought to restrict Warren Court activism just as Justices Black and Douglas initially had sought to stifle the activism of their predecessors—by using the Constitution rather than heart's desire as a standard for determining what interests are fundamental (and thus deserving of special court protection under the Fourteenth Amendment).

For good or bad that amendment in explicit terms forbids only *state*

---

[80] *Harper* v. *Virginia Bd. of Elections*, 383 U.S. 663 (1966).

[81] Twenty Fourth Amendment (1964).

[82] *Breedlove* v. *Shuttles*, 302 U.S. 277 (1937); *Butler* v. *Thompson*, 341 U.S. 937 (1951).

[83] 397 U.S. 471 (1970). Justices Douglas, Marshall and Brennan dissented.

[84] See W. Mendelson, "From Warren to Burger: The Rise and Decline of Substantive Equal Protection," 66 *The American Political Science Review* 1226, (1972).

action; like the First Amendment it does not cover private conduct.   At least since World War II the Court has been quite lenient in finding forbidden state action.   Indeed in 1967 a competent observer noted that for years no Court decision had rejected a discrimination claim because of the state-action standard.   He thought that obstacle was dying, if not dead.[85]   Since then four crucial decisions make it plain that barrier is still vital.[86]   In all four instances Mr. Justice Douglas (and at least one other) dissented.   Indeed in no case has he ever found the state-action limitation insurmountable.   To put it differently, he has consistently reached results that would be required by an amendment directed at private (as well as state) conduct.

CONCLUSION

The problem of access to the federal courts is, among other things, a problem in the separation of powers.   How much social conflict shall be resolved by the judiciary and how much shall be left for the political processes?   Mr. Justice Douglas leaned markedly in one direction, just as Mr. Justice Brandeis leaned in the other.   But, if they differed on access to the judiciary, they shared at least at the verbal level a deep respect for democratic government.   Both seemed devoted to freedom of speech and press.   But free utterance is important mainly as a device to facilitate problem-solving by the political process.   For all his outspoken concern for government by the people Mr. Justice Douglas seemed strangely anxious to diminish it by multiplying—and using—opportunities for government by judges.   The more patient Brandeis took the opposite tack.   He espoused free utterance, and he sought to maximize the area in which it might serve as the effective policy maker. The old liberalism resented government by judges; neo-liberalism embraces it.   Mr. Justice Douglas started out in the one camp and ended up in the other.

---

[85] C. E. Black, "Foreword: 'State Action', Equal Protection, and California's Proposition 14," 81 Harvard Law Review 69 (1967).

[86] *Evans* v. *Abney*, 396 U.S. 435 (1970); *Moose Lodge* v. *Irvis*, 407 U.S. 163 (1972); *Lloyd Corp.* v. *Tanner*, 407 U.S. 551 (1972).   *Jackson* v. *Metropolitan Edison Co.*, 95 Sup. Ct. 449 (1974).   See also *Bell* v. *Maryland*, 378 U.S. 226 (1964).

5   A Response to Professor Goldman

I hate justice.

O. W. Holmes, Jr.

P<small>ROFESSOR</small> <small>GOLDMAN</small> has undertaken to defend Justice. Leaving such matters to those who are better equipped, I will try to answer some of the more mundane—merely legal—"problems" that he raises.

I

Professor Goldman agrees with the view expressed in my "Conclusion" that Brandeis had high regard for freedom of communication. On this basis plus *Olmstead* he is willing to "wager" that Brandeis would have been a "liberal activist" in the 1960s and 1970s. I leave prophecy to others. I do know, however, that Brandeis was with the majority, for example, in *Palko* and the *Poll Tax Case* both of which the activists of the 1960s overruled.[1] He was also with the

---

[1] *Benton* v. *Maryland*, 395 U.S. 784 (1969); *Duncan* v. *Louisiana*, 391 U.S. 145 (1968); *Harper* v. *Virginia Bd. of Elections*, 383 U.S. 663 (1966).

majority in upholding compulsory military training in peace-time for male students at a state university, and in upholding compulsory sterilization.[2] Nor did he dissent when on two occasions the Court found no substantial federal question in a compulsory flag salute.[3] For Brandeis free utterance was crucial, but it was not an abstract end in itself. It was the *means* for achieving the ultimate goal of government by the people. In sum the function of the open market for ideas is to generate laws under which the community shall live. That is why Brandeis practiced strict restraint in non-speech cases involving the validity of legislation—no matter how offensive such legislation might be to his own liberal outlook. To put it in language of the 1920s, he rejected the divine right of judges. It is noteworthy that *Olmstead* is the only non-speech case cited by Professor Goldman to support his view that Brandeis was an activist. That case did not involve the validity of legislation! Thus it was one of the few in which Brandeis felt relatively free of his ethic of judicial restraint.

If I make much of the Brandeis matter, it is basic to my theme: the difference between the old and the new "liberalism." The one stressed the sanctity of the *processes* by which the people govern (well or badly); the other demands far more. Neo-lib judges make much of democracy, yet, no matter how free the speech, no matter how well apportioned the legislature, and no matter what the language of the Constitution, they insist with Professor Goldman upon *Justice*—as they perceive it. Douglas made the point quite openly when he wrote of a book, "It makes a mockery of judges who insist that, if they were not imprisoned by the law, they could do justice."[4] Unless he thought himself a "mockery," he must have felt unimprisoned by, i.e., above, the law. What his outlook means in operation we saw in the 1920s and the 1960s: rule by the most elite among elites—nine (or five) lawyers governing the lives of millions without political or judicial accountability. This is not democracy! It is the context in which Holmes quipped, "I hate justice."

Afterthought: those who are comfortable with Truth and Justice

---

[2] *Hamilton* v. *Regents*, 293 U.S. 245 (1934); *Buck* v. *Bell*, 274 U.S. 200 (1927).

[3] *Leoles* v. *Landers*, 302 U.S. 656 (1937); *Hering* v. *State Bd. of Education*, 303 U.S. 624 (1938).

[4] New York Times, Sec. 7, p. 3 (19 Feb. 1961).

may find Brandeis a bit troubling; they should avoid Holmes at any cost, particularly the essays on "Ideals and Doubts" and "Natural Law" in his *Collected Legal Papers* (1920).

II

Certiorari

To come at once to the heart of the matter: does Professor Goldman really think the Court does not have a backlog of some 800 undecided cases, a more than fivefold increase in the past 25 years? Does he really believe (per Douglas) the Court could decide twice the number of cases it now decides?   Nothing in Casper and Posner even hints that it could; they deal with a quite different problem (the burden of applications for review).   The Douglas stand on certiorari is so far out of line with reality, so radically incompatible with anything any other judge has done or proposed that it must be deemed at most a bargaining position—more likely, a calculated "shocker" (in the manner of Holmes' quip above quoted).

Professor Goldman chided me for finding the length of a school boy's hair trivial in the context of certiorari policy.   If in the Term in question the Court had seen fit to hear one additional case, it would have had—as usual—to select it from hundreds that were pressed upon it for review.   I think that, if Profesor Goldman would examine those hundreds of cases, he would find many which *in terms of his values* would make the youngster's hair seem trivial indeed.   The short of the matter is that every year for various reasons—including the Court's limited time and energy—many worthy cases cannot be reviewed.   Finally to shift from the relative to the absolute: if a child's coiffure raises such weighty problems in human freedom as Professor Goldman insists, why is it that Douglas could not even get such thoroughgoing libs as the Warren Court's Brennan and Marshall to join him in dissent, as they so often did in other cases?

As to the Viet Nam War: unless one is to stand on formalities, all the Constitution requires is that we fight no war without the acquiescence of Congress.   Obviously Congress acquiesced in the Viet Nam disaster time after time in draft, appropriation, and other measures without which there could have been no war.   Obviously too, Congress could have stopped the tragedy by withholding troops

and money—as in fact it did with respect to Cambodia.[5] **In short**
the substance of the constitutional requirement having been met—
and no doubt for other reasons too—even the Warren Court could
not bring itself to meddle in matters of foreign policy. But suppose
it had. Suppose following the reasoning of *Orlando* v. *Laird*,[6]
Massachusetts v. *Laird II*,[7] and the *Prize Cases*,[8] it had upheld, i.e.,
"legitimized," the Viet Nam War. Perhaps that possibility alone
was enough to discourage the required minority from granting certiorari in the Viet Nam cases.

Standing to Sue

Of course Toqueville's insight is not a constitutional mandate.
And if he said (I doubt he did) that social issues winding up in
court are necessarily decided on the merits, he was plainly wrong—
as *Frothingham* and a host of other cases indicate. It is here that
Professor Goldman lets the cat escape. He recognizes (apparently
with approval) that, if the Douglas view of standing were adopted,
it would "certainly facilitate . . . the process of transforming political
issues into judicial controversies. . . ." This is precisely what I
meant by the "neo-liberal goal" of shunting policy issues from the
democratic, to the judicial, process. It is also precisely what
Brandeis opposed because he believed so deeply in government by
the people via open public discussion and the legislative process.
This is what his free speech and *Ashwander* views are all about.

Ripeness

Here again is the Douglas-Goldman view as to hypothetical cases,
i.e., advisory opinions, at the expense of the democratic processes.
With respect to *Griswold*, the professor finds nothing therein that
would prevent government from attempting to influence birth rates
by taxation or monetary rewards and punishments. But *Griswold*
creates a new *constitutional* privacy right. How could such a right—
any more than the right to free speech—be restricted by taxation or
monetary pressures? Then he argues that in any case government

---

[5] Special Foreign Assistance Act of 1971, 84 Stat. 1943.
[6] 443 F. 2nd. 1039 (1971).
[7] 451 F. 2nd. 26 (1971).
[8] 67 U.S. 635 (1862).

has never wanted to control births. How can he possibly know that in the future we and government will not want, or need, to do just that? His concern about Griswold's conviction seems misplaced. As I pointed out with citation, it would have been a fit subject for abatement—to say nothing of the pardoning power. And of course killing the Connecticut law would not automatically kill anti-birth control laws in other states—if there are such laws.

As to *Tatum*, there is absolutely no basis for what he charges me with thinking in his "Unlike Mendelson . . ." sentence. I expressed not my views but the Court's. Professor Goldman finds *Tatum* and the *Little Rock* case have nothing in common. Others may find them alike in this: in both cases army surveillance was used in an effort to forestall law violations and serious violence (remember the bombings and burnings in both contexts). And no doubt, if sufficient violence erupted, the army would have been used in both cases to quell it.

Mootness

Here again is the hypothetical, or advisory opinion, problem. The major subject of my paper is the neo-liberal's special willingness to remove policy issues from the democratic, to the judicial, process. This attitude is obvious in the Douglas position in both *Griswold* and *DeFunis*. That on the merits in these cases Douglas took what Professor Goldman considers a "right wing" stand is beside my point.

Political Questions . . .

Substantive Law

Professor Goldman's difficulties here spring from his failure to recognize the difference between the Black-Douglas dissent and the Murphy-Rutledge dissent in *Adamson*. The one sought to tame Due Process in the Fourteenth Amendment by tying it to the "specific" provisions of the Bill of Rights. The other rejected this as too narrow, holding that Due Process did indeed incorporate the Bill of Rights *but also more*. Douglas of course supported the narrower dissenting view—but later, as I pointed out, he shifted to the broader Murphy-Rutledge position. Black did not shift in this way. That is why he and Douglas were on opposite sides in *Griswold*.

Of course I nowhere said, "Black remained a restraintist." What

I said was that as a "matter of doctrine" he never departed from his *Adamson* dissent. As I have observed elsewhere, however, he often departed from it *in practice,* at least until the early 1960s. For that and other reasons I referred to him in the early 1960s as "a leader—perhaps the backbone—of the Court's . . . 'liberal' wing." Thereafter (no doubt disgruntled by what he must have thought were the growing excesses of the Warren Court) Black retreated to *Adamson* in practice as, for example, in *Griswold* and *Harper.*

This brings me to a point I find thoroughly offensive in Professor Goldman's "Defense," i.e., the allegation of my "vigorous defense of poll taxes." Of course, I did not, and do not, defend poll taxes. What I defended was the Constitution as written, and as amended by the American people in Article XXIV—not as amended by Douglas *et. al.* (nor for that matter by his activist predecessors of the early 1930s and before). In short, I argued not that the poll tax is desirable but that it *is* constitutional—as have most Justices who have passed upon it, including such heroic figures as Brandeis, Stone, Cardozo, and Black (even in his early libertarian era).[9]

Professor Goldman is mad at the Fourteenth Amendment because of its unequivocal "No state" limitation. He wants it to cover some or all private affairs. Could it just be that the Amendment was written as it was out of respect for the right to privacy? Or in the alternative, could it be mere coincidence that all of the great liberty-protecting restrictions of the Constitution are similarly addressed only to governmental conduct—including even those relating to speech, press, and religion? None of them imposes restraints on private people. Is it not the function of constitutions (certainly ours) to define what *government* may and may not do—leaving to legislation (within constitutional bounds) what private individuals may do? Now after generations of discussion and Goldman-fashioned criticism of the "state action" limitation, ERA—which is nothing, if it is not modern and "progressive"—adopts that limitation fully and without qualification. In short, its limitations too prohibit only governmental conduct.

Finally Professor Goldman finds a "conservative-activist" majority on the "Nixon-Burger" Court. A few paragraphs earlier he had favored expediting "the process of transforming political issues into legal controversies." Has he considered the meaning of these two

---

[9] See *Breedlove* v. *Shuttles,* 302 U.S. 277 (1937) and *Butler* v. *Thompson,* 341 U.S. 937 (1951).

thoughts in combination? What they jointly mean, and therefore what Professor Goldman supports throughout his "Defense," is that "conservative-activist" judges should be free to pass upon the validity, for example, of welfare measures in moot cases; in premature cases; in cases as to which plaintiffs have only such platonic interests as Ms. Frothingham had; and in political-question cases where, for example, there is no relevant constitutional guide. Or is it that only "liberal" activists are free to water down or ignore gateway questions? The fact is that—however the present judges are to be characterized—they have restored much of what the Warren Court cut down in gateway matters (and of course the Warren Court did not go nearly as far as Douglas did).

Conclusion

The hysterical 1960's have served their function and passed into history. It seems to me high time that political *scientists*—at least in their professional work—distinguish between the Constitution, between law in general, and those passionate, personal commitments they call Justice. Surely the result would be a more adequate, a more rational, view of the meaning and function of law in a democratic society.

6 ✺ *Was Chief Justice Marshall an Activist?*

Rampant law making by the Warren Court antagonized many, indeed most, Americans, according to the Gallup polls.[1] It also attracted numerous outspoken admirers. Not a few of the latter undertook to justify Warrenism on the basis of a comparable aggressiveness they claimed to find in Chief Justice Marshall.[2] More accurately, perhaps, they did not find, but rather derived, it from the Progressive Historians whose views had germinated in the incredible era of laissez faire justice from the 1890s until 1937. As though bent upon proving that all history is contemporary history, the Progressives read back into Marshall's day the activism they saw in the judges of their own time. For them judicial review was at least suspect—a device that Marshall in an artful opinion[3] foisted upon the nation, and then used extravagantly for his own purposes; namely, to promote nationalism at the expense of local self-government, and property at the expense of human or personal rights. All this, if true, surely was what it was called: "Government by Judiciary."[4]

It has long been implicit in praise for the Warren Court that in principle nothing was wrong with government by the "nine old men." They erred, it seems, only in governing us unwisely. This we have on the high authority of Mr. Justice Douglas.[5] Similarly, learned professors—including Charles Black and Eugene Rostow—have recently insisted that judicial review and democracy go hand in hand. This in the face of *Dred Scott,*[6] the *Income Tax,*[7] *Sugar Trust,*[8] *Child Labor*[9] cases, *Plessy,*[10] *Lochner,*[11] and all the rest! Many seem to have forgotten that not very long ago the academic world was overwhelmingly skeptical of judicial supremacy, as it was then called. Learned professors in the 1920s and early 1930s found "the divine right of judges" (to use a then familiar term) entirely out of place in a nation dedicated to democracy and striving for its perfection. Obviously there are fashions in scholarship, as in hemlines.

The Progressive Historians, one wants to believe, would reject the Douglas-Rostow-Black vogue out of hand, for a basic premise of their stance was that government by judges is a poor substitute for government by the people. It is difficult for one who knew them well to believe they would find nothing wrong with elitist oligarchy, or dictatorship in general, provided it were in their view benevolent. Still for them as for some others much might depend upon whose sacred cow is gored.

What follows here is a suggestion that Chief Justice Marshall was not, as charged, an activist with respect to the powers of the federal courts, the sovereignty of the nation, or the claims of property.

Regarding Federal Measures

Five years before John Marshall became a judge the Supreme Court exercised the power of judicial review in *Hylton* v. *United States*.[12] Each of the participating justices recognized explicitly that the issue before them was the constitutionality of a federal statute, and each explicitly based his opinion (upholding the act) on constitutional grounds. There was no fanfare of explanation or justification. The power of review was taken for granted. Only Mr. Justice Chase indicated doubt as to whether the Court "has the power to declare an act of Congress void. . . ." Four years later (well before *Marbury*) he observed in *Cooper* v. *Telfair* that "[i]t is, indeed, a general opinion, it is expressly admitted by all this bar, and some of the Judges have, individually, in the circuits, decided, that the Supreme Court can declare an act of Congress unconstitutional, and therefore invalid. . . ."[13]

What after all can the Constitution possibly mean in Article III that grants to the federal courts jurisdiction of cases "arising under this Constitution" (as well as under federal statutes and treaties), if it does not mean that such courts shall have power to pass upon the meaning of the Constitution with respect to measures challenged as unconstitutional? Article VI refers to the Constitution as "law." Are we to assume that this law somehow is not subject—as is law generally—to judicial interpretation and application? Article VI dubs the Constitution not only "law," but "supreme" law; though it gives Acts of Congress supremacy only when they are "made in pursuance" of the Constitution.[14] Read in conjunction with the Article III provision just quoted, does this not plainly authorize federal courts to decide in appropriate cases whether particular acts of Congress are "in pursuance of" the Constitution?

Obviously, the *Hylton* Court accepted the implication of these questions; namely, that what we have come to call judicial review is a constitutionally authorized power of the federal courts. On this point the pre-Marshall judges were not alone. In Section 25 of the Judiciary Act of 1789 the first Congress (including nearly a score of the Founding Fathers) explicitly authorized Supreme Court review of state decisions "where is drawn in question the validity of a treaty or statute . . . of the United States, and the decision is against their validity" (or where a state measure is questioned and upheld). Of course a state decision invalidating a federal law (or upholding a state law) may be found quite correct on review; state decisions on constitutional issues are not inevitably erroneous. Thus Congress went on to provide in Section 25 that all such state decisions "may be reexamined and reversed or affirmed by the Supreme Court. . . ." Obviously, Congress, in adopting this legislation twelve years before Marshall went to the bench, explicitly recognized the power of both the federal Supreme Court and state courts to declare national (as well as state) laws unconsitutional. How, then, can it be said that judicial review as such—whether with respect to state or federal measures—was an activist innovation of the Marshall Court?

Marbury v. *Madison*[15] simply followed congressional and judicial precedent. It was not a case of first instance with respect to judicial review; it did not entail the indispensable element of judicial activism; namely, innovation.

Early in the *Marbury* opinion there is extensive discussion which concludes that the plaintiff was entitled to what he requested, and that *mandamus* was a proper vehicle for getting it. This is said to be an abusive use of the judicial function, since, as the Court concluded, it lacked jurisdiction of the case. Exploration of those preliminary issues was perfectly compatible with a major principle of judicial restraint; namely, that before judges delve into a constitutional problem, they should make sure that there is no other basis for decision.

Finally, even if the fabrication, or usurpation, charge is valid with respect to *Marbury* (does any serious scholar now so insist?), what Marshall and his colleagues *held* bears no relation whatsoever to the blatant political function activist judges later undertook in the name of judicial review. The fact is the Marshall Court over a period of some thirty-four years vetoed only one congressional act—a very narrow technical one at that. What *Marbury* held after all is simply that Congress may not enlarge the original jurisdiction of the Supreme Court—a matter of little significance in the life and well-being of the Republic. To find in such a narrow holding anything comparable to, or precedent for, Warren Court activism is to make a vast mountain range out of an anthill.

As we shall see, Congress did not give general federal-question jurisdiction to federal courts until after the Civil War. It follows that, apart from Section 25, the only general occasion for judicial review in Marshall's day arose out of the diversity-of-citizenship jurisdiction, authorized in Section 11 of the 1789 Judiciary Act.[16] An activist Court presumably would have construed this jurisdiction broadly. Marshall's Court did the opposite, reading it strictly in three important cases.[17] Similarly one would not expect aggressive judges to repudiate federal jurisdiction of common-law crimes;[18] to take a narrow view of admiralty jurisdiction;[19] to construe strictly their own appellate authority;[20] or to hold the Bill of Rights inapplicable to the states.[21] Yet Marshall's Court—exercising what would now be called judicial restraint—did all of these things.

Before the Civil War only two federal laws suffered Court veto; the first in *Marbury*, the second in *Dred Scott* v. *Sandford*.[22] While the holding in the former was innocuous, that in the latter was a major disaster.

If antebellum judicial history was destined to inspire later Court attitudes, surely the *Dred Scott* catastrophe would have eclipsed *Marbury*. It must follow that neither had much effect upon judicial things to come; that the rampant activism which prevailed from the 1890s until 1937, and again in the 1960s, must have been sui generis springing from new sociopolitical conditions;[23] and that *Marbury* was influential, if at all, only as an excuse or rationalization.

Some may conclude that the Warren, and the laissez faire, justices had more in common with each other than either had with those who decided *Marbury* v. *Madison*.

Regarding State Measures

Several years before Marshall became a judge, the Supreme Court struck down a state law on constitutional grounds. That case—*Ware* v. *Hylton*[24]—held that a Virginia law discharging debts owed enemy aliens conflicted with a federal treaty and was thus void by virtue of Article VI of the Constitution. The latter provides that federal measures, including treaties, "shall be the supreme law of the land." Here too the power of judicial review was taken for granted.[25]

As we have seen, Article III of the Constitution gives federal courts jurisdiction of cases arising under the Constitution or other federal law. But with few exceptions nothing in federal law makes this jurisdiction an exclusive function of federal tribunals. State courts may and do decide such cases. Indeed it was not until 1875 that Congress gave federal trial courts a general jurisdiction to decide federal-law questions. Before then, such matters had to be heard initially by state judges (which is still the fashion in all other federal systems). Inevitably, then, Section 25 of the Judiciary Act of 1789 authorized Supreme Court review of state decisions challenged as not giving full effect to the Constitution, laws, or treaties of the United States. For example, when a state tribunal upheld a state law in the face of constitutional objection, the decision was (and still is) subject to Supreme Court review.

The reason and basis for Section 25 is clear. The Constitution in Article VI imposes upon state judges a duty to treat federal law as supreme, "anything in the constitution or laws of any state to the contrary notwithstanding." Section 25 was an effort to ensure via Supreme Court supervision that this obligation would be honored. Thus judicial review of state—as well as federal—measures was the creature of Congress, not of the Supreme Court. It was perceived and explicitly authorized by statue in accordance with Congressional understanding of the Constitution—and exercised by the Court—long before Marshall became a judge.

If "the Great Chief Justice" was an activist, support for that view must come not from his recognition of the power of review, but from how he used it in state-law cases. For it was in these that he made all of his famous constitutional pronouncements save that in *Marbury*.

National Sovereignty

The crux of the difficulty under the Articles of Confederation was that each state (per Article II) "retains its sovereignty." What little central authority there was—confined to foreign affairs, a postal system, coinage of money, and standard weights and measures—depended entirely upon the goodwill of the states. For the overall "government" had no way to enforce its policies, and only such funds as the constituent sovereignties were willing to contribute via "requisitions." The result, as the Founding Fathers saw it by 1787, was impending disaster. To them the tenuous confederation seemed about to break under the stress of a crushing debt, an empty treasury, and paralysis for lack of authority to raise taxes, regulate trade, enforce laws and treaties, or attain respect from foreign nations. Conflict among the states with respect to commerce and boundary disputes, state intrusions upon contractual and property interest, loose monetary practices, and finally Shay's Rebellion, convinced the Founders that the states had to be curbed; that sovereignty had to be transferred from the parts to the whole. George Washington put it succinctly in a letter to John Jay on August 1, 1786:

> Your sentiments, that our affairs are drawing rapidly to a crisis, accord with my own. What the event will be is also beyond the reach of my foresight. . . . I do not conceive we can exist long as a nation without having lodged somewhere a power which will pervade the whole Union in as energetic a manner, as the authority of the State Governments extends over the several States. . . . Requisitions are a perfect nullity, where thirteen sovereign, independent, disunited States are in the habit of discussing and refusing compliance with them at their option. Requisitions are actually little better than a jest and a byeword throughout the land. If you tell the Legislatures they have violated the treaty of peace and invaded the prerogatives of the Confederacy, they will laugh in your face. What then is to be done? Things cannot go on in the same train forever. It is much to be feared, as you observe, that the better kind of people, being disgusted with the circumstances, will have their minds prepared for any revolution whatever. We are apt to run from one extreme into another. To anticipate and prevent disastrous contingencies, would be the part of wisdom and patriotism.[26]

James Madison's explanation of the "Origin of the Constitutional Convention" (1835) describes the problem in some detail:

> At the date of the Convention, . . . the political condition of the U.S. could not but fill the public mind with gloom. . . . It was seen that the public debt . . . remained without any provision for its payment. The reiterated and elaborate efforts of Congress to procure from the States a more adequate payment had failed. The effect of the ordinary requisitions of Congress had only displayed the inefficiency of the authority making them. . . .
>
> The want of authority in Congress to regulate commerce had produced in foreign nations . . . a monopolizing policy injurious to the trade of the U.S., and destructive to their navigation. . . .

> The same want of power over commerce led to an exercise of the power separately, by the States, which not only proved abortive, but engendered rival, conflicting and angry regulations. . . .
>
> In certain cases the authority of the Confederacy was disregarded, as in violation not only of the treaty of peace, but of treaties with France and Holland. . . .
>
> As a natural consequence of this distracted and disheartening condition of the union, the federal authority had ceased to be respected abroad. . . . At home it had lost all confidence and credit; the unstable and unjust career of the States had also forfeited the respect and confidence essential to order and good government. . . . [27]

Such views—justified or not—were the views of those who convened at Philadelphia in 1787 to devise "a more perfect union." There is said to have been only one states' righter among them. It was the overwhelming consensus that national authority had to be substantially enlarged (Constitution, Article I, Section 8) and made supreme vis-à-vis the states (Article VI); that the states' power to harm one another and the country as a whole must be severely cut down (Article I, Section 10, and Articles IV and VI); and that the old Congress (merely a meeting of the ambassadors of sovereign states) had to be replaced by a true government including a legislature, an executive, and a judiciary (Articles I, II, and III). This—the commitment of the Founding Fathers to national sovereignty—permeates the pronouncements of the Marshall Court.

Each of its great decisions in this context—*Martin* v. *Hunter's Lessee*,[28] *McCulloch* v. *Maryland*,[29] and *Gibbons* v. *Ogden*[30]—involved a state act which impinged upon national interests. In *Hunter*, Virginia's highest judges refused to honor a Supreme Court judgment. In *McCulloch* a state tax threatened operations of the Bank of the United States. In *Gibbons* a state-authorized steamboat "monopoly" hindered traffic in New York waters—a link in the trade route between the East Coast, the Midwest, and New Orleans via the Hudson River, the Erie Canal, the Great Lakes, and the Ohio and Mississippi rivers. In each case the Supreme Court removed the state impediment. To have done otherwise would have been a return to state sovereignty and the problems of the Confederation. As Felix Frankfurter observed, the Marshall Court "was on guard against every tendency to [treat] the new union as though it were the old confederation." Even Thomas Jefferson—hardly an ardent nationalist—agreed in principle, if a priori, that such measures could not stand. For in his view

> the States should severally preserve their sovereignty in whatever concerns themselves alone, and that whatever may concern another State or any foreign nation, should be made a part of the federal sovereignty; . . . some peaceful means should be contrived [judicial review?] for the federal head to force compliance on the part of the states.[31]

The only question, then, in the cases just mentioned, was how to eliminate the offending measures. Each of them had been upheld by a state tribunal in the face of constitutional objections. This per Section 25 of the Judiciary Act brought the appellate jurisdiction of the Supreme Court into play.

Initially in *Hunter* the Court had struck down a Virginia confiscation act as a denial of the supremacy which Article VI of the Constitution gives to federal treaties. The problem was that Virginia's high court had refused to honor the Supreme Court's decision. The rationale for the refusal was that Virginia being a sovereign entity, there could be no appeal from the edict of its highest court. The issue was starkly presented: was it to be state or national sovereignty; were we a confederacy or a nation; did the Supremacy Clause of Article VI mean what it says? Let James Madison give the answer:

> The jurisdiction claimed for the Federal Judiciary [under Section 25] is truly the only defensive armor of the Federal Government, or rather for the Constitution and laws of the United States. Strip it of that armor and the door is wide open for nullification, anarchy and convulsion, unless twenty-four States, independent of the whole and of each other, should exhibit the miracle of a voluntary and unanimous performance of every injunction of the parchment compact.[32]

Mr. Justice Story, for a unanimous Court in *Hunter*—like the Great Chief Justice in *Cohens* v. *Virginia*[33] —spelled out the Madisonian view in constitutional terms:

> That the United States form, for many and for most important purposes, a single nation, has not yet been denied. In war, we are one people. In making peace, we are one people. In all commercial regulations, we are one and the same people. In many other respects, the American people are one; and the government which is alone capable of controlling and managing their interests in all these respects, is the government of the Union. It is their government, and in that character they have no other. America has chosen to be, in many respects, and to many purposes, a nation; and for all these purposes, her government is complete; to all these objects, it is competent. The people have declared that in the exercise of all powers given for these objects it is supreme. It can, then, in effecting these objects, legitimately control all individuals or governments within the American territory. The constitution and laws of a state, so far as they are repugnant to the Constitution and laws of the United States, are absolutely void. These states are constituent parts of the United States. They are members of one great empire—for some purposes sovereign, for some purposes subordinate.[34]

In a government so constituted, national review of state decisions on questions of national law was indispensable because

> Judges of equal learning and integrity, in different states, might differently interpret a statute, or a treaty of the United States, or even the constitution itself. If there were no revising authority to control these jarring and discordant judgments, and harmonize them into uniformity, the laws, the treaties, and the Constitution of the United States would

be different in different states, and might, perhaps, never have precisely the same construction, obligation, or efficacy, in any two states. The public mischiefs that would attend such a state of things would be truly deplorable; and it cannot be believed that they could have escaped the enlightened convention which formed the constitution. What, indeed, might then have been only prophecy, has now become fact, and the appellate jurisdiction must continue to be the only adequate remedy for such evils.[35]

Far from exercises in judicial activism, *Hunter* and *Cohens* involve no more than a literal application of the explicit terms of the Constitution and an act of Congress--an application completely compatible with their spirit as well. Though endlessly pressed in the antebellum era to strip down Section 25 jurisdiction, Congress steadfastly refused to do so.[36]

Gibbons presents more complex problems. It involved inter alia a claim that the New York steamboat monopoly was incompatible with the Commerce Clause itself. This entailed an inquiry into the meaning and scope of congressional authority to "regulate commerce . . . among the several States. . . ." Few would insist the meaning of this provision standing alone is obvious in the context of *Gibbons* v. *Ogden*. In that impasse Marshall for the Court sought help in an old principle of interpretation: the *Rule in Heydon's Case*.[37] As Marshall put it:

If from the imperfection of human language, there should be serious doubts respecting the extent of any given power, it is a well-settled rule that the objects for which it was given, especially when those objects are expressed in the instrument itself, should have great weight in the construction.[38]

A basic "object" of the Constitution was "to form a more perfect Union."[39] One of the most vexing imperfections of the old one was the problem of state interference with interstate commerce, and lack of national authority to do anything about it.[40] An expansive view of congressional power under the Commerce Clause was thus required if a more perfect union was to be achieved—that is, if we were to avoid a return to the trade barriers that were so familiar during the Confederation. Thus, following an ancient rule of construction, Marshall read the doubtful language of the Commerce Clause in the light of the well-known circumstances that produced it. The result was a broad view of the congressional commerce power, a view that has prevailed throughout our history except in that tragic era of judicial activism that ran from 1895 until 1937.[41] What the Marshall Court did in *Gibbons* was simply this: it resolved (a mainly linguistic) doubt in favor of Congress and the democratic process. This is a far cry indeed from activism. It would seem rather that to have minimized congressional authority, to have ignored the origins of the Commerce Clause—as the 1895-1936 Court did—would have been an abuse.

Counsel for the steamboat monopoly next argued that, even if the commerce power was to be read broadly, it should be treated as a concurrent power, that is, one available to the states as well as to Congress. In this view the New York law would stand (absent an incompatible federal regulation). On this point Marshall found no help in *Heydon's* rule. Quite obviously he was sympathetic to the argument that the commerce power was not concurrent, but exclusively national: "There is great force in this argument—and the court is not satisfied that it has been refuted."[42]

Still, given the magnitude of the consequences of a judgment either way, and the lack of *Heydon* clues, judicial restraint was called for. And so, anticipating one of the *Ashwander*[43] rules, he avoided a critical constitutional issue by finding an alternative basis for decision; namely, a Supremacy Clause conflict between the New York steamboat law and an act of Congress. The result was to postpone a crucial question of constitutional law that might more wisely be settled with the benefit of further experience under our new federal system of government. Meanwhile the ball was in the congressional court. For *Gibbons* left Congress free to alter, if it chose, the measure found to be in conflict with the New York law. What was this, if not judicial restraint? Only Mr. Justice Johnson was prepared to accept the exclusive view. He, it will be recalled, was Jefferson's appointee and "representative" on the bench. Neither of these gentlemen could be deemed entirely unsympathetic to states' rights.

McCulloch v. *Maryland*[44] involved a state tax plainly and completely incompatible with the continued operation of the Bank of the United States (BUS) in Maryland. Thus the tax ran afoul of the Supremacy Clause, if congressional enactment of the bank law was "pursuant to the Constitution." The Marshall Court found that it was; that congressional authority to create it was implicit in, and incidental to, the powers expressly given to the national government. This was fully in accord with the view of "the father of the Constitution." "In . . . debate on the tenth amendment, Madison successfully resisted an attempt to insert one word, to make it say that powers not *expressly* delegated to the United States are reserved to the states or the people. No government, he contended, could be limited to express powers: 'There must necessarily be admitted powers by implication.' "[45]

Recall that BUS had been proposed initially by Alexander Hamilton, a member of the Constitutional Convention and an author of the *Federalist Papers*. It had been chartered by a Federalist Congress which included several of the Founding Fathers, and then approved by President Washington who had been president of the Constitutional Convention. In 1811 it was rechartered by a Republican Congress and approved by President Madison. Surely judges would have to be high-handed to override such impressive credentials—as Marshall's opinion of the Court suggests. But impressive credentials or not, how can judges rationally be charged with activism when they defer to Congress, when they leave major policy issues to the processes of democracy? It is noteworthy that a

few years after the decision in *McCulloch*, BUS expired when Congress sustained
President Jackson's veto of a recharter bill. The people had the first, and the
people had the last, word on BUS. This is light-years away from government by
judges as we came to know it beginning in the 1890s and again in the 1960s.

If in *Hunter, Gibbons,* and *McCulloch* the Marshall Court honored federal
law and the national democratic process, in each of those cases *pari passu* it
struck down a state measure and to that extent intruded upon state self-government. Marshall for the Court responded to this problem in *McCulloch* when
counsel argued that, if a state tax on federal operations is invalid, then a federal
tax on state operations must also fail:

> But the two cases are not on the same reason. The people of all the
> states have created the general government, and have conferred upon
> it the general power of taxation. The people of all the states, and the
> states themselves, are represented in Congress, and, by their representa-
> tives exercise this power. When they tax the chartered institutions of
> the states, they tax their constituents; and these taxes must be uniform.
> But, when a state taxes the operations of the government of the United
> States, it acts upon institutions created, not by their own constituents,
> but by people over whom they claim no control. It acts upon the meas-
> ures of a government created by others as well as themselves, for the
> benefit of others in common with themselves. The difference is that
> which always exists, and always must exist, between the action of the
> whole on a part, and the action of a part on the whole—between the
> laws of a government declared to be supreme, and those of a govern-
> ment which, when in opposition to those laws, is not supreme.[46]

As though supplementing these thoughts (they are the same as those that inform
the Supremacy Clause itself). Marshall in reference to the national commerce
power observed in *Gibbons:*

> If, as has always been understood, the sovereignty of Congress, though
> limited to specified objects, is plenary as to those objects, the power
> over commerce with foreign nations, and among the several States, is
> vested in Congress as absolutely as it would be in a single government,
> having in its constitution the same restrictions on the exercise of the
> power as are found in the Constitution of the Untied States. The wis-
> dom and the discretion of Congress, their identity with the people, and
> the influence which their constitutents possess at elections, are, in this,
> as in many other instances . . . the sole restraints on which they have
> relied, to secure them from its abuse. They are the restraints on which
> the people must often rely solely, in all representative governments.[47]

Generations later Mr. Justice Holmes would say:

> I do not think the United States would come to an end if we lost our
> power to declare an Act of Congress void. I do think the Union would

be imperiled if we could not make the declaration as to the laws of the several States. For one in my place sees how often a local policy prevails with those who are not trained to national views and how often action is taken that embodies what the Commerce Clause was meant to end.[48]

Guided by the Founders, Marshall's nationalistic opinions laid the foundation for the American common market. They were not oblivious to state interests. In *Gibbons,* though Marshall favored the exclusive conception of the national commerce power, he left the issue open. Later in *Willson* v. *Blackbird Creek Marsh Co.*[49] he upheld "states' rights" in an interstate commerce setting. Delaware had authorized a dam across a small yet navigable stream thus hindering interstate commerce as had New York in *Gibbons.* Except for a difference in the importance of the two waterways as trade routes, the two cases seem quite alike. Yet the Court's judgments ran in opposite directions: the New York law was struck down, the Delaware law upheld. The one was treated as a regulation of commerce, the other as a police measure to protect local health and reclaim local land from a marsh infestation. Of course the difference in terminology is not decisive; a rose by any other name would smell as sweet. What Marshall must have been groping for (but lacked enough cases to spell out) was a dividing line between undue local interference with national interests, and state protection of legitimate local claims. How he might have solved the problem, if he had been given adequate opportunity for a rounded answer, we do not know. One supposes the difference in the outcome of the two cases is not unrelated to the fact that New York's law reflected the same self-seeking provincialism that had devastated the Confederation; the Delaware law did not. For it is one thing to seek a selfish local advantage simply by imposing burdens on outsiders, but quite another to cure local evils though at some cost to others. Especially is this so because (as Marshall recognized in *Gibbons*) the local problem which by hypothesis "concerns more states than one" may be regulated (preempted) by Congress, if it finds the local solution noisome from the national point of view. Similarly, in *Brown* v. *Maryland*[50] Marshall recognized that while the Constitution outlaws state duties on imports (Article I, Section 10), this does not mean that an imported item is forever immune from state taxation. At some point, he recognized, the import like local goods must be subject to state levys. Groping again, he tentatively drew a line via the original package doctrine. Marshall's was not a dogmatic nationalism, blind to local needs.

Property Interests

If, as charged, Marshall favored ownership interests, much might be said in extenuation of such a tendency. In his day property had not yet become suspect.

Das Kapital would not appear for years to come. Great disparities in wealth had not yet developed in this country. Most Americans owned a farm or had reasonable expectations of acquiring one. Rich and poor alike respected ownership, knowing that property was the key to personal and family well-being. Indeed in a poor, developing nation private property was a social security system protecting against the pitfalls of sickness, old age, widowhood, and orphanage. Especially for Thomas Jefferson—the lion of liberalism—property was indispensable to liberty. As he saw it, the widespread ownership of farms saved us from the misery and bitter class conflicts of the Old World. "When we get piled up upon one another in large cities, as in Europe, we shall become as corrupt as in Europe and go to eating one another as they do there."[51] The urban mobs of Paris, he thought, were in effect slaves because, being propertyless, they were dependent upon their "betters." As Brandeis would say later, "The necessitous man is not free." It was largely to ensure a continuing "Empire of Liberty" which comes with individual private ownership of farms that Jefferson—unconstitutionally, he thought—made the Louisiana Purchase.

According to Irving Brant—James Madison's inspired biographer—the great accomplishment of the Founding Fathers was that "[a] convention dominated by devotees of property rights was able to write a democratic Constitution. Save for two or three delegates, the whole convention desired to protect property . . . by the strength and form of the national government, and to strike down state laws designed to wipe out debt or impair financial contracts."[52] It follows from all this that, if Marshall was indeed especially sensitive to proprietary claims, he was in full accord with the temper of the American people of his day and with the outspoken purposes of those who gave us the Constitution. But do *Fletcher* v. *Peck*[53] and the *Dartmouth College* case[54]—endlessly cited to support the charge of property bias—in fact support it?

Fletcher arose when land speculators cheated the people of Georgia out of millions of acres of public land by bribing state legislators. When Georgia voters discovered this they compelled a new legislature to rescind the transaction. Meanwhile innocent buyers had acquired some of the land from the wrongdoers. They attacked the rescinding act as a violation of the Contract Clause.[55] Marshall, for the court, upheld the challenge. The effect was to sustain the property claims of the innocent buyers. The alternative would be to sustain the property claims of the innocent people of Georgia. Either way, the Court would be deciding proproperty—and also antiproperty. Either way, an innocent party would be hurt. There seems to have been no way to escape a decision upholding the plaintiff's, or the defendant's, ownership claim. One fails to see how *Fletcher* can be said to involve a property bias. Was there, however, bias of another sort in deciding for the ultimate buyers rather than for the initial owners? Far from arbitrary, the choice was informed by a long-settled (and still prevailing) rule of Anglo-America equity jurisprudence. While a fraudulent purchaser takes a good title *at law*, it is subject to cancellation by a chancery decree. Thus in a clash between a cheating buyer and his innocent victim the latter prevails. But *Fletcher* involved a clash between the innocent victim and an equally innocent subsequent purchaser for value. As between the two guiltless parties the chancellor—finding the moral claim of the one no better than that of the other—does not intervene. The equities being balanced, he lets the chips fall as they may (the victim's recourse being an action for damages against the fraudulent party). In short Marshall and the Court read the Contract Clause in the light of a long familiar, time-tested rule of equity. If this be activism, it is not property biased, and it is not a brand similar to that of the Warren Court.

Critics press two allegations: The Contract Clause was not intended to apply to state contracts, nor to grants (as distinct from contracts). The fact is, the language of the clause literally covers *all* contracts in explicit terms. There is no hint of limitation in the written words of the Constitution, nor have critics revealed any discussion in the Constitutional Convention or in the *Federalist* in support of an unwritten limitation. Had the Founders wanted to protect only private (as distinct from state) agreements, they need only have said so—as indeed the Continental Congress had just done in the Northwest Ordinance. (Earlier in England *An Agreement of The People* (1649) had undertaken to protect only *public* contractual obligations.) On August 28, 1787, Rufus King moved to insert the private-contract provision of the Northwest Ordinance into the Constitution. After brief discussion, it was rejected. Some two weeks later (September 14), at the suggestion of the Committee of Style, the Constitutional Convention adopted the present Contract Clause. We have no record of any here relevant discussion either in the Committee or in the Convention. Strictly all that we know of the *Convention's* intent, then, is that it was invited to adopt the private-contract approach and refused to do so. Shortly thereafter it adopted a similar provision which refers merely to contracts in general as distinct from *private* contracts per the Northwest Ordinance (and as distinct from *public* contracts per *An Agreement of The People*).

Surely this bespeaks rejection of one view in favor of another. Those who favor the apparently rejected position rely essentially on the proposition that the great contract problem of the time was a host of state debtor-relief laws which went far to obliterate private debtor obligations. This clearly was a major and notorious problem. Yet it is no basis for holding that related matters, though literally covered by the Contract Clause, are somehow excluded. After all, state negligence with respect to state obligations was hardly unknown! The Founders wrote broadly; we are urged to assume they thought narrowly, that they used unqualified language of principle to deal only with quite limited, easily definable specifics. The argument moreover leads to the proposition that the Contract Clause applies only in a debtor-relief context—a position seemingly without significant support in any quarter. Even if we knew absolutely that every one of the Framers individually intended their written words to apply only to private compacts, this would not justify adopting that view judicially. Those who ratified can hardly be said to have ratified something other than the words of the document itself.

The other anti-Marshall point—that grants are not contracts—entails an anachronism. Certainly today a grant and a contract are two quite different things. But in the late eighteenth century the term "contract" had far broader connotations than it does today, embracing not only executory, but executed, agreements as well.[56] Alexander Hamilton's view in his well-known pamphlet on the subject clearly anticipated the Court's position in *Fletcher*, as did the highest court of Massachusetts in *Darby* v. *Blake*.[57] The broad language of Madison's 44 *Federalist* also supports both the public-contracts and the grants aspect of *Fletcher*. Nowhere does it even dimly suggest the restrictive outlook.

It is worth noting that the land problem involved in *Fletcher* was so troublesome that President Jefferson appointed an investigatory commission—James Madison, Albert Gallatin, Levi Lincoln. The recommendations of that most distinguished body of Jeffersonians agreed with Marshall (though by a different route) that the innocent purchasers should prevail.[58]

The *Dartmouth* case involved these circumstances: a group of philanthropists agreed (contracted) that each in consideration of the donations of the others would contribute to a fund for the education of American Indians, among others. By their agreement the fund was to be administered by trustees selected in a prescribed manner. The British King approved and gave these arrangements legal sanction in a charter for Dartmouth College—whereupon the promised contributions were made. Later (after Independence) the State of New Hampshire tried by legislation to take over and govern the school contrary to the donors' agreements as set out in the charter. Marshall's Court blocked the effort via the Contract Clause. Viewed narrowly the trustees won the case, but they had no beneficial interest in the property. They won on behalf of the donor-philanthropists (presumably deceased) and generations of students. Were these really property interests—does the decision reveal a prejudice in favor of material wealth?

The traditional Progressive answer is that the *Dartmouth* decision was a crafty gambit purposefully designed to an ulterior purpose: protection of corporation charters from legislative interference. That it was highly successful is demonstrated, we are told, by the enormous growth of corporate enterprise thereafter. This is make-believe. Mr. Justice Story in *Dartmouth* pointed out that no state need grant irrevocable or nonamendable charters; that the power to alter, amend, or revoke may be reserved. In fact this became standard practice over the years after *Dartmouth*, and was not unknown before. Also the granting of corporation charters by special legislation (which was the real basis of abuse) gave way following the Jacksonian reform movement to general-law, standard-provision incorporation.

It is strange that those who charge Marshall with proproperty bias seem always to ignore his "antiproperty" decisions. *Gibbons*, for example, destroyed an enormously valuable ownership interest when it killed the New York steamboat charter.[59] How is *Gibbons* to be reconciled with *Fletcher* and *Dartmouth*? The two latter, one suggests, are not proproperty, but rather protransaction, cases. They mean that when the equities are not plainly imbalanced (there being no clearly overriding public interest, as in *Gibbons*), judges will not disturb the "contracts," or transactions by which men and women conduct their personal affairs—be they philantrhopists (*Dartmouth*) or land speculators and farmers (*Fletcher*).[60] An inclination toward unfettered human activity was deep in the temper of the times. It was apparently accepted as so natural, so inevitably right, as not even to rise to the level of awareness. Americans were on the make. They had escaped the Old World fetters: king, feudal aristocracy, and established church. They were the "new men." A vast spiritual, as well as geographic, frontier provoked ingenuity and initiative. The standard of living was low, but natural resources were great. This put a high premium on constructive, developmental human effort. That legal support for such interests came via the Contract Clause was not by chance. As Sir Henry Maine would later observe, the transition from medieval to modern civilization was a shift from "status to contract."[61] Under feudalism a person acquired a fixed social status by birth; all of his rights and duties were determined thereby. Thus if a man were born a serf, he and his descendents were serfs for life. Each status had reciprocal, or mutually supplementary, rights and duties—the serf, for example, provided the community's food; the military man its protection from marauders. With the decline of feudalism this reciprocal right-duty system faded away in favor of a network of voluntary contractual relationships. This was the "new freedom." This was how men—according to their talents rather than birth—made their way in life. And so in the new social milieu it was crucial that contractual arrangements be honored, and not lightly disturbed. This was the spirit that informed Marshall's construction of the Contract Clause. He recognized in *Dartmouth* that such a case probably "was not particularly in the view of the framers of the Constitution." What was immediately in their minds, he seemed to say, was the old problem of debtor-relief laws. Yet, as he noted, they used language far broader than would be required if they were concerned only with that familiar problem. Accordingly he saw no reason why the broad terms used should not be read as they were written—to cover the "rare case" of *Dartmouth.* This reasoning would apply also to the state-agreement aspect of *Fletcher.*[62]

It is revealing that the Progressive critique shifts ground according to the progressiveness of the case under discussion. Marshall is charged with activism in *Fletcher* and *Dartmouth* for not confining the Contract Clause to the debtor-relief problem which he and all others agreed was its prime target. In *Ogden* v. *Saunders*[63] he insisted (in dissent) on using it in this prime intended sense to kill a debtor-relief law. For this he is accused of being a "supreme conservative"—obviously because his progressive critics like the "liberal" Jacksonian relief law in question. If late in its day the Marshall Court—succumbing to Jacksonian fever—indulged in a bit of activism, the Chief Justice did not. Ironically the liberal tradition lampoons him for not following the minimum (debtor-relief) meaning in *Fletcher* and in *Dartmouth,* and for following it in *Saunders.* This of course indicates less about Marshall than about his critics.

It is not hardheartedness that led the framers (and Marshall) to outlaw state interference with debtor-creditor relationships. Experience under the Confederation convinced them such matters should be handled by the national government. That is why the bankruptcy power was given to Congress in Article I, Section 8 of the Constitution, and seemingly denied to the states in the Contract Clause.

Conclusion

There is substantial reason to believe—and some to doubt—that the Founding Fathers embraced the power of judicial review.[64] No matter, the "arising under" language of the Constitution plainly authorizes it. So at least the first Congress thought—and explicitly provided in Section 25 of the Judiciary Act of 1789. The pre-Marshall Court, obviously agreeing, exercised the power as a matter of course. Chief Justice Marshall and his colleagues, then, can hardly be said to have invented judicial review. Did they, however, abuse it, or use it in an activist manner? They struck down only one act of Congress in almost two generations—a narrow inconsequential measure of no general interest whatsoever. This does not constitute much of a case for abuse or activism. Nor does acquiescence in, and deferral to, all other congressional measures that came before the Court—certainly not, if activism is defined by the conduct of judges in the laissez faire and Warren eras.

All of the state measures that suffered veto because they clashed with extra-state interests (for example in *Gibbons, McCulloch, Hunter,* and *Brown*) reflected the same narrow state provincialism that had proven so costly during the Confederation—and which was indeed the chief reason for calling the Constitutional Convention. The Supremacy Clause and Section 25 were aimed specifically at curing that problem. To have upheld the state measures in question would have been to ignore the Constitution, congressional legislation, and the history that produced them. It would have constituted a return to state sovereignty and the old Confederation.

Fletcher and *Dartmouth,* which are said to show a proproperty bias in the Marshall Court were, as suggested, not proproperty but protransaction, that is, personal liberty, cases. It is significant that before *Fletcher*—the first of the contract cases—only four states had contract clauses in their constitutions. Thereafter, in the Marshall era, eight more states adopted them. So also did fourteen others in the next thirty years. In each instance save one the clause was included in the state's bill of rights. Obviously, the prohibition against contract impairment as interpreted by the Supreme Court was widely "viewed as one of those restrictions upon governmental power which serve to protect the most valuable rights of the citizen."[65]

Finally, modern activists can find no support or satisfaction in Marshall's vigorous self-restraint in the jurisdiction cases,[66] nor in his allegedly activist nationalism; for his opinions in that context merely reflect the outlook of those who produced the Constitution. In sum, he followed their basic design to create a system in which the parts could no longer emasculate the whole. To put it in more modern (economic) terms, he gave us what they wanted: a common market. Moreover, as *Blackbird, Brown,* and *Gibbons* make clear, he was far from dogmatic in his antiparochialism. *Gibbons* is particularly interesting because, while in that case Marshall was markedly nationalistic on the scope of the Commerce Clause, he was plainly nonnationalistic (despite his expressed personal inclination) on the exclusive-concurrent problem. The desideratum, it would seem, was not nationalism but the purpose (or nonpurpose) of the Founders as deduced via *Heydon's* rule. Finding in that approach no clue to the Founders' design with respect to the exclusivity problem, Marshall and his colleagues exercised judicial restraint. That is, they decided the case on a less momentous ground, leaving the crucial issue for resolution in the light of such further wisdom as additional experience and discussion might provide.

It was not Marshall who set precedent for Warren Court imperialism; it was rather the laissez faire activists beginning in the 1890s. The father of that movement was Mr. Justice Field.[67] His son-in-law (so to speak) was Mr. Justice Black who passed the torch to the Warren Court activists[68] —and lived to regret it.[69]

Notes

1. "High Court Seen Losing Backers," *New York Times,* June 15, 1969, p. 43.

2. See Philip B. Kurland, *Politics, the Constitution and the Warren Court* (Chicago: University of Chicago Press, 1970), pp. 10-12.

3. *Marbury v. Madison,* 1 Cranch 137 (1803).

4. Louis B. Boudin, *Government by Judiciary* (New York: Goodwin, 1932).

5. *Poe v. Ullman,* 367 U.S. 496, 517-518 (1961).

6. *Dred Scott v. Sandford,* 19 Howard 393 (1857).

7. *United States v. E.C. Knight Co.,* 156 U.S. 1 (1895).

8. *Pollock v. Farmers' Loan & Trust Co.,* 158 U.S. 601 (1895).

9. *Hammer v. Dagenhart,* 247 U.S. 251 (1918).

10. *Plessy v. Ferguson,* 163 U.S. 537 (1896).

11. *Lochner v. New York,* 198 U.S. 45 (1905).

12. 3 Dallas 171 (1796).

13. 4 Dallas 14, 19 (1800).

14. "This Constitution, and the Laws of the United States which shall be made in Pursuance thereof; and all Treaties made, or which shall be made, under the Authority of the United States, shall be the supreme Law of the Land; and the Judges in every State shall be bound thereby, any Thing in the Constitution or Laws of any State to the Contrary notwithstanding."

15. 1 Cranch 137 (1803).

16. *Fletcher v. Peck,* 6 Cranch 87 (1810), was a diversity case.

17. *New Orleans v. Winter,* 1 Wheaton 91 (1816); *Bank of the United States v. Deveau,* 5 Cranch 61 (1809); *Hepburn v. Ellzey,* 2 Cranch 445 (1804).

18. *United States v. Hudson and Goodwin,* 7 Cranch 32 (1812).

19. To the surprise of the admiralty bar, *The Steamboat Thomas Jefferson,* 10 Wheaton 438 (1825), confined the admiralty jurisdiction of the federal courts to cases involving tidal waters. The Taney Court adopted a more expansive view in *Genesee Chief v. Fitzhugh,* 12 Howard 443 (1851).

20. *Durousseau v. United States,* 6 Cranch 307 (1810).

21. *Barron v. Baltimore,* 7 Peters 243 (1833).

22. 19 Howard 393 (1857).

23. Wallace Mendelson, "The Politics of Judicial Activism," *Emory Law Journal* 24 (Summer 1975):43–66.

24. 3 Dallas 199 (1796).

25. The Marshall Court explored the basis of review in such cases at length in *Martin v. Hunter's Lessee,* 1 Wheaton 304 (1816), and *Cohens v. Virginia,* 6 Wheaton 264 (1821), discussed below.

26. George Washington, *The Writings of George Washington,* ed. John Fitzpatrick (Washington, D.C.: Government Printing Office, 1938), 28:502–503.

27. James Madison, "Origin of the Constitutional Convention," 1835.

28. 1 Wheaton 304 (1816).

29. 4 Wheaton 316 (1819).

30. 9 Wheaton 1 (1824).

31. Jefferson to G. Wythe, 16 Sept. 1787.

32. Madison to J.C. Cabell, 1 April 1833.

33. 6 Wheaton 264 (1821).

34. Ibid., pp. 413–414.

35. *Martin v. Hunter's Lessee,* 1 Wheaton 304, 348 (1816).

36. Henry M. Hart, ed., *Henry M. Hart and Herbert Wechsler's The Federal Courts and the Federal System* (Mineola, N.Y.: Foundation Press, 1973). p. 455.

37. Heydon's Case, 3 Co. Rep. 7a, 76 Eng. Rep. 637 (Exch. 1854).

38. *Gibbons v. Ogden,* 9 Wheaton 1, 188–189 (1824).

39. Preamble to the Constitution.

40. See *Hughes v. Oklahoma,* 99 S. Ct. 1727, 1731 (1979).

41. Robert G. McCloskey, *The American Supreme Court* (Chicago: University of Chicago Press, 1960), pp. 144–150.

42. Madison also was inclined toward the exclusive view. See Max Farrand, ed., *The Records of the Federal Convention of 1787* (New Haven: Yale University Press, 1911), 2:625.

43. See the Brandeis opinion in *Ashwander v. Tennessee Valley Authority,* 297 U.S. 288, 346–348 (1936).

44. 4 Wheaton 316 (1819).

45. Irving Brant, "The Madison Heritage," in *The Great Rights,* ed. Edmund Cahn (New York: Macmillan, 1963). p. 34. As president, Madison approved the rechartering of BUS.

46. 4 Wheaton 316, 435–436 (1803).

47. 9 Wheaton 1, 197 (1824).

48. "Law and the Court" in Oliver Wendell Holmes, *Collected Legal Papers,* 295–296 (1920).

49. 2 Peters 245 (1829).

50. 12 Peters 419 (1827).

51. Thomas Jefferson, *Notes on the State of Virginia* (New York: Harper and Row, 1964).

52. Irving Brant, *James Madison: Father of the Constitution, 1787-1800* (New York: Bobbs-Merrill, 1950), 3:45,61.

53. 6 Cranch 87 (1810).

54. 4 Wheaton 518 (1819).

55. U.S. Constitution, Article 1, Section 10: "No State shall . . . pass any law . . . impairing the obligation of contracts. . . . "

56. As Dean Roscoe Pound has explained, "Contract was then used, and was used as late as Parsons on Contracts in 1853 to mean [what] might be called "legal transaction". . . . Not merely contract as we now understand it, but trust, will, conveyance, and grant of a franchise are included. . . . The writers on natural law considered that there was a natural legal duty not to derogate from one's grant. . . . This is the explanation of *Fletcher,* . . . and no doubt is what the [contract clause] meant to those who wrote it into the Constitution." ("The Charles River Bridge Case," *Massachusetts Law Quarterly* 27, no. 4, at pp. 19-20.)

57. 226 Mass. 618 (1799).

58. See C. Peter Magrath, *Yazoo: Law and Politics in the New Republic* (New York: Norton, 1966), pp. 35-37.

59. See also, for example, *Barron v. Baltimore,* 7 Peters 243 (1833), holding the Fifth Amendment does not require compensation for *state* confiscation of private property; *Providence Bank v. Billings,* 4 Peters 514 (1830), undermining valuable economic interests by strict construction of a public grant; and *Mason v. Haile,* 12 Wheaton 370 (1827), which diminished protection for creditors by upholding even retroactive abolition of imprisonment for debt.

60. *Gibbons* also promoted transactional freedom by destroying the steamboat monopoly.

61. Sir Henry Maine, *Ancient Law* (New York: Scribner, 1864), p. 165.

62. It is noteworthy that Alexander Hamilton, too, believed the Contract Clause applied to state as well as private-party agreements. See his brief with respect to the Yazoo claims, reproduced in Magrath, *Yazoo.*

63. 12 Wheaton 213 (1827).

64. Raoul Berger, *Congress v. The Supreme Court* (Cambridge: Harvard University Press, 1969).

65. Benjamin F. Wright, *The Contract Clause of the Constitution* (Cambridge: Harvard University Press, 1938), p. 61. See also ibid., pp. 60, 86-88.

66. See notes 17-21 and related text.

67. See Wallace Mendelson, "Mr. Justice Field and Laissez Faire," *Virginia Law Review* 36 (February 1950):45–58.

68. Wallace Mendelson, *Justices Black and Frankfurter: Conflict in the Court*, 2d ed. (Chicago: University of Chicago Press, 1966).

69. Ibid., pp. 132 ff. See also Mr. Justice Black's dissent in *Harper v. Virginia Board of Elections*, 383 U.S. 663 (1966).

ADDENDUM

As indicated above, one premise of the 1789 judiciary act was that state courts would have the power of judicial review. Accordingly, to protect national interests Section 25 gave the Supreme Court appellate judicial-review authority when a state tribunal struck down an act of Congress or upheld a state measure in the face of constitutional objection.

What of judicial review in the lower federal courts? Having given them severely restricted jurisdiction, the first Congress apparently saw no judicial-review problem there comparable to what it feared in state courts. Later, however, the Judiciary Act of 1801, drawing on the language of the Constitution, enlarged the authority of the lower federal judges to include *inter alia* cases "arising under the Constitution." At least five of the Founding Fathers (Yates, Martin, Wilson, Mason, and Randolph) had acknowledged in various state ratification conventions what that phrase quite plainly says. As Yates put it: "The cases arising under the Constitution must include such, as bring into question its meaning, and will require an explanation of the nature and extent of the powers of the different departments under it." No one in the federal or any state convention appears to have rejected, or even questioned, this understanding. See R. Berger, *Congress v. The Supreme Court* (1969), chap. 7.

Largely because of the "midnight appointments," the Jeffersonians repealed the 1801 statute. In 1875 Congress "reversed" the Jeffersonians and again enlarged the jurisdiction of the federal courts. Ever since, they have had broad power to decide cases arising under the Constitution and other federal law. The point is simply this: Long before *Marbury* v. *Madison*, Congress and the President on two occasions recognized in legislation that judicial review was a basic element of American government. Like Jefferson in the Declaration of Independence, Marshall in *Marbury* was not an innovator, but a gifted spokesman for a widely held view.

7 ❧ *The Judge's Art*

When men act on the principle of intelligence, they go out to find the facts and to make their wisdom. When they ignore it, they go inside themselves and find only what is there. They elaborate their prejudice, instead of increasing their knowledge.

—WALTER LIPPMANN

Plato's ancient question will not down. Is it "more advantageous to be subject to the best man or the best laws?"[1] We have long since settled on the Rule of Law, but that catch-phrase hardly meets the problem. As Plato observed, laws by definition are *general* rules; their generality is their essence and their weakness. For generality contemplates averages—the stuff of books. It falters before the complexities of life and must usually concern itself with form rather than substance. Accordingly, in Plato's ideal view, laws are a rough makeshift far inferior to the discretion of the philosopher king, whose pure wisdom would render real justice by giving each man *his* due, not the due of some nonexistent "average man."[2]

Aristotle anticipated our choice by rejecting the allwise ruler: "[T]o invest man with authority is to introduce a beast, as desire is something bestial, and even the best of men in authority are liable to be corrupted by anger." Law, in contrast, is "intelligence without passion." Yet Aristotle knew with Plato that:

All law is universal but about some things it is not possible to make a universal statement which shall be correct. In those cases then in which it is necessary to speak universally but not possible to do so correctly, the law takes the usual case, though it is not ignorant of the possibility of error. And it is none the less correct; for the error is not in the law nor in the legislator but in the nature of the thing, since the matter of practical affairs is of this kind from the start.[3]

---

[1] Aristotle posed the problem in *Politics* after Plato had explored it in *Statesmen.* See 4 THE DIALOGUES OF PLATO 496-507 (Jowett ed. 1892).

[2] This and the next paragraph have drawn heavily from MCILWAIN, THE GROWTH OF POLITICAL THOUGHT IN THE WEST (1932).

[3] ARISTOTLE, NICOMACHEAN ETHICS, book V, ch. 10, at 1137, in 9 THE WORKS OF ARISTOTLE (Ross ed. 1925).

And so, having rejected the philosopher king in favor of the Rule of Law, we call him back to limited service and name him judge.[4] In this capacity he fills the gap between the generalities of law and the specifics of life. Holmes put it in a thimble: "general propositions do not decide concrete cases." [5] Thus judges must. We have synthesized the wisdom of Plato and the wisdom of Aristotle. An inclination one way rather than the other is the difference between our "activists" and our "humilitarians"—only the names are new. How much informed discretion, how much "law," is appropriate to the peculiarities of each concrete case? What are the proper proportions for each of the myriad contexts in which a court must resolve the discrepancy between the generic directives given it and the unanticipated or imperfectly foreseen controversies that demand adjudication? As Lord Wright put it, "notwithstanding all the apparatus of authority, the judge has nearly always some degree of choice." [6]

Such is the judge's burden. In its discharge he is plagued by all the frailties, not just the "bestiality" of desire, passion, and anger that Aristotle mentioned. He must clear his endless dockets and somehow maintain the stability and predictability of the Rule of Law without losing the flexibility implicit in the sound discretion of the philosopher king. He must mediate between the letter and the spirit; between the traditions of the past and the convenience of the present; between society's need for stability and its need for change; between liberty and authority; between the whole and its parts—all this in contexts that no lawmaking assembly could be expected to foresee. Plainly this entails high art. How may the job be done?

How, indeed, does one create a poem, or a symphony? If our literature on such matters is as sparse as it is on the judge's art, it is virtually nonexistent. Cardozo's famous effort—*The Nature of the Judicial Process*—stands almost alone and somewhat dated. Was it not, after all, a tract for the times directed to the last vestige of pretense that judges are mere mimics—that creativity is not for them? Thanks to Cardozo, supplemented by the innuendoes of "the great dissenters" after World War I and the Court crisis of the mid-1930's, we are more sophisticated now. Yet, while the legislative, executive, and administrative processes have been examined endlessly, few have proceeded further—and only modestly—in the thicket where Cardozo pioneered.[7] What we have for the most part are scattered insights in

---

4 In another, more modern capacity, we call him "administrator."
5 Lochner v. New York, 198 U.S. 45, 76 (1905) (dissenting opinion).
6 WRIGHT, LEGAL ESSAYS AND ADDRESSES xxv (1939).
7 See Chafee, *Do Judges Make Or Discover Law?*, 91 PROCEEDINGS AM. PHIL. SOC'Y 405 (1947); Frankfurter, *Some Observations on the Natures of the Judicial Process of Supreme Court Litigation*, 98 PROCEEDINGS AM. PHIL. SOC'Y 233 (1954).

writings directed to other ends.   Some of these are gathered below in the hope that they may stimulate further thought on one of the pressing problems of our day: the role of judges in democratic government.

Of course, some "laws" are so clear that they preclude litigation, as, for example, the constitutional provision with respect to the number of senators from each state.   Others are so vague, so lacking in standards, as to foreclose adjudication.   Thus Holmes ventured to think that:

> every time . . . a judge declines to rule whether certain conduct is negligent or not he avows his inability to state the law; and that the meaning of leaving nice questions to the jury is that while if a question of law is pretty clear we can decide it, as it is our duty to do, if it is difficult it can be decided better by twelve men at random from the street.[8]

Similarly, Judge Learned Hand observed that a jury verdict as to whether the accused had violated an obscenity statute "is not the conclusion of a syllogism of which they are to find only the minor premiss, but really a small bit of legislation ad hoc, like the standard of due care." [9]   Putting such issues to a jury is not unlike leaving inscrutable constitutional standards for application (read incarnation) by the political branches of government.[10]

Between these extremes where the law is neither so clear nor so obscure as to preclude adjudication, judges must find or make criteria for judgment.   We have it on Mr. Justice Frankfurter's authority that:

> The decisions in the cases that really give trouble rest on judgment, and judgment derives from the totality of a man's nature and experience.   Such judgment will be exercised by two types of men, broadly speaking, but of course with varying emphasis— those who express their private views or revelations, deeming them, if not *vox dei,* at least *vox populi;* or those who feel strongly that they have no authority to promulgate law by their merely personal view and whose whole training and proved performance substantially insure that their conclusions reflect understanding of, and due regard for, law as the expression of the views and feelings that may fairly be deemed representative of the community as a continuing society.[11]

It will be noted that here even a convinced humilitarian recognizes that the problem is not whether judges shall make or find the law, but whether internal or external data shall guide their creativity.   Mr.

---

[8] Holmes, *The Path of the Law,* in Collected Legal Papers 164, 233 (1920).
[9] United States v. Levine, 83 F.2d 156, 157 (2d Cir. 1936).
[10] See, *e.g.,* Coleman v. Miller, 307 U.S. 433 (1939); Luther v. Borden, 48 U.S. (7 How.) 1 (1849).
[11] Frankfurter, *supra* note 7, at 237.

Justice Stone's less challenging language may be more generally acceptable:

> [T]he great constitutional guarantees and immunities of personal liberty and of property, which give rise to the most perplexing questions of constitutional law and government, are but statements of standards to be applied by courts according to the circumstances and conditions which call for their application. The chief and ultimate standard which they exact is reasonableness of official action . . . . They are not statements of specific commands. They do not prescribe formulas as to which governmental action must conform . . . .
>
> Whether the constitutional standard of reasonableness of official action is subjective, that of the judge who must decide, or objective in terms of a considered judgment of what the community may regard as within the limits of the reasonable, are questions which the cases have not specifically decided. Often these standards do not differ. When they do not, it is a happy augury for the development of law which is socially adequate. But the judge whose decision may control government action, as well as in deciding questions of private law, must ever be alert to discover whether they do differ and, differing, whether his own or the objective standard will represent the sober second thought of the community, which is the firm base on which all law must ultimately rest.[12]

For humilitarians, of course, there can be no doubt—the judge's personal views have no proper place in his official life. "It comes down to this," Cardozo said:

> There are certain forms of conduct which at any given place and epoch are commonly accepted under the combined influence of reason, practice and tradition, as moral or immoral. If we were asked to define the precise quality that leads them to be so characterized, we might find it troublesome to make answer, yet the same difficulty is found in defining other abstract qualities, even those the most familiar. The forms of conduct thus discriminated are not the same at all times or in all places. Law accepts as the pattern of its justice the morality of the community whose conduct it assumes to regulate. In saying this, we are not to blind ourselves to the truth that uncertainty is far from banished. Morality is not merely different in different communities. Its level is not the same for all the component groups within the same community. A choice must still be made between one group standard and another. We have still to face the problem, at which one of these levels does the social pressure become strong enough to convert the moral norm into a jural one? All that we can say is that the line will be higher than the lowest level of

---

[12] Stone, *The Common Law in the United States*, 50 HARV. L. REV. 4, 23-25 (1936).

moral principle and practice, and lower than the highest.   The law will not hold the crowd to the morality of saints and seers. It will follow, or strive to follow, the principle and practice of the men and women of the community whom the social mind would rank as intelligent and virtuous.[13]

This, of course, is an elaboration of the old common-law "reasonable man" standard which different judges may express in different terms. Thus Lord Haldane observed:

> I think that there are many things of which judges are bound to take judicial notice which lie outside the law properly so called, and among those things are what is called public policy and the changes which take place in it.   The law itself may become modified by this obligation of the judges.   [Some law, like the Rule Against Perpetuities, has become] . . . a crystalized proposition forming part of the ordinary common law, so definite that it must be applied without reference to whether a particular case involves the real mischief to guard against which the rule was originally introduced.   [But between such rules and those] . . . in which the principle of public policy has never crystalized into a definite or exhaustive set of propositions, there lies an intermediate class. Under this third category fall the instances in which public policy has partially precipitated itself into recognized rules which belong to law properly so called, but where these rules have remained subject to the moulding influence of the real reasons of public policy from which they proceeded.[14]

Chief Judge Learned Hand put it with a different emphasis:

> There is a hierarchy of power in which the judge stands low; he has no right to divinations of public opinion which run counter to its last formal expressions.   Nevertheless, the judge has, by custom, his own proper representative character as a complementary organ of the social will, and in so far as conservative sentiment, in the excess of caution that he shall be obedient, frustrates his free power by interpretation to manifest the half-framed purposes of his time, it misconceives the historical significance of his position and will in the end render him incompetent to perform the very duties upon which it lays so much emphasis.   The profession of the law of which he is a part is charged with the articulation and final incidence of the successive efforts toward justice; it must feel the circulation of the communal blood or it will wither and drop off, a useless member.[15]

Finally, in Professor Swisher's words:

> The Supreme Court is able to lead in constitutional development, then, only by virtue of the fact that its leadership is of such a

---

[13] Cardozo, Paradoxes of Legal Science 36-37 (1928).
[14] Rodriguez v. Speyer Bros., 88 L.J.K.B. (n.s.) 147, 157-59 (1918) (Haldane, L.J.).
[15] Hand, *The Speech of Justice*, 29 Harv. L. Rev. 617-18 (1916).

character that the people and their representatives are willing to follow. To put the matter more simply, the Supreme Court succeeds in leading largely to the extent of its skill not merely as a leader but as a follower. Since the medium of its leadership is the law, or the decision of cases in terms of law, we can go further and say that the effectiveness of the Court's leadership is measured by its ability to articulate deep convictions of need and deep patterns of desire on the part of the people in such a way that the people, who might not have been able themselves to be similarly articulate, will recognize the judicial statement as essentially their own. The Court must sense the synthesis of desire for both continuity and change and make the desired synthesis the expressed pattern of each decision.[16]

In short, troublesome legal issues shall be settled in harmony with the sense of the community, whether in the judge's view the community be right or wrong. Accordingly, when doubtful matters cannot be avoided, they may be referred to a jury, to the political processes, or to the "reasonable man." But who is this creature? Like jury and legislature, he symbolizes all of us. He is a standard, an American Everyman, whereby a hard-pressed judge seeks to capture the "views and feelings that may fairly be deemed representative of the community as a continuing society" (Frankfurter); "the sober second thought" of the body politic (Stone); the "forms . . . which are commonly accepted under the combined influence of reason, practice and tradition" (Cardozo); "public policy" (Haldane); "half formed [community] purposes" (Hand); or the basic "convictions of need and deep patterns of desire on the part of the people" (Swisher). The underlying thought, of course, is plain:

> [T]he judge must always remember that he should go no further than he is sure the government would have gone, had it been faced with the case before him. If he is in doubt, he must stop, for he cannot tell that the conflicting interests in the society for which he speaks would have come to a just result, even though he is sure that he knows what the just result should be. He is not to substitute even his juster will for theirs; otherwise it would not be the common will which prevails, and to that extent the people would not govern.[17]

The "reasonable man" approach is orthodox. A not entirely incompatible guide to decision—equally mundane, if less rational—is the informed "hunch" which Judge Ulman describes in action:

---

[16] SWISHER, THE SUPREME COURT IN MODERN ROLE 179-80 (1958).

[17] HAND, *Is a Judge Free in Rendering a Decision?*, in THE SPIRIT OF LIBERTY 109 (1952).

On the morning of my third day of solitary work on this [rate] case the familiar hunch came to me. Quite suddenly, while reading an opinion of the Supreme Court, I discovered that I was going to have to decide in favor of the railway company. This discovery came to me with a shock; for not until then had I realized fully the strength of my bias the other way . . . .

Therefore I determined to test to the utmost the validity of my hunch. The way to do it was to write an opinion. If the half-thoughts and partial conclusions which were forming in my mind would go down on paper and stay there, then they were my deliberate judgement. Otherwise I might erase what I should first write and decide the case the way I wanted to decide it . . . . There had developed within me a clear-cut issue between the emotions and the intellect.[18]

But is the mundane never to be enlightened by frankly transcendental values? Must we, insofar as courts are concerned, live forever in a moral *status quo*? Is judicial law to be perpetually confined by the morals of the masses?

When a case comes before a court for decision, it may be that nothing can be drawn from the sources heretofore mentioned; there may be no statute, no judicial precedent, no professional opinion, no custom, bearing on the question involved, and yet the court must decide the case somehow . . . . The French Code Civil [art. 4] says: "Le juge qui refusera de juger sous prétexte du silence, de l'obscurité ou de l'insuffisance de la loi, pourra être poursuivi comme coupable de déni de justice." And I do not know of any system of law where a judge is held to be justified in refusing to pass upon a controversy because there is no person or book or custom to tell him how to decide it. He must find out for himself; he must determine what the Law ought to be; he must have recourse to the principles of morality.[19]

Or in the rather more sophisticated language of Lord MacMillan:

It is thus clear that the judiciary are constantly confronted with the necessity of making a choice between the doctrines of the law which they are to hold applicable to a particular case, and the choice which they make in the particular instance results inevitably in the expansion or restriction of the doctrine applied or rejected. It is at this point that what may, I think, quite properly be called ethical considerations operate and ought to operate. I hope I shall be acquitted of any suggestion that judges should allow themselves to be swayed by sentiment to wrest the law,

[18] ULMAN, A JUDGE TAKES THE STAND 197-98 (1933). See also Hutcheson, *The Judgment Intuitive: The Function of the "Hunch" in Judicial Decisions*, 14 CORNELL L.Q. 274 (1929).

[19] GRAY, NATURE AND SOURCES OF THE LAW 302 (2d ed. 1921).

and I should deprecate as strongly as any the admission of the motives of the social reformer into the counsels of the Bench. I am no friend of that spurious kind of equity which Lord Bramwell robustly denounces as consisting in "A disregard of general principles and general rules in the endeavor to do justice more or less fanciful in particular cases." Other eminent judges in equally vigorous language, to which I am quite prepared to subscribe, have condemned the impropriety of allowing other than purely legal considerations to influence the decisions of the Courts. But when, as happens from time to time, the law itself presents a choice, and when it is a question whether one or other principle is to be applied, then it seems to me that it is impossible, as it is undesirable, that the decision should not have regard to the ethical motive of promoting justice.[20]

Other judges may be inclined to go further as the following quotations from Chief Justice Waite, Chief Justice Reid of the Supreme Court of Georgia, and Judge Medina, respectively, suggest:

I have read with interest your brief . . . and am satisfied the case is by no means as desperate as I thought it was. Justice is on your side certainly and that is nine points in every law suit. I never realized this so much as since I have been on the bench.[21]

[I]f he [the lawyer] arrives at a sound solution, in his interminable quest for it, it will finally rest upon the eternal principles of what is right and wrong, and, if he finds that some judicial precedent is to the contrary, either he or those ministers of justice who are to follow him will come back again to those principles that lie eternally in what is right and wrong. Thus, pursuit of the law, glamorous as it is, is very little different on the bench from what it is in the practice.[22]

I do not see why a judge should be ashamed to say that he prays for divine guidance and for strength to do his duty. Indeed, there came a time . . . when I did the most sincere and the most fervent praying that I ever did in my life.

I suddenly found myself in the midst of that trial of the Communists. It took me a long time to realize what they were trying to do to me. But as I got weaker and weaker and found the burden difficult to bear, I sought strength from the one source that never fails . . . . my unguided will alone and such self-control as I possess were unequal to this test.[23]

---

[20] MacMillan, *Law and Ethics*, 49 Scot. L. Rev. 61, 69 (1933).

[21] Letter From Chief Justice Waite to H. Newbegin, June 16, 1877, quoted in Trimble, Chief Justice Waite 266 (1938).

[22] Reid, *What a Lawyer Discovers on Becoming a Judge*, 1940 Ala. Bar Ass'n Proceedings 316, 323-24.

[23] Medina, *The Judge and His God: "We Are Not the Masters,"* 38 A.B.A.J. 661, 662-63 (1952).

The virtues and dangers of extrarational intrusions upon the judicial process are suggested in the philosophies of Lon Fuller and John Dickinson:

> The solution for the problem of rationalism *versus* irrationalism as it affects human conduct is, I think, to be found in a balance in which man's rational nature and the unrationalized side of his being reciprocally check and counterpoise one another.   In such a state of balance, intuitive insight tempers reason and preserves it from excesses, while at the same time there is no relaxing of the effort to force intuition and instinct into the patterns of articulate thought.   I believe it is not going too far to say that it was such a state of balance which sustained Western civilization during its progressive periods.[24]

> Under the name "law of nature," this ideal law, derived from currently active moral aspirations by philosophers, divines and judges, has supplied not merely a pattern and model, but a powerful stimulus for changes in and additions to the law of a given time and place.   Of course, such ideal law can only influence the actual insofar as portions of it are from time to time adopted by judges and legislators.   Naturally the ideal has varied, and not merely from period to period, but from individual thinker to individual thinker; yet in the large, the pursuit of it has usually represented an effort to discover and give effect to fundamental underlying human values, and the judge who has been influenced by the concept in his decisions has for the most part been doing what he could to build the law according to the better lights of his own age . . . .

> [The hostility of the "realists"] to rules arises precisely from the element of stability which rules necessarily involve, and they, therefore, seek to eliminate the rule-element in law in favor of a conception of law as consisting essentially of intelligent discretion . . . . This view, stripped of its contemporary phraseology and modernistic trappings, is nothing but a return to the age-old idea that the best government is government by philosopher-kings. This idea long ago lost out in the competition of the market-place to the more pedestrian idea of government by law, because law, although at the expense of a certain amount of flexibility, can at least institutionalize the common sense wisdom of mankind, while the wisdom of the philosopher-king can often be proved to be wisdom only by the persuasive force of bullets and bombs. Whether the wisdom of modern philosopher-kings can be made to rest on any different kind of proof remains to be seen.[25]

If doubt invites and often compels judicial "legislation," doubt is not a self-defining quality.   One trait of the activists—old

---

[24] Fuller, *My Philosophy of Law*, in MY PHILOSOPHY OF LAW 113, 122 (1941).
[25] Dickinson, *My Philosophy of Law*, in MY PHILOSOPHY OF LAW 91, 101-02, 106 (1941).

and new—is their relative freedom from uncertainty. They do not question the judicial duty of deference to the community when the law is foggy, but they have a marked ingenuity for scattering the clouds of doubt. Often, where colleagues are troubled, the activist finds (or, as it seems to some, legislates) certitude. His characteristic gambit is to discover or revive the "true purpose" of the Fathers—for he dare not openly repudiate the orthodox view that judgment should spring from some objective, external standard. Thus, as Jerome Frank put it,

> All judges exercise discretion, individualize abstract rules, make law . . . . The fact is, and every lawyer knows it, that *those judges who are most lawless, or most swayed by the "perverting influences of their emotional natures," or most dishonest, are often the very judges who use most meticulously the language of compelling mechanical logic, who elaborately wrap about themselves the pretense of merely discovering and carrying out existing rules, who sedulously avoid any indication that they individualize cases.*[26]

Thomas Reed Powell expressed it differently: "I think that what I most object to in many Justices is something that springs from a feeling of judicial duty to try to make out that their conclusions come from the Constitution." [27]

Even Plato recognized that a philosopher king would be unacceptable unless he could hide his naked power by a "noble fiction." It follows, of course, that platonists on the bench do not avow, but only practice, activism. When Mr. Justice Field needed a broad constitutional tool to restrain state regulation of business he "discovered" that the natural rights listed in the Declaration of Independence had been embedded in the fourteenth amendment:

> Among these inalienable rights, as proclaimed in that great document [the Declaration], is the right of men to pursue their happiness, by which is meant the right to pursue any lawful business or vocation, in any manner not inconsistent with the equal rights of others, which may increase their prosperity or develop their faculties so as to give them their highest enjoyment.[28]

Modern activists find that Field was quite wrong; that the Fathers intended to "incorporate" the Bill of Rights (rather than the Declaration) into the fourteenth amendment.[29] The effective difference, of

---

[26] Frank, Law and the Modern Mind 137-38 (1949).

[27] Powell, Vagaries and Varieties in Constitutional Interpretation 179 (1956).

[28] Butchers' Union Co. v. Crescent City Co., 111 U.S. 746, 754, 757 (1884) (concurring opinion).

[29] See Adamson v. California, 332 U.S. 46, 68 (1947) (Black, J., dissenting).

course, is that the one view gave business interests a "preferred place," while the other would give it—rather selectively—to libertarian interests.

Of course, one can be as creative in gauging the sense of the community as in discovering the true meaning of the Fathers. But there is this great difference: the community can talk back. Few, and modern activists least of all, would be willing to accept as generally binding the dead hand of past "intentions." [30]   To do so would be, in Mr. Justice Mathews words, "to deny every quality of the law but its age." [31]   Moreover, in view of the changing and contradictory purposes that have been attributed to the Fathers, it would appear that their meaning is at least as uncertain in the face of modern problems as is our thinking.   Given the present activist's progressive bent, one suspects that when he pleads past purposes—always selectively—to justify his conception of present needs, he does so because he is reasonably sure his views would not be presently acceptable on their own merits.

Must it be either a "psychoanalysis" of the present with the humilitarians, or of the past with the activists?   Max Radin proposed a more direct approach:

> [I]n that great mass of transactions which do not fit readily or quickly into established types, or will fit into one just as easily as another, the judge ought to be a free agent.   We need not fear arbitrariness.   Our Cokes and Mansfields and Eldons derive their physical and spiritual nourishment from the same sources that we do.   They will find good what we find good, if we will let them. And if they had not prescribed to themselves the curious necessity of putting the transactions to be regulated into one type-form rather than another—assuming that it could go into either and will not without pushing go into any—they would have no need of their relations and imputations, their presumptions and suppositions, their gyrations and concatenations, and could cut straight to the desirable result which they in common with ourselves as members of the community prefer . . . .

> It is an undoubted fact that the chief purpose courts fulfill in giving us not merely a judgment but a classification of the judgment by types and standards, is to make it easy for us to find out how they think.   The technique which has become traditional in Europe and America seems to me to make it hard.[32]

---

[30] With modern activist views on freedom of expression and right to counsel, contrast the "intentions" of the Fathers as set out in LEVY, LEGACY OF SUPPRESSION (1960), and BEANEY, THE RIGHT TO COUNSEL IN AMERICAN COURTS ch. 3 (1955).

[31] Quoted in Bickel, Book Review, New Republic, May 12, 1958, pp. 16, 19.

[32] Radin, *The Theory of Judicial Decision: Or How Judges Think*, 11 A.B.A.J. 357, 362 (1925).

John Dewey propounded a similar thought in more pragmatic terms:

> On the view here presented, the standard is found in consequences, in the *function* of what goes on socially. If this view were generally held, there would be assurance of introduction on a large scale of the rational factor into concrete evaluations of legal arrangements. For it demands that intelligence, employing the best scientific methods and materials available, be used, to investigate, in terms of the context of actual situations, the consequences of legal rules and of proposed legal decisions and acts of legislation. The present tendency [1941], hardly more as yet than in a state of inception, to discuss legal matters in their concrete social setting, and not in the comparative vacuum of their relations to one another, would get the reinforcement of a consistent legal theory. Moreover, when it is systematically acknowledged in practice that social facts are going concerns and that all legal matters have their place *within* these ongoing concerns, there will be a much stronger likelihood than at present that new knowledge will be acquired of a kind which can be brought to bear upon the never-ending process of improving standards of judgment.[33]

Some will insist that whatever the proclaimed standard a judge cannot long escape his own sense of values—his own bias. Perhaps detachment is an illusion. Maybe it belongs only to the gods. "Be that as it may," Learned Hand admonishes,

> we know that men do differ widely in this capacity; and the incredulity which seeks to discredit that knowledge is a part of the crusade against reason from which we have already so bitterly suffered. We may deny—and, if we are competent observers, we will deny—that no one can be aware of the danger [of his bias] and in large measure provide against it.[34]

Cardozo's attitude was not entirely different:

> If reasoning is vitiated at times by adhering to abstractions, it is vitiated also by starting with a prepossession and finding arguments to sustain it. The weakness is inherent in the judicial process. The important thing, however, is to rid our prepossessions, so far as may be, of what is merely individual or personal, to detach them in a measure from ourselves, to build them, not upon instinctive or intuitive likes and dislikes, but upon an informed and liberal culture, a knowledge (as Arnold would have said) of the best that has been thought and said in the world, so far as that best has relation to the social problem to be solved. Of course, when our utmost effort has been put forth, we shall be far from freeing ourselves from the empire of inarticulate

---

33 Dewey, *My Philosophy of Law,* in MY PHILOSOPHY OF LAW 73, 84-85 (1941).
34 HAND, *Thomas Walter Swan,* in THE SPIRIT OF LIBERTY 209, 218 (3d ed. 1960).

emotion, of beliefs so ingrained and inveterate as to be a portion of our very nature . . . . The best that we can hope for is that from the knowledge of our weakness there will come the exercise of strength.[35]

Judge Frank may have been a bit more pessimistic:

> In the many cases where the testimony is in conflict, can there ever be much "objectivity" in judicial decisions, or . . . much of uniformity in the translation of community ideals into those decisions? I confess that I do not know the answer. To some extent, the difficulty can be surmounted by self-knowledge on the part of the judge, by a self-scrutiny revealing to him his personal biases, followed by an effort on his part to bring them into line with acceptable moral ideals. But that is no complete solution. Perhaps there is none; perhaps there is.[36]

In the end we must recognize that law is not a bucket of ready-made answers, but a process, or technique, for easing an endless flux of changing social tensions. It "is always approaching, and never reaching, consistency. It is forever adopting new principles from life at one end, and it always retains old ones from history at the other, which have not yet been absorbed or sloughed off. It will become entirely consistent only when it ceases to grow." [37] Legal reasoning then involves more than logic. Judge Bok described it at its best as "the play of an enlightened personality within the boundaries of a system." [38] Under a facade of formal symmetry it must synthesize established rules, pragmatic needs, and moral yearnings. It must honor reasonable expectations born of the past and yet allow adequate *Lebensraum* for the present and the future. It must have daring moments and moments politic, moments of hope, moments of fear, and moments of doubt. Plainly the stolid satisfaction of the hedgehog, bristling upon a single postulate, is not for judges. They must pursue the fox—the reason that is many reasons, the truth that cannot be caught without destroying its vitality. In short, as Dean Levi insists,

> The emphasis should be on the process. The contrast between logic and the actual legal method is a disservice to both. Legal reasoning has a logic of its own. Its structure fits it to give meaning to ambiguity and to test constantly whether society has come to see new differences or similarities. Social theories and other changes in society will be relevant when the ambiguity has to be

[35] CARDOZO, *op. cit. supra* note 13, at 126-27.
[36] Frank, Book Review, 59 HARV. L. REV. 1004, 1011 (1946).
[37] HOLMES, THE COMMON LAW 36 (1881).
[38] BOK, BACKBONE OF THE HERRING 9 (1941).

resolved for a particular case. Nor can it be said that the result of such a method is too uncertain to compel. The compulsion of the law is clear; the explanation is that the area of doubt is constantly set forth. The probable area of expansion or contraction is foreshadowed as the system works. This is the only kind of system which will work when people do not agree completely. The loyalty of the community is directed toward the institution in which it participates. The words change to receive the content which the community gives to them. The effort to find complete agreement before the institution goes to work is meaningless. It is to forget the very purpose for which the institution of legal reasoning has been fashioned. This should be remembered as a world community suffers in the absence of law.[39]

Holmes tells us he once heard an eminent judge say that he never let a decision go until he was sure it was right:

> This mode of thinking is entirely natural. The training of lawyers is training in logic . . . and the logical method and form flatter that longing for certainty and for repose which is in every human mind. But certainty generally is illusion, and repose is not the destiny of man. Behind the logical form lies a judgment as to the relative worth and importance of competing legislative grounds, often an inarticulate and unconscious judgment, it is true, and yet the very root and nerve of the whole proceeding. You can give any conclusion a logical form. You always can imply a condition in a contract. But why do you do it? It is because of some belief as to the practice of the community or of a class, or because of some opinion as to policy, or, in short, because of some attitude of yours upon a matter not capable of exact quantitative measurement, and therefore not capable of founding exact logical conclusions.[40]

From this it is an easy step to Cardozo's view that "a judge must think of himself as an artist . . . who, although he must know the handbooks, should never try to use them for his guidance; in the end he must rely upon his almost instinctive sense of where the line [lies] between the word and the purpose . . . behind it; he must somehow manage to be true to both." [41]

Great artistry on the bench as elsewhere means creative response to the evolving processes of social life. It entails respect for existing forms and values, but immunity from their strangulating grasp. Above all, it demands a sense of paradox. For in the words of Mr. Justice Frankfurter:

---

[39] LEVY, AN INTRODUCTION TO LEGAL REASONING 73-74 (1949).
[40] HOLMES, *The Path of the Law*, in COLLECTED LEGAL PAPERS 167, 180-81 (1920).
[41] Hand, *Mr. Justice Cardozo*, 52 HARV. L. REV. 361-62 (1939).

The core of the difficulty is that there is hardly a question of any real difficulty before the Court that does not entail more than one so-called principle. Anybody can decide a question if only a single principle is in controversy. Partisans and advocates often cast a question in that form, but the form is deceptive. In a famous passage Mr. Justice Holmes has exposed this misconception:

> All rights tend to declare themselves absolute to their logical extreme. Yet all in fact are limited by the neighborhood of principles of policy which are other than those on which the particular right is founded, and which become strong enough to hold their own when a certain point is reached . . . . The boundary at which the conflicting interests balance cannot be determined by any general formula in advance, but points in the line, or helping to establish it, are fixed by decisions that this or that concrete case falls on the nearer or farther side.

This contest between conflicting principles is not limited to law. In a recent discussion of two books on the conflict between the claims of literary individualism and dogma, I came across this profound observation: ". . . But when, in any field of human observation, two truths appear in conflict it is wiser to assume that neither is exclusive, and that their contradiction, though it may be hard to bear, is part of the mystery of things." But judges cannot leave such contradiction between . . . conflicting "truths" as "part of the mystery of things." They have to adjudicate. If the conflict cannot be resolved, the task of the Court is to arrive at an accommodation of the contending claims. This is the core of the difficulties and misunderstandings about the judicial process. This, for any conscientious judge, is the agony of his duty.[42]

42 Frankfurter, *supra* note 7, at 238.

Freedom of Expression:
Words Enlighten, Words Deceive,
Words Injure

8   *Clear and Present Danger —*
From Schenck to Dennis

Some legal doctrines are more important as manifestations of attitude than as guides to decision in specific cases. Not long ago "liberty of contract" was little more than a shorthand symbol for Spencerian sociology. More happily, in recent years "clear and present danger" has embodied a deeply democratic instinct favoring the free expression of ideas. But like "economic due process," it has been more significant as a pervasive atmospheric pressure, than as a reliable standard for the decision of a specific case or as a rationale for a line of cases.[1] The policy decision implicit in the choice of one legal doctrine over another often explains more than does the chosen doctrine itself.

The influence of danger doctrine can hardly be overrated; indeed, it has become one of our democratic traditions. But we are not without evidence that protection for civil liberties is least available when needed most. It may be that the apparent softening at present of judicial concern for free utterance—like the demise of "economic due process"—indicates that doctrines which are long on atmosphere and short on concrete standards find themselves at a disadvantage in time of crisis. Yet even in less troubled times danger doctrine has not been a reliable guide. The step from general ideal to specific application is always difficult. And, since the departure of Mr. Justice Holmes, "clear and present danger" has suggested all things to all justices.

Notwithstanding its admitted influence as an ideal, analysis of free expression opinions suggests that, as a judicial instrument, the danger test has never had more than four enthusiasts on the Supreme Court at any one time. Given a lack of doctrinal agreement among the remaining justices and the economy of effort which the pressure of Supreme Court business imposes, a vigorous minority of four will often find a fifth to endorse its language—

---

1. See Latham, *The Theory of the Judicial Concept of Freedom of Speech*, 12 J. POL. ECON. 637 (1950).

especially, though perhaps not exclusively, if the fifth is not averse to the conclusion reached:

> The considerations that move a judge to yield concurrence in an opinion reaching an approved result through uncongenial doctrine are among the most teasing mysteries. . . . Long-term strategy or immediate fatigue, hopelessness of opposition or deprecation of the importance of the pronouncement, bonhommie of common labors or avoidance of undue division [all may be involved].[2]

But harmony so achieved is highly volatile for, as Mr. Justice Frankfurter has noted, "different nuances in phrasing the same conclusion lead to different emphasis and thereby eventually may lead to different conclusions in slightly different situations."[3]

To test the more important of these hypotheses and to uncover the hard core of meaning behind Mr. Justice Holmes' danger rhetoric is the object of what follows—for it may be that by returning to his position we can combine the power of an ideal with the stability that is implicit in a rule of law.

I. 1919 TO 1930

The danger rule was born in *Schenck v. United States*,[4] in March, 1919. By urging resistance to the draft Schenck had run afoul of the Espionage Act of 1917; he defended on free speech grounds. Mr. Justice Holmes, for a unanimous Court, observed:

> the character of every act depends upon the circumstances in which it was done. . . . The most stringent protection of free speech would not protect a man in falsely shouting fire in a theatre, and causing a panic. It does not even protect a man from an injunction against uttering words that may have all the effect of force. . . . The question in every case is whether the words used are used in such circumstances and are of such a nature as to create a clear and present danger that they will bring about the substantive evils that Congress has a right to prevent. It is a question of proximity and degree.[5]

The test was found to have been met—given the intent and the tendency of Schenck's words.

The *Schenck* decision was cited by the Court as controlling in six subsequent cases during 1919 and 1920,[6] but the danger test was not mentioned

---

2. FRANKFURTER, THE COMMERCE CLAUSE 56 (1937).
3. American Communications Ass'n, CIO v. Douds, 339 U.S. 382, 418 (1950) (concurring in part and dissenting in part).
4. 249 U.S. 47 (1919).
5. *Id.* at 52.
6. Gilbert v. Minnesota, 254 U.S. 325 (1920); Pierce v. United States, 252 U.S. 239 (1920); Schaefer v. United States, 251 U.S. 468 (1920); Abrams v. United States, 250 U.S. 616 (1919); Debs v. United States, 249 U.S. 211 (1919); Frowerk v. United States, 249 U.S. 204 (1919).

nor was the evidence analyzed in danger terms. A conviction was sustained in each instance. Throughout the next ten years the rule was mentioned in only one majority opinion and then it was merely distinguished to permit upholding a conviction.[7] Justices Holmes and Brandeis alone kept "clear and present danger" alive in a series of six concurring or dissenting opinions.[8] This is the full history of the rule down to 1930.[9] For all but two justices it seems to have been nothing more than a device enabling the Court to send men to jail. Nevertheless, because of the brilliance with which they wrote, Justices Holmes and Brandeis left a deep mark upon the law of free expression.

In origin "clear and present danger" was a rule of evidence designed to keep the application of espionage and criminal syndicalism statutes within constitutional bounds. Drawing upon the common law of incitement to crime, Mr. Justice Holmes used the danger test to determine where discussion ends and incitement or attempt begins.[10] The core of his position was that the First Amendment protects only utterance that seeks acceptance via the democratic processes of discussion and agreement. "Words that may have all the effect of force"[11]—that is, utterance calculated to achieve its goal by circumventing the democratic processes—are not so protected. Falsely shouting fire in a crowded theater does not invite debate; it incites panic in which force and injury are inevitable. But how is the line to be drawn between discussion and incitement on the border where, as Mr. Justice Cardozo observed, "thought merges into action"?[12] The common law of incitement to crime suggested an answer. The danger test, as Justices Holmes and Brandeis used it, assumes that the normal cure for allegedly harmful talk is time and debate. Repression is permissible only if

> the evil apprehended is so imminent that it may befall before there is opportunity for full discussion. If there be time to expose through discussion the falsehood and fallacies, to avert the evil by the process of education the remedy to be applied is more speech, not enforced silence.[13]

---

7. Gitlow v. New York, 268 U.S. 652 (1925).

8. *See* Whitney v. California, 274 U.S. 357, 372 (1927); Gitlow v. New York, 268 U.S. 652, 672 (1925); Gilbert v. Minnesota, 254 U.S. 325, 334 (1920); Pierce v. United States, 252 U.S. 239, 253 (1920); Schaefer v. United States, 251 U.S. 468, 482 (1920); Abrams v. United States, 250 U.S. 616, 624 (1919).

9. Fiske v. Kansas, 274 U.S. 380 (1927), which turned on the inadequacy of the charge and the evidence, is the only case during this period in which a First Amendment claim was sustained. The other civil liberties cases are: New York *ex rel.* Bryant v. Zimmerman, 278 U.S. 63 (1928); Burns v. United States, 274 U.S. 328 (1927); United States *ex rel.* Milwaukee Social Democratic Pub. Co. v. Burleson, 255 U.S. 407 (1921).

10. See CHAFEE, FREE SPEECH IN THE UNITED STATES 82 (1942).

11. Schenck v. United States, 249 U.S. 47, 52 (1919).

In Masses Publishing Co. v. Patten, 244 Fed. 535, 540 (S.D.N.Y. 1917), Judge Learned Hand noted a distinction between words used as "keys of persuasion" and as "triggers of action."

12. Cardozo, *Mr. Justice Holmes*, 44 HARV. L. REV. 682, 688 (1931).

13. Whitney v. California, 274 U.S. 357, 377 (1927) (concurring opinion).

Mr. Justice Holmes, however, did not suppose that a context of force constitutes the sole ground for cutting off or punishing discourse. There are other abuses of democratic freedoms—abuses that cannot be measured in terms of danger that goals will be reached without running the gauntlet of community discussion. When Nebraska's legislature sought to foster cultural unity by forbidding grade school teachers to teach in foreign languages, the Court balked.[14] Mr Justice Holmes, dissenting, did not attempt to weigh the conflicting interests in danger terms as did some of his successors in the comparable flag salute litigation.[15] Of course there is no threat of bypassing democratic processes in either situation. That the danger test reveals none is just as meaningless as the failure of a barometer to record the imminence of an avalanche.

The Constitution does not protect the utterance of "force words"; neither does it prohibit majorities from being "foolish." It requires only that dissenters be free to exploit such "foolishness" in argument. Prohibiting a teacher's "free speech" in German represses no ideas, blocks no one's participation in democratic politics, and forecloses no efforts to change the public mind. In short, the purpose of the First Amendment is not violated. On the Massachusetts bench Mr. Justice Holmes upheld state efforts to forbid certain political activities by policemen[16] and to outlaw speech-making on Boston Commons.[17] Democratic processes are not materially impeded, nor are reasonable men necessarily offended, when policemen are deterred from mixing politics and law enforcement or a park is set aside as a haven for repose free from political and religious polemics. The most that a court may ask in such circumstances is whether there are reasonable opportunities for adequate public discussion elsewhere or by other means.

All the evidence indicates that Mr. Justice Holmes distinguished between restrictions on the mind and regulation of modes of expression. Only when a government's thrust was against an idea itself did he use the danger test, his purpose being to give all ideas complete freedom to seek acceptance in the democratic forum. But when the public animus was not calculated to suppress ideas, but merely to regulate the time, place, or manner of expressing them, Mr. Justice Holmes' guide was the less stringent reasonable basis rule.[18] "Congress [like the states] certainly cannot forbid

---

14. *See* Meyer v. Nebraska, 262 U.S. 390, 412 (1923).
15. West Virginia State Board of Education v. Barnette, 319 U.S. 624 (1943). See CHAFEE, *op. cit. supra* note 10, at 321.
16. McAuliffe v. New Bedford, 155 Mass. 216, 29 N.E. 517 (1891), *cf.* Kovacs v. Cooper, 336 U.S. 77 (1949); Saia v. New York, 334 U.S. 558 (1948).
17. Commonwealth v. Davis, 162 Mass. 510, 39 N.E. 113 (1895).
18. Mr. Justice Holmes' vote in Pierce v. Society of Sisters, 268 U.S. 510 (1925), may be explained on the ground that he saw in the Ku Klux Klan-inspired restriction there at issue far more than a mere time, place, or manner regulation.

all effort to change the mind of the [community];"[19] democracy requires substantial opportunity for full discussion of all ideas. But it does not require that everyone be free to say anything he wants anywhere, anytime, and at any place. The great contribution of Mr. Justice Holmes was that he looked through the deceptively simple language of the First Amendment to its plain purpose—the safeguarding of society's thinking processes.

II. 1930 TO 1940

The chief justiceship of Mr. Hughes clearly marks a new dispensation. The decade of the thirties far surpasses all prior decades in the number of Supreme Court decisions vindicating civil liberties. The danger rule, however, was mentioned only twice—once as an oblique underpinning for the Court's position[20] and once in a dissent by Mr. Justice Cardozo.[21] Despite his position of leadership in the struggle to protect civil liberties, neither as associate nor as chief justice did Mr. Hughes ever write an opinion in which the danger test was used. Blackstone's old doctrine of "prior restraint" as the essence of forbidden censorship served in several cases;[22] the others were handled largely *ad hoc* with no discernible thread of doctrinal continuity.[23]

III. THE EARLY ROOSEVELT COURT—1940 TO MAY, 1943

Mr. Justice Murphy's first civil liberties opinion, delivered in 1940, marks the beginning of another cycle. *Thornhill v. Alabama*[24] concerned the validity of a conviction under a general statutory prohibition against picketing. Building on a famous remark of Mr. Justice Brandeis,[25] and speaking for all but Mr. Justice McReynolds, Mr. Justice Murphy observed:

> In the circumstances of our times the dissemination of information concerning the facts of a labor dispute must be regarded as within that area of free discussion that is guaranteed by the Constitution. . . . Free discussion concerning the conditions in indus-

---

19. Abrams v. United States, 250 U.S. 616, 628 (1919) (dissenting opinion).
20. Herndon v. Lowry, 301 U.S. 242 (1937).
21. Herndon v. Georgia, 295 U.S. 441, 448 (1935).
22. Schneider v. Irvington, 308 U.S. 147 (1939); Lovell v. City of Griffin, 303 U.S. 444 (1938); Near v. Minnesota, 283 U.S. 697 (1931); *cf.* Hague v. CIO, 307 U.S. 496 (1939); see 1 BL. COMM. *151.
23. Associated Press v. NLRB, 301 U.S. 103 (1937); DeJonge v. Oregon, 299 U.S. 353 (1937); Hamilton v. University of California, 293 U.S. 245 (1934); Stromberg v. California, 283 U.S. 359 (1931); Grosjean v. American Press Co., 297 U.S. 233 (1926).
24. 310 U.S. 88 (1940).
25. The dictum quoted is: "Members of a union might, without special statutory authorization by a State, make known the facts of a labor dispute, for freedom of the press is guaranteed by the Federal Constitution." *Id.* at 103. Mr. Justice Murphy failed, however, to quote Mr. Justice Brandeis' next sentence, which is: "The State may, in the exercise of its police power, regulate the *methods and means* of publicity as well as the use of public streets." Senn v. Tile Layers Protective Union, 301 U.S. 468, 478 (1937) (emphasis added).

try and the causes of labor disputes appears to us indispensable to the effective and intelligent use of the processes of popular government to shape the destiny of modern industrial society.[26]

Granting that discussion of the subject matter involved, "the facts of a labor dispute," is constitutionally protected, what of picketing as a mode of expression? Mr. Justice Murphy cited a group of "police power" (reasonable basis) decisions[27] in support of the proposition that

the rights of employers and employees to conduct their economic affairs and to compete with others for a fair share in the products of industry are subject to modification or qualification in the interests of the society in which they exist. . . . This is but an instance of the power of the state to set the limits of permissible contest open to industrial combatants.[28]

Thus, following Mr. Justice Holmes, the Court drew a distinction between the form and the content of expression and, as indicated by the line of decisions cited, took the position that the validity of restraints on form should be tested by the reasonable basis rule.

But, continued Mr. Justice Murphy:

It does not follow that the State in dealing with the evils arising from industrial disputes may impair the *effective* exercise of the right to discuss freely industrial relations which are matters of public concern. A contrary conclusion could be used to support abridgment of freedom of speech and of the press concerning almost every matter of importance to society.[29]

The key word is "effective" which bridges the distinction between form and content. For if the effective way of expressing "the facts of a labor dispute" —that is, peaceful picketing—is prohibited, the prohibition becomes in fact a substantive restraint.[30] In that event the danger test is relevant.[31]

In a word, the *Thornhill* case brought both aspects of the Holmesian approach back into the law, for it recognized as constitutionally significant the difference between censorship and reasonable time, place, or manner regulations. Indeed, *Thornhill* went a step farther and made explicit what Mr. Justice Holmes had only implied, namely, that a regulation of the manner of expression may in some circumstances be a serious impediment to ideas themselves.

---

26. Thornhill v. Alabama, 310 U.S. 88, 102 (1940).

27. *Id.* at 103. The cases cited begin with Holden v. Hardy, 169 U.S. 366 (1898), and include Nebbia v. New York, 291 U.S. 502 (1934), and West Coast Hotel Co. v. Parrish, 300 U.S. 379 (1937).

28. Thornhill v. Alabama, 310 U.S. 88, 103 (1940).

29. *Id.* at 104 (emphasis added).

30. *Cf.* Bakery & Pastry Drivers v. Wohl, 315 U.S. 769, 775 (1942). There the Court expressly recognized that an unusual form of picketing was justified by the unavailability of any other practical method for petitioners to make their case known to the public.

31. See Thornhill v. Alabama, 310 U.S. 88, 104 (1940).

Four more decisions during this period followed *Thornhill* in striking down general restraints on peaceful picketing.[32] Two others, following the implication of *Thornhill*, approved restricted limitations upon picketing on reasonable basis grounds.[33] Finally, in *Cox v. New Hampshire*[34] and *Minersville School District v. Gobitis*,[35] the early Roosevelt Court upheld a "license" requiriment for parades and a compulsory public school flag salute, both of which had been attacked by Jehovah's Witnesses on First Amendment grounds. In each instance the Court treated the restraint involved as a reasonable time, place, or manner regulation which did not hinder substantially either freedom of religion or democratic political processes.[36]

The early Roosevelt Court did not, however, always follow Mr. Justice Holmes' path. In *Cantwell v. Connecticut*,[37] decided unanimously less than a month after *Thornhill*, a statutory requirement of advance discretionary approval for religious canvassing was invalidated on prior restraint grounds. The same result might have been reached via Mr. Justices Holmes' approach. Presumably historical tradition and the recent glory of *Near v. Minnesota*[38] explain this Court's retention of "prior restraint" in the limited factual context where it is applicable.[39] But its implication that expression may be penalized on a *post hoc* basis makes it a hopeless anachronism. Apparently "clear and present danger" was revived to supplement Blackstone in *Thornhill* and other subsequent punishment cases. In the preceding decade, under the leadership of Chief Justice Hughes, the Court had relied largely upon *ad hoc* tactics when the facts of a case could not be brought within the narrow limits of the prior restraint rule.

While the year 1940 marks at least a partial fruition of Mr. Justice Holmes' efforts in the area of civil liberties, it also marks the beginning of an entirely different cycle. In that year Mr. Justice Stone, writing his first civil liberties opinion, dissented alone in the first flag salute case.[40] By 1941 Justices Black and Douglas were in dissent;[41] by 1942 Mr. Justice Murphy had joined them.[42] The common element in all these dissents is disenchantment with the reasonable basis approach in civil liberties cases. Finally, in

---

32. Bakery & Pastry Drivers v. Wohl, 314 U.S. 769 (1942); Hotel & Restaurant Employees v. Wisconsin Employment Relations Bd., 315 U.S. 437 (1942); AFL v. Swing, 312 U.S. 321 (1941); Carlson v. California, 310 U.S. 106 (1940).

33. Carpenters & Joiners Union v. Ritters Cafe, 315 U.S. 722 (1942); Milkwagon Drivers v. Meadowmoor Dairies, 312 U.S. 287 (1941).

34. 312 U.S. 569 (1941).

35. 310 U.S. 586 (1940).

36. *See id.* at 593, 594, 599.

37. 310 U.S. 296 (1940).

38. 283 U.S. 697 (1930).

39. See Largent v. Texas, 318 U.S. 418 (1943); Jamison v. Texas, 318 U.S. 412 (1943).

40. Minersville School District v. Gobitis, 310 U.S. 586, 601 (1940).

41. Milkwagon Drivers v. Meadowmoor Dairies, 312 U.S. 287, 299 (1941).

42. Carpenters & Joiners Union v. Ritters Cafe, 315 U.S. 722, 729 (1942).

Jones v. Opelika,[43] Justices Black, Douglas, and Murphy not only joined in a dissent by Chief Justice Stone, but wrote a separate opinion to announce "gratuitously" that they now conceived themselves to have been in error in the first flag salute case, the leading modern exposition of the reasonable basis rule. By the spring of 1943, when Mr. Justice Byrnes resigned from the bench, four of its members were unmistakably out of sympathy with the reasonable basis aspect of the Holmesian approach—the aspect which so often seemed to justify imposition of governmental restraints on expression. Conversely, Justices Frankfurter and Roberts, as well as Chief Justice Stone on occasion, had shown signs of sharp displeasure with the manner in which the others had, as they thought, improperly used danger rhetoric to achieve results that Mr. Justice Holmes could not have contemplated.[44] Chief Justice Stone was to be found sometimes in one camp and sometimes in the other; he seemed satisfied with neither the danger nor the reasonable basis test in civil liberties cases.

IV. The Mature Roosevelt Court—May, 1943 to July, 1949

The tenure of Mr. Justice Rutledge marks the era *par excellence* of civil liberties—some would say civil anarchy—in American jurisprudence. An increasingly libertarian attitude on the part of Justices Black, Douglas, and Murphy had been indicated during the formative period of the Roosevelt Court. To that bloc was now added another. Since four votes are decisive in the disposition of writs of certiorari, it is not surprising to find more decisions involving First Amendment freedoms during this period than in the entire previous history of the Supreme Court. If "clear and present danger" was ever "the law," it was while the four libertarians, Justices Black, Douglas, Murphy, and Rutledge, were together on the bench.

During these six years forty-one expression decisions were handed down.[45] Seven may be dismissed at the outset as involving only specious

43. 316 U.S. 584 (1942).
This case, like Chaplinsky v. New Hampshire, 315 U.S. 568 (1942), and Valentine v. Christensen, 316 U.S. 52 (1942), went on the ground that commercial activities and offensive language are not protected by the First Amendment.
44. *See* Bridges v. California, 314 U.S. 252, 279 (1941) (dissenting opinion).
Hartzel v. United States, 322 U.S. 680 (1944), indicates that neither Chief Justice Stone nor Justices Black, Murphy, Roberts, and Rutledge would have joined in Mr. Justice Holmes' opinion in the *Schenck* case.
45. Terminiello v. Chicago, 337 U.S. 1 (1949); Giboney v. Empire Storage & Ice Co., 336 U.S. 490 (1949); Fisher v. Pace, 336 U.S. 155 (1949); Railway Express Co. v. New York, 336 U.S. 106 (1949); Kovacs v. Cooper, 336 U.S. 77 (1949); Doubleday & Co. v. New York, 335 U.S. 848 (1948); AFL v. American Sash & Door Co., 335 U.S. 538 (1949); Lincoln Federal Labor Union v. Northwestern Iron Co., 335 U.S. 525 (1949); United States v. CIO, 335 U.S. 106 (1948); Saia v. New York, 334 U.S. 558 (1948); United States v. Paramount Pictures, 334 U.S. 131 (1948); Winters v. New York, 333 U.S. 507 (1948); Donaldson v. Read Magazine, 333 U.S. 178 (1948); Musser v. Utah, 333 U.S. 95 (1948); United States v.

claims:[46] for example, a group of newspaper publishers sought exemption from the Sherman Antitrust and Fair Labor Standards Acts on free press grounds.[47] Without dissent, the Court refused to treat such claims seriously. Another five were disposed of without reaching a First Amendment question.[48] Three of these cases involved acts of Congress;[49] there freedom of expression was sustained either by a strained interpretion of the statutes[50] or by finding insufficient evidence.[51] The result, of course, reflects the Roosevelt Court's reluctance to invalidate national legislation. Indeed since the judicial revolution of 1937 no act of Congress has been invalidated on First Amendment grounds—demonstrating that sometimes one may eat one's cake and have it too.

That the substitution of Mr. Justice Rutledge for Mr. Justice Byrnes would bring changes in the law was made clear on May 3, 1943, when the *Opelika* decision was reversed on rehearing[52] and two other important cases were decided.[53] The four dissenters in the original *Opelika* case had gained an ally—at least when decision could be based on what were essentially prior restraint considerations. In the following month the Court did an about-face on the flag salute issue.[54] Simultaneously it abandoned Mr.

Petrillo, 332 U.S. 1 (1947); Craig v. Harney, 331 U.S. 367 (1947); Oklahoma v. United States Civil Service Comm'n, 330 U.S. 127 (1947); United Public Workers v. Mitchell, 330 U.S. 75 (1947); Pennekamp v. Florida, 328 U.S. 331 (1946); Oklahoma Press Pub. Co. v. Walling, 327 U.S. 186 (1946); Mabee v. White Plains Pub. Co., 327 U.S. 178 (1946); Tucker v. Texas, 326 U.S. 517 (1946); Marsh v. Alabama, 326 U.S. 501 (1946); May Dep't Stores v. NLRB, 326 U.S. 376 (1945); Associated Press v. United States, 326 U.S. 1 (1945); *In re* Summers, 325 U.S. 561 (1945); Thomas v. Collins, 323 U.S. 516 (1945); Keegan v. United States, 325 U.S. 478 (1945); Hartzel v. United States, 322 U.S. 680 (1944); United States v. Ballard, 322 U.S. 78 (1944); Follett v. Town of McCormick, 321 U.S. 573 (1944); Prince v. Massachusetts, 321 U.S. 158 (1944); Cafeteria Employees Union v. Angelos, 320 U.S. 293 (1943); West Virginia State Board of Education v. Barnette, 319 U.S. 624 (1943); Taylor v. Mississippi, 319 U.S. 583 (1943); NLRB v. Virginia Electric & Power Co., 319 U.S. 533 (1943); National Broadcasting Co. v. United States, 319 U.S. 190 (1943); Douglas v. City of Jeanette, 319 U.S. 157 (1943); Martin v. Struthers, 319 U.S. 141 (1943); Murdock v. Pennsylvania, 319 U.S. 105 (1943); Jones v. Opelika, 319 U.S. 103 (1943).

Danger language was used in two non-expression cases: Korematsu v. United States, 323 U.S. 214 (1944); Bridges v. Wixon, 326 U.S. 135 (1945).

46. AFL v. American Sash & Door Co., 335 U.S. 538 (1949); Lincoln Federal Labor Union v. Northwestern Iron & Metal Co., 335 U.S. 525 (1949); United States v. Paramount Pictures, 334 U.S. 131 (1948); Oklahoma Press Pub. Co. v. Walling, 327 U.S. 186 (1946); Mabee v. White Plains Pub. Co., 327 U.S. 178 (1946); Associated Press v. United States, 326 U.S. 1 (1945); National Broadcasting Co. v. United States, 319 U.S. 190 (1943).

47. Associated Press v. United States, *supra* note 46.

48. United States v. CIO, 335 U.S. 106 (1948); Winters v. New York, 333 U.S. 507 (1948); Musser v. Utah, 333 U.S. 1 (1948); Keegan v. United States, 325 U.S. 478 (1945); Hartzel v. United States, 322 U.S. 680 (1944). *Cf.* United States v. Petrillo, 332 U.S. 1 (1947); Douglas v. City of Jeanette, 319 U.S. 157 (1943).

49. United States v. CIO, Keegan v. United States, Hartzel v. United States, *supra* note 48.

50. United States v. CIO, *supra* note 48.

51. Keegan v. United States, Hartzel v. United States, *supra* note 48.

52. Jones v. Opelika, 319 U.S. 103 (1943).

53. Martin v. Struthers, 319 U.S. 141 (1943); Murdock v. Pennsylvania, 319 U.S. 105 (1943).

54. West Virginia State Board of Education v. Barnette, 319 U.S. 624 (1943), *overruling* Minersville School District v. Gobitis, 310 U.S. 586 (1940).

Justice Holmes' distinction between suppression of ideas and mere regulation of the time, place, or manner of expressing them. "Reasonable basis" was discarded in First Amendment cases and "clear and present danger" expanded to fill the resulting vacuum. A test originally intended to detect the point at which discussion ripens into illegal conduct became the criterion for permissible grade school curricula:

> here the power of compulsion is invoked without any allegation that remaining passive during a flag salute ritual creates a clear and present danger. . . . The right of a state to regulate, for example, a public utility, may well include, so far as the due process test is concerned, power to impose all of the restrictions which a legislature may have a "rational basis" for adopting. But freedoms of speech and of press, of assembly and of worship may not be infringed on such slender grounds. They are susceptible of restriction only to prevent grave and immediate danger to interests which the state may lawfully protect.[55]

Of course a test designed to deal with serious criminality would be insensitive to the conduct of moppets in their school rooms. To make "clear and present danger" the sole test in First Amendment cases is to imply that incitement to crime is the only abuse of free expression.[56]

Cut loose from its anchor in the distinction between discussion and incitement, the danger rule lost its intrinsic meaning. No longer a guide to decision, it became a cloak for "vague but fervent transcendentalism." During the remainder of the Rutledge era only two cases presented problems of incitement and censorship,[57] though danger talk occurs in at least fifteen of the opinions.[58] But having "reinterpreted" the rule and thereby stretched it far beyond its original meaning, the Court failed, as we shall see, to use it in all cases logically within its new ambit. To have done so would often have led to results apparently too unreasonable even for the libertarians.

A. *Opinions in which the Danger Rule Was Mentioned*

During the period from 1943 to 1949 danger language was used in fifteen opinions in thirteen cases.[59] Twelve of these were written by either

---

55. West Virginia State Board of Education v. Barnette, 319 U.S. 624, 633, 639 (1943).
56. See *id*. at 654, 655, 663 (Justice Frankfurter dissenting).
57. Musser v. Utah, 333 U.S. 95 (1948); Taylor v. Mississippi, 319 U.S. 583 (1943).
58. See cases cited notes 59-61, 65-69, *infra*.
59. See note 58 *supra*.
The following cases or opinions are not included for the reasons indicated: Giboney v. Empire Storage & Ice Co., 336 U.S. 490 (1949) (a single danger phrase used); Hartzel v. United States, 322 U.S. 680 (1944) (danger rule mentioned with approval but not used to decide case); Schneiderman v. United States, 320 U.S. 118 (1943) (same); Cafeteria Employees Union v. Angelos, 320 U.S. 293 (1943) (a clear and present danger case cited); Terminiello v. Chicago, 337 U.S. 1, 13 (1949) (dissenting opinion; danger test mentioned to show majority wrong even by its own standard); Craig v. Harney, 331 U.S. 367, 384 (1947) (same).

Justices Black, Douglas, Murphy, or Rutledge; the remaining three by Justices Roberts, Reed, and Jackson, none of whom can be called a clear and present danger enthusiast. Mr. Justice Roberts and Mr. Justice Reed, each in turn, resorted to danger language on an occasion when the result was obvious enough to get unanimous approval. In one case a newspaper's citation for contempt was challenged, the crux of the decision being that publication had occurred too late to be contumacious.[60] The other case put in issue a dragnet statute which, as construed by the state court, made it a crime "to communicate views and opinions respecting governmental policies, and prophesies concerning the future of our own and other nations."[61]

While Mr. Justice Jackson, speaking for the Court, used danger language in the second flag salute case,[62] it is difficult to imagine a mind less congenial to the new approach than his. Apparently Mr. Justice Jackson was chosen to write the opinion as a compromise between the libertarians' danger views and Chief Justice Stone's *Gobitis* position. Not unnaturally he threw a few bones in both directions, but his own rule for drawing the line between liberty and authority is mentioned first[63]—a rule which he has been at pains to express on other occasions[64] and which is quite unlike the danger test.

In addition to the two already-mentioned unanimous opinions, there are four divided opinions of the Court employing danger language. In all four, Justices Black, Douglas, Murphy, and Rutledge supported it. But who would supply the other vote to make a majority was difficult to predict; only Mr. Justice Reed voted with them as often as twice. In the second flag salute case the libertarian quartet had the support of Justices Stone and Jackson; in *Thomas v. Collins*[65] they could not get a fifth to join in their language, though Mr. Justice Jackson joined in their result; in *Craig v. Harney*[66] the fifth and sixth votes came from Justices Burton and Reed; in the *Terminiello* case[67] Mr. Justice Reed made a fifth. These cases involved respectively a compulsory flag salute in public schools, a statutory requirement of advance registration for union organizers, another newspaper contempt citation, and a "lunatic fringe" hate speech which caused some public disturbance.

---

60. Pennekamp v. Florida, 328 U.S. 331 (1946).
61. Taylor v. Mississippi, 319 U.S. 583, 589 (1943).
62. West Virginia State Board of Education v. Barnette, 319 U.S. 624 (1943).
63. *Id.* at 630.
64. See American Communications Ass'n, CIO v. Douds, 339 U.S. 382, 443 (1950); Douglas v. City of Jeanette, 319 U.S. 157, 180 (1943).
65. 323 U.S. 516 (1945).
66. 331 U.S. 367 (1947).
67. Terminiello v. Chicago, 337 U.S. 1 (1949).

Finally, each of the three concurring[68] and five dissenting[69] opinions (in seven cases) that employ danger language was written and supported only by one or more of the libertarians. Since the latter were themselves divided in all the cases in which the danger test was referred to in dissent, it is not surprising that "conservative" views prevailed. These cases passed on the Hatch Act prohibition on the political activities of certain federal and state employees,[70] a conviction for advocacy of plural marriage,[71] the application of a child labor law to religious activities,[72] and the war-time exclusion from the West Coast of persons of Japanese ancestry.[73]

Of the three cases in which the danger test is found in concurring opinions, one is the second flag salute case where Justices Black and Douglas, joining fully in the Court's views, added a few words merely to explain their shift in position since the earlier flag litigation. But in *Bridges v. Wixon*[74] only Mr. Justice Murphy ventured to assert that the national power to deport aliens is limited by the danger test.[75] A majority, including Justices Black, Douglas, and Rutledge, were satisfied to reach the same result by means of statutory construction. On the other hand, in *United States v. CIO*[76] where the constitutional possibilities were not so far-fetched, all the libertarians were willing to strike down a part of the Taft-Hartley Act on danger grounds[77]—a result which the majority again reached via statutory construction.

The striking thing about these fifteen opinions is that all were written in support of First Amendment claims. Thus, just as in the early Roosevelt period, "clear and present danger" was a one-way ticket. When First Amendment arguments were rejected, other linguistic formulae were used.

B. *Cases Sustaining First Amendment Claims Without Resort to the Danger Rule*

Seven cases sustained First Amendment claims without mention of "clear and present danger." All turned more or less clearly on prior restraint grounds. Six are the well known proselytizing cases in which Jehovah's Witnesses ran afoul of tax or license impediments, or outright prohibitions,

---

68. United States v. CIO, 335 U.S. 106, 129 (1948); Bridges v. Wixon, 326 U.S. 135, 157 (1945); West Virginia State Board of Education v. Barnette, 319 U.S. 624, 644 (1943).
69. Musser v. Utah, 333 U.S. 95, 98 (1948); United Public Workers v. Mitchell, 330 U.S. 75, 105, 115 (1947); Korematsu v. United States, 323 U.S. 214, 233 (1944) (a case not involving the First Amendment); Prince v. Massachusetts, 321 U.S. 158, 171 (1944).
70. United Public Workers v. Mitchell, *supra* note 69.
71. Musser v. Utah, *supra* note 69.
72. Prince v. Massachusetts, *supra* note 69.
73. Korematsu v. United States, *supra* note 69.
74. 326 U.S. 135 (1945).
75. *Id.* at 157.
76. 335 U.S. 106 (1948).
77. *Id.* at 129.

on their door-to-door activities.[78] The seventh was a challenge to the constitutionality of an ordinance requiring that permission be obtained before using a sound truck.[79] In each, the Court's opinion was written by one of the libertarians, and supported by all the others participating. At first Chief Justice Stone supplied the deciding vote. By the time he felt the libertarians had gone too far, Mr. Justice Frankfurter had joined them because he thought the precedent of the earlier decisions binding. Unlike the Chief Justice, he could not distinguish them.[80] Mr. Justice Reed went over one case earlier than his brother Frankfurter and for similar reasons,[81] but along with the Chief Justice he was able to distinguish the last two proselytizing cases. In the *Saia* sound truck case a new chief justice furnished the vote necessary to make a majority.

Obviously these cases were decided by the barest margin; Chief Justice Stone cast the decisive vote in the first instance and thus established the precedent later deemed controlling by other justices. This may be the clue to the use of the prior restraint approach in these decisions. Having no more patience with subsequent punishment than with prior restraints on expression, Justices Black, Douglas, Murphy, and Rutledge doubtless would have preferred to frame these decisions in terms of "clear and present danger." Indeed they did exactly that in another advance permission case[82] in which a separate concurring opinion by Mr. Justice Jackson relieved them of the necessity to compromise on methodology. But in *Jones v. Opelika*, the first of the Jehovah's Witnesses' proselytizing cases, the price of Chief Justice Stone's crucial vote presumably was abandonment of that approach. In his long judicial career Mr. Justice Stone did not once write an opinion using danger language; as a matter of fact, during the twenties he voted with the majority in a decision from which Justices Holmes and Brandeis dissented on clear and present danger grounds.[83] Chief Justice Stone joined in only two opinions using danger language—one in a unanimously-decided case,[84] the other in the second flag salute case.[85] But his real views on saluting the flag are to be found in his lone dissent in the *Gobitis* case.[86]

---

78. Tucker v. Texas, 326 U.S. 517 (1946); Marsh v. Alabama, 326 U.S. 501 (1946); Follett v. Town of McCormick, 321 U.S. 573 (1944); Martin v. Struthers, 319 U.S. 141 (1943); Murdock v. Pennsylvania, 319 U.S. 105 (1943); Jones v. Opelika, 319 U.S. 103 (1943). *Cf.* United States v. Ballard, 322 U.S. 78 (1944).
79. Saia v. New York, 334 U.S. 558 (1948). This is the only case during this period which explicitly follows the prior restraint doctrine.
80. Tucker v. Texas, 326 U.S. 517 (1946); Marsh v. Alabama, 326 U.S. 501 (1946).
81. *See* Follett v. Town of McCormick, 321 U.S. 573, 578 (1944).
82. Thomas v. Collins, 323 U.S. 516 (1945).
83. Gitlow v. New York, 268 U.S. 652 (1925). *Cf.* Whitney v. California, 274 U.S. 357 (1927). According to Professor Alpheus Mason, Mr. Justice Stone did not participate in the *Gitlow* decision, the official report notwithstanding.
84. Pennekamp v. Florida, 328 U.S. 331 (1946).
85. West Virginia State Board of Education v. Barnette, 319 U.S. 624 (1943). *Cf.* Herndon v. Georgia, 295 U.S. 441, 451 (1935).
86. Minersville School District v. Gobitis, 310 U.S. 586, 601 (1940).

Vote "purchasing" is only one possible explanation for the choice of "prior restraint" rather than "clear and present danger" as the rationale for these decisions. Perhaps the latter was abandoned because in its new non-Holmesian version it would have led to results the libertarians did not like—for *a priori* much of the proselytizing would seem to have occurred "in such circumstances . . . as to create a clear and present danger that . . . [it would] bring about the substantive evils [for example, violation of privacy of the home] that [state legislatures have] . . . a right to prevent."[87] The same is true in regard to the sound truck case. Just as "reasonableness" had been used by the early Roosevelt Court in *Cox v. New Hampshire* to avoid the prior restraint rule, so the latter may have been used here to avoid the unwelcome implications of "clear and present danger." To complete the circle, moreover, not all previous impediments to free expression were disposed of via the prior restraint rule; the danger test did the job in *Thomas v. Collins*.

C. *Cases in Which the Danger Rule Was Ignored and First Amendment Claims Denied Protection*

In six of the remaining nine expression cases during this period, First Amendment claims were rejected more or less clearly on reasonable basis grounds. At issue in five of these cases were: the Hatch Act's prohibition,[88] a "test-oath" used to preclude a pacifist from practicing law,[89] a contempt citation of a lawyer whose talk had offended a trial judge,[90] and another sound truck regulation.[91] Significantly, in each case the majority opinion was written by Mr. Justice Reed. Every vote of Justices Black, Douglas, Murphy, and Rutledge was cast in dissent. The loss of the vote of the chief justice,[92] and the inability to attract a replacement, lost the day for the libertarians. In dissent, where it was no longer necessary to appease a fifth colleague, they were free to indulge in clear and present danger language.[93]

---

87. Schenck v. United States, 249 U.S. 47, 52 (1918).
88. Oklahoma v. United States Civil Service Comm'n, 330 U.S. 127 (1947); United Public Workers v. Mitchell, 330 U.S. 75 (1947).
89. *In re* Summers, 325 U.S. 561 (1945).
90. Fisher v. Pace, 336 U.S. 155 (1949).
91. Kovacs v. Cooper, 336 U.S. 77 (1949). *Cf.* Railway Express Co. v. New York, 336 U.S. 106 (1949) (commercial advertising not within First Amendment); Donaldson v. Read Magazine, 333 U.S. 178 (1948) (use of the mails not within First Amendment).
Doubleday & Co. v. New York, 335 U.S. 848 (1949), upheld censorship of a collection of short stories, but is not included in the list of nine cases discussed in the text because it was decided per curiam by an evenly divided bench, Mr. Justice Frankfurter not participating.
92. In his last years on the bench, Chief Justice Stone often disagreed with the libertarian quartet. Nevertheless, upon him probably rested their chief hope of gaining a majority. His replacement in the spring of 1946 by Chief Justice Vinson made the prospect of obtaining the necessary vote less likely.
93. The dissents in Fisher v. Pace, 336 U.S. 155 (1949), are *ad hoc*, relying on the par-

On their facts four of these cases differ so greatly from the cases previously discussed in which First Amendment claims were sustained in terms of prior restraint doctrine that the significance of the Chief Justice's vote is obscured. But the *Kovacs* sound truck case removes the obscurity. There Mr. Justice Reed, speaking also for Chief Justice Vinson and Mr. Justice Burton, made a brave show of distinguishing the *Saia* case in the course of sustaining the regulation, but at least four justices in concurrence or dissent recognized that it had been abandoned.[94]

Prince v. Massachusetts[95] is the remaining and most fascinating of this group of six cases. It presented a typical Jehovah's Witness proselytizing problem, except that here the proselytors were children who had violated a child labor law. Of course, the four "conservatives" voted to uphold the conviction, just as they had in the earlier proselytizing cases. But in the *Prince* case they were joined not only by Chief Justice Stone, but by Justices Black, Douglas, and Rutledge as well. Indeed, Mr. Justice Rutledge, undismayed, wrote the opinion for the Court, distinguishing the previous decisions on the ground that the proselytors in *Prince* were children—without commenting on the childhood of those who had previously refused to salute the flag.[96] This was too much for Mr. Justice Murphy, who dissented in clear and present danger terms.[97] In a concurring opinion, Justices Frankfurter, Jackson, and Roberts did not fail to note that the activity at issue was exactly what the libertarians a few months earlier had held to "occupy the same high estate" as worship in a church.[98] One can only speculate as to whether Justices Black, Douglas, and Rutledge withheld dissent in exchange for the privilege of writing for the Court. By doing so Mr. Justice Rutledge at least had an opportunity to save the earlier proselytizing cases from the subsequent fate of the *Saia* sound truck decision.

Three labor relations cases[99] complete this group of nine. "Clear and present danger" was ignored; the decisions turned on the proposition that freedom of speech may not be used to shield illegal conduct. Yet, oddly enough, this is the exact situation for which Mr. Justice Holmes designed the present danger test: namely, to determine when utterance ceases to be mere discussion and becomes a "trigger of action." Certainly some picket

---

ticular facts involved. Those in Kovacs v. Cooper, 336 U.S. 77 (1949), are based largely on the first sound truck case, Saia v. New York, 334 U.S. 558 (1948). Dissenting opinions in the remaining cases employ danger language or citations.

94. *See* Kovacs v. Cooper, 336 U.S. 77, 97 (1949).

95. 321 U.S. 158 (1944).

96. See West Virginia State Board of Education v. Barnette, 319 U.S. 624 (1943); Minersville School District v. Gobitis, 310 U.S. 586 (1940).

97. Prince v. Massachusetts, 321 U.S. 158, 171 (1944).

98. *Id.* at 176.

99. Giboney v. Empire Storage & Ice Co., 336 U.S. 490 (1949) [see note 59 *supra*]; May Dep't Stores v. NLRB, 326 U.S. 376 (1945); Virginia Electric & Power Co. v. NLRB, 319 U.S. 533 (1943); NLRB v. Virginia Electric & Power Co., 314 U.S. 469 (1941).

lines and some employer's speeches to workmen are calculated not to enlighten but to compel immediate, unreasoned action.

V. The Truman Court

The substitution of Justices Minton and Clark for Justices Rutledge
and Murphy seems to introduce another epoch in civil liberties litigation.
In the six relevant decisions during its 1949 Term, the Court rejected all
claims based on freedom of expression. Three cases,[100] following the implications of *Thornhill* and *Giboney*, sustained limited restrictions on picketing.
So thoroughly was reasonableness emphasized that Mr. Justice Black found
it necessary to disassociate himself from the Court's language in two instances[101] and to dissent in the third.[102] Mr. Justice Douglas did not participate in these cases nor in another in which the Court unanimously upheld a conviction under a state statute which had been construed to prohibit persons acting in concert from assembling to prevent others by force or
violence from engaging in lawful occupations.[103] Danger language was used
in none of the opinions in these cases.

But in the two Taft-Hartley non-communist oath cases[104] the danger
test got a "new" twist. Speaking for the Court, Chief Justice Vinson observed that Congress clearly has the power to attempt to prevent political
strikes and other direct burdens upon interstate commerce. "But the more
difficult problem here arises because, in drawing lines on the basis of beliefs
and political affiliations . . . Congress has undeniably discouraged the
lawful exercise of political freedoms as well."[105] Such a problem

> is not the same one that Justices Holmes and Brandeis found con-
> venient to consider in terms of clear and present danger. The Gov-
> ernment's interest here is not in preventing the dissemination of
> Communist doctrine or the holding of particular beliefs . . .
> [The legislation] is designed to protect the public not against what
> Communists . . . advocate or believe, but what Congress has
> concluded they have done and are likely to do again [*i.e.*, disrupt
> interstate commerce by political strikes].[106]

Having found the danger approach inapplicable when the regulation of
conduct "results in an indirect, conditional, partial abridgment of speech,"

---

100. Building Service Employees v. Gazzam, 339 U.S. 532 (1950); International
Brotherhood of Teamsters v. Hanke, 339 U.S. 470 (1950); Hughes v. Superior Court, 339
U.S. 460 (1950).
101. Building Service Employees v. Gazzam; Hughes v. Superior Court, *supra* n. 100.
102. International Brotherhood of Teamsters v. Hanke, *supra* n. 100.
103. Cole v. Arkansas, 338 U.S. 345 (1949).
104. American Communications Ass'n, CIO v. Douds, 339 U.S. 382 (1950); Osman v.
Douds, 339 U.S. 846 (1950). A "non-communist oath" was required of the officers of a labor
union as a condition precedent to the enjoyment by their union of the benefits of the Taft-
Hartley Act.
105. American Communications Ass'n, CIO v. Douds, 339 U.S. 382, 392 (1950).
106. *Id.* at 396.

the Chief Justice proceeded to uphold the oath requirement on reasonable basis grounds.[107]

On the record before it, the Court undoubtedly was justified in finding that Congress had sought only to control political strikes and not to censor political views. In that event Mr. Justice Holmes, too, presumably would have used the reasonable basis rule to uphold the statute—provided he were also satisfied that, regardless of purpose, such a regulation of conduct did not in effect constitute a censorship of ideas. Chief Justice Vinson's rather cavalier treatment of the latter point weakens the Court's position in the Taft-Hartley oath cases. Nevertheless, these two decisions constitute a somewhat inarticulate return to the Holmesian distinction between regulation and censorship. Of course, the two remaining libertarians dissented[108]— not to mention the partial dissents of Justices Jackson and Frankfurter (with whom Mr. Justice Holmes doubtless would have agreed) on the part of the oath concerning beliefs. None of the dissenters used danger language, however, and there is a hint in the opinions of Justices Black and Douglas that they may be abandoning the danger approach altogether in favor of one which would protect all utterance not connected with overt criminal action.[109]

During its 1950 Term the Court disposed of *Niemotko v. Maryland*[110] and *Kunz v. New York*[111] on prior restraint grounds. Both involved advance permit requirements for the use of public parks or streets by religious proselytizers. Mr. Justice Jackson, dissenting in the *Kunz* case, found it "peculiar that today's opinion makes no reference to the 'clear and present danger' test."[112] He argued that if it had been adopted the decision would have been otherwise, for "the approach will determine the result."[113] In short, as already intimated, Holmes and Blackstone are not logically complementary. The choice of one instead of the other in a particular case involves a *tour de force*.[114]

In *Feiner v. New York*[115] the Chief Justice, speaking for the Court, used "clear and present danger" for the first time since 1920 to justify punishment for speech-making which the Court and some members of the audience

---

107. *Id.* at 399 *et seq.*
108. *Id.* at 445 (Justice Black dissenting). Mr. Justice Douglas participated only in the second decision, but his position there clearly covers both cases. *See* Osman v. Douds, 339 U.S. 846, 848 (1950).
109. *See* American Communications Ass'n, CIO v. Douds, 339 U.S. 382, 452 (1950); Osman v. Douds, 339 U.S. 846, 848 (1950).
110. 340 U.S. 268 (1951).
111. 340 U.S. 290 (1951).
112. *Id.* at 300.
113. *Id.* at 301.
114. *See* Cantwell v. Connecticut, 310 U.S. 296, 308 (1940). The Court there recognizes that a clear and present danger would justify a prior restraint.
115. 340 U.S. 315 (1951).

found overstimulating. Justices Black and Douglas dissented on *ad hoc* grounds, indicating a somewhat dimmed enthusiasm for the danger test when used to send a man to jail.

In *Breard v. Alexandria*[116] the Court upheld a conviction under a municipal ordinance which restricted door-to-door solicitation for the sale of merchandise. The merchandise in question was magazine subscriptions. Again Justices Black and Douglas dissented. For them the Court's reasonableness approach could not be reconciled with *Opelika*, *Murdock*, and *Struthers*,[117] the three crucial cases of early 1943 which, thanks to the vote of Mr. Justice Rutledge, had introduced the libertarian phase of the Roosevelt Court. Once more there was no reference to the danger test. The same can be said of *Garner v. Board of Public Works*,[118] which upheld a non-communist oath requirement for municipal employees—Justices Black and Douglas dissenting altogether and Justices Burton and Frankfurter in part.

Finally, in *Dennis v. United States*[119] Chief Justice Vinson, for the Court, sustained the conviction of eleven Communist Party leaders for conspiring to teach and advocate the violent overthrow of the government. Following the dicta and implications of the non-communist oath cases, the plurality opinion held that because here Congress had put a "direct restriction upon speech"[120] the clear and present danger rule was applicable. But the Chief Justice found it necessary to adopt Judge Learned Hand's "reinterpretation" to the effect that

> In each case . . . [courts] must ask whether the gravity of the "evil," discounted by its improbability, justifies such invasion of free speech as is necessary to avoid the danger.[121]

As Judge Hand explained below, "improbability" was substituted for "remoteness" because "that must be the right interpretation. Given the same probability, it would be wholly irrational to condone future evils which we should prevent if they were immediate. . . ."[122]

The remoteness element, however, is the heart of the danger test; it was Mr. Justice Holmes' answer to the "bad tendency" attitude of most of his colleagues. The question is, did the Communist leaders conspire to "teach and advocate" under conditions allowing free play for the democratic corrective of counter-discussion? An overwhelming preponderance of evidence indicates that they did not. They sought to bypass the democratic processes,

---

116. 341 U.S. 622 (1951).
117. See p. 321 *supra*. Chief Justice Vinson dissented in the principal case on commerce clause grounds.
118. 341 U.S. 716 (1951).
119. 341 U.S. 494 (1951).
120. *Id.* at 508.
121. *Id.* at 510.
122. Dennis v. United States, 183 F.2d 201, 212 (2d Cir. 1950).

not to use them. They tried to attain their ends "without advocacy or persuasion that seeks acceptance in the competition of the market."[123] Taking into account their widespread and highly organized activities, largely *sub rosa*, this constituted the danger. In short, democracy and free speech provide a testing ground for ideas, but not for conspiracies. The law would be "a ass" not to notice the distinction. What Judge Hand really did was to hold that in the circumstances, application of the clear and present danger test would be "irrational." That he did so by means of "reinterpretation" is what may be expected when a great, creative lower court judge is caught between the demands of good sense in the case before him and the pressure of the unwieldy danger-language precedents of the Supreme Court—to say nothing of the position of the trial judge. The difference between "clear and probable danger" and "reasonable basis" certainly is not obvious. It may be that the former will be reserved for use in cases involving restraints upon conspiratorial, underground "discussion."

In any event, the probable danger rule was accepted by only four members of the Supreme Court. Mr. Justice Clark did not participate in the decision. Justices Frankfurter and Jackson, though they concurred in the result, took pains to disassociate themselves from the "reinterpretation." Justices Black and Douglas dissented. Again there is an indication that Mr. Justice Black has more to say on the subject: "At least as to speech in the realm of public matters, I believe that the 'clear and present danger' test does not mark the furthermost constitutional boundaries of protected expression" but does "no more than recognize a minimum compulsion of the Bill of Rights."[124] Thus while the Court's apparent return to Mr. Justice Holmes in the non-communist oath cases had the support of six out of eight participating justices, "reinterpretation" of the master had the support of but four out of eight participants. In only one other case, *Feiner v. New York*, has the Truman Court, or any of its members, used danger language, and there four justices thought it improperly applied. It may be that now, as in Mr. Justice Holmes' day, the danger approach is to be a one-way road leading only to jail.

VI. Conclusion

If by law we mean a reasonably accurate prediction as to how a court will dispose of a given controversy, the clear and present danger test has never been law. Mr. Justice Holmes himself suggested that he was chosen to write for the Court in the *Schenck* case in part because he would "go further probably than the majority in favor of" free speech.[125] Apparently

---

123. Dennis v. United States, 341 U.S. 494, 502 (1951).
124. Dennis v. United States, 341 U.S. 494, 580 (1951).
125. 2 Howe, Holmes-Pollock Letters 7 (1941). See Chafee, *op. cit. supra* note 10, at 86.

Mr. Justice Holmes' associates were willing to use his heroic liberal reputation to sugarcoat an unpleasant decision. In all other First Amendment cases decided while Mr. Justice Holmes was on the bench, the danger rule found expression only in dissenting or concurring opinions joined in by at most two judges. Thereafter until 1940 it was mentioned, and then obliquely, only twice, notwithstanding the flood of expression cases during the tenure of Chief Justice Hughes.

Early in the forties Mr. Justice Holmes' dual approach of "clear and present danger" and "reasonable basis" was revived by a virtually unanimous Court. Almost immediately, however, a vigorous quartet of libertarians purported to reject "reasonable basis" and put all expression eggs in the danger basket. But lacking reliable accompaniment, they could never depend on getting their truncated approach into a majority opinion. Get it in they sometimes did, but voting records suggest that this was accomplished only by the kind of horse trading "Court opinions" encourage and not because of general acceptance of the new view as a rule of law. Often Justices Black, Douglas, Murphy, and Rutledge were out-traded and found themselves either dissenting or supporting prior restraint language, as though for them prior restraint was worse than subsequent punishment of expression.

But while the "liberal" quartet loved freedom well, even they sometimes found it abused. In such cases they rather pointedly refused to blemish "clear and present danger" by finding its test to have been met. Other linguistic formulae were employed for the dirty work. "Reasonable basis," having been ruled out of court, was on occasion surreptitiously readmitted. If the associates of Justices Holmes and Brandeis used the danger doctrine only to send men to jail, its ardent supporters in the 1940's used it only to get them out. Chief Justice Stone's early inclination to vote "liberal" coupled with his distaste for the libertarians' doctrinaire approach accounts for a large part of the judicial maneuvering during the period in which he presided. The picture is further complicated by the tendency of the Roosevelt Court to avoid questioning the constitutionality of national legislation.

With the death of Justices Rutledge and Murphy and the emergence of the Truman Court, the libertarians' conception of the danger rule was clearly dead. Recent opinions seem to trace at least some of the steps back to Holmes—or perhaps merely back to *Gitlow*. But as before, the Court is too obviously divided to warrant prediction. At any rate, decisions since the demise of two of the four libertarians have been quite different—as Terminiello might attest upon contemplation of Feiner's fate. Meanwhile Justices Black and Douglas, finding their favorite rule now turned against them when it is used at all, show signs of looking elsewhere for a suitable vehicle for their ideas.

All this suggests that except in the hands of Justices Holmes and Brandeis "clear and present danger" has been something less than a guide to decision. Nevertheless it reflects a great ideal, tarnished somewhat in its service as a mask to cover disagreements and perplexities on the bench.[126]

126. *See* Kunz v. New York, 340 U.S. 290, 299 (1951).

Addendum

The explosive perversion of the clear and present danger test in the 1940s brought disillusionment and contraction (see W. Mendelson, "Clear and Present Danger—Another Decade," 30 *Texas Law Review* 449 [1961]). The result was a number of "new" approaches—experiments perhaps—until after years in the desert the Warren Court in its final months produced *Brandenburg* v. *Ohio,* 395 U.S. 444 (1969). That case seems to have synthesized the Holmes-Brandeis position with Learned Hand's approach in *Masses Publishing Co.* v. *Patten,* 244 Fed. 535 (1917). Thus (see Hand) only words of *explicit* incitement are unprotected; yet even they are not punishable unless (see Holmes-Brandeis) they are likely to produce immediate harm. The Burger Court seems to have accepted the *Brandenburg* synthesis (see *Hess* v. *Indiana,* 414 U.S. 105 [1973]; *NAACP* v. *Claiborne Hardware Co.,* 102 S. Ct. 3409 [1982]; and G. Gunther, "Learned Hand and the Origins of Modern First Amendment Doctrine: Some Fragments of History," 27 *Stanford Law Review* 719 [1975]).

9 ❧ Clandestine Speech and the First Amendment — A Reappraisal of the Dennis Case

In a comment[1] written at the conclusion of the Communist leaders' trial[2] Professor Nathanson noted that Judge Medina's instructions required for a verdict of guilty that the jury "find only that the defendants intended to accomplish the overthrow of government 'as speedily as circumstances would permit it to be achieved.' "[3] This, wrote Professor Nathanson, was "inconsistent with the clear-and-present-danger test as formulated by Holmes and Brandeis, unless there were other circumstances in the facts actually presented which made that test inapplicable."[4] A major part of the balance of the comment is an attempt to refute a suggestion[5] that clandestine, underground utterance (unlike that which is openly directed to the public) is not entitled to the protection of the Holmesean clear and present danger test.

It is the purpose of what follows to suggest that under the princi-

---

[1] Comment, The Communist Trial and the Clear-and-Present Danger Test, 63 HARV. L. REV. 1167 (1950).

[2] United States v. Foster, 9 F.R.D. 367 (1949).

[3] 63 HARV. L. REV. 1167 at 1170 (1950). The indictment charged a violation of the "Smith Act" [18 U.S.C. (1946) §11, now §§2385, 2387], that is, for "knowingly and willfully" conspiring to organize the Communist Party of the United States as a group to "teach, advocate, or encourage the overthrow or destruction" of the government "by force or violence," and "knowingly and willfully . . . to advocate . . . or teach the duty, necessity, [or] desirability . . . of overthrowing or destroying" the government "by force or violence."

[4] 63 HARV. L. REV. 1167 at 1170 (1950).

[5] One theme in the government's brief response to the defendants' motion for a directed verdict on the grounds that there had been no showing of a clear and present danger was expressed in the following terms:

"When Holmes talked about freedom of speech, he said he meant the right of men to get their ideas accepted in the market place of thought. Holmes was talking from the background of a life and an experience where there was the freest possible discussion, in the town meetings of New England, in the public taverns, in the public squares, in the public halls, where men frankly and fearlessly stated their ideas. He was not talking about the kind of propaganda speakeasy that we heard about in this case, where persons went to school under assumed names or using only their first names, coming through a doctor's or a dentist's office into rooms some place else. This is not the kind of freedom of speech Holmes said could be protected." NEW YORK TIMES, May 21, 1949, p. 6, col 3.

ples espoused by Justices Holmes and Brandeis there is a constitutionally significant difference between clandestine and other utterance and
that this difference was a crucial factor in the *Dennis* decision.[6] If this
position is valid, *Dennis* is restricted to narrow quarters and is not, as it
otherwise must be, a precedent for virtual abandonment of the clear
and present danger test.

Examination of all of their opinions in which danger language is
used leads inevitably to Professor Nathanson's own conclusion that
Justices Holmes and Brandeis "were trying to suggest basic lines of
distinction between an appeal to reason and an incitement to action,
recognizing that the two might overlap, but also taking the position
that so long as the action contemplated by the appeal to reason was
sufficiently remote to permit time for counterappeals to reason, the
advocacy, even of the right of violence, should be treated as within the
protection of freedom of speech."[7]

The rationale of such a position must be that, if in the process of
social adjustment the deliberative forces are to prevail over the arbitrary,
the community must have access to all available ideas; that a major
purpose of the First Amendment is to safeguard such access; and that
the only legitimate way for bringing on changes in public policy is
through the peaceful devices of democracy, i.e., by public discussion
and acceptance or rejection of all available proposals. As Justice
Brandeis, his brother Holmes concurring, observed, "Those who won
our independence believed . . . that the fitting remedy for evil counsels
is good ones. Believing in the power of reason as applied through
public discussion, they eschewed silence coerced by law. . . . To courageous, self-reliant men, with confidence in the power of free and
fearless reasoning applied through the *processes of popular government,* no danger flowing from speech can [justify repression unless]
it may befall before there is opportunity for full discussion."[8] Or as
Justice Holmes, referring to suppression as a cure for noxious doctrine,
observed, "the ultimate good desired is better reached by free trade in
ideas . . . the best test of truth is the power of the thought to get itself
accepted in the competition of the market. . . . That at any rate is the
theory of our Constitution."[9]

---

[6] Dennis v. United States, 341 U.S. 494, 71 S.Ct. 857 (1951).

[7] 63 HARV. L. REV. 1167 at 1174 (1950).

[8] Whitney v. California, 274 U.S. 357 at 375-377, 47 S.Ct. 641 (1927), concurring
opinion (emphasis added).

[9] Abrams v. United States, 250 U.S. 616 at 630, 40 S.Ct. 17 (1919), dissenting
opinion.

In short, *democratic give-and-take is the antidote for bad doctrine*—
"the fitting remedy for evil counsels is [the] good ones" which according to the basic democratic faith will spring from public discussion.
Then what of him whose speech, intentionally or otherwise, threatens
to bring on changes without first proposing them for public discussion?
How are we to be protected from "evil counsels" which we do not have
an opportunity to refute? Surely the answer lies in the proposition—
of which the danger test is merely a special application—that only
utterance which is subject to the antidote of public discussion comes
within the very special immunity from public control that the First
Amendment does, and democracy must, afford. As Professor Freund
puts it, "The state may not punish open talk, however hateful; not for
the hypocritical reason that Hyde Parks are a safety valve, but because
a bit of sense may be salvaged from the odious by minds striving to be
rational, and this precious bit will enter into the amalgam which we
forge."[10]

In all of the cases in which Justice Holmes and Brandeis used the
danger test the utterance at issue was open and directed to a broad
public. Consequently the crucial question for them was whether the
threatened danger was sufficiently remote to provide ample "opportunity for full discussion . . . to avert the evil by the processes of education. . . ."[11] But surely the same principle would apply in a case where,
although there is ample *time* "for counter appeals to reason" other circumstances foreclose opportunity for them. The crucial issue is not
whether a threatened danger is present or remote, but whether there
is opportunity to forestall it by the rational processes of democracy.

Suppose, for example, a Smith Act[12] prosecution for conspiracy to
teach and advocate the violent overthrow of government. The evidence
(obtained by F.B.I. infiltration tactics) indicates that the teaching and
advocacy in question was intended to, and did, take place only in a
widespread, network of secret underground "study groups" open only
to carefully selected totalitarian party members, such "study groups"
being in design incipient cells for revolutionary action whenever the
propitious moment might arrive. Suppose further that, as clearly as
such things may be, "the propitious moment" was, at the time of the

---

10 Freund, On Understanding the Supreme Court 26 (1949).
11 Whitney v. California, 274 U.S. 357 at 377, 47 S.Ct. 641 (1927), concurring
opinion.
12 18 U.S.C. (1946) §11 (now §§2385, 2387).

indictment, still so far away that there was no clear and present danger of an eruption.

Assuming in short that so far as time alone is concerned there was ample occasion to refute in the market place of reason what the defendants conspired to teach and advocate, still reasonable men could conclude there was no real opportunity for refutation because the "evil counsels" at issue were hidden from the public. What is there in such a context for "the power of reason as applied through public discussion" to deal with? Surely adequate time to refute an argument, i.e., the absence of a clear and present danger, is not significant free-speech-wise unless we know what the argument is!

In this view a crucial question in any free expression case would be this: is the challenged utterance calculated to bypass the process of public discussion and to attain its ends, if at all, by other means? If the answer is no, the danger test would be relevant—the utterance would be protected "unless the incidence of the evil apprehended is so imminent that it may befall before there is opportunity for full discussion."[13] If on the other hand the answer is yes, i.e., if the speaker is not willing, or if for other reasons there is no opportunity, to test "the power of [his] thought to get itself accepted in the competition of the market,"[14] then some other rule would apply. The *Dennis* case suggests the applicability of what may be called the probable danger test, i.e., "courts must ask whether the gravity of the 'evil' discounted by its improbability, justifies such invasion of free speech as is necessary to avoid the danger."[15] The merits or demerits of this test and to what extent, if at all, it differs from the reasonable basis test is not our present concern. It will be enough here to suggest that in a society that stakes its life on *unfettered intellectual exchange,* with public control of action in accordance with those ideas that prevail in the market place of reason, clandestine utterance is not entitled to the same high level of protection that must be accorded its open counterpart.

Assuming that there is constitutional significance in the difference between clandestine and other utterance, was there in the *Dennis* case such a finding of secrecy on the part of the defendants as to justify rejection of the clear and present danger test in favor of some other

---

[13] Whitney v. California, 274 U.S. 357 at 377, 47 S.Ct. 641 (1927), concurring opinion.

[14] Abrams v. United States, 250 U.S. 616 at 630, 40 S.Ct. 17 (1919), dissenting opinion.

[15] Dennis v. United States, 341 U.S. 494 at 510, 71 S.Ct. 857 (1951).

rule?[16] The government's suggestion of this approach to the case has already been noted. This suggestion was at least partially reflected in Judge Medina's charge to the jury:

> "No such [necessary] intent could be inferred from the open and aboveboard teaching of a course on the principles and implications of communism in an American college or university, where everything is open to scrutiny of parents and trustees and anyone who may be interested to see what is going on. That is why it is so important for you to weigh with scrupulous care the testimony concerning secret schools, false names, devious ways, general falsification and so on, all alleged to be in the setting of a huge and well disciplined organization, spreading to practically every state of the union and all the principal cities and industries."[17]

To be sure there was no special or express jury finding that defendants had conspired *secretly* to teach and advocate the overthrow of government.[18] But in view of the quoted instructions it is arguable that a general verdict of guilty implies a finding of significant secrecy on the part of defendants. In any case the Supreme Court's plurality opinion does note that for purposes of review under the limited grant of the writ of certiorari "the record in this case [must be considered] amply [to support] the necessary finding of the jury that petitioners . . . were unwilling to work within our framework of democracy, but intended to initiate a violent revolution whenever the propitious occasion appeared."[19] What is the significance of this reference to a finding of unwillingness "to work within our democratic framework," if it does not refer to a refusal of the Communist leaders to submit their views for acceptance or rejection via constitutional processes?[20] Justice Frank-

---

[16] The Supreme Court's plurality opinion does not purport to reject; it merely endorses the court of appeals' "reinterpretation" of the clear and present danger test—a "reinterpretation," one submits, that in effect produces a different rule. See Dennis v. United States, 341 U.S. 494 at 510, 71 S.Ct. 857 (1950).

[17] NEW YORK TIMES, October 14, 1949, p. 15, col. 6.

[18] I am assuming here with Professor Nathanson that a jury rather than a court finding would be necessary.

[19] 341 U.S. 494 at 497, 71 S.Ct. 857 (1951).

[20] In his dissenting opinion Justice Douglas said, "So far as the present record is concerned, what petitioners did was to organize people to teach and themselves teach the Marxist-Leninist doctrine contained chiefly in four books . . ." all of which are available to the public. Dennis v. United States, 341 U.S. 494 at 582, 71 S.Ct. 857 (1951). At most these books disclose the strategy of the defendants. I suggest the Dennis record indicates tactical teachings that are not accessible to the public. But even if the books in question tell the whole story, is that sufficient free-speech-wise when the teachers and pupils involved are hidden from anyone who might want to refute their position? Is the

furter's concurring opinion contains similar language:

"The Communist Party was not designed by these defendants as an ordinary political party. For the circumstances of its organization, its aims and methods, and the relation of the defendants to its organization and aims we are concluded by the jury's verdict. The jury found that the Party rejects the basic premise of our political system—that change is to be brought on by nonviolent constitutional process."[21]

Whether the jury did in fact find that the defendant's teaching and advocacy was clandestine is not important for present purposes. But it is crucial that on review five members of the Supreme Court majority used language which at the very least gives color to the view that their position rested upon such a finding by the jury.[22] On this basis *Dennis* is not, as it otherwise must be, a precedent for complete annihilation of the position for which Justices Holmes and Brandeis fought. Rather it is authority for a complementary rule which, like the pristine danger approach, is not an expression of anarchic individualism, but a recognition of the need for preserving self-government from the shoals where words cease to be keys of public discussion.[23] The purpose of the First Amendment is to protect the right of every man to offer his thoughts as an ingredient in "that public opinion which is the final source of government in a democratic state."[24] It would be a perversion of that purpose to give special constitutional protection to expressions of thought which are not so offered. To the extent that "citizens who are to decide an issue are denied acquaintance with information or opinion or doubt or disbelief or criticism which is relevant to that issue, just so far the result must be ill-considered [and] ill-balanced. . . . It is that mutilation of the thinking process of the community against which the First Amendment is directed."[25] By keeping open the channels of communication for ideas, democracy seeks to make full use of the community's total thinking power—in striking

---

requirement of public discussion that Justices Holmes and Brandeis had in mind satisfied by blind gropings after the needle in the haystack?

[21] 341 U.S. 494 at 514, 546, 71 S.Ct. 857 (1951).

[22] The Justices may have been more than usually willing to discover a necessary jury finding to avoid imposing upon another trial court the kind of ordeal that the defendants had inflicted upon Judge Medina's court. If there is merit in this suggestion, the defendants set their own trap.

[23] See Judge L. Hand in Masses Publishing Co. v. Patten, (D.C. N.Y. 1917) 244 F. 535 at 540.

[24] Ibid.

[25] MEIKLEJOHN, FREE SPEECH AND ITS RELATION TO SELF-GOVERNMENT 26 (1948).

contrast to the totalitarian reliance upon the intellectual resources of a dictator and his small circle of henchmen.

ADDENDUM

Most or all of our great founts of free speech doctrine seem to have anticipated the Court's apparent view in *Dennis;* namely, that the crux of freedom of speech is *open public* discussion, not underground activity calculated to achieve its goals by circumventing rather than by winning community consent. Thus in *Abrams* v. *United States*, 250 U.S. 616 (1919), Holmes and Brandeis referred to freedom of utterance as "free trade in ideas" in the "competition of the market," where the community is offered exposure to conflicting views so that it can choose intelligently among them. Recall Milton's famous line in *Areopagitica:* "[W]ho ever knew truth put to the worse in a free and open encounter?" Mills's *On Liberty* rests on what he called "the morality of public discussion." Jefferson put it briefly: Truth is "the proper and sufficient antagonist to error, and has nothing to fear from the conflict unless by human interposition [e.g., secrecy, she is] disarmed of her natural weapons, free argument and debate." Benjamin Franklin has it thus: [W]hen men differ in opinion, both sides ought equally to have the advantage of being heard by the publick." In Chafee's view, "The fundamental policy of the First Amendment [is] the open discussion of public affairs." For Meiklejohn the old New England town meeting suggested the meaning of the First Amendment (see W. Mendelson, *The American Constitution and Civil Liberties* [1981], p. 197).

The underground speech problem seems not to have surfaced again in the Supreme Court since *Dennis.* Nothing in *Brandenburg* (p. 141) suggests that it equates clandestine with open, public utterance. After all, as suggested above, *Brandenburg* is a synthesis of Hand-Holmes-Brandeis doctrine. Hand of course wrote the opinion that the Supreme Court endorsed in *Dennis* and also the opinion in the *Masses* case (p. 141).

10 ⟨⟨⟨ On the Meaning of the First Amendment: Absolutes in the Balance

Doctrines are the most frightful tyrants to which men ever are subject, because doctrines get inside of a man's reason and betray him against himself. —W. G. Sumner[1]

IN A RECENT article, Mr. Laurent Frantz criticizes the Supreme Court's "balancing of interests" approach in free speech cases. In the course of his argument, he also lampoons the "absolutist" approach of the dissenters, and chides its chief spokesman for putting his argument "largely in the form that the first amendment 'means what it says.'"[2] Yet in criticizing the Court, Mr. Frantz himself rests largely on what he seems to assume is a clear meaning in the "constitutional text"—and its history.[3]

In support of the Court's balancing position, I suggest that the language of the first amendment is highly ambiguous, and that this ambiguity is at best compounded by history. Professor Chafee put it in a thimble: "The truth is, I think, that the framers had no very clear idea as to what they meant by 'the freedom of speech or of the press.'"[4] Indeed, perhaps it is not going too far to suggest that there is no more equivocal word in the English language than "freedom." What Lincoln said of "liberty" is relevant here: "The world has never had a good definition of [it]." He also pointed out that what is freedom for the lion is death for the lamb. In short, however clear the thou-shalt-not part of the amendment may be, its chain of meaning cannot transcend the fogginess of its weakest link. Surely the framers would have communicated more clearly if they had omitted the weasel-word, and provided simply, "Congress shall pass no law abridging (or restricting) speech." This suggests, of course, that they used the word "freedom" as a limiting or qualifying, not an enlarging, term—a reference presumably to the narrow conception of free utterance that prevailed in the late eighteenth century. Finally, it is noteworthy that even so stout a libertarian as Alexander Meiklejohn has chided those who insist that the words "abridging the freedom of speech or of the press" are "plain words, easily understood."[5]

---

[1] HITCHNER & HARBOLD, MODERN GOVERNMENT 509 (1962).

[2] Frantz, *The First Amendment in the Balance*, 71 YALE L.J. 1424, 1432 (1962).

[3] *Id.* at 1433–44, 1446.

[4] Chafee, Book Review, 62 HARV. L. REV. 891, 898 (1949).

[5] Meiklejohn, *The First Amendment Is an Absolute*, 1961 SUP. CT. REV. 245, 247.

Of course, as Mr. Frantz suggests, we are entitled to seek clarification in history. Doing so, he cites Jefferson's statement that "it is time enough for the rightful purposes of civil government for its officers to interfere when principles break out into overt acts against peace and good order."[6] But this is not only selective history, it is selective Jefferson. Referring to the "licentiousness" of the press that opposed him, the first of the Jeffersonians observed:

> This is a dangerous state of things, and the press ought to be restored to its credibility if possible. The restraints provided by the laws of the States are sufficient for this, if applied. And I have, therefore, long thought that a few prosecutions of the most prominent offenders would have a wholesome effect. . . . Not a general prosecution, for that would look like persecution; but a selected one.[7]

Some of us may be excused for finding in these combined statements as much equivocation as in the undefined terms of the first amendment itself.

Holmes presumably was one of the greatest of legal historians. Yet he gave at different times opposite interpretations of the historic meaning of the amendment. Speaking for himself and Brandeis, he observed that "History seems to me against the notion [that] the First Amendment left the common law of seditious libel in force."[8] A few years earlier he had written for the Court: "[T]he main purpose of such constitutional provisions is 'to prevent all such *previous restraints* . . . as had been practiced by other governments,' and they do not prevent the subsequent punishment of such as may be deemed contrary to the public welfare."[9] In this statement Holmes had the support of Cooley, who maintained that its Blackstonian outlook "has been followed by American commentators of standard authority as embodying correctly the idea incorporated in the constitutional law of the country by the provisions in the American Bill of Rights."[10] To support this proposition Cooley justifiably cites Kent, Story, and Rawle.

While Holmes' switch suggests that the historic purpose of the first amendment is something less than obvious, Mr. Frantz may find comfort in the fact that the Justice's later position was the more liberal one. Professor Chafee also seems to support the charge of vagueness, but by a switch from a generous to a more restricted view. Thus he first asserted that the framers intended "to wipe out the common law of sedition, and

---

[6] Frantz, *supra* note 2, at 1446.

[7] Letter from Thomas Jefferson to Thomas McKean, Feb. 19, 1803, in 8 THE WRITINGS OF THOMAS JEFFERSON 216, 218–19 (Ford ed. 1897). For extensive evidence of the restricted conception of free utterance of Jefferson, and indeed of many of the Founding Fathers, see Levy, *Liberty and the First Amendment: 1790–1800,* 78 AM. HIST. REV. 22 (1962).

[8] Abrams v. United States, 250 U.S. 616, 630 (1919).

[9] Patterson v. Colorado, 215 U.S. 454, 462 (1907).

[10] COOLEY, CONSTITUTIONAL LIMITATIONS 420 (3d ed. 1874).

make further prosecutions for criticism of the government, without any incitement to law-breaking, forever impossible."[11]

It would be ironical if Holmes reversed himself under the influence of Chafee,[12] because Chafee later appears to have altered his own position:

> [The] argument that all the freedoms within the First Amendment are not open to any governmental restrictions . . . leans far too heavily on the absolute nature of its language. . . . Especially significant is the contemporaneous evidence that the phrase "freedom of the press" was viewed against a background of familiar legal institutions which men of 1791 did not regard as objectionable, such as damage suits for libel. Many state constitutions of this time included guarantees of freedom of speech and press which have been treated as having approximately the same scope as the federal provisions. Some of these, as in Massachusetts, were absolute in terms, while others . . . expressly imposed responsibility for abuse of the right. The precise nature of the state constitutional language did not matter; the early interpretation was much the same. *Not only were private libel suits allowed, but also punishments for criminal libel and for contempt of court.* For instance, there were several Massachusetts convictions around 1800 for attacking the conduct of the legislature and public officials. . . .
>
> The truth is, I think, that the framers had no very clear idea as to what they meant by "the freedom of speech or of the press," but we can say . . . with reasonable assurance . . . . [that] the freedom which Congress was forbidden to abridge was not, for them, some absolute concept which had never existed on earth.[13]

Henry Schofield's "Freedom of the Press in the United States," which appeared in 1914, seems to be the seedbed of the modern libertarian conception of the first amendment. It begins, however, with the admission that the "nearly if not quite unanimous expressed view of our judges always has been, and is, that the constitutional declarations of liberty of the press are only declaratory of the English common-law right protected by the English courts at the time of the Revolution. . . ."[14] Of course, it may be that Professor Schofield, writing 123 years after adoption of the amendment, had a truer insight into that history than judges and commentators who witnessed or participated in it, but surely there is room for respectful doubt.

So far, I have meant only to suggest that at best (from the liberal point of view) history is a somewhat less than obvious key to the meaning of the first amendment. Surely, however, no such discussion can fail to men-

---

11 Chafee, *Freedom of Speech in Wartime*, 32 HARV. L. REV. 932, 947 (1919).

12 Chafee's initial position appeared in the June issue of the *Harvard Law Review* in 1919. Holmes' switch found expression in the *Abrams* case which was argued in October, and decided in November, 1919.

13 Chafee, Book Review, 62 HARV. L. REV. 891, 897–98 (1949). (Emphasis added.)

14 Schofield, *Freedom of the Press in the United States,* in 2 ESSAYS ON CONSTITUTIONAL LAW AND EQUITY 510, 511 (1921).

tion Leonard Levy's powerful (if reluctant) case that history speaks clearly in these matters—but in a way that contradicts the libertarian position.[15]

For those who are not moved by his "textual and historical" arguments, Mr. Frantz offers three "fundamental policy reasons" for a more active judicial role in expression, than in economic, cases:

> An economic mistake or injustice [by Congress] does not interfere with the political process and that process therefore remains open for its correction or redress if the courts refuse relief. The same cannot be said where legislation results in infringement of political rights, for the injured can hardly rely for redress on the very weapons of which they are deprived.[16]

This is difficult to follow. By the Interstate Commerce Act, Congress deprives a railroad owner of his "freedom" to charge what the traffic will bear. By the Smith Act, Congress deprives a Communist of his "freedom" to teach and advocate violent overthrow of government. *Yet both the railroad owner and the Communist are perfectly free to seek political redress, i.e., repeal of the measure deemed offensive.* Both may speak freely in favor of a change in the law. Any substantial legislative interference with that kind of freedom would certainly have hard going in the Supreme Court.[17] Even the leader of the antiactivists has made his position clear on that point.[18]

Mr. Frantz's second policy reason for giving free utterance a "preferred place" is that

> economic interests are typically represented in legislative bodies—or are able to obtain a hearing from them. Despised ideological minorities typically are not. In extreme situations such as those which give rise to first amendment test cases, their political influence may be less than zero, for it may be better politics for a legislator to abuse them than to listen to their grievances.[19]

Surely we cannot pretend that all economic interests have substantial "political influence," nor that all other interests are politically impotent. Mr. Frantz's distinction then is not between the economic and the noneconomic, but between claims which have much political leverage and those which have little or none. On this basis, some economic interests ought to enjoy a "preferred place" (including perhaps a presumption of unconstitutionality for offending legislation), just as some spiritual interests should have only a second-class status. This might entail some difficul-

---

[15] LEVY, LEGACY OF SUPPRESSION (1960).

[16] Frantz, *supra* note 2, at 1446.

[17] See De Jonge v. Oregon, 299 U.S. 353, 365–66 (1937).

[18] West Virginia Bd. of Educ. v. Barnette, 319 U.S. 624, 664 (1943) ; Minersville School Dist. v. Gobitis, 310 U.S. 586, 600 (1940).

[19] Frantz, *supra* note 2, at 1447.

ties in application. Would the crucial test refer to absolute or relative political influence? How would such values be measured? How much political strength would be required to justify a "deferred" judicial place? Would a politically negligible religious group enjoy an advantage in the courts that would be denied to the Catholic Church? Would the latter have a "preferred place" vis-à-vis protestantism? Ideally, of course, legislators and all of us would give every "despised minority" a respectful hearing, but surely *the first amendment* does not require it.

The final policy reason presented on behalf of libertarianism on the Bench is that while "activism" in economic cases restricts the scope of "popular choice," activism in utterance cases expands it.[20] But surely a judicial veto of anticommunist legislation limits the range of popular government just as effectively as a judicial veto of minimum-wage legislation. Both say to the people these are choices you may not make. And is it absolutely clear that democracy is poisoned by suppressing those who preach violence when all the avenues of peaceful change are open? Men of the Weimar Republic, like those of pre-1948 Czeckoslovakia, might have some interesting thoughts on that question.

Having bludgeoned both the balancing and the absolutist gambits in speech cases, Mr. Frantz concludes by insisting that constitutionally protected freedom of speech ought to be "defined."[21] Yet strangely (for one who is so concerned for freedom of popular choice) he thinks this should be done not by a constitutional convention, nor by Congress, but by the Supreme Court. To insist that "freedom of speech" needs defining is to concede what I have been arguing: that it is not adequately defined either in the language of the Constitution, or by history, or by considerations of public policy so unquestionable as to be fit subjects for judicial notice.

It is largely because of the absence of defining standards, I suggest, that the Court has resorted openly to balancing in free speech cases. We have had too many opinions that hide the inevitable weighing process by pretending that decisions spring full-blown from the Constitution—a document written generations ago by men who had not the slightest conception of the world in which *we* live. "It will ever remain a mystery to me," Thomas R. Powell observed, "how intelligent jurists can make these professions of nonparticipation in the judicial process."[22] Open balancing compels a judge to take full responsibility for his decisions, and promises a particularized, rational account of how he arrives at them—more particularized and more rational at least than the familiar parade of hallowed abstractions, elastic absolutes, and selective history. Moreover, this approach should make it more difficult for judges to rest on their pre-

---

[20] *Ibid.*

[21] *Id.* at 1449–50.

[22] Powell, Vagaries and Varieties in Constitutional Interpretation 28 (1956).

dispositions without ever subjecting them to the test of reason. It should also make their accounts more rationally auditable. Above all, the open balancing technique is calculated to leave "the sovereign prerogative of choice" to the people—with the least interference that is compatible with our tradition of judicial review. Absent that tradition in utterance cases, the Court might logically accept Learned Hand's view that the first amendment (like the republican-form-of-government clause[23]) is too uncommunicative—too lacking in guidelines—to be treated as law.[24]

Those who find these thoughts offensive may recall that even modern libertarians are far from agreement on the meaning of free speech. Thus its two leading academic advocates—Chafee and Meiklejohn—are deeply divided on matters of scope and limitation.[25] Similarly, Justices Black and Douglas have found themselves on opposite sides of utterance issues.[26] Indeed the first amendment idea is so obscure that both of them apparently failed to see a free-expression problem in the compulsory flag salute until it was pointed out by Mr. Justice Jackson.[27] This obscurity is also revealed in Mr. Justice Black's change of heart with respect to the validity of libel laws[28]—and in the disagreements of Holmes and Brandeis.[29] So too, as we have seen, Jefferson could not agree with himself on the meaning of free communication. Finally, even those two well springs of Anglo-American freedom, Milton's *Areopagitica* and Mill's *On Liberty*, are deeply at odds on the thing that they both eulogize. For surely Mill could not accept Milton's principle that only "neighboring differences, or rather indifferences" are entitled to toleration.[30]

This brings us to the anguished question that Mr. Frantz puts at least by implication: What good is the first amendment, if it is not to be given a "preferred place" by "activist" magistrates? Madison long ago gave the answer: It is futile to rely on judges and "parchment barriers"; politics is the only reliable protection for basic substantive interests.

Of course, Madison introduced and fought for the Bill of Rights—and, in so doing, referred to judicial review in support of it, as libertarians

---

[23] See Luther v. Borden, 48 U.S. (7 How.) 1 (1849).

[24] HAND, THE SPIRIT OF LIBERTY 177–78 (1st ed. 1952).

[25] See Chafee, Book Review, 62 HARV. L. REV. 891 (1949).

[26] See, *e.g.*, Communist Party v. Subversive Activities Control Bd., 367 U.S. 1 (1961); Barr v. Mateo, 360 U.S. 564 (1959); Tenney v. Brandhove, 341 U.S. 367 (1951).

[27] *Compare* their position in Minersville School Dist. v. Gobitis, 310 U.S. 586 (1940), *and* Jones v. Opelika, 316 U.S. 584 (1942), *with* West Virginia Bd. of Educ. v. Barnette, 319 U.S. 624, 643 (1943).

[28] *Compare* his position in Chaplinsky v. New Hampshire, 315 U.S. 568, 572 (1942), *with Justice Black and First Amendment "Absolutes": A Public Interview,* 37 N.Y.U.L. REV. 549, 557 (1962).

[29] See Meyer v. Nebraska, 262 U.S. 390 (1923); Gilbert v. Minnesota, 254 U.S. 325, 334 (1920).

[30] 4 THE WORKS OF JOHN MILTON 349–50 (Patterson ed. 1931).

emphasize ad infinitum.[31] What they fail to mention is that this was
Madison under pressure. If the "father of the Constitution" had really
wanted a bill of rights, why did he not introduce and fight for one in the
constitutional convention? Here is his answer:

> I have never thought the omission [of a bill of rights from the original
> Constitution] a material defect, nor been anxious to supply it even by
> *subsequent* amendment, for any other reason than that it is anxiously
> desired by others. . . .
>
> I have not viewed it in an important light . . . because [among other
> things] experience proves [its] inefficiency on those occasions when its
> controul is most needed. . . . In Virginia I have seen the bill of rights vio-
> lated in every instance where it has been opposed to a popular current. . . .[32]

Before he was pressured into supporting a bill of rights, Madison insisted the only use of a formal declaration was that "the political truths
declared in that solemn manner acquire by degrees the character of fundamental maxims of free government, and as they become incorporated with
the national sentiment, counteract the impulses of interest and passion."[33]
If the government should act improperly, a bill of rights would be "a good
ground for an appeal to the sense of the community."[34] How far this is
from judicial review! And how close to Learned Hand's thought that the
Bill of Rights is not law, but a moral admonition.[35]

Madison was unenthusiastic about the Bill-of-Rights-Judicial-Review
approach because he foresaw a far more reliable, and far more sophisticated, shield for civil liberty: the structure and process of politics.[36] For
him the constitutional diffusion of power and the vast expanse of the nation
with its multiplicity of regional, economic, religious, and other interests
were the true safeguards. Faction would resist faction; ambition would
weigh against ambition. The hopes and fears of each subgroup would
check and balance those of all the others. Government could act only after
political compromise had found the common denominator of a host of
mutually suspicious minorities. In the extended, pluralistic republic of the
United States this could not be an easy, overnight venture. No program
that had survived the give and take necessary to attain support by a concurrent majority of our incredibly varied factional interests could depart

---

[31] See, *e.g.*, Frantz, *supra* note 2, at 1448 n.100.

[32] Letter from James Madison to Thomas Jefferson, Oct. 17, 1788, in PADOVER, THE
COMPLETE MADISON 253–55 (1953).

[33] *Id.* at 254.

[34] *Id.* at 255.

[35] See note 24 *supra*. Even after Madison had brought himself to argue in favor of a
national bill of rights, he did not link it with judicial review until Jefferson suggested that he
do so. On this, and Jefferson's subsequent disillusionment with judicial review, see Mendelson,
Jefferson on Judicial Review: Consistency Through Change, 29 U. CHI. L. REV. 327 (1962).

[36] His thoughts on this, very inadequately summarized below, will be found in THE
FEDERALIST Nos. 10, 51 (Madison).

substantially from the Nation's moral center of gravity. No governmental system could be expected to achieve more; certainly not by idealistic fiats from the Bench that fly in the face of deeply felt community needs. In short, as Madison saw it, majority rule—given a vast empire of diffused sociopolitical power—was the only reliable security against governmental inhumanity.[37]

Of course, some free speech "indiscretions" might survive the sifting of the social and political processes—the Sedition Act of 1798, the Espionage Act of 1917, the Smith Act of 1940 come to mind. But these (assuming they were unjustified) would necessarily reflect such deep and widespread feelings as to defy judicial veto. The upshot is that Congress has killed thousands of bills reflecting every imaginable form of bigotry, intolerance, and demagogery; the Supreme Court has not yet struck down a national measure on the basis of any provision in the first amendment.[38] As Madison anticipated, the congressional batting average is about .999; the Court's is .000.

My point is that liberals appreciate the political processes far too little, and expect far more from judicial review than it has ever been able to deliver. Conservatives no longer make this mistake. They know the cost and frailty of a preferred place in court. Accordingly, since 1937, they have concentrated on legislatures, and have carried off all but a few of the prizes.

Meanwhile a select little company of libertarians—with far less social support than conservatives had in the old days—is trying to repeat all of the Old-Guard mistakes: the twisted history, the tortured parchment, the sugar-coated bias called public policy, the preferred place that can hope only to delay defeat. Sooner or later libertarians will have to face it—the real victories are won in legislatures and at the polls.[39] Man after all is a political, not a legal, animal.

---

[37] Madison recognized that the sociopolitical check and balance system might not be an adequate restraint upon a state because of the relative paucity of interests at play within its boundaries. This may explain why the Supreme Court has been more willing to impose first amendment ideals upon the states than upon the Nation.

[38] Mr. Frantz criticizes the Court for not enforcing the first amendment as "absolutely" as it enforces some other Bill-of-Rights provisions. Frantz, *supra* note 2, at 1436–38. The answer is presumably that these other provisions are directed largely against judges, administrators, and police officers. It is one thing for the Supreme Court to override them; it is quite another to override the National Legislature *acting in its lawmaking capacity*. See also note 37 *supra*.

[39] Brown v. Board of Educ., 347 U.S. 483 (1954), was costly indeed, if it convinced libertarians that the judicial process is an effective tool of libertarianism. Eight years after the original decision, *all the public schools of one of the defendants* (Prince Edward County, Virginia) *remained closed*. Only .4% of the South's Negro public school pupils were in classes with whites—and they were concentrated largely in the border states. Alabama, Mississippi, and South Carolina still had no integrated public schools. What Georgia and Louisiana had achieved could not fairly be called even token integration. See generally *Is the South Really Integrating Now?*, U.S. News & World Report, Dec. 10, 1962, p. 78.

ADDENDUM TO FOOTNOTE 39

On the tenth anniversary of *Brown*, "a head count . . . showed that only 1.17 percent of black school children in the eleven states of the Confederacy were attending public school with white classmates" (R. Kluger, *Simple Justice* [1975] p. 758). Notable southern desegregation did not come until Congress enacted the Civil Rights Act of 1964, along with the Voting Rights Act and the Elementary and Secondary Education Act of 1965. Revolutionary changes followed. Within six years, according to a Health, Education, and Welfare report (1971), an estimated 43.9 percent of black pupils attended white-majority public schools in the South. Yet even this improvement was confined to Dixie. The same HEW study estimated that only 27.8 percent of black pupils attended white-majority schools in the North and West. The percentage of blacks who attended schools that were more than 80 percent black was 91.3 in Cleveland, Ohio; 97.8 in Compton, California; 78.1 in Dayton, Ohio; 78.6 in Detroit, Michigan; 95.7 in Gary, Indiana; 86.6 in Los Angeles, California; 78.8 in Milwaukee, Wisconsin; and 89.8 in St. Louis, Missouri.

"Nationwide, in the last decade about . . . four in ten black children have been in a 90 percent (or more) minority school. . . . In spite of the elimination of legal segregation . . . segregation remains the obvious pattern in U.S. schools" (J. Feagin, *Social Problems* [1982], pp. 220–21).

11 🐾 The First Amendment and the Judicial Process: A Reply to Mr. Frantz

In a wide-ranging debate, Mr. Laurent Frantz and I have singled out two key issues on which we—and perhaps activists and anti-activists generally—are divided.[1] One concerns the meaning of the first amendment; the other the "balancing of interests" in free utterance cases.

THE MEANING OF THE FIRST AMENDMENT

To come at once to the heart of the problem: Mr. Frantz assumes that the first amendment incorporates Meiklejohn's book, *Political Freedom*.[2] This wise little study suggests that

> When men govern themselves, it is they—and no one else—who must pass judgment upon unwisdom and unfairness and danger. . . . Just so far as, at any point, the citizens who are to decide an issue are denied acquaintance with information or opinion or doubt or disbelief or criticism which is relevant to that issue, just so far the result must be ill-considered, ill-balanced planning for the general good. *It is that mutilation of the thinking process of the community against which the First Amendment . . . is directed.*[3]

Surely no one dedicated to democracy and human decency could fail to find inspiration in these words. But philosophy is one thing, and history another. Dean Levy and others have shown that at best (in the libertarian view) the historic meaning of free utterance is found in Blackstone.[4] In short it permitted prosecution for seditious libel.

---

1. Frantz, *The First Amendment in the Balance*, 71 YALE L.J. 1424 (1962); Mendelson, *On the Meaning of the First Amendment: Absolutes in the Balance*, 50 CALIF. L. REV. 821 (1962); Frantz, *Is the First Amendment Law?—A Reply to Professor Mendelson*, 51 CALIF. L. REV. 729 (1963).

2. *Id.* at 735. See also Emerson, *Toward a General Theory of the First Amendment*, 72 YALE L.J. 877, 878, 916 (1963).

3. MEIKLEJOHN, POLITICAL FREEDOM 27 (1960).

4. LEVY, LEGACY OF SUPPRESSION (1960). For further evidence, see Mendelson, *supra* note 1, at 822-24.

This view stands unrefuted; even Chafee ultimately accepted it.[5] Mr. Justice Iredell—appointed to the Supreme Court by President Washington—gave the gist of the matter in charging a grand jury with respect to the Sedition Act of 1798:

> That objection is, that the act is in violation of this amendment of the Constitution.
>
> "Congress shall make no law respecting an establishment of religion, or prohibiting the free exercise thereof; or abridging the freedom of speech, or of the press, or the right of the people peaceably to assemble, and to petition the government for a redress of grievances."
>
> The question then is, whether this law has abridged the freedom of the press?
>
> Here is a remarkable difference in expressions as to the different objects in the same clause. They are to make no law *respecting* an establishment of religion, or prohibiting the free exercise thereof, or *abridging* the freedom of speech, or of the press. When, as to one object, they entirely prohibit any act whatever, and, as to another object, only limit the exercise of the power, they must, in reason, be supposed to mean different things. I presume, therefore, that Congress may make a law *respecting* the press, provided the law be such as not to *abridge its freedom*. What might be deemed the freedom of the press, if it had been a new subject, and never before in discussion, might indeed admit of some controversy. But, so far as precedent, habit, laws, and practices are concerned, there can scarcely be a more definite meaning than that which all these have affixed to the term in question.[6]
>
> . . . .
>
> It is believed that, in every State in the Union, the common law principles concerning libels apply; and in some of the States words similar to the words of the Amendment are used in the Constitution itself, or a contemporary Bill of Rights, of equal authority, without ever being supposed to exclude any law being passed on the subject. So that there is the strongest proof that can be of a universal concurrence in America on this point, that the freedom of the press does not require that libellers shall be protected from punishment.[7]

Of course, we are not inevitably obliged to honor the purposes of those who gave us the Bill of Rights. What then of judicial precedent? I suggest that in first amendment cases pure and simple no decision of the Supreme Court goes beyond Blackstone (though perhaps some of its language does). Indeed, no act of Congress has ever been held invalid on first amendment grounds.

What kind of law is it that was never enacted by the political processes, nor adopted by the judges? By what authority does Mr. Frantz get Mr. Meiklejohn into the First Amendment? Both history

---

5. Chafee, Book Review, 62 Harv. L. Rev. 891 (1949).

6. See Wharton, State Trials of the United States During the Administration of Washington and Adams 477-78 (1849). For a similar view see the Report of a House Committee, 38 Annals of Cong., 5th Cong., 3d Sess. 2985-93 (1799).

7. Wharton, *op. cit. supra* note 6, at 479.

and judicial precedent (federal and state) are overwhelmingly against him—to say nothing of the other agencies of government. And surely he can claim no social support remotely comparable to the forces that put Herbert Spencer's *Social Statics* into the fourteenth amendment. Law cannot support itself by its own bootstraps, or thrive on the dreams of a few idealists. Moreover, even so ardent a libertarian—and so competent a lawyer—as Chafee found Meiklejohn's approach judicially unworkable.[8]

Of course, on his *philosophic* premise much of what Mr. Frantz says would have to be accepted. And only on that premise can he ask such paradoxical questions as "Is the First Amendment Law?," and why does the Court not enforce it?[9] The answer is that the amendment *is* law, and (insofar as it goes) *is* judicially enforced. It is Meiklejohn's book that is not law and not enforced.

In effect Mr. Frantz is chiding the Court for not legislating Meiklejohn into, and something else out of, the Constitution. This, perhaps, a court may do when it "feels behind it the weight of such general acceptance as will give sanction to its pretension to unquestioned dictation."[10] Meanwhile, "it must be content to lag behind the best inspiration of its time"—as reflected in men like Alexander Meiklejohn.[11]

BALANCING AND FREEDOM

Mr. Frantz rejects the "balancing of interests" as a general approach in utterance cases. He let go of the cat when he confessed about Meiklejohn. I now confess that (except perhaps in simple cases which seldom reach the Supreme Court) balancing seems to me the essence of the judicial process—the nexus between abstract law and concrete life. Lawmakers cannot anticipate all the combinations and permutations of circumstance. What Cardozo called "the great generalities of the Constitution" are no more amenable to mechanistic application by liberals than they were by Mr. Justice Roberts in his famous squaring analogy.[12] Moreover, balancing would seem to be implicit in an adversary system which inevitably contemplates at least two sides to every case—the lopsided ones being weeded out in law offices and the lower courts. As T. R. Powell observed long ago, "It will ever remain a mystery to me how intelligent jurists can make . . . professions of nonparticipation in the judicial process."[13] Surely the choice is

---

8. Chafee, Book Review, 62 HARV. L. REV. 891 (1949).
9. FRANTZ, *supra* note 1, 51 CALIF. L. REV. at 738.
10. HAND, THE SPIRIT OF LIBERTY 15-16 (2d ed. Dilliard 1953).
11. *Id.* at 15.
12. See United States v. Butler, 297 U.S. 1 (1936).
13. POWELL, VAGARIES AND VARIETIES IN CONSTITUTIONAL INTERPRETATION 28 (1956).

simply this: shall the balancing be done "intuitively" or rationally; covertly or out in the open? Of course, it should always be done in the light of accepted legal principles[14]—and obviously the light of Meiklejohn is quite different from that of Blackstone.

Di Santo v. Pennsylvania[15] is a classic example of covert, and probably "intuitive," balancing. There the old Court held invalid a state regulation of commerce as a "direct burden"—and that is virtually all there was in the opinion. No observer could tell what interests were weighed against what. Ostensibly the Court merely applied a well-known rule of law. But who outside the Court could know, and thus appraise, the decisive considerations that marked the burden in question as "direct" rather than "indirect"? Mr. Justice Stone, joined by Holmes and Brandeis, observed in dissent:

> In this case the traditional test of the limit of state action by inquiring whether the interference with commerce is direct or indirect seems to me to be too mechanical, too uncertain in its application, and too remote from actualities, to be of value. In thus making use of the expressions, "direct" and "indirect interference" with commerce, we are doing little more than using labels to describe a result rather than any trustworthy formula by which it is reached.[16]

What a world of difference between the Court's approach in *Di Santo,* and its approach in *Southern Pacific Co. v. Arizona!*[17] There Stone gave the positive side of his earlier dissent, revealing in detail factors considered on each side of the judicial scale. Appraisal of the process could then proceed rationally. Perhaps even more important, the open balancing operation itself tends to focus the attention of all concerned on actualities and away from the never-never land of private, and perhaps unconscious, preconceptions.[18]

---

14. How much weight should be given to congressional judgment is another matter. Apparently modern, overt balancers find that the step from a general and ancient constitutional precept to the problems of modern life is largely legislative. Hence, presumably, their special deference (via the reasonable man approach) for legislative policy. Learned Hand put it briefly: "If a court be really candid, it can only say: 'We find that this measure will have this result; it will injure this group in such and such ways, and benefit that group in these other ways. We declare it invalid, because after every conceivable allowance for differences of outlook, we cannot see how a fair person can honestly believe that the benefits balance the losses.'" HAND, THE SPIRIT OF LIBERTY 179 (2d ed. Dilliard 1953).

15. 273 U.S. 34 (1927).

16. *Id.* at 44.

17. 325 U.S. 761 (1945).

18. It is noteworthy that Mr. Justice Black, who in first amendment cases believes in absolutes and repudiates balancing (see Konigsberg v. California, 366 U.S. 36, 65-76 (1962); Cahn, *Justice Black and First Amendment "Absolutes": A Public Interview,* 37 N.Y.U.L. REV. 549 (1962)), dissented in *Southern Pacific.* There too he repudiated the Court's balancing technique, and thought the case should have been decided by an absolute rule which the Court had never accepted as law.

It seems a fair guess that if in *Di Santo* the Court had felt compelled to reveal the ingredients of its decision, there would have been less Herbert Spencer in the scales, and more of the real-life considerations mentioned in the Brandeis dissent. In short, the Court might have been compelled either to reach a different result, or reveal for all to see a vulnerable exercise in the accommodation of law and life.

Mr. Frantz does not like the balancing that occurred in *Barenblatt*.[19] The Court could easily have reached the same result via the *Di Santo* route. But in balancing openly, it gave Mr. Frantz an opportunity for *reasoned* criticism of the proffered weighing process. The *Di Santo* technique hides the inevitable balancing behind a verbal, and often Platonic, barrier. Strictly followed, it means a Mr. Frantz must argue that the burden on commerce "'taint," while the Court holds "'tis," direct (whatever that means). Our debt to Holmes, Brandeis, and Stone is that they cut through the net of formality, and encouraged us to "think things, not words." This, I believe, is the crux of the open balancing approach. It is not foolproof and certainly will not make a great judge of a little man. But it offers hope of progress for inquiring minds. What Walter Lippmann said in another context is relevant here: "When men act on the principle of intelligence, they go out to find the facts. . . . When they ignore it, they go inside themselves and find only what is there. They elaborate their prejudice instead of increasing their knowledge."

Dean Griswold has suggested that the balancing approach is misnamed, that it might better be called the "comprehensive" or "integral" approach.

> Instead of focusing on a few words, and ignoring all else, including the effect and meaning of those words, as distinguished from their apparent impact when isolated from everything else . . . the comprehensive or integral approach accepts the task of the judge as one which involves the effect of all the provisions of the Constitution, not merely in a narrow literal sense, but in a living, organic sense, including the elaborate and complex governmental structure which the Constitution, through its words, has erected.[20]

In any event, the essence of balancing is realism—a repudiation of the modern activists' rhetorical, or magic phrase, technique. The latter characteristically begins with an honored phrase or doctrine—the clear and present danger rule, for example; knocks the brains out of it, by stretching it so broadly as to deprive it of any ascertainable meaning;[21] and then uses it in talismanic fashion to "resolve" all manner of difficul-

---

19. Barenblatt v. United States, 360 U.S. 109 (1959); Frantz, *supra* note 1, 51 CALIF. L. REV. at 746.

20. Griswold, *Absolute Is in the Dark*, 8 UTAH L. REV. 167, 172 (1963).

21. See Mendelson, *Clear and Present Danger—From Schenck to Dennis*, 52 COLUM. L. REV. 313, 317 (1952).

ties—from non-utterance by moppets in their classrooms,[22] to trial by newspaper,[23] to a struggle between lunatic fringe hate groups for what Hitler called "the conquest of the streets."[24] Paul Freund gave the epitaph for this cycle of activist word-play when he wrote

> No matter how rapidly we utter the phrase "clear and present danger," or how closely we hyphenate the words, they are not a substitute for the weighing of values. They tend to convey a delusion of certitude when what is most certain is the complexity of the strands in the web of freedom which the judge must disentangle.[25]

Or, as Mr. Justice Jackson observed in the *Terminiello* case (after his conversion at Nuremberg), the activists reverse

> this conviction by reiterating generalized approbations of freedom of speech with which, in the abstract, no one will disagree. Doubts as to their applicability are lulled by avoidance of more than passing reference to the circumstances of Terminiello's speech and judging it as if he had spoken to persons as dispassionate as empty benches, or like a modern Demosthenes practicing his Philippics on a lonely seashore.[26]

Cut loose from its foundation in the distinction between discussion and incitement, the clear and present danger test lost its rational meaning and became a cloak for "vague but fervent transcendentalism."[27] In short, the activists destroyed it as an intelligible guide to decision—and then abandoned it about a dozen years ago.[28] Meanwhile they have tried, and apparently discarded, one "new" verbalism after another. The latest is Mr. Justice Black's absolutist concentration on two untroubled words in the first amendment: "no law."[29] This gambit—"no law means no law"—again begs all the difficulties simply by ignoring them. As Dean Griswold has suggested, it reminds one of the fundamentalist church sign which proclaimed, "God said it. We believe it. That's all there is to it."[30]

CONCLUSION

The need for judicial balancing, I suggest, results from the imperfection of mundane law. In a better world, no doubt, clear and precise legal rules would anticipate all possible contingencies. No wonder,

---

22. West Virginia Bd. of Educ. v. Barnette, 319 U.S. 624 (1943).
23. Bridges v. California, 314 U.S. 252 (1941).
24. Terminiello v. Chicago, 337 U.S. 1 (1949).
25. FREUND, ON UNDERSTANDING THE SUPREME COURT 27-28 (1949).
26. 337 U.S. at 13.
27. Mendelson, *supra* note 21, at 322.
28. Mendelson, *Clear and Present Danger—Another Decade,* 39 TEXAS L. REV. 449 (1961).
29. Cahn, *supra* note 18.
30. Griswold, *supra* note 20, at 172.

then, that idealists are impatient with the balancing process. Mr. Frantz' solution has a familiar ring. He suggests that law precedes, and apparently even transcends, politics.[31] Here is our old friend "the brooding omnipresence"—"the higher law"—that Holmes and Brandeis among others fought so hard to kill. Surely *in a democracy* law is a creature of the political processes, constitutional and legislative. Judges, of course, cannot avoid legislating in some degree, but to repeat Holmes' much quoted phrase they must do so only interstitially—lest they rather than the people govern. For judges now to treat Meiklejohn's book as "higher law" seems at least as far from mere gap-filling as was their predecessors' treatment of Herbert Spencer.

If libertarians are convinced that the Court is wrong, and that Meiklejohn's views reflect the community consensus, surely a constitutional amendment would be a feasible and proper remedy. If there is no such consensus, how could we justify imposing a minority view upon the people? The old Court tried that in the 1930s and destroyed itself. Obviously most of the "nine old men" and their supporters were just as certain as libertarians are today that their values were "fundamental" and indeed indispensable to freedom—as well as inherent in "higher law." Holmes' answer was that "certitude is not the test of certainty."[32] Another response was the Brandeis brief with its invitation to open balancing as a substitute for word-play and Platonic abstraction in court opinions.

I end where I began, amused yet troubled by the continuing activist-idealist pretense that all answers to all problems are in (or above) the Constitution—and that the judicial process for extracting them is largely mechanical or automatic.

---

31. Frantz, *supra* note 1, 51 Calif. L. Rev. at 754.
32. Holmes, *Natural Law*, in Collected Legal Papers 310, 311 (1920).

Addendum

It is said here and elsewhere in these essays that the Supreme Court has never vetoed an act of Congress on First Amendment grounds. This remained true until the case of *Lamont* v. *Postmaster,* 381 U.S. 301 (1965). That decision was qualified in *Rowan* v. *Post Office,* 397 U.S. 728 (1970). Since *Lamont* the Supreme Court has vetoed five congressional measures on First Amendment grounds. Four were speech or association measures, two of which Congress could reinstate by curing an overbreadth and a *Freedman* v. *Maryland* problem.

12 🦋 Mr. Justice Black, the Supreme Court, and the Bill of Rights

In a recent article in *Harper's Magazine*, Professor Charles Black sought to explain and buttress Mr. Justice Black's position on the Bill of Rights. The argument is so new and appealing—its implications with respect to the judicial process are so provocative—as to invite consideration in a learned journal. Since Professor Black wrote in broad and non-professional terms, it seems appropriate to respond in kind.

No past or present Justice, and no responsible commentator, has ever suggested that the Bill of Rights gives an absolute right to say whatever one might choose to say at any time and any place. To quote Professor Black, "No one would argue, for example, that . . . 'free speech' . . . includes mere personal slander, or fraudulent oral misrepresentation of goods offered for sale, or perjury on the witness stand. . . ." or (in Holmes' famous phrase) shouting "fire" falsely in a dark and crowded theater. It follows then, that in close cases the essence of the judicial function is to balance conflicting interests in the context of the circumstances in which they clash. This is what the Court purports to do, and what Professor Black agrees it must do. His point (bluntly put) is that the Court should insist (pretend?) that free speech is an absolute —while it does the inevitable balancing by manipulating the definition of "free speech." Professor Black admits that "in a *purely logical* sense" it really makes no difference which approach is used. In either case "free speech" gets balanced off against more mundane interests. We must look, then, for an extra-logical—perhaps irrational—justification for the unorthodox position. Its value is said to be psychological: "what is really on the scale is attitude." A judge who talks in terms of absolutes (even though with tongue in cheek) reveals a more reliable attitude, it seems, than one who makes no bones about what he is doing, who balances openly and not under the guise of defining.

Of course, Professor Black has no sympathy for subterfuge and he knows that in this world compromise cannot be avoided. Yet his argument has little point unless it contemplates that by talking absolutes a court will delude itself—if only a little bit—into thinking and acting in absolute terms. And what of the layman who hears high talk of unqualified rights—which, as it turns out, are somewhat less than unqualified?

Verbalisms are important—largely because they are so misleading. That is why Justice Holmes admonished us to think things, not words, and why in his long fight for human freedom he carefully avoided absolutes. That also is why Brandeis fought so heroically to shift the focus of judicial attention from word-play to the facts of life. The old Court that goaded Holmes and Brandeis into dissent wasn't cruel; it was blinded by absolutes. Preoccupied with the definition and meaning of its preconceptions, it failed to see the human meaning of such things as child labor, sweat-shops, and "yellow-dog" contracts. The whole purpose of the Brandeis Brief was to cure this blindness by blocking the very thing that Professor Black now advocates: judicial opinions founded on platonic absolutes and closet exercises in the art of definition.

If the balancing of concrete human claims is at, or near, the heart of the judicial process, let it be done directly and openly for all to see—not at second hand, behind a verbal barrier. For the great merit of the frankly factual (as distinct from the verbal) emphasis is that it tends to keep us close to reality and away from the never-never land of our private hopes and fears. What Walter Lippman said in another context is relevant here: "When men act on the principle of intelligence, they go out to find the facts and make their own wisdom. When they ignore it, they go inside themselves and find only what is there. They elaborate their prejudice instead of increasing their knowledge."

We are told that: "Attitude is what is at stake between Justice Black and his adversaries." Since that Judge's reverential treatment of the Bill of Rights is shown to be "correct," it would seem to follow that the Court's attitude is hostile, or at least "wrong." What, then, is that attitude? Of course, Justice Black's "adversaries" on the bench respect the principle of free speech. But they know that the Bill of Rights was not designed, and has never been held, to protect every word that might come out of a man's mouth. The great difficulty is that the Constitution does not tell us which words in what contexts are protected and which are not. Accordingly, the thing that we have called "balancing" inevitably involves an element of *choice, i.e., an element of law-making.* To cry "fire" falsely when one is alone on a desert island is one thing; to do so in a crowded theater is another. Somewhere between these obvious extremes lies the line between protected and unprotected speech. Since the Constitution does not locate that boundary for us, some mortal agency must. Unfortunately we have none that is immune from the possibility of human error. Under our system, unlike the British, the judiciary has the final word (short of constitutional amendment). But this is a bit galling to some who believe deeply that democracy cannot exist for a people that is not free to choose for itself when choice must be made. After all, voters have relatively direct and immediate control over Congress, but only the remotest power to correct judicial error. It is not that Justice Black's "adversaries" like free speech less, but that they like democracy—*in all its aspects*—more. Accordingly, when the two responsible, *i.e.*, elected, branches (Congress and the President) agree upon a line in the area of doubt or choice, the Court hesitates to interfere. (The Constitution, remember, does not provide an unmistakable boundary.) This is to say, the Court is reluctant to intrude upon the democratic processes unless it is convinced beyond reasonable doubt that the legislative balance has no rational foundation. To put it differently: the Court starts with a presumption that the people, speaking through their elected representatives, are "right"; Justice Black presumes that they are "wrong." Each side, of course, will consider arguments in rebuttal of its presumption.

In short, both Justice Black and his "adversaries" believe deeply in free speech—probably more deeply than any comparable group of their predecessors. They differ mainly in their attitude toward the judicial role in a democracy. It comes, perhaps, to this: How can democracy work, if its fundamentals (free speech, for example) are not preserved? Yet, how can democracy prosper, how deep is our respect for it, if we do not trust it with fundamentals? We practice intolerance and expect the Court to preserve the Bill of Rights. Should judges try to save us from ourselves even in the area where the Constitution leaves room for doubt and choice; or should they leave us free to gain the strength that grows with the burden of responsibility—the wisdom that comes with self-inflicted wounds? That is the oldest, most basic, and most tantalizing problem in American constitutional law. We have no solution, unless it be this: we almost always manage to have both attitudes represented on the bench.

13   Mr. Justice Rutledge's Mark upon the Bill of Rights

The constitutional revolution which began in the spring of 1937 had run a six year course when Wiley Blount Rutledge was called to the Supreme Court bench. For the sharp-eyed, there had been intimations as early as 1938 of things to come in civil liberty cases. Buried in a footnote was Justice Stone's now famous observation that there "may be narrower scope for operation of the presumption of constitutionality when legislation appears on its face to be within a specific prohibition . . . of the first ten amendments. . . ."[1] In due course Justice Rutledge was to turn a decision upon that hint, but first came the preliminary Flag Salute Case. There Justice Frankfurter spoke for the majority:

> It is not our province to choose among competing considerations in the subtle process of securing effective loyalty to the traditional ideals of democracy. . . . So to hold would in effect make us the school board for the country. . . . Except where the transgression of constitutional liberty is too plain for argument [i.e., where the legislation in question has no reasonable basis], personal freedom is best maintained—so long as the remedial channels of the democratic process remain open and unobstructed—when it is ingrained in a people's habits and not enforced against popular policy by the coercion of adjudicated law.[2]

This was the "reasonable basis" rule, from which only Justice Stone dissented. By 1941 the disintegration of its eight-fold support began. Thus for Justices Black and Douglas, who dissented in the *Milk Wagon Drivers* case,[3] picketing even in a "context of violence" was a constitutionally protected freedom of expression and might not be prohibited merely because a state had a "reasonable basis" for doing so. It was not enough that judges might find no plain "transgression of constitutional liberty," for freedom of speech and press stand on a higher footing and may be denied only upon a showing—not here made—of "clear and present danger." Then in 1942, after hawkers of religious tracts had refused to pay an ordinary and non-discriminatory tax on peddling, Justices Black, Douglas, and Murphy, dissenting with Chief Justice Stone, not only supported the claimed exemption on

---

1. United States v. Carolene Products Co., 304 U.S. 144, 152 n.4 (1938).
2. Minersville School District v. Gobitis, 310 U.S. 586, 598 (1940).
3. Milk Wagon Drivers Union v. Meadowmoor Dairies, 312 U.S. 287, 299 (1941). Justice Reed also dissented.

freedom of religion grounds, but also announced the abandonment of their position in the *Flag Salute* case.[4]

When shortly thereafter Mr. Justice Rutledge joined the Court, the former minority attained majority status. In *Murdock v. Pennsylvania*[5] the denial of tax immunity for vendors of religious "literature" was reversed. Equality of tax treatment in such cases was not enough for Justices Rutledge, Black, Douglas, Murphy and Chief Justice Stone, for in their view "freedom of the press, freedom of religion are available to all, not merely to those who can pay their own way."[6] Mr. Justice Frankfurter in dissent felt that interpreting the First Amendment to require "a subsidy in the form of fiscal exemption" was transmutting freedom of religion from government encroachment into religious encroachment upon government. Moreover, he thought that it "is irrelevant that a tax can suppress or control, if it does not."[7] Mr. Justice Jackson lampooned the majority's approach. He urged that difficult constitutional problems should not be decided "by a vague but fervent transcendentalism . . . unless we are to reach judgments as did Plato's men who were chained in a cave so that they saw nothing but shadows. . . ." As to the danger in adopting such an approach, he pointed to the history of the contract clause, "which was discredited by being overdone."[8]

A few weeks later refusal to salute the flag was vindicated. Justice Jackson, now out of the cave, found for a majority that the exact purpose of the Bill of Rights was to remove certain basic rights from the reach of legislatures and popular majorities:

> The right of a state to regulate, for example, a public utility may well include, so far as the due process clause is concerned, power to impose all of the restrictions which a legislature may have a "rational basis" for adopting. But freedoms of speech and of press, of assembly, and of worship may not be infringed on such slender grounds. They are susceptible of restriction only to prevent grave and immediate danger to interests which the state may lawfully protect.[9]

Justice Frankfurter, with the concurrence of Justices Reed and Roberts, held his position. Citing Holmes' admonition that legislatures as much as courts are the guardians of the liberty and welfare of the people,[10] he reiterated that the Court's "only and very narrow function is to determine whether within the broad grant of authority vested in legislatures they have exercised a judgment for which reasonable justification can be offered. . . ."[11]

It fell to Mr. Justice Rutledge to give the new majority position full

---

4. Jones v. Opelika, 316 U.S. 584, 623-24 (1942).
5. 319 U.S. 105 (1943).
6. *Id.* at 111.
7. *Id.* at 137.
8. *Id.* at 166, 179, 181.
9. West Virginia Bd. of Education v. Barnette, 319 U.S. 624, 639 (1943).
10. Missouri K. & T. Ry. v. May, 194 U.S. 267, 270 (1904).
11. West Virginia Bd. of Education v. Barnette, 319 U.S. 624, 646-47, 649 (1943).

body. In *Thomas v. Collins*[12] he examined the validity of a Texas statute requiring registration of union organizers before they could solicit members. Writing at length, Rutledge spoke of the "indispensible democratic freedoms secured by the First Amendment," and declared that "any attempt to restrict those liberties must be justified by clear public interest, threatened not doubtfully or remotely, but by clear and present danger." He rejected, the "reasonable basis" rule and concluded that a requirement of registration prior to making an otherwise lawful public speech was wholly incompatible with the requirements of the First Amendment. But the crucial importance of the opinion came in his "preferred place" language, which seems to deny even the normal presumption of constitutionality to a statute which on its face appears to abridge free speech, press, religion or assembly :

> Choice on that border [between freedom and authority], now as always delicate, is perhaps more so where the usual presumption supporting legislation is balanced by the preferred place given in our scheme to the great, the indispensible democratic freedoms secured by the First Amendment. . . .[13]

There are those who see in this a presumption of unconstitutionality for statutes which prima facie impinge upon First Amendment principles[14]—a presumption which can be overcome only by convincing the Court that the legislation is justified by a "clear and present danger." In any case this famous test, designed by Mr. Justice Holmes for judges in the quicksand where words shift from "keys of thought" into "triggers of action," becomes equally a measure of legislative power to control words themselves.

How far would "individual liberty" take the new majority along the Transcendental Road in the direction of anarchy? Justice Stone, whose lone dissent in the First Flag Salute case had touched off the controversy, stopped when the majority in the name of free speech denied state power to license labor organizers[15] and when it laid down the "novel Constitutional doctrine" that in the name of freedom of religion "one may remain on private property [a company town] against the will of the owner and contrary to the law of the State. . . ."[16] Justice Jackson, who spoke for the Court in the Second Flag Salute Case, stopped when the public purse[17] and privacy of the home[18]

---

12. 323 U.S. 516 (1945).

13. *Id.* at 529-30. See also Justice Rutledge's "preferred position" language in Prince v. Massachusetts, 321 U.S. 158, 164 (1944).

14. *E.g.,* Cushman, *Civil Liberties* in *Ten Years of the Supreme Court: 1937-1947,* 42 AM. POL. SCI. REV. 32, 42, 43 (1948). *Cf.* Justice Frankfurter's remarks in Kovacs v. Cooper, 93 L. Ed. 381, 387 *et seq.* (1949) ; Mosher, *Mr. Justice Rutledge's Philosophy of Civil Rights,* 24 N.Y.U.L.Q. REV. 661, 667 (1949).

15. Thomas v. Collins, 323 U.S. 516, 548 (1945).

16. Marsh v. Alabama, 326 U.S. 501, 511 (1946) ; *cf.* Tucker v. Texas, 326 U.S. 517 (1946).

17. Murdock v. Pennsylvania, 319 U.S. 105, 134 (1943).

were invaded in the name of religious freedom. But it was Justice Rutledge who led the Court in a strategic retreat when it stood on the border between a state's interest in protecting child welfare and "freedom" of children to hawk religious tracts on the streets at night. Speaking for all but his Brother Murphy, Justice Rutledge carved a quaint exception into the Court's new "transcendentalism":

> Concededly a statute or ordinance identical in terms with . . . [that here involved], except that it is applicable to adults or all persons generally, would be invalid . . . [But] the states' authority over children's activities is broader than over like action of adults.[19]

The result, if not the language, was certainly a concession to the wisdom of Justice Frankfurter's "reasonable basis" rule, as were both result and language in the Hirabayashi,[20] Korematsu[21] and Hatch Act[22] cases. Indeed Frankfurter has had the satisfaction, if any there be, of seeing one after another of his associates call a halt to "transcendentalism" in civil freedom cases,[23] though to date in only a few instances has their apostasy been concurrently broad enough to turn the decision.[24]

At the time when Hitler's star was at its zenith, Mr. Justice Rutledge brought to the Court a vote that changed the whole trend of decision and gave to civil liberty a latitude unequaled in American judicial history. And while he could not always follow the logic of his position, in the log of history Rutledge's name must be associated with the "preferred place" doctrine— that *beau geste* which would give Americans "better" government than they are at the moment able to give themselves and take from them (perhaps merely dilute) moral responsibility for their acts, which is the indispensable matrix of human freedom.[25]

---

18. Martin v. Struthers, 319 U.S. 141, 166 (1943).
19. Prince v. Massachusetts, 321 U.S. 158, 167-68 (1944). Justice Rutledge does not mention the Flag Salute cases, where children were also involved.
20. Hirabayashi v. United States, 320 U.S. 81 (1943).
21. Korematsu v. United States, 323 U.S. 214 (1944).
22. United Public Workers v. Mitchell, 330 U.S. 75 (1947).
23. *See, e.g.*, the dissenting opinions in cases cited notes 15-18 *supra*.
24. *E.g.*, cases cited notes 19-22 *supra; cf. In re* Summers, 325 U.S. 561 (1945).
25. For discussion of Mr. Justice Rutledge's mark upon the commerce clause, see Mendelson, *Recent Developments in State Regulation and Taxation of Interstate Commerce*, 98 U. OF PA. L. REV. 57 (1949).

 III

The Fourteenth Amendment:
Judicial Catchall

14 🦋 A Note on the Cause and Cure of the Fourteenth Amendment

Raoul Berger's *Government by Judiciary* (1977)[1] offers the latest of a long series of incompatible interpretations of the Fourteenth Amendment. His thesis is that the heart of the matter is the Privileges or Immunities Clause, which for the 39th Congress (whence it came) ". . . had [a] clearly defined and narrow compass" revealed in the "rights . . . enumerated" in the Civil Rights Act of 1866.[2] The Due Process and Equal Protection Clauses, it seems, were meant merely as adjuncts for implementing the privileges clause.[3]

No doubt there were some in the 39th Congress who held this view. Yet each of the three sponsors of the Fourteenth Amendment found more in it than that. Congressman John Bingham, its chief architect, observed in his final summation in the House,[4]

---

[1] A "Symposium" on this book appears in 6 *Hastings Constitutional Law Quarterly* 403 (1979).

[2] *Government by Judiciary*, 18, 36. The Civil Rights Act of 1866 (42 Stat. 27) provided that persons born in the United States and not subject to any foreign power were citizens of the United States; that such citizens, without regard to color, were entitled in every state and territory to the same right to contract, sue, give evidence, and take, hold, and convey property, and to the equal benefit of all laws for the security of person and property, as was enjoyed by white citizens; and that any person who under color of law caused any such civil right to be denied would be guilty of a federal offense.

[3] Berger, *Government by Judiciary*, 166-220.

[4] *Congressional Globe*, 30th Congress, 1st Session 2542 (1866).

. . . there remains a want now, in the Constitution of our country, which the proposed amendment will supply. What is it? It is the power in the people . . . to do that by Congressional enactment which hitherto they have not had the power to do . . . that is to protect by national law the privileges and immunities of all the citizens of the Republic and the inborn rights of every person . . . whenever the same shall be abridged or denied by the [already] unconstitutional acts of any State.

Allow me . . . in passing, to say that this amendment takes from no State any right that ever pertained to it. No State ever had the right, under the forms of law or otherwise, to deny to any freeman the equal protection of the laws or to abridge the privileges or immunities of any citizen of the Republic, although many of them have assumed and exercised the power. . . .

Thus Bingham saw in "his" amendment not only protection for the "privileges and immunities" of *citizens*, but also for the "inborn rights" of *persons* (whatever that means). All this, however, he thought was already in the Constitution. The Fourteenth Amendment would add only a new remedy (a congressional enforcing power) — to safeguard something that both preceded and exceeded the Civil Rights Act of 1866. Obviously Bingham — the so-called James Madison of the Fourteenth Amendment — would not agree with Mr. Berger.

Congressman Thaddeus Stevens, a major force in Congressional Reconstruction, introduced the measure in the House on behalf of the Joint Committee on Reconstruction. For him the theme of its first section was equality:[5]

I can hardly believe that any person can be found who will not admit that every one of these provisions is just. They are all asserted, in some form or other, in our Declaration or organic law. But the Constitution limits only the action of Congress, and is not a limitation on the States. This amendment supplies that defect, and allows Congress to correct the unjust legislation of the States, so far that the law which operates upon one man shall operate *equally* upon all. Whatever law punishes a white man for a crime shall punish the black man precisely in the same way. . . . Whatever law protects the white man shall afford "equal" protection to the black man. Whatever means of redress is afforded to one shall be afforded to all. Whatever law allows the white man to testify in court shall allow the man of color to do the same.

Then he noted, "Some answer, 'Your civil rights bill does the same things.' That is partly [note *only partly*] true. . . ."[6] Thus for Stevens, too, the amendment went farther than the 1866 legislation.

Certainly, as Mr. Berger shows, Stevens recognized that his "bright dream" of freedom "from every vestige of . . . inequality" was not then politically possible — that he had to accept less than the

---

[5] *Ibid.*, 2459.

[6] *Ibid.*, 2459.

"principles of [the] great Declaration [of Independence]."[7] Still Mr. Berger offers no evidence, and I find none, indicating that in Stevens' view the proposed amendment fell short of full equality for Blacks except with respect to suffrage.[8] That short-fall of course was immediately made good by the Fifteenth Amendment.

Senator Jacob Howard introduced the proposed Fourteenth Amendment in the Senate on behalf of the Joint Committee. His position is light years away from Mr. Berger's. First the Senator discussed at length the Privileges and Immunities Clause of Article IV, Section 2, of the Constitution as interpreted in the old opinion in *Corfield* v. *Coryell*.[9] From this he thought "we may gather some intimation of what probably" the clause will ultimately be found to mean. Then he continued,[10] "To these privileges and immunities, whatever they may be — for they are not and cannot be fully defined in their entire extent and precise nature — to these should be added the personal rights guarantied and secured by the first eight amendments of the Constitution. . . ." Obviously Senator Howard was unaware of the view that the new privileges clause constituted merely a reference to the 1866 Civil Rights Act. He saw far more in it than that — and he, like Stevens and Bingham, were members of the Joint Committee on Reconstruction which produced the amendment.

What these three gentlemen — the chief congressional sponsors of the Fourteenth Amendment — had in common was that none of them supposed that they were merely constitutionalizing the provisions of the Civil Rights Act. They obviously were far from agreement, however, on what in fact the proposed amendment meant. Indeed, in view of their mutually incompatible explanations, one would think they were talking about three different measures. This variance no doubt reflects disagreement within the Joint Committee and within the Republican Party itself. This dissension apparently is the reason why the Republican majority — in the midst of the Senate debates — in effect adjourned the Senate and transferred the discussion from the Senate floor to the secrecy of their party caucus. There, it seems, they agreed to disagree, but to do so silently. For

---

[7] *Ibid.*, 2459.

[8] "In all probability, the disappointment of . . . Stevens centered on failure to make any provision for negro suffrage. . . ." Alexander Bickel, "The Original Understanding and the Segregation Decision," 69 *Harvard Law Review* 1, 45-46 (1955).

[9] 6 *Fed. Cas.* 546 (No. 3, 230) (1825).

[10] *Congressional Globe*, 39th Congress, 1st Session 2765 (1866).

thereafter one finds — apart from vague generalities — no Republican floor discussion of the meaning of Section 1 of the proposed amendment.

As Senator Hendricks, a Democrat, put it:[11]

A caucus was called, and we witnessed the astounding spectacle of the withdrawal, for the time, of a great legislative measure, touching the Constitution itself, from the Senate, that it might be decided in the secret councils of a party. For three days the Senate Chamber was silent, but the discussions were transferred to another room of the Capitol, with closed doors and darkened windows, where party leaders might safely contend for a political and party policy.

And so it was that at the end of the Senate debate, Hendricks — referring *inter alia* to Howard's initial speech — observed,[12] ". . . I have not heard any Senator accurately define, what are the rights and immunities of citizenship. . . . We do not know, the Senator from Michigan says."

So, too, Senator Reverdy Johnson, perhaps the leading constitutional lawyer of his day, said,[13]

I am decidedly in favor of the first part of the section which defines what citizenship shall be, and in favor of that part of the section which denies to a State the right to deprive any person of life, liberty, or property without due process of law, but I think it quite objectionable to provide that 'no State shall make or enforce any law which shall abridge the privileges or immunities of citizens of the United States,' simply because I do not understand what will be the effect of that.

Earlier, just before the House concluded its debate on the proposed amendment, Congressman Robert S. Hale, a Moderate Republican, had been highly critical of its "extremely vague, loose, and indefinite provisions. . . ."[14] He tried hard and skillfully to get Bingham to face that problem. One must conclude that he succeeded only in demonstrating that his colleague was either muddleheaded or (like the Senate later) determined to avoid divisive issues.[15]

The vexing problem for the framers and sponsors of the Fourteenth Amendment was to surmount Radical, Moderate, and Conservative Republican disagreements and to achieve ratification by three-fourths of the states with all their varied views and interests.

---

[11] *Ibid.*, 2938. See also Senator Saulsbury's remarks at *ibid.*, 2869.

[12] *Ibid.*, 3039.

[13] *Ibid.*, 3041.

[14] *Ibid.*, 1063, 1064. Later in a few hours on a single day, the House would approve Senate changes without major discussion.

[15] *Ibid.*, 1063 *et seq.*

The solution, it seems, was calculated ambiguity with high-blown rhetoric that promised to protect Blacks somehow in some unspecified degree.

Given this confusion and unresolved discord among those who produced the amendment, no wonder scholars and judges have found so many conflicting meanings in it. For example, Mr. Justice Field discovered that it incorporated "the pursuit of happiness" which in turn included laissez-faire economics.[16] Horace Flack and Mr. Justice Black found rather that it incorporated the Bill of Rights[17] — while Professor Charles Fairman found that it did not.[18] Professor William Crosskey repudiated Fairman's findings and conclusions, but in a manner completely incompatible with the views of Messrs. Flack and Black.[19] Howard Jay Graham and Jacobus ten Broek — unlike Field, Flack, Black and Crosskey — find the key to the amendment in its "antislavery origins," which include a large tincture of natural law.[20] Mr. Berger finds the key in the Civil Rights Act of 1866. "Most constitutional lawyers" think Section 1 of the amendment has nothing to do with suffrage;[21] the Warren Court thought otherwise.[22] Mr. Justice Bradley found it compatible with blatant male chauvinism;[23] others have found the opposite[24] — to say nothing of "liberty of contract,"[25] the "fair value" doctrine,[26] "separate but equal,"[27] busing,[28] obscenity,[29] and so on *ad infinitum*.

---

[16] *Butchers' Union Co.* v. *Crescent City Co.*, 111 U.S. 746, 757 (1884).

[17] H. Flack, *The Adoption of the Fourteenth Amendment* (1980); *Adamson* v. *California*, 332 U.S. 46, 68 (1947).

[18] "Does the Fourteenth Amendment Incorporate the Bill of Rights?" 2 *Stanford Law Review* 5 (1949).

[19] "Charles Fairman, 'Legislative History', and the Constitutional Limitations on State Authority," 22 *University of Chicago Law Review* 1 (1954). For Fairman's "Reply" see *ibid.* at 144.

[20] See ten Broek, *The Antislavery Origins of the Fourteenth Amendment* (1951).

[21] Mr. Berger agrees with what Professor Gerald Gunther sees as the view of "most constitutional lawyers" that Mr. Justice Harlan (the second) was correct in concluding that Section 1 of the Fourteenth Amendment does not cover suffrage rights. See Gunther, Book Review, *Wall Street Journal*, November 5, 1977, at 4.

[22] For example, *Reynolds* v. *Sims*, 377 U.S. 533 (1964).

[23] *Bradwell* v. *Illinois*, 83 U.S. 130, 141 (1872).

[24] See, for example, *Frontiero* v. *Richardson*, 411 U.S. 677 (1973).

[25] *Lochner* v. *New York*, 198 U.S. 45 (1895).

[26] *Smyth* v. *Ames*, 169 U.S. 466 (1898).

[27] *Plessy* v. *Ferguson*, 163 U.S. 537 (1896).

[28] *Swann* v. *Charlotte-Mecklenburg Board of Education*, 402 U.S. 1 (1971).

[29] *Miller* v. *California*, 413 U.S. 5 (1973).

The babel of voices in the 39th Congress provides at least scattered support for many different views, but a consensus on very little.[30]   On one thing there was genuine agreement; namely, the citizenship-by-birth provision.   Beyond that, in Section 1 of the Fourteenth Amendment the "fathers" seem to have recognized that, if they were to accomplish anything, they had to eschew specifics. Thus the Privileges or Immunities Clause protects something that is nowhere defined.   It is an empty vessel, meaning only as much as one is willing to pretend it means.[31]   The 39th Congress might just as well have provided, "No state shall make or enforce any law abridging X with respect to citizens of the United States."   The Equal Protection Clause can hardly be taken to mean what it seems to say: that *no* legislative classification of people — according to their different needs, faults, virtues, or whatever — is permissible.   Obviously it must mean less than that, if the legislative process is not to be gutted, but how much less is not revealed.   The Due Process Clause — vague in itself — had been quite clearly defined by a common-law tradition running back to Magna Carta.   But is that definition what the 39th Congress had in mind?   What was there in the mid-1860s to suggest that either Congress or the American people felt a great need — so suddenly out of the blue — for *general*, federal supervision of state court procedure, ie. in matters unrelated to race?[32]

---

[30] This seems equally true of the press understanding of the amendment and therefore, presumably, of the public (and perhaps the ratifiers') understanding.   See K. C. Cerny, "Appendix to the Opinion of the Court," 6 *Hastings Constitutional Law Quarterly* 455 (1979).

[31] The privileges clause is so devoid of meaning that with one exception, *Colgate* v. *Harvey*, 296 U.S. 404 (1935) — soon overruled in *Madden* v. *Kentucky*, 309 U.S. 83 (1940) — the Supreme Court has never upheld any claim based upon it.

[32] One does not forget that in this era the Supreme Court was at a very low point in public esteem because of its disastrous decision in *Dred Scott* v. *Sandford*, 19 Howard 393 (1857).   It was hardly then deemed a bastion of freedom.   Professor R. G. McCloskey refers to this time as the "judicial ice age."   *The American Supreme Court*, 98 (1960).   Few would deny that the first sentence of the Fourteenth Amendment was designed to wipe out whatever remained of *Dred Scott*.   One must remember, too, the hostility of the 39th Congress vis-a-vis the judiciary, which ultimately brought no glory for the judges.   See *Ex parte McCardle*, 7 Wallace 506 (1869).   It is not by chance that the Bingham, Stevens, and Howard speeches, cited above, all emphasized that the proposed amendment would satisfy a special need; namely, *congressional* power to protect whatever it was that the proposal covered.   Congress sought to give itself full enforcing power.   Few in the 39th seem to have contemplated that the judiciary would play the chief, or even a major, enforcing role.

My own conclusion is that, apart from its first sentence, Section 1 of the Fourteenth Amendment is inherently meaningless, and that it can be saved rationally (if at all), only by reading it as part of a pattern manifest in all three Civil War Amendments, and in the vast array of other anti-racist measures of its era — especially the Civil Rights Acts of 1866, 1870, 1871, and 1875, the five Reconstruction Acts, and the various Freedmen's Bureau measures. In the long view surely each of these — like Jefferson's Declaration and Lincoln's Address at Gettysburg — reflect the abiding American dream: a dream we do not always honor, yet never quite forget.

In sum, the only reliable key we have to the meaning of the Fourteenth Amendment is that it was aimed at racism. This view is sustained by one of the oldest principles of construction; namely, the Rule in Heydon's Case[33] which holds that a clue to the meaning of ambiguous language in a formal document may properly be found in the circumstances that begot the document and the language in question. The immediate circumstance that produced both the Civil Rights Act of 1866 and the Fourteenth Amendment was the racism rampant in the southern Black Codes. Every one of them "confessed a determination to keep the freedmen in a permanent position of inferiority" — to substitute a kind of peonage for the slavery outlawed by Amendment Thirteen.[34]

Surely all will agree that only in Wonderland could the Fourteenth Amendment be said to mean what in fact it has meant: that nine (or five) lawyers in Washington are authorized to govern the rest of us as they see fit — be it in the *Plessy-Lochner*,[35] or the more recent manner.

---

[33] 3 Co. Rep. 7a, 76 Eng. Rep. 637 (Exch. 1584).

[34] S. E. Morison, H. S. Commager, and W. E. Leuchtenburg, *A Concise History of the American Republic*, Vol. 2, 328-329 (1977). Certainly the Fourteenth Amendment was adopted among other reasons to quiet doubts as to the constitutionality of the Civil Rights Act of 1866. What Mr. Berger seems to ignore is that the 39th Congress, which drafted that act, was not the same 39th Congress that drafted the amendment. The watershed was the presidential veto of the act, which enraged many, including not a few Moderates, and drove some of them into the arms of the Radicals. This defection strengthened the latter and apparently permitted them to use broader language in the amendment than in the act. Of course the veto did not give the Radicals a free hand. There was still much opposition in and out of Congress, and much need for bargaining. See J. A. Garraty, *The American Nation*, Chapter 16, and appended bibliography (1966).

[35] *Plessy* v. *Ferguson*, 163 U.S. 537 (1896); *Lochner* v. *New York*, 198 U.S. 45 (1805). Mr. Justice Holmes could see "hardly any limit but the sky" upon judicial abuse of the Fourteenth Amendment as the decisions stood in his day — which was only the beginning. *Baldwin* v. *Missouri*, 281 U.S. 586 (1930).

ADDENDUM

A generation ago Mr. Justice Brandeis and Professor Felix Frankfurter found so much judicial abuse of the Fourteenth Amendment that in their view one of its provisions (along with a similar provision in the Fifth Amendment) should be deleted. See Frankfurter's memoranda of his conversations with Brandeis in the Library of Congress. As Frankfurter put it to the public in 1924 (*Law and Politics*, 1939, p. 16),

An informed study of the work of the Supreme Court of the United States will probably lead to the conclusion that no nine men are wise enough and good enough to be entrusted with the power which the unlimited provisions of the due process clauses confer. We have had fifty years of experiment with the Fourteenth Amendment, and the centralizing authority lodged with the Supreme Court over the domestic affairs of forty-eight widely different states is an authority which it simply cannot discharge with safety either to itself or to the states. The due process clauses ought to go. It is highly significant that not a single constitution framed for English-speaking countries since the Fourteenth Amendment has embodied its provisions.

15 🎐 Foreign Reactions to American Experience with "Due Process of Law"

IT is not often that we are able to see our institutions as others see them. Among the most fundamental, and most characteristically American, of our constitutional provisions are the "due process of law" clauses. During the period of their existence, numerous basic laws have been adopted by English-speaking nations. Many, perhaps all, of them have drawn upon American governmental experience—but not one has ever adopted a "due process" clause. This is all the more striking because of the thoroughly English origins of "due process" in the universally revered Magna Charta.[1] Our experience with this ancient safeguard seems to have spoiled the British taste for it!

To put the matter shortly: the term "due process of law" does not appear in any past or present constitution of any British Dominion (including Ireland); in four instances, available evidence discloses that "due process" provisions were considered and expressly rejected; in four more cases, though no direct evidence of rejection has been found, provisions actually adopted suggest that "due process" must have been considered and found wanting. Furthermore, outside the British Dominions, it will be observed that the Japanese Constitution of 1946, the United Nations Universal Declaration of Human Rights, and the Draft Covenant on Civil and Political Rights—in the making of which the United States played a crucial role—rather conspicuously circumlocute in avoidance of "due process."

I

CONSTITUTIONAL PROCEEDINGS IN WHICH THERE IS EVIDENCE OF REJECTION OF DUE PROCESS

In connection with Clause 110 of a Draft Bill submitted to the

---

1. Chapter 29 of Magna Charta, 9 HEN. 3 (1225), uses the phrase "law of the land," but by Coke's time this was considered to be the equivalent of "due process of law," and thereafter the two were used interchangeably. See 2 Co. INST. *50-*51.

states by the Australian Federal Convention, the legislature of Tasmania suggested a due process provision obviously taken directly from our Fourteenth Amendment.[2] This proposal apparently reflects the influence of Mr. A. Inglis Clark, then Attorney General of Tasmania, who has been called "more American than the Americans in his admiration of American institutions."[3] But under the leadership of Mr. Isaacs, eventually to become one of the most powerful members of Australia's highest court, brisk opposition defeated it on the following grounds: (1) The origin of the provision was the Fourteenth Amendment, which "has given [the Americans] a great deal of trouble";[4] (2) It results in undue interference with the rights of the states;[5] (3) Its meaning is vague;[6] (4) "We do not want a clause in our Constitution which could only be carried in America by force of arms";[7] and, (5) "Why should these words be inserted? They would be a reflection on our civilization. Have any of the colonies of Australia ever attempted to deprive any person of life, liberty, or property without due process of law?"[8]

The Government of Ireland Bill of 1893 as originally introduced by His Majesty's Government contained a clause clearly inspired by the due process language of our Fifth Amendment.[9] Opposition to it in the House of Commons was extremely vigorous. One opponent objected that "Nobody seemed to understand what . . . [the words 'due process of law'] really meant. No American lawyer had yet been able absolutely to tell how much they embraced."[10] Another hoped to "elicit from the Government the meaning of those mysterious words. . . . they had it on good authority that this particular safeguard operated very badly in . . . [the American] Constitution."[11]

Unsuccessful in their attempts to strike out "due process" entirely, the opposition offered a series of amendments for the purpose of add-

---

2. 1 OFFICIAL RECORD OF THE DEBATES, AUSTRALIAN FEDERAL CONVENTION, THIRD SESSION, MELBOURNE, 1898, at 664.

3. WISE, THE MAKING OF THE AUSTRALIAN COMMONWEALTH 75 (1913).

4. 1 OFFICIAL RECORD OF THE DEBATES, AUSTRALIAN FEDERAL CONVENTION, THIRD SESSION, MELBOURNE, 1898, at 667.

5. *Id.* at 667, 675, 682, 683.

6. *Id.* at 678, 683, 687-688.

7. *Id.* at 685-686.

8. *Id.* at 688.

9. Cl. 4, Subsec. 6.

10. 13 PARL. DEB. 1083 (4th ser. 1893).

11. *Id.* at 1113-1114.

ing clarifying language to it. The Government finally agreed to insert the words "in accordance with settled principles and precedents" after "due process of law."[12] The debate on these "clarifying" proposals is particularly interesting because in the course of it, Mr. James Bryce, who was generally understood to be the author of the original provision,[13] was induced to give the following explanation of due process:

> [This expression] . . . is one that cannot be defined. [Opposition cheers]. Yes, it cannot be defined, and it ought not to be defined, because a definition would destroy its value. . . . We are not dealing here with a new matter—with an ambiguous matter. We are dealing with words which have received in the Courts of the United States a perfectly clear, perfectly uniform, perfectly definite, and perfectly unambiguous construction.[14]

Though the result in the House of Commons was something of a standoff ("due process" stayed in, but only after the addition to it of taming language), the entire measure came to defeat in the House of Lords.[15] And the next Government of Ireland Bill was introduced in 1914 without the offending provision. But Mr. Astor, "the son of an expatriated American," moved to insert a "due process" clause including the "clarifying" language of the 1893 Bill.[16] This time the Government took the floor against it, and in doing so called out some of its most powerful members, including Prime Minister Asquith himself and the Solicitor General, Sir John Simon. According to Sir John:

> . . . we are . . . raising a number of questions which may involve litigation and judicial decisions hereafter. . . . The first thing . . . to consider is whether or not . . . this Clause is . . . reasonably susceptible of judicial determination from time to time. . . .
> We do regard it as a serious thing to introduce into the Bill matters which, it seems to us, are not really susceptible of judicial examination, which undoubtedly would increase the amount of litigation and disputes, and which really would not lead ultimately, as it seems to us, to definiteness and precision in the powers of this [the Irish] Parliament. . . .

---

12. *Id.* at 1119, 1125, 1130, 1198, 1206-1218.
13. See, for example, *id.* at 1082-1083.
14. *Id.* at 1153-1154.
15. 17 *id.* at 649.
16. 42 H.C. DEB. 2082 (5th ser. 1912).

Inasmuch as these words, as we believe, cannot do other than lead to fantastic disputations in the Courts of Justice . . . [they should be omitted].[17]

The Prime Minister pointed out that language of this type does not appear in any Dominion constitution. To use it here

. . . would be an acknowledgment that in the case of . . . Ireland alone . . . it is necessary to fetter the free action of the responsible legislature. . . . [This language is] full of ambiguity abounding in pitfalls and certainly provocative of every kind of frivolous litigation. . . . If you introduce into your Bill a limitation of this kind . . . you are really enthroning the judiciary as the ultimate tribunal of appeal. There is no question whatever about that. Look at what is going on now in the United States. . . .
[He then refers to the language as] . . . ambiguous and dubious . . . the ultimate interpretation of which must fall on the judicial bench, with the result that you may have one of the most undesirable conflicts it is possible to contemplate, a conflict between the judiciary on the one side and the Legislature and public opinion on the other.[18]

Mr. Munro-Ferguson observed that:

It is in order to remove those grave scandals and difficulties which have resulted from those words being in the American Constitution, that is the primary cause of Colonel Roosevelt's campaign at the present time. . . . the rule of lawyers in a purely professional capacity has a really bad effect.[19]

The socio-economic implications of the problem were stressed by Mr. John Ward, who said:

. . . we may take it for granted that this amendment is put forward more for the purpose of opposing democratic legislation, and for the purpose of stifling democratic effort with reference to social reform and the great economic disputes which are raging at the present time between different classes of society, than for protecting any immediate vested interest. . . .
[What the Gentlemen] . . . are suggesting now is that we should have

17. *Id.* at 2085-2088.
18. *Id.* at 2230-2232.
19. *Id.* at 2266.

... not a detailed Constitution, but a sort of general provision so as to enable the Courts . . . to question and decide whether any law passed . . . dealing with the subject of individual liberty and great economic questions, such as have been similarly decided in the United States, may be taken from the floor of that House . . . and be decided by pundits on the benches. . . .[20]

Mr. Astor's proposed "due process" amendment was defeated by a vote of 299 to 197.[21]

In the course of the post-World-War II constitution-making efforts in India, the Constituent Assembly's Advisory Committee on Fundamental Rights recommended the following in Clause 9:[22]

No person shall be deprived of his life or liberty without due process of law.

But the Drafting Committee inserted the word "personal" before the word "liberty," and substituted "except according to procedure established by law" for "without due process of law."[23] "The only reason which was given by the Drafting Committee [for the substitution] was that the words 'due process of law' is [sic] not specific and the . . . [substituted language] as used in the Japanese Constitution is more specific."[24]

On the convention floor, a motion was made to reinstate the due process language.[25] Thereupon Mr. S. A. K. Ayyar, a member of the Drafting Committee, pointed out that the English interpretation of "due process" as relating only to procedure had not been followed in the United States:[26]

To-day, according to Professor Willis, the expression means what the Supreme Court says what [sic] it means in any particular case. It is just possible, some ardent democrats may have a greater faith in the judiciary than in the conscious will expressed through the enactments of a popular legislature. Three gentlemen or five gentlemen, sitting as a court of law, and stating what exactly is due process ac-

---

20. *Id.* at 2217-2218.
21. *Id.* at 2268.
22. 7 INDIAN CONSTITUENT ASSEMBLY DEBATES 854. See also SHUKLA, THE CONSTITUTION OF INDIA 34 (1950).
23. *Ibid.*
24. *Id.* at 855.
25. *Id.* at 843.
26. *Id.* at 853-854.

cording to them in any particular case . . . may appeal to certain democrats more than the expressed wishes of the legislature or the action
of an executive responsible to the legislature. In the development of
the doctrine of "due process", the United States Supreme Court has
not adopted a consistent view at all and the decisions are conflicting.
One decision very often reversed another decision. I would challenge
any member of the Bar with a deep knowledge of the cases in the
United States Supreme Court to say that there is anything like uniformity in regard to the interpretation of "due process" . . . .

After further remarks in similar vein,[27] the proposal to reinstate the
challenged language was defeated.[28]

The United Nations' Universal Declaration Of Human Rights is
not a constitution, of course, but simply a statement of principles.
Still it is noteworthy that due process language does not appear in the
Declaration, though it was considered for use during the draft stages
of the following articles:[29]

Article 9:

No one shall be subjected to arbitrary arrest, detention or exile.

Article 17:

1. Everyone has a right to own property alone as well as in association with others.
2. No one shall be arbitrarily deprived of his property.

Unlike the Declaration, the United Nations Draft Covenant On
Civil And Political Rights, when completed, will contemplate the imposition of legal obligations upon signatory nations. It does not yet
contain provisions with respect to property, but Article 9(1) of the latest
version, like the corresponding provision in the Declaration, rather
pointedly avoids due process terminology:[30]

Everyone has the right to liberty and security of person. No one shall

---

27. *Id*. at 843-853, 855-857.

28. *Id*. at 1001.

29. *Draft Outline of an International Bill of Rights* E/CN.4/21 (U.N. Econ. & Social
Council Official Records, 10th Sess.) 43 (1947). See also *id., Annex F.*

30. See *Report of the Tenth Session of the Commission on Human Rights* E/2573,
E/CN.4-705 (U.N. Econ. & Social Council Official Records, 18th Sess., Supp. 7) 67
(April 16, 1954).

be subjected to arbitrary arrest or detention. No one shall be deprived of his liberty except on such grounds and in accordance with such procedure as are established by law.

A rejected provision of the Draft Covenant relating to property did include a due process clause. Surely it is significant that during discussion thereof the United States moved to substitute the term "arbitrarily" for the phrase "without due process of law."[30a]

II

Constitutional Proceedings in Which It May Be Inferred That Due Process Was Considered and Rejected

The Irish Constitutions of 1922 and 1937, the Government of India Act of 1935, and the current Draft Constitution of Pakistan all contain provisions resembling our due process clauses. Unfortunately, the draftsmen of these provisions seem to have left no explanation of the origin of those provisions; nor do the recorded proceedings of the adopting assemblies throw any light upon the matter. But surely it is not unreasonable to suppose that, when draftsmen used such phrases as "save in accordance with law,"[31] "save in due course of law,"[32] and "save by authority of law"[33] in clauses obviously inspired by Magna Charta and its offshoots, they must have been trying to avoid the well-known pitfalls of due process language.

The case perhaps may be put a bit more strongly with respect to the Government of India Act of 1935. With respect to it, Parliament's Joint Committee to "consider the future Government of India" reported that:[34]

> The question of so-called fundamental rights, which was much discussed at the three Round Table Conferences, was brought to our notice. . . . [Cynicism aside] there are . . . strong practical arguments against the proposal, which may be put in the form of a dilemma: for either the declaration of rights is of so abstract a nature that it has no

---

30a. *Id* at 7-9.

31. Irish Free State Const. Art. 6 (1922); Const. of Ireland Art. 40, § 4 (1), Art. 40, § 5 (1937); see 2 Peaslee, Constitutions of Nations 259 (1950).

32. Const. of Ireland Art. 38, § 1 (1937); see Peaslee, *supra* note 31 at 258.

33. Government of India Act of 1935 § 299.

34. 1 Report of the Joint Committee on Indian Constitutional Reform pt. 1, at 215 ¶ 366 (1934).

legal effect of any kind, or its legal effect will be to impose an em-
barrassing restriction on the powers of the Legislature and to create a
grave risk that a large number of laws may be declared invalid by the
Courts. . . . An examination of the lists [of proposed fundamental
rights] shows very clearly indeed that this risk would be far from
negligible.

A later paragraph observed that:

> . . . some general provision should be inserted in the Constitution
> Act safeguarding private property against expropriation, in order to
> quiet doubts . . . aroused . . . [by certain Indian utterances]. [But]
> . . . much the same difficulties would be presented as those which we
> have discussed above in relation to fundamental rights.[35]

Accordingly, there was no general provision concerning life and liberty
in the Government of India Act of 1935. It did, however, contain
the following in Section 299:

> No person shall be deprived of his property in British India save by
> authority of law.

It has already been seen that the Japanese Constitution of 1946
influenced the Indians in their avoidance of due process language.
The drafting of the pertinent provision in Japan is unusually interesting because there can be no doubt of the great weight of American influence upon the whole project. In September of 1945, the Japanese
Prime Minister "was informed that the Supreme Commander [General
MacArthur] regarded revision of the constitution as a matter of first
importance."[36] The Japanese responded with a "tentative plan," which
was rejected by SCAP. The latter thereupon prepared and presented
to the Japanese Government for its consideration a proposed draft.[37]
This is still classified as "Secret" in the Defense Department's Records
Branch, but we may judge of its contents and SCAP's—as well as the
Japanese—attitude toward due process from the redrafts (in the official English translation) as resubmitted by the Japanese to the Supreme Commander:[38]

---

35. *Id* at 217 ¶ 369.
36. 1 POLITICAL REORIENTATION OF JAPAN 91 (Rep. of Gov't Sec., SCAP 1950).
37. *Id* at 101-105.
38. 2 *id.* (app.) at 626, 632, 638.

1. First Japanese Government Draft:

> Article 28.   All of the people shall not be deprived of life or liberty, nor shall any criminal penalty be imposed upon them, except according to law.

2. Second Japanese Government Draft:

> Article XXX.   No person shall be deprived of life or liberty, nor shall any criminal penalty be imposed, except according to procedure established by the Diet, nor shall any person be denied the right of access to the courts.

3. Third Japanese Government Draft:

> Article XXVIII.   No person shall be deprived of life or liberty, nor shall any other criminal penalty be imposed, except according to procedure established by law.

The latter is the final form of the provision as it appears in Article 31 of the present Japanese Constitution.   It will be noted that, probably as a further precaution against any repetition of our due process experience, the term "property" is not included in this provision along with "life" and "liberty."[39]

The draft Constitution of Israel provides that "No one shall be tried save by due process of law."[40]   But this cannot be considered an import from America.   The Israelis have used the phrase in a context which makes clear their effort to avoid our experience by confining the term to its orthodox, procedural meaning in criminal trials.

Finally it may be noted that the constitution of Liberia (1847), in Article I, Section 8, provides that "No person shall be deprived of life, liberty, property or privilege, but by judgment of his peers or the law of the land."[41]   This version of due process, a rather literal translation from Magna Charta,[42] had commonly been used in our early state constitutions.   While no record of the proceedings which produced the Liberian Constitution seems to be available in this

---

39. See JAPANESE CONST. Art. XXIX, XXX (1946), *id.* at 672-673.

40. Art. 13, § 6 (1946), as reproduced in 3 PEASLEE, CONSTITUTIONS OF NATIONS 745 (1950).

41. See 2 PEASLEE, *supra* note 40 at 365.

42. See note 1 *supra.*

country, we do know that the document's principal author was a
famous American law professor—Simon Greenleaf.[43] It is significant
that our difficulties with due process had not yet materialized when
Professor Greenleaf offered his constitutional suggestions to the people
of Liberia. To complete the story, we may note that one constitution, now long dead, did contain a due process clause taken directly
from our Fifth Amendment—that of the Confederate States of
America.[44]

CONCLUSION

If in view of our experience the outside world has shown skepticism
with respect to an ancient precept, that same attitude is not unknown
at home. When the due process clause of the Fourteenth Amendment
was first pressed upon the Supreme Court in what was to become the
peculiarly American, *i.e.*, substantive sense, the argument was dismissed as frivolous:

> We are not without judicial interpretation, therefore, both State
> and National, of the meaning of this clause. And it is sufficient to say
> that under no construction of that provision that we have ever seen, or
> any that we deem admissible, can the restraint imposed by the State
> . . . upon the exercise of their trade by the butchers . . . be held to be a
> deprivation of property within the meaning of that provision.[45]

Only two of the four dissenters in the case relied heavily upon due
process.[46]

Four years later, in the crucial case of *Munn* v. *Illinois*,[47] questions
which counsel raised under the newly improvised construction of the
Fourteenth Amendment were dismissed as essentially political in
character.[48] But dissent was persistent. The plain fact is that laissez-
faire economics had engulfed the bar, and due process was its constitutional handmaiden.[49] Where the bar led, the bench was soon to
follow. First by dicta,[50] and then at the turn of the century by de-

---

43. 1 HUBERICH, THE POLITICAL AND LEGISLATIVE HISTORY OF LIBERIA 823, 836 (1947).
44. Art. I, § 9, cl. 16; see Va. Acts app. (1861-1862).
45. The Slaughter House Cases, 16 Wall. 36, 80-81 (U.S. 1873).
46. *Id.* at 116, 122.
47. 94 U.S. 113 (1877).
48. *Id.* at 134.
49. For an interesting account, see TWISS, LAWYERS AND THE CONSTITUTION (1942).
50. See, *e.g.*, Powell v. Pennsylvania, 127 U.S. 678, 684 (1888); Mugler v. Kansas, 123
U.S. 623, 661 (1887).

cision,[51] due process as the embodiment of laissez-faire economics became the law of the land—but not without dissent.

Mr. Justice Holmes' thirty-year war against that new construction of the ancient concept is a twice-told tale.[52] It will be enough to note that since 1937 Holmes' position has been accepted by the Supreme Court without dissent[53]—though the older tradition still prevails in some state tribunals.[54] But if at the national level "due process" has been emptied of its controversial economic content, it is now the center of a civil liberty storm.[55] A new generation of judges is in the process of putting another heady new brew into the ancient vessel.

---

51. *The Minnesota Rate Case*, Chicago, M. & St. P. Ry. v. Minnesota, 134 U.S. 418 (1890), is generally considered to be the turning point.

52. See, for example, Holmes' famous dissenting opinions in Baldwin v. Missouri, 281 U.S. 586, 595 (1930); Adkins v. Children's Hospital, 261 U.S. 525, 567 (1923); Lochner v. New York, 198 U.S. 45, 74 (1905).

53. See Lincoln Fed. Labor Union v. Northwestern Iron and Metal Co., 335 U.S. 525 (1949).

54. See Mendelson, *Smyth v. Ames in State Courts, 1942-1952*, 37 MINN. L. REV. 159, 161-166 (1953); Paulsen, *The Persistence of Substantive Due Process in the States*, 34 MINN. L. REV. 91, 92-93 (1950).

55. See, *e.g.*, Irvine v. California, 347 U.S. 128 (1954); Wolf v. People, 338 U.S. 25 (1949); Adamson v. People, 332 U.S. 46 (1947).

16 ⚜ A Missing Link in the Evolution of Due Process

On the eve of the American Revolution Blackstone could comment that "so great . . . is the regard of the [English] law for private property . . . it will not authorize the least violation of it; no, not even for the general good of the whole community."[1] A similar concern for proprietary interests soon found expression on this side of the Atlantic in what Professor Corwin has called "The Basic Doctrine of American Constitutional Law";[2] namely, the "doctrine of vested interests." The general purport of this concept was that "the effect of legislation on existing property rights was a primary test of its validity. . . ."[3]

In brief a sense of insecurity among the comfortable classes in the face of early American democracy led courts at first to invoke natural law and social contract[4] principles for the insulation of vested interests from legislative regulation. But extra-constitutional restraints upon government were hardly compatible with written constitutions. For this and other reasons, after flirting with ex post facto[5] and contract clauses[6] and with the separation of powers[7], the doctrine of vested interests finally settled in the law of the land or due process[8] provisions that were (and are) ubiquitous in American constitutions.

Granting all this as accepted learning, the present thesis is that by the end of the eighteenth century the orthodox procedural meaning of due process was too thoroughly established semantically, contextually[9] and historically[10] to accommodate a radically new, i.e. substantive,

---

1. 1 BLACKSTONE, COMMENTARIES 139.
2. Corwin, *The Basic Doctrine of American Constitutional Law*, 12 MICH. L. REV. 247 (1914). See also Corwin, *The Doctrine of Due Process of Law before the Civil War*, 24 HARV. L. REV. 366, 460 (1911).
3. CORWIN, LIBERTY AGAINST GOVERNMENT 72 (1948).
4. See, *e.g.*, Calder v. Bull, 3 U.S. (3 Dall.) 386 (1798); Goshen v. Stonington, 4 Conn. 209, 225 (1822).
5. See, *e.g.*, Calder v. Bull, 3 U.S. (3 Dall.) 386 (1798); *cf.* Satterlee v. Matthewson, 27 U.S. (2 Pet.) 380, 415 (1829) (note appended to Mr. Justice Johnson's opinion).
6. See, *e.g.*, Fletcher v. Peck, 10 U.S. (6 Cranch) 87 (1810); *cf.* Charles River Bridge v. Warren Bridge, 36 U.S. (11 Pet.) 420 (1837).
7. See Lewis v. Webb, 3 Maine 326 (1825); Bayard v. Singleton, 1 N.C. (1 Mar.) 42 (1787); Bowman v. Middleton, 1 S.C. 252 (1792); Staniford v. Barry, 1 Aik. 314 (Vt. 1825).
8. The term "law of the land" is a literal translation from the original Magna Charta. In later versions, *i.e.* reissues, the term becomes "due process of law." By Coke's time the two phrases had become interchangeable. See 2 COKE, INSTITUTES 50-51. In general our earliest constitutions contained the former expression while later usage tended to adopt the latter.
9. In our Federal Bill of Rights and in all of the early state constitutions "due process" and "law of the land" clauses are found in the midst of purely procedural provisions.
10. See, *e.g.*, 2 KENT, COMMENTARIES ON AMERICAN LAW 13 (14th ed. 1896); 2 STORY, CONSTITUTION § 1789 (3d ed. 1858). Professor Strong, running counter

meaning without some respectable constitutional go-between; namely, the separation of powers. Professor Corwin was well aware of the importance of separation principles in the development of the doctrine of vested interests.[11] But neither he nor his followers appear to have noticed the importance of those principles in the metamorphosis of due process.[12] The burden of the present effort is to show how that ancient procedural concept got its initial substantive impetus by absorbing separation of powers ideas—an impetus great enough to carry on eventually without recourse to separation doctrine. So viewed the latter was a vital link in the evolution of due process, not merely one of several fumbling steps that were tried and found wanting before vested interests finally found sanctuary in the fourteenth amendment.

To put it shortly orthodox due process meant that government could not punish, or "go against," a person except in a procedurally proper manner. Of course certain powers and processes belong to legislatures and others to the courts. In the old phraseology "To . . . compare the claims of the parties with the laws of the land before established, is in its nature a judicial act. But to . . . pass new rules for the regulation of new controversies, is in its nature, a legislative act; and if those rules interfere with the past, or the present, and do not look wholly to the future, they violate the definition of a law, 'as a rule of civil conduct'; because no rule of conduct can with consistency operate upon what occurred before the rule itself was promulgated."[13] Moreover while courts are created to apply the law retrospectively to *particular* persons in *particular* circumstances, the legislative function is to make "*general* and *public* law [of future application] equally binding upon every member of the community * * * under similar circumstances."[14]

---

to what he admits is the accepted view, undertakes to show that there were some threads of substantive meaning in due process in England prior to the Glorious Revolution and also in Colonial America. See STRONG, AMERICAN CONSTITUTIONAL LAW 43-49, 307 (1950).

11. Corwin, *The Basic Doctrine of American Constitutional Law*, 12 MICH. L. REV. 247, 259 (1914).

12. In a recent recapitulation of his previous efforts Professor Corwin appends a short footnote to his discussion of an early due process case to say, "It will be observed again how the principle of the separation of powers helps out this [due process?] argument," namely, that "when anybody is deprived of his conceded property rights . . . it is with a view to *punishing* him, which can only be done by judicial—i.e., 'due'—process . . . ." CORWIN, LIBERTY AGAINST GOVERNMENT 93 (1948). Interested in a much broader problem, Professor Corwin thus casually passes over the relationship which is the crux of the present paper. Indeed it is not clear to me that even the above quoted remarks refer to the connection between due process and separation. For his word "again" is supported by reference to another page where clearly Professor Corwin is not talking about due process at all, but rather about the connection between separation and the doctrine of vested interests. See also text and note 60 *infra*.

13. Merrill v. Sherburne, 1 N.H. 199, 204 (1818). See also Ogden v. Black-ledge, 6 U.S. (2 Cranch) 272, 277 (1804); Opinion of the Judges, 4 N.H. 565, 572 (1829).

14. Vanzant v. Waddell, 10 Tenn. 259, 270 (1829). See also Holden v. James, 11 Mass. 396 (1814).

(Emphasis added.) Accordingly if a legislature acts not in general and prospective terms, but retrospectively for a particular case, it encroaches upon the judicial process. This is the old problem of attainder and bills of pains and penalties. One whose vested right is disturbed by such "legislation" is hurt (punished) as the result of improper procedure. In striking it down a court merely enforces *process* requirements—though the substance of the measure is incidentally destroyed. This approach was especially relevant in the formative era of American law when, as Dean Pound has shown, legislatures deemed themselves "omnicompetent" even in the judicial domain. They "did not hesitate to enact statutes reversing judgments of the courts in particular cases. They sought to probate wills rejected by the courts. . . . By special laws they directed the details of local government for particular instances. They validated particular invalid marriages. They suspended the statute of limitations for a particular litigant in a particular case. They exempted a particular wrongdoer from liability for a particular wrong for which his neighbors would be held by the general law."[15] Such measures of special rather than general, and retrospective rather than prospective, application smack of the judicial decree. Some of them in essence are legislative adjudications. In disturbing vested rights they would be procedurally vulnerable for taking property by improper process, being among other things a repudiation of trial by jury and in effect bills of pains and penalties.

This problem and the separation approach to it are illustrated as early as 1787 in *Bayard* v. *Singleton*.[16] There, after confiscating by special act the land of certain royalists, the North Carolina legislature provided that actions for the recovery of such property should be dismissed by the courts upon motion. After some outside observations by Ashe, J.,[17] concerning the separation of powers, the court refused to honor the dismissal statute, observing according to the reporter:

> That by the constitution every citizen had undoubtedly a right to a decision of his property by a trial by jury. For that if the Legislature could take away this right, and require him to stand condemned in his property without a trial, it might with as much authority require his life to be taken away without a trial by jury. . . .[18]

Soon thereafter Magna Charter (Due Process?) was introduced into the formula. In *Bowman* v. *Middleton*[19] a South Carolina statute,

---

15. Pound, The Formative Era of American Law 39-40 (1950).
16. 1 N.C. (1 Mar.) 42 (1787).
17. *Id.* at 43.
18. *Id.* at 45.
19. 1 S.C. 252 (1792).

purporting to quiet title by confirming the claim of one of the contestants, was held invalid on the ground that:

> [P]laintiffs could claim no title under the act in question, as it was against common right, as well as against magna charta, to take away the freehold of one man and vest it in another, and that, too, to the prejudice of third persons, without any compensation, or even a trial by the jury of the country, to determine the right in question.[20]

Skipping for the moment some twenty-seven years brings us to the celebrated argument of Daniel Webster as counsel for Dartmouth College. His case was before the Supreme Court on federal question (contract clause) grounds which precluded consideration of state constitutional restraints.[21] Recognizing "the limits which bound the jurisdiction of the Court," Webster observed nevertheless that "it may assist in forming an opinion of [the] true nature and character [of the statutes altering Dartmouth's charter] to compare them with those fundamental principles, introduced into State governments for the purpose of limiting the exercise of legislative power. . . ."[22]

> One prohibition [Art. 15 of the New Hampshire Constitution] is "that no person shall be deprived of his property . . . but by judgment of his peers, or the law of the land". . . .
>
> Have the plaintiffs lost their franchises by "due course and due process of law?" On the contrary, are not these acts "particular acts of the legislature, which have no relation to the community in general, and which are rather sentences than laws?" By the law of the land, is most clearly intended, the general law; a law, which hears before it condemns; which proceeds upon inquiry, and renders judgment only after trial. The meaning is, that every citizen shall hold his life, liberty, property and immunities, under the protection of the general rules which govern society. Everything which may pass under the form of an enactment, is not, therefore, to be considered the law of the land. If this were so, acts of attainder, bills of pains and penalties, acts of confiscation, acts reversing judgments, and acts directly transferring one man's estate to another, legislative judgments, decrees and forfeitures, in all possible forms, would be the law of the land.[23]

In support of this argument that a legislature's performance of quasi-judicial acts is a violation of "the law of the land" and due process Webster cited *University v. Foy*.[24] There legislation purported to repeal an earlier grant of land to the university. Striking down the repealing measure the North Carolina Supreme Court had said:

---

20. *Id.* at 254.
21. Webster was uneasy about going to "Washington on a single point" and took steps to broaden his base in later litigation should he lose on the federal issue. 1 FUESS, DANIEL WEBSTER 225 (1930).
22. Dartmouth College v. Woodward, 17 U.S. (4 Wheat.) 518, 557-58 (1819). It is, of course, interesting and perhaps significant that the Court permitted such argument.
23. *Id.* at 561, 581.
24. 5 N.C. 58 (1805).

But one great and important reason which influences us in deciding this question is [the constitutional provision] "that no freeman ought to be . . . deprived of his life, liberty or property, but by the law of the land". . . . It seems to us to warrant a belief that members of a corporation as well as individuals shall not be so deprived . . . unless by a trial by Jury in a Court of Justice, according to the known and established rules of decision. . . . The property vested in the Trustees must remain for the uses intended for the University, until the Judiciary of the country in the usual and common form, pronounce them guilty of such acts, as will, in law, amount to a forfeiture of their rights or a dissolution of their body.[25]

The other case cited by Webster on this point was *Dash v. Van Kleeck*[26] in which both Thompson, J., and the great Kent, C. J., had used the separation of powers as a cloak to protect vested interests against legislative interference.[27] And they in turn had cited *Ogden v. Blackledge*[28] in which the Supreme Court of the United States had, as Kent put it, "considered the point too plain for argument, that a statute could not retrospect, so as to take away a vested civil right."[29] The supererogatory argument referred to began as follows:

To declare what the law is, or has been, is a judicial power; to declare what the law shall be, is legislative. One of the fundamental principles of all our governments is that the legislative power shall be separated from the judicial.[30]

The full significance of Webster's position can be appreciated only in contrast to the opinion below. There the Supreme Court of New Hampshire in then orthodox fashion had categorically rejected an unqualified substantive due process argument:

What statute does not either directly or indirectly interfere with property rights? The principle urged would probably make our whole statute book a dead letter.[31]

Webster's genius was that he saw in separation a device for giving due process a *manageable,* if expanded, meaning in an age not yet prepared to recognize only the sky as its limit. No court in 1819 could be expected to hold, and few lawyers to argue, that due process embodied (as Holmes later put it) Mr. Herbert Spencer's *Social Dynamics,* or anything like it. But imaginative lawyers could see that a court might be induced to give the old provision such familiar, quasi-procedural overtones as were implicit in separation and the old struggle against bills of attainder and bills of pains and penalties.

---

25. *Id.* at 87, 88, 89.
26. 7 Johns. 477 (N.Y. 1811).
27. *Id.* at 497-98, 507-08.
28. 6 U.S. (2 Cranch) 272 (1804).
29. 7 Johns. at 507-08.
30. 6 U.S. (2 Cranch) at 277.
31. Dartmouth College v. Woodward, 1 N.H. 111, 131 (1818).

Once this step was accomplished more expansive constructions might be in order!

Of course for jurisdictional reasons the Supreme Court in the *Dartmouth* case could not make use of a "law of the land" or "due process" clause, but a famous lawyer had made a point in a forum where all judges and lawyers could take notice of it. Within a decade the Tennessee Supreme Court, perhaps fastening upon Webster's emphasis on generality as a necessary characteristic of legislation, had started a line of cases the crux of which was that special or "partial" laws directly or indirectly interfering with property rights violate "the law of the land" clause of the state constitution.[32] In due course the Tennessee court made more plain—what doubtless was implicit from the beginning—that while talking "law of the land," it was thinking separation.[33]

Meanwhile amalgamation of separation and due process had been accomplished in the jurisprudence of states far more influential in the legal world than Tennessee. When South Carolina tried to create a new medical school by transferring the "rights, powers and duties" of an existing institution to a new one, it met a "law of the land" barrier in *State v. Heyward*.[34] There, after noting that while in England Parliament was supreme, in South Carolina the separation of powers prevailed, the court said:

> An Act of the Legislature which takes from one man his property, or rights, and gives it, or them, to another, on a claim of right, is the exercise of Judicial power, which is [vested in the judiciary] * * * the State . . . cannot resume her grant, or transfer it to another, until a forfeiture of the grant is judicially ascertained. . . . It would hence seem that . . . a corporation can only be deprived of its powers, rights, privileges, and immunities by a judgment of forfeiture, obtained according to the *law of the land.*—By this, I understand a trial had, and a judgment pronounced, in the court of law of this State.[35] (Emphasis added.)

In the following year (1833) Chief Justice Ruffin in *Hoke v. Henderson*[36] delivered the classic separation-due process opinion. By general act North Carolina had made certain public offices elective rather than appointive as they had been previously. The effect was to deprive Hoke of an appointive position. Finding that Hoke had had a property right in his office, the Chief Justice for his court held that

> Whenever an act of Assembly therefore is a decision of titles between individuals, or classes of individuals, although it may in terms purport to be the introduction of a new rule of title, it is essentially a judgment against the old claim of right; which is not a legislative, but a judicial

---

32. Vanzant v. Waddell, 10 Tenn. 259, 270-71 (1829).
33. Jones v. Perry, 18 Tenn. 59, 71-80 (1836).
34. 15 S.C. 389 (1832).
35. *Id.* at 410, 412.
36. 15 N.C. 1 (1833).

function. . . . The Legislature cannot act in that character; and therefore, although their act has the forms of law, it is not one of those *laws of the land,* by which alone a freeman can be *deprived* of his *property.*[37]

In the original edition of his *Commentaries on American Law* in 1826 Kent had defined due process in what appears to be purely ortho-dox, procedural terms: "it means law in its regular course of adminis-tration through the courts of justice."[38] In the editions that appeared after Hoke's case Kent added a footnote to the above definition in which he commended Ruffin's "elaborate opinion" as being "replete with sound constitutional doctrines." So indorsed in the *Commentaries Hoke v. Henderson* was insured a wide circulation. Under the authority of such great names as Ruffin and Kent it could not fail to carry enormous weight.

Within a decade Chief Justice Gibson of Pennsylvania in *Norman v. Heist,*[39] without citing any of the foregoing cases, wrote an opinion in which he came to similar conclusions:

> [T]he Constitution . . . declares that no citizen shall be deprived of his life, liberty or *property,* unless by the judgment of his peers or the law of the land. What law? Undoubtedly, a pre-existent rule of conduct, declarative of a penalty for a prohibited act; not an *ex post facto* rescript or decree made for the occasion. The design of the convention was to exclude arbitrary power from every branch of the government; and there would be no exclusion of it, if such rescripts or decrees were allowed to take effect in the form of a statute.[40]

Thus a full generation before adoption of the fourteenth amendment three of the four leading ante-bellum state court judges, Kent, Ruffin and Gibson, had put their stamps of approval upon the absorption of the separation concept by due process.[41]

Professor Corwin considers the "great case of *Wynehamer v. State of New York*[42] . . . a new starting point in the history of [substantive] due process . . . ."[43] The difficulty with this evaluation is that in hold-ing a prohibition act invalid on due process grounds the court empha-sized the failure of the measure to distinguish between "liquors existing when it took effect as a law, and such as might thereafter be acquired . . . all the judges [being] of opinion that it would be competent for the Legislature to pass such an act [that] should be plainly and dis-

---

37. *Id.* at 13, 15.
38. 2 KENT, COMMENTARIES ON AMERICAN LAW 13 (14th ed. 1896).
39. 5 W. & S. 171 (Pa. 1843).
40. *Id.* at 173. See also Sharpless v. Philadelphia, 21 Pa. 147 (1853).
41. Chief Justice Shaw comes quite close to this position in Commonwealth v. Alger, 61 Mass. (7 Cush.) 53, 102-04 (1851). Earlier in Holden v. James, 11 Mass. 396 (1814), a special, retrospective statute had been invalidated via a constitutional clause similar to the more common due process provision.
42. 13 N.Y. 378 (1856).
43. See CORWIN, LIBERTY AGAINST GOVERNMENT 101-02 (1948).

tinctly prospective as to the property on which it should operate."[44] Thus like all of the cases discussed above *Wynehamer* turns on the judicial, i.e., particular or retrospective, nature of the legislation in question.

Perhaps a better candidate for a "new starting point" in substantive due process would be the earlier New York case of *Taylor v. Porter*.[45] There relying on *Hoke v. Henderson* and the later of the two Tennessee cases referred to above, Bronson, J., for his court struck down a *general* act authorizing, under limited circumstances, the construction of private roads on property owned by third parties.

> The meaning of the [law of the land] section then seems to be, that no member of the state shall be . . . deprived of any of his rights or privileges, unless the matter shall be adjudged against him upon trial had according to the course of the common law. It must be ascertained judicially that he has forfeited his privileges, or that some one else has a superior title to the property he possesses, before either of them can be taken from him. It cannot be done by mere legislation.[46]

While the language used is much like that in the earlier cases (fusing separation and due process concepts) there is no specific mention of retroactivity or particularity. In fact the act at issue was general in nature and the reported facts suggest that it long ante-dated plaintiff's acquisition of the property for which he claimed and received protection.[47] It is noteworthy that in this case Judge Bronson's language was not endorsed by his colleagues. One of them concurred separately without opinion, the other dissented.

The suggestion that *Taylor v. Porter* marks a new departure comes simply to this: in all prior cases the retrospective or "partial" application of the challenged legislation had been emphasized as the basis of invalidity. When Bronson, J., silently dispensed with both of these elements he was in effect holding—perhaps without awareness of what was involved—that separation was no longer the essential content of due process in vested interest cases. For the elements of retroactivity and particularity are important only when it is deemed necessary to show the judgment-like, or "pains and penalties" quality, of a legisla-

---

44. 13 N.Y. at 487 (1856). See text and note 60 *infra*.
45. 4 Hill 140 (N.Y. 1843). *Cf. In re* Jacobs, 98 N.Y. 98 (1885) in which substantive due process in the modern sense first reached full and unequivocal bloom.
46. 4 Hill at 146.
47. See dissenting opinion of Nelson, C. J., 4 Hill at 148-51. Professor Corwin at first mistakenly read *Taylor v. Porter* as involving only a special, or private, statute. See Corwin, *The Doctrine of Due Process of Law before the Civil War*, 24 HARV. L. REV. 366, 460, 465 (1911). On that basis of course there would be nothing unusual about the case. In his recapitulation thirty-seven years later Professor Corwin apparently recognized his mistake as to the nature of the statute in question. See CORWIN, LIBERTY AGAINST GOVERNMENT 97-98 (1948). But meanwhile, thanks to his earlier efforts, *Wynehamer* had become such a famous landmark that there was perhaps no retreating from it.

ture's act. If Bronson, J., could do without either or the old crutches, it is noteworthy that Ruffin, C. J., in *Hoke's* case had expressly dispensed with one of them, namely, particularity.[48] Consciously or not Judge Bronson was clearly ahead of his own court and ahead of his era.

In the only pre-Civil War majority opinion of the Supreme Court of the United States in which due process was substantively conceived both the special and the retrospective nature of the legislation at issue were stressed.[49] Congress by special act had extended the life of a patent on planing machines. *Bloomer v. McQuewan*[50] raised the question of whether an assignee under the original patent continued to enjoy his assigned rights under the extension. Construing the statute so as not to "interfere with rights of property before acquired."[51] Chief Justice Taney for the Court observed that, if the measure were construed otherwise,

> the power of Congress to pass it would be open to serious objection . . . .
> The right to construct and use these planing machines, had been purchased
> and paid for . . . . They were the property of the respondents. Their only
> value consists in their use. And a special act of Congress, passed after-
> wards, depriving the appellees of the right to use them, certainly could
> not be regarded as due process of law.[52]

So much for the ante-bellum cases. If not universally recognized, so well established was the nexus between separation and due process on the eve of the Civil War that the two could be presented in Sedgwick's well-known treatise as virtual equivalents. Thus, referring to the separation of powers, Sedgwick continues:

> This idea is sometimes conveyed in the phrase . . . that a legislature
> can do no judicial act; and it is almost identical with the constitutional
> declaration which insures to all persons attacked or charged, the protec-
> tion of the law of the land. If, as we have seen, by the right to the law

---

48. See Hoke v. Henderson, 15 N.C. 1, 13 (1833). Rejecting a broad due process argument in 1854 the Supreme Court of Illinois observed, "The framers of Magna Charta and of the constitutions of the United States and of the states never intended to modify, abridge, or destroy the police powers of government. They only prohibited its exercize by ex post facto [i.e. retrospective] laws and regulated the mode of trial for offences." Goddard v. Jacksonville, 15 Ill. 589 (1854).

49. I have passed over two minority opinions, one per Mr. Justice Baldwin in Groves v. Slaughter, 40 U.S. (15 Pet.) 449, 510-15 (1841); the other per Chief Justice Taney in Dred Scott v. Sanford, 60 U.S. (19 How.) 393, 450 (1856), in which due process is used in a purely substantive sense without reliance upon separation factors. In view of what went before and after, these must be considered sports. The fact that both deal with slavery suggests that they are the product of the abolitionists' peculiar political usage. See Graham, *Procedure to Substance—Extra-Judicial Rise of Due Process*, 1830-1860, 40 CALIF. L. REV. 483 (1952); Graham, *The Early Anti-Slavery Backgrounds of the Fourteenth Amendment*, 1950 WIS. L. REV. 479, 610.

50. 55 U.S. (14 How.) 539 (1852).

51. *Id.* at 554.

52. *Id.* at 553.

> of the land is meant the right to judicial procedure, investigation, and determination, whenever life, liberty, or property is attacked; and if it be conceded, as it must be, that our legislatures are by our fundamental law prohibited from doing any judicial acts,—then it would seem . . . that the rights of the citizens are as perfectly protected by the guarantee of the law of the land, as they can be by a preemptory distribution of power. *In fact, the special clause works a division of power.* . . . This, however, is merely a circuitous statement of the proposition that vested rights are sacred.[53] (Emphasis added.)

After the Civil War the Supreme Court's first brush with substantive due process came in *Hepburn v. Griswold*.[54] There, striking down national legal tender legislation on due process grounds *interalia*, Chief Justice Chase for his Court emphasized the retrospective character of the offending measure.[55] Shortly afterwards counsel first used the fourteenth amendment to press the unqualified, *i.e.*, non-separation, substantive position upon the Court in the *Slaughter House* cases.[56] The response was a categorical repudiation. Indeed the Court had never heard of such a claim.

> We are not without judicial interpretation . . . both State and National, of the meaning of this clause. And it is sufficient to say that under no construction of that provision that we have ever seen, or any that we deem admissible, can the restraint imposed by the State . . . upon the exercise of their trade by the butchers . . . be held to be a deprivation of property within the meaning of that provision.[57]

But counsel's position found support in dissenting opinions by Justices Bradley and Swayne.[58] Both of them, however, rested more heavily upon the "privileges and immunities" clause than on due process. But this emphasis was soon to be reversed. The "privileges and immunities" of citizenship proviso perhaps was too slender a tool in the expanding world of corporate enterprise, or was it that due process was a more familiar, and hence handier, instrument thanks to its long tempering in the flames of separation doctrine at the state level? In any case we know that only a few months after rejecting a purely substantive due process argument in the *Slaughter House* cases, a majority in *Bartemeyer v. Iowa*,[59] sustaining a prohibition act, cited *Wynehamer* with the observation that, if the prosecution had involved the sale of liquor owned *prior* to prohibition, it would have raised "very grave" due process questions.[60] The narrowness of this separa-

---

53. Sedgwick, Statutory and Constitutional Law 676-77 (1857). See also Dwarris, Construction of Statutes 165, 428 (Potter ed. 1874).
54. 75 U.S. (8 Wall.) 603 (1869).
55. *Id.* at 624-25.
56. The Slaughter-House Cases, 83 U.S. (16 Wall.) 36 (1872).
57. *Id.* at 80-81.
58. *Id.* at 111, 124 (Mr. Justice Field's dissent does not mention due process).
59. 85 U.S. (18 Wall.) 129 (1873).
60. *Id.* at 133. Professor Corwin calls this reasoning an "evasion" of the true issue which again suggests that he was oblivious to the role of separa-

tion concession to due process was emphasized in the following year when, Mr. Justice Miller, speaking for the Court (as he had in the two preceding cases), struck down a tax measure on the basis of "limitations which grow out of the essential nature of all free governments."[61] This atavistic reliance upon "natural law" must have amused Justices Field, Swayne and Bradley, but it certainly did not impede the fight to put the heady brew in the old "due process" bottle.[62] Perhaps they remembered that extra-constitutional limitations without more had long since been tried and found wanting.[63]

After a long and cautious flirtation with the Field-Swayne-Bradley position,[64] the Court finally in the *Minnesota Rate* case of 1890[65] took what is generally considered the decisive turn.[66] But, it is noteworthy that the challenged rate order of a regulatory commission in this case was not found to be unreasonable or confiscatory. Rather the holding was that, since under the authorizing statute the commission's order was final, the railroad had been denied a judicial hearing on the reasonableness of the rate which is "eminently a question for judicial investigation, requiring due process of law for its determination."[67] Here again is a resort to "separation of powers" help for giving content to due process.

Not until six years later in *Missouri Pacific Ry v. Nebraska*[68] does one find a Supreme Court majority invalidating legislation on nonprocedural due process grounds without reliance upon some element of separation.[69] The highest court of the land had now caught up with

---

tion in the rise of substantive due process. CORWIN, LIBERTY AGAINST GOVERNMENT 128 (1948). If there is evasion here, what of *Wynehamer?*

61. Loan Ass'n v. Topeka, 87 U.S. (20 Wall.) 655, 663 (1874).

62. See Hamilton, *The Path of Due Process of Law,* in THE CONSTITUTION RECONSIDERED (Read. ed. 1938).

63. See, *e.g.,* the dissenting opinion of Mr. Justice Iredell in Calder v. Bull, 3 U.S. (3 Dall.) 386, 398 (1798).

64. While sustaining challenged legislation, the Court made linguistic concessions in each of the following: Munn v. Illinois, 94 U.S. 113, 125, 134 (1876); Davidson v. New Orleans, 96 U.S. 97, 102 (1877); Stone v. Farmers' Loan & Trust Co., 116 U.S. 307, 331 (1886); Mugler v. Kansas, 123 U.S. 623, 661 (1887); Powell v. Pennsylvania, 127 U.S. 678, 684 (1888).

65. 134 U.S. 418 (1890).

66. See Federal Power Comm'n v. Natural Gas Pipeline Co., 315 U.S. 575, 600, 609 (1942).

67. 134 U.S. at 458.

68. 164 U.S. 403 (1896). After Hepburn v. Griswold, 75 U.S. (8 Wall.) 603 (1869), the fifth amendment's due process clause first drew blood in Noble v. Union River Logging R.R., 147 U.S. 165, 176 (1893), in which separation elements are prominent.

69. The following extract from a letter written by Mr. Justice Miller in 1875 suggests what happened on the bench between Slaughter House and the principal case:

"It is vain to contend with judges who have been at the bar the advocates for forty years of railroad companies, and all the forms of associated capital, when they are called upon to decide cases where such interests are in contest. All their training, all their feelings are from the start in favor of those who need no such influence. I am losing interest in these matters. I will do my duty but will *fight* no more. I am perhaps beginning

Judge Bronson. A long cycle in the evolution of due process had been fulfilled. But after the *Missouri Pacific* denouement what content was due process to have in vested interest cases? If separation was no longer to be its essence what would be? For neither language, nor context, nor history provide a touchstone when the ancient term is freed both of its procedural and separation moorings.[70] This, of course, is a classic riddle of American constitutional law. The first answer— for their have been many—came only months after the *Missouri Pacific* case. Laissez-faire had long been in the air. At least since the Civil War it had been the real stimulant, the substance behind the separation-due process form of protection for vested interests. In *Allgeyer v. Louisiana*[71] "liberty of contract" formally moved into the "void of due process" as separation faded out. The immediate fountainhead of this development, as Dean Pound has shown, was Mr. Justice Field's separate opinion a few years earlier in *Butcher's Union Co. v. Cresent City Co.*[72] Rejected by the highest court of the land, Field's position was treated in the more "advanced" New York, and other state, courts as of the highest authority.[73] Having been farmed out and proven in the minor leagues, so to speak, "liberty of contract" was taken up in the unanimous *Allgeyer* opinion by Mr. Justice Peckham who himself had come up from New York. Then, after all but wrecking the Supreme Court, the "liberty of contract" yardstick gave way to others. Indeed there have been so many others that it is quite plain the true measure of substantive due process is the length of the judge's foot. And there's the rub!

To summarize: Separation with its procedural connotations had been a ready, if narrow, bridge between orthodox procedural due process and the doctrine of vested interests in an age when legislatures habitually interfered with property by crude retrospective and special, *i.e.*, quasi-judicial, measures. But as legislation entered the broad police power domain (and showed more respect for the line between court and legislature) protection that hinged on separation offered little comfort for the claims of property. And so, having accomplished their intermediary purpose, the separation elements in due process were gradually abandoned in favor of principles better fitted to the needs of a new age. What remained constant in the transition from separation to laissez-faire as the nub of due process was substantive

to experience that loss of interest in many things which is the natural result of years. . . ." FAIRMAN. MR. JUSTICE MILLER AND THE SUPREME COURT 1862-1890, 374 (1939).

70. Traces of the mingling of separation and due process may be found as late as 1936, *i.e.*, as long as substantive due process lived in the realm of economic affairs. See Carter v. Carter Coal Co., 298 U.S. 238, 311-12 (1936) and cases cited therein.

71. 165 U.S. 578 (1897).

72. 111 U.S. 746, 754 (1884).

73. See Pound, *Liberty of Contract*, 18 YALE L.J. 454, 470 (1909).

protection for established proprietary interests. As usual, with judge-made law changing social pressures were accommodated, not by the sudden introduction of strange, new concepts, but by subtle, usually imperceptible, changes in the meaning of old, familiar principles.[74]

---

74. See POUND, THE SPIRIT OF THE COMMON LAW 166-92 (1921).

IV

Judicial Review: Shield or Sword?

17 🦚 *Democracy and the Divine Right of Judges — A Review of Eugene V. Rostow,* The Sovereign Prerogative *(1962)*

W HATEVER Jefferson may have thought at first, he ultimately repudiated judicial review.[1] And as recently as thirty years ago, few if any liberals could be found to argue in favor of "the democratic character" of that institution. Obviously there are fashions in liberalism; what only yesterday it found untenable is now a major article of its faith. This book is largely an effort to justify the new position. Among a host of moving arguments on what for me are collateral topics, Dean Rostow meets the basic difficulty with this: "Where judges are carrying out the functions of constitutional review, the final responsibility of the people is appropriately guaranteed by the provisions for amending the Constitution . . ." (p. 153). But, like judicial review itself, the amending process puts awesomely disproportionate policy power in minority hands. This may be good or bad, but let us not pretend that it is democratic.

Dean Rostow is brutally critical of the *Dennis* decision. What satisfaction could he — an avowed realist — find in the possibility of its reversal by the cumbrous, minority-controlled process of constitutional amendment? If *Dennis* were an isolated event, libertarians perhaps could swallow it, and still maintain their new faith. The fact is that despite numerous opportunities, the Supreme Court has never vetoed an act of Congress on free-speech — or any other First Amendment — grounds. I stand in awe of a realist who in the face of such a record can maintain his faith. And, of course, this is only a small part of the record. Have liberals so soon forgotten Professor (later Judge) Edgerton's conclusions in a 1937 study of all relevant cases?[2]

In one who identifies the country with the well-to-do minority of its population, enthusiasm for judicial review over Congress is as logical as enthusiasm can be. It is hard to see why, apart from convention, one who does not make that identification should share that enthusiasm. . . . I

---

[1]Mendelson, "Jefferson on Judicial Review: Consistency Through Change," 29 University of Chicago Law Review 327 (1962).

[2]"The Incidence of Judicial Control Over Congress," 22 Cornell Law Quarterly 299 (1937).

wonder what cases [are] so valuable as to outweigh the *Dred Scott* case, which helped to
entrench slavery; the *Civil Rights* and related cases, which protected the oppression of Negroes;
the employers' liability and workmen's compensation cases, which denied relief to injured
workmen; the child labor and minimum wage cases, which protected the hiring of women and
children at starvation wages; the income tax cases, which prevented the shifting of [some] tax
burdens from the poor to the rich; and the many minor instances in which the Court's review
has done harm to common men.

Professor Charles Black has recently argued (and his colleague Dean
Rostow seems to agree—p. 117) that an important function of judicial
review is to "legitimate" questionable legislative measures.[3] On that basis
the Smith Act and all similar measures sustained on review have been
"legitimatized." Congress has recognized this—or to quote libertarianism
against itself, judicial review is indeed "educational." It is no accident, for
example, that the Smith Act was drawn in terms similar to those previously
upheld by the Court in *Gitlow.* Nor is it by chance that in providing for
what Dean Rostow calls *"concentration camps"* (p. 167), the McCarran Act
of 1950 draws upon the precedent of *Korematsu*—which to his everlasting
glory Dean Rostow publicly condemned at a time when it was somewhat less
than popular to do so.

In the face of these "legitimating" precedents, what decisions are there
to sustain the new liberal faith in judicial review? Surely the courageous
Segregation Cases will not bear so heavy a load—*after all they only repudiate
what the Court had made "legitimate" some generations earlier.* One of the
Dean's arguments in favor of court review is "the benign influence of time
which changes the personnel of courts" (p. 153). Or as Brandeis put it, no
case is finally decided until it is rightly decided. True and wise no doubt, but
that argument would prove "the democratic character" even of a Hitler.

Apparently, then, the only *realistic* basis for liberalism's new confidence
in judicial review is a handful of cases (mostly modern) which impose First-
Amendment and fair-trial principles upon the states. But even here the
Court has disappointed libertarians by its caution. And even at best such
cases could not support the "democracy" of judicial review in general. For
surely as Marshall, Holmes, and others have indicated—and as Swiss practice
recognizes—there is a vast and relevant difference between court review of
acts of the whole body politic, and acts of merely a subdivision thereof.

It goes without mention that Dean Rostow rejects the anti-activist philosophy of Justices Hand and Frankfurter. And, while he favors Mr. Justice
Black's results, he repudiates the conviction or pretense that they spring
from clear and absolute provisions of the Constitution. Indeed, as he sees it,
Black's "judicial philosophy has not proved to be a workable rule of judicial
action" (p. xvii). The Justice is constantly stumbling over his own absolutes.

[3]*The People and the Court,* Chapter 3 (1960).

Yet having repudiated the Frankfurterian philosophy Dean Rostow embraces Mr. Justice Frankfurter's balancing approach (p. 177). It comes to this: the Dean is too good a lawyer to accept the activist technique, and too impatient with the political process to accept anti-activist results. In short, his trained legal mind rejects what his heart desires. Try as it may, his book (I think) does not resolve that dilemma. We cannot be on both sides of the fence. A judge cannot be true to the ideal of detachment and also keep a libertarian — or a proprietarian — thumb on the scales of justice.

Judicial review was born of Federalist distrust of democracy. All told, it has served its purpose well. Of course, even an absolute monarch may on occasion promote freedom — as when the Russian Czar abolished slavery — but that does not give monarchy a democratic character. Indeed, even a consistently benevolent philosopher-king would be the antithesis of democracy. The essence of self-government after all, is self-government — not a nursemaid who lets the children play, if they behave. Freedom includes freedom to make mistakes — a far too important function to be exercised by guardians. To rely upon others to save us from our faults is to repudiate the moral foundation of freedom. Surely all this is implicit in democracy. If so, libertarians have sold their birthright for a few decisions — which may be reversed tomorrow.

Maybe it is realistic to doubt or despise the political processes. Maybe the masses cannot be fully trusted with self-government. But let us not pretend that guardianship is synonymous with democracy. It may be naïveté on my part, but I have thought that one goal of liberalism was to expose, not refurbish, the "noble fictions" that frustrate government by the people. Surely we can answer the radical right without betraying the liberal tradition — without pretending that judicial review in all its aspects has suddenly become a democratic institution.

18 ✾ *Professor Cahn on Jefferson, Commager, and Learned Hand*

In a recent article Professor Edmond Cahn finds that after "several decades" Chief Judge Learned Hand has confessed error and "finally changed" his mind about judicial review vis-a-vis the first amendment.[1] In expounding this thesis Cahn finds occasion to bisect Thomas Jefferson and assail a famous historian, H. S. Commager, on a matter of history. The victims deserve a few words of consolation.

Jefferson would not be in this trouble if he had not after 1789 changed his mind about judicial review. Cahn is aware of the change but refuses to recognize it. For him the earlier view is the vintage article. "The genuine Jeffersonian is one who agrees with Jefferson's views of 1789 . . . ."[2] Professor Commager's difficulty, it seems, is that he sees Jefferson whole. He discounts the younger, in favor of the more mature, master of Monticello. He refuses, that is, to cut off and ignore the later phase of Jefferson's intellectual development.

Cahn admits, of course, that "agreeing with the Jeffersonian position of 1789 does not automatically make one right; it only makes one comfortable."[3] But such comfort is only for those who are not troubled with why Jefferson altered his view. What reconsideration, what new experience, explains the shift? Who can say? I only suggest that the earlier stand was a priori. It preceded experience with judicial review as a going institution in the federal courts. Later, after discovering what judicial review meant in practice, Jefferson denounced it roundly and without exception for the Bill of Rights.[4] He recognized no "preferred position." It is just possible that Jefferson made no distinction in his strictures because he came to fear that property and the judicial heart have a special affinity around which judicial review inevitably gravitates. After all, in Jefferson's day vicious court enforcement of the Sedition Act was not ancient history, nor was the contrasting vindication of property "rights," even those grounded in fraud as in *Fletcher v. Peck.*[5] If, in fact, it was Jefferson's ultimate conclusion that judicial review inevitably would give economic interests a "preferred place," subsequent experience does not repudiate that view. Indeed, in the entire history of the first amendment there is not one Supreme Court decision which vindicates any of its great freedoms by striking down an act of Congress. As a matter of experience,

---

[1] Cahn, *The Doubter and the Bill of Rights*, 33 N.Y.U.L. Rev. 903 (1958).
[2] *Id.* at 908.
[3] *Ibid.*
[4] See COMMAGER, MAJORITY RULE AND MINORITY RIGHTS. Ch. II (1943).
[5] 10 U.S. (6 Cranch) 87 (1810).

judicial review has been much kinder to economic interests.

Refusing to accept Jefferson's shift in view, Professor Cahn next strains to demonstrate that Learned Hand has shifted his. The judge's old position, as Cahn explains it, was that "the guarantees of the First Amendment and most of the remainder of the Bill of Rights are not really law at all . . . [but] only 'admonitions of moderation,' 'moral adjurations,' 'a mood rather than a command,' 'not jural concepts at all, in the ordinary sense.' "[6]

Has all this been abandoned? In the last chapter of his recent book on *The Bill of Rights,* Hand undertakes to weigh the advantages and disadvantages of judicial review of the merits of legislation. To do this he lists considerations on both sides. *One part of one item* in the account is this: "I agree that they [who favor review on the merits] have the better argument so far as concerns Free Speech."[7] For Cahn this and the reasons offered in support are the "clearest and most significant" evidence of Hand's "departure" from his earlier position.[8] But this is not the judge's final balance. It is only one item on one side of the ledger.

Cahn's point is that Hand has not only abandoned his old view, but that he has finally come around to the "preferred position" doctrine at least with respect to free speech.[9] This requires a rather special interpretation of Hand's conclusion:

I have tried to strike a balance between the advantages of our own system and one in which we might enjoy at least the protection of judges against our frailties. To me, it seems better to take our chances that such constitutional restraints as already exist may not sufficiently arrest the recklessness of popular assemblies.[10]

Any doubts as to what this means must vanish when it is read in conjunction with the opening paragraph of the chapter in which it appears. There Hand outlines what he proposes to do in this part of the book. "I shall say first why I do not think that the interests mentioned in the First Amendment are entitled in point of constitutional interpretation to a measure of protection different from other interests. . . ."[11] Can this be reconciled with Cahn's idea that Hand has abandoned his old skepticism and stands "in the presence of a dawning faith"?[12]

Professor Cahn is a man of principle. He does not, as the old saw admonishes, "join 'em when he can't lick 'em." His short way with opponents is more comfortable. Refusing to let one change his mind, he insists that another has done so. This removes two old heroes from the

[6] CAHN, *op. cit. supra* note 1, at 903.
[7] HAND, THE BILL OF RIGHTS 69 (1958).
[8] CAHN, *op. cit. supra* note 1, at 915.
[9] *Ibid.*
[10] HAND, *op cit. supra* note 1, at 74.
[11] *Id.* at 56. The remainder of the sentence poses a second problem: "and then [I shall] conclude by considering whether, even assuming that I am right in thinking that the Constitution does not warrant the courts in annulling any legislation because they

opposition and puts them in Cahn's camp. Professor Commager's perversity is handled differently: when that "distinguished historian" opposed Cahn he must have been "extremely provoked" and thus presumably befuddled.[13]

Judicial review has been a storm center in American history because it involves exercise of political power (*i.e.*, policy determination) without commensurate political responsibility. It involves in short what Holmes called the "sovereign prerogative of choice." Despite unqualified language in some parts of the Bill of Rights, no past or present member of the Supreme Court has even suggested that any of its freedoms are absolute. As with property interests the only question has been when and how they may be qualified. Whom do we fool by pretending that this is a matter of constitutional *interpretation?* Is it not in fact policy-making and not less so when done by liberals than when done by conservatives? Both are quite capable of rationalizing their value preferences. Not only are Justices Sutherland and Black in disagreement as to what human arrangements deserve preferred treatment—so are Justices Black and Douglas.[14] And so were Justices Sutherland, Van Devanter, McReynolds and Butler.[15]

Protesting our faith in government by the people, we resort when hard pressed to government by judges. Perhaps the basic difficulty is that while we believe in Democracy, we also fear it. If so, until this inner conflict is resolved, we are not apt to find either judges or doctrines that will give more than partisan satisfaction. Meanwhile, Chief Judge Hand's half-way house has much to offer. For him, the judicial veto should be confined to those cases in which the court is prepared to say:

We find that this measure will have this result; it will injure this group in such and such ways, and benefit that group in these other ways. We declare it invalid, because after every conceivable allowance for differences of outlook, we cannot see how a fair person can honestly believe that the benefits balance the losses.[16]

This, I take it, is essentially the old reasonable man rule with which we all agree—until our special preferences are at stake.

---

disapprove it on the merits, nevertheless it is desirable that they should exercise such an authority on extreme occasions." Even if Hand's answer to this proposition is conceded to be affirmative, limiting judicial intervention to "extreme occasions" seems plainly a repudiation of the "preferred position," in favor of the "reasonable man" or "rational basis," test. Moreover the judge's now famous repudiation of "Platonic Guardians" in favor of the political processes, *Id.* at 73–74, suggests again that he is still doing business at the same old stand.

[12] CAHN, *op. cit. supra* note 1, at 909.

[13] *Id.* at 906. For Commager's criticism of Cahn see *Id.* at 905; N.Y. Times, Feb. 23, 1958, § 7, p. 44.

[14] See, *e.g.*, Zorach v. Clauson, 343 U.S. 306 (1952).

[15] See, *e.g.*, United States v. Curtiss-Wright Export Corp., 299 U.S. 304 (1936); Village of Euclid v. Ambler Realty Co., 272 U.S. 365 (1926).

[16] HAND, THE SPIRIT OF LIBERTY 179 (1952).

19   *Jefferson on Judicial Review: Consistency through Change*

RECENT AMERICAN history suggests that the "liberal" attitude toward judicial review varies with the relative "liberalism" of the Supreme Court. When in the years just prior to 1937 the Court was generally more conservative than the legislative branches of government, "liberals" found judicial review quite undemocratic. More recently—and particularly since the *School Segregation Cases*[1]—"liberals" have found judicial review a useful adjunct to democracy.[2] Conversely, of course, the "conservative" view of the Court has shifted from veneration to distrust. Thomas Jefferson's attitude toward the judiciary seems to have been similarly flexible, though his "inconsistency" is better explained not in terms of the comparative "liberalism" of the various agencies of government, but in terms of their changing, relative tendencies towards "tyranny." Finding that Jefferson was at first more hospitable toward judicial review than he was later on, Dumas Malone offers this explanation:

> he generally opposed such tyrannies as seemed most menacing at a particular time. . . . [At first] the danger of judicial supremacy was exceedingly remote. Also, the American government was heavily overbalanced on the side of the states, and neither here nor elsewhere in this period of constitutional discussion did he appear as a notable champion of the latter. The dangers of the new system [a Federalist judiciary headed by John Marshall] which impressed him most, when he finally learned just what it was to be, were those relating to the liberty of individuals.[3]

Mr. Malone does not spell out the details of the alleged Jeffersonian switch. A recent critic argues that there was no switch; that Jefferson consistently rejected judicial review, and steadfastly supported what may be called "concurrent review."[4] The latter contemplates that each of the three branches of government "is truly independent of the others, and has an equal right to decide for itself what is the meaning of the Constitution in the cases submitted to its action . . . ."[5] The present thesis is that while Jefferson

---

[1] Brown v. Board of Educ., 347 U.S. 483 (1954).

[2] See Roche, Book Review, 2 MASS. REV. 573 (1961).

[3] MALONE, JEFFERSON AND THE RIGHTS OF MAN 163–64 (1951).

[4] Krislov, *The Alleged Inconsistency: A Revised Version*, 10 J. PUB. L. 117 (1961). This was a response to Mendelson, *Jefferson on Judicial Review*, 10 J. PUB. L. 113 (1961).

[5] Letter to Judge Roane, Sept. 6, 1819, 15 THE WRITINGS OF THOMAS JEFFERSON 212, 214 (Bergh ed. 1904).

undoubtedly advocated concurrent review after 1800, earlier he favored a far more important role for the judiciary.

In his famous *Notes on Virginia* (1782), Jefferson examined his state's government and found it wanting, particularly in that its constitution (1776) was only a legislative act and as such alterable by legislation.[6] Thus, in his view there was "no legal obstacle to the assumption by the assembly of all the powers legislative, executive, and judiciary...."[7] In 1783 he proposed a new constitution to be adopted by a constitutional convention whose product would be supreme vis-à-vis ordinary legislation—the new document to contain the following provision: "The General Assembly shall not have power to infringe this constitution...."[8] To enforce this, *i.e.*, to provide a safeguard against legislative tyranny of the kind that he feared under the existing constitution, he provided a "legal obstacle." This was a special Council of Revision made up of representatives of the executive and judicial branches, and armed with the power to veto legislation.[9] Obviously in this era Jefferson was not satisfied to let a simple legislative majority enjoy the freedom from an outside, *over-ruling* power that concurrent review contemplates.

In 1784 he listed the "rational and necessary" objects for the attainment of which he had "long wished to see a [state constitutional] convention called." Among the objects listed was "making our constitution paramount [vis-à-vis] ... the ordinary legislature so that all acts contradictory to it may be *adjudged* null...."[10]

By 1786 he seemed to consider judicial review an accepted principle throughout the country: "I have not heard that in the other states they have ever infringed their constitutions; and I suppose they have not done it; as the judges would consider any law as void, which was contrary to the constitution."[11] Shortly thereafter in 1787 he wrote Madison with respect to the proposed Constitution of the United States: "I like the negative [veto] given to the Executive, conjointly with a third of either House; though I should have liked it better, had the judiciary been associated for that purpose,

---

[6] 2 *Id.* at 1, 165–74.

[7] *Id.* at 173.

[8] Jefferson's Draft of a Constitution for Virginia (1783), 6 THE PAPERS OF THOMAS JEFFERSON 294, 298 (Boyd ed. 1952).

[9] *Id.* at 302–03.

[10] Letter to Pendleton, May 25, 1784, 7 THE PAPERS OF THOMAS JEFFERSON 292, 293 (Boyd ed. 1952). (Emphasis added.) As Mr. Krislov recognizes, *supra* note 4, at 121, concurrent review contemplates that a court may refuse to enforce a measure which it deems unconstitutional. Unlike judicial review, this does not mean that the court may invalidate the measure, *i.e.*, adjudge it null and void.

[11] Letter to Demeunier, Jan. 24, 1786, 10 THE WRITINGS OF THOMAS JEFFERSON 11, 18 (Bergh ed. 1904).

or invested separately with a similar power."[12] Obviously Jefferson wanted the judiciary to have some part in a veto, or "legal obstacle," against legislative tyranny—whether it was the council-of-revision type, *or* a separate judicial veto, did not seem to matter. Obviously, too, at this juncture Jefferson thought the judiciary was to have no veto power at all either "conjointly" or "separately"—otherwise he would not have written that "he should have liked it better," if the Constitution had provided for one or the other.

Shortly thereafter in *The Federalist, No. 78,* Hamilton demonstrated that a judicial veto (judicial review) was implicit in the Constitution. Indeed the views thus expressed are reflected in large part in *Marbury v. Madison.*[13] Then evidently accepting Hamilton's position,[14] though of course he may have come upon it elsewhere, Jefferson reversed himself by recognizing the existence of a judicial veto—which he endorsed in rather lyrical terms. Writing Madison in 1789 about the proposed Bill of Rights, he counseled:

> In the arguments in favor of a declaration of rights, you omit one which has great weight with me; the legal check which it puts into the hands of the judiciary. This is a body, which, if rendered independent and kept strictly to their own department, merits great confidence for their learning and integrity. In fact, what degree of confidence would be too much, for a body composed of such men as Wythe, Blair and Pendleton?[15]

It seems clear that the "legal check" here contemplated was the exact equivalent in *purpose and desired effect* of the "legal obstacle" that he had mentioned in conjunction with the Virginia constitution; namely, a device to enforce the principle that the legislature "shall not have power to infringe this constitution. . . ." After all, in the 1787 letter to Madison, Jefferson refers to the council-of-revision type of *veto* and the separate judicial *veto* as though he deemed them equally desirable *alternatives* as checks upon legislative abuse. It may well be that, given a choice, Jefferson would have preferred the former —as his draft proposal of a constitution for the State of Virginia suggests. But with respect to the federal constitution he had little choice. It came to him largely as a *fait accompli*, and plainly there was far more likelihood of finding in it a judicial veto than a council of revision.

---

[12] Letter to Madison, Dec. 20, 1787, 6 *id.* at 385, 387. Emphasis added to those words which Mr. Krislov appears to have overlooked—overlooking them results in a distorted understanding of the letter, and a gratuitous mistake about an "overnight" change of mind. Krislov, *supra* note 4, at 119, 122.

[13] 5 U.S. (1 Cranch) 137 (1803).

[14] Mr. Krislov asserts that Jefferson had not read the *Federalist* carefully, *supra* note 4, at 122. Jefferson wrote, "I read it with care, pleasure and improvement . . . ." Letter to Madison, Nov. 18, 1788, 7 THE WRITINGS OF THOMAS JEFFERSON 183 (Bergh ed. 1904).

[15] Letter to Madison, March 15, 1789, 7 *id.* at 309. Speaking of an exchange of thoughts that culminated in this letter, Irving Brant said, "Thus it was through Jefferson that Madison was brought to the doctrine of judicial review, and it was from Madison that Jefferson derived the idea (but not the details) of the Kentucky Resolutions." 3 JAMES MADISON: FATHER OF THE CONSTITUTION 267 (1950).

It is suggested that the "legal check" which Jefferson had in mind at this juncture was nothing more than concurrent review. But the latter means merely that while the judiciary may construe the Constitution in matters that come before it, such constructions are not binding upon other branches of government. In short the legislature is its own independent judge of the validity of its own conduct. This was precisely the defect of the Virginia constitution against which Jefferson had fought—the defect he proposed to cure by a super-legislative provision that the "General Assembly shall not have power to infringe this constitution . . . ."[16] (This provision of course was to be enforced by an *outside* "legal obstacle.") Similarly concurrent review does not seem to jibe with either the "conjoint" negative, or the "negative . . . invested separately" in the judiciary, one or the other of which Jefferson felt should have been in the federal constitution as a device for *overriding* Congress.[17] Nor does concurrent review sound like an argument of such "great weight" that Jefferson would suggest Madison should use it in support of the proposed Bill of Rights.[18] If Madison had argued concurrent review publicly and been questioned on the point, he would have had to admit that it would have no binding effect upon Congress, the executive, or any other agency of government (including the states?)—that, whatever the Supreme Court might hold, no other branch of government would be under any legal or moral obligation to follow anything but its own conception of the limits of its own power. For example, the Court might hold a particular established church unconstitutional, nevertheless it would be perfectly legal for Congress and the executive to maintain the establishment. I suggest that this was not the "weighty argument" that Jefferson thought should be used in support of the Bill of Rights—but rather that he had in mind the kind of argument he himself had used with respect to the need for a "legal obstacle" to restrain the Virginia legislature from violating state constitutional limitations.

Having suggested that Jefferson believed in judicial review (or something quite similar) prior to 1800, and that he abandoned it in favor of concurrent review thereafter, I must now attempt to account for the change. My position like Dumas Malone's, comes to this: Jefferson's means changed in the face of changing circumstances; his ends remained constant. When in the beginning "the danger of judicial supremacy seemed exceedingly remote," when Congress seemed dangerous and the federal judiciary the most "harmless" branch of government,[19] a beefing-up of judicial power would promote balanced government. Later, when in Jefferson's view judicial supremacy became a

---

[16] Jefferson's Draft of a Constitution for Virginia (1783), 6 THE PAPERS OF THOMAS JEFFERSON 294, 298 (Boyd ed. 1952).

[17] See text at note 12 *supra*.

[18] See text at note 15 *supra*.

[19] See text at notes 21 & 23 *infra*.

reality, a reduction of court power would promote balance. If he was flexible as to means, Jefferson's "deeper consistency lay in his continued advocacy of a balanced government."[20]

In the same 1789 letter to Madison in which he expressed "great confidence" in a properly organized judiciary, Jefferson observed that: "The executive, in our governments, is not the sole, it is scarcely the principal object of my jealousy. The tyranny of the legislatures is the most formidable dread at present, and will be for many years. That of the executive will come in its turn; but it will be at a remote period."[21] Since, as he saw it then, the danger lay in the legislature and the executive, he would naturally look for protection in other quarters. He found it not only in a "legal check" (as we have seen), but also in state check: "The jealousy of the subordinate governments is a precious reliance."[22] This of course found expression later in the Virginia and Kentucky Resolutions. The point is that Jefferson's attention prior to 1800 was oriented toward Congress and the executive as the dangerous branches of government. It cannot be said that he was thinking only of the moment, for he observed that while the one was immediately dangerous, the other would be a threat later. Yet he foresaw no trouble from the judiciary. Later he recognized his error:

> At the establishment of our constitutions, the judiciary bodies were supposed to be the most helpless and harmless members of the government. Experience, however, soon showed in what way they were to become the most dangerous; that the insufficiency of the means provided for their removal gave them a freehold and irresponsibility in office.[23]

What had happened in the interval between these two letters that changed Jefferson's mind about the relative danger of the courts and the other branches of government is plain. The Federalists had adopted the Alien and Sedition Acts (1798) in an effort to defeat Jefferson's Republican Party. Federalist judges had enforced the sedition provisions viciously. When these moves had failed to secure the great election of 1800 for the Federalist Party, it used its last days in office to expand and pack the federal bench (1801). As Jefferson saw it, the Federalists:

> have retired into the judiciary as a stronghold. There the remains of federalism are to be preserved and fed from the treasury, and from that battery all the works of republicanism are to be beaten down and erased. By a fradulent use of the Constitution, which has made judges irremovable, they have multiplied useless judges merely to strengthen their phalanx.[24]

---

[20] MALONE, *op. cit. supra* note 3, at 163.

[21] Letter to Madison, *supra* note 15, at 312.

[22] *Id.* at 311.

[23] Letter to Coray, Oct. 31, 1823, 7 THE WRITINGS OF THOMAS JEFFERSON 318, 322 (Washington ed. 1854).

[24] Letter to Dickinson, Dec. 19, 1801, 10 THE WRITINGS OF THOMAS JEFFERSON 301, 302 (Bergh ed. 1904).

These fears of an overriding judiciary were confirmed some two years later in *Marbury v. Madison*.[25] The Jeffersonians had defeated their Federalist rivals in the political arena—only to find them entrenched in the judiciary with the formidable power of judicial review. Under such circumstances, perhaps, a Jeffersonian change in attitude as to the extent of judicial power is not quite the "needless and redundant" change in principle "at a moment of triumph" that Mr. Krislov has suggested.[26]

I do not find that Jefferson ever formulated the doctrine of concurrent review prior to 1801, *i.e.*, prior to his discovery that the judicial lamb had become in fact a wolf. As late as September, 1798, he wrote to a friend that despite the "alarm and jealousy" then sweeping the country "the laws of the land, administered by upright judges, would protect you from any exercise of power unauthorized by the Constitution of the United States."[27] Is it likely that Jefferson would have spoken thus of "unauthorized" power, if at that time he believed at least three agencies had the power—independently and concurrently—to determine what was authorized and what was not?

Concurrent review may have been an afterthought inspired by the Federalist threat to destroy Jeffersonianism from a stronghold in the judiciary. The most immediate difficulty from the Jeffersonian point of view was that Federalist judges, including some Supreme Court Justices on Circuit, abused the Bill of Rights by abetting persecution in a series of Sedition Act cases.[28] The judiciary having failed to provide the "legal check," Jefferson (with Madison) turned to his second line of defense (the state check) in the Virginia and Kentucky Resolutions (1798–1799). When this also failed, and *after he became President*, he may have hit upon concurrent review. In any case what seems to have been his first enunciation of that doctrine appeared in the draft of a message to Congress (December, 1801). But, for whatever reason, it was deleted before delivery.[29]

It is noteworthy that in the context of the Sedition Act convictions concurrent review is not entirely unlike political supremacy. If the courts had gone along with Jefferson's understanding of the Bill of Rights, well and good. When they failed to do so concurrent review provided the rationale for a "final" check via the executive pardoning power and the legislative power to repay fines. It may be significant that in what appears to be Jefferson's first "published" exposition of the doctrine (the year after *Marbury v. Madison*), he illustrated his point by reference to the Sedition Act prosecutions:

---

[25] 5 U.S. (1 Cranch) 137 (1803).

[26] Krislov, *supra* note 4, at 123.

[27] Letter to Rowan, Sept. 26, 1798, 10 THE WRITINGS OF THOMAS JEFFERSON 59, 61 (Bergh ed. 1904).

[28] See SWISHER, AMERICAN CONSTITUTIONAL DEVELOPMENT 88–98 (1954).

[29] 1 WARREN, THE SUPREME COURT IN UNITED STATES HISTORY 265–66 (1935).

nothing in the Constitution has given [the judges] a right to decide for the Executive, more than to the Executive to decide for them. Both magistrates are equally independent in the sphere of action assigned to them. The judges, believing the [Sedition] law constitutional, had a right to pass a sentence of fine and imprisonment; because the power was placed in their hands by the Constitution. But the Executive, believing the law to be unconstitutional, were [*sic*] bound to remit the execution of it; because that power has been confided to them [*sic*] by the Constitution.[30]

As a matter of fact, President Jefferson did pardon all who had been convicted and stopped all pending Sedition Act prosecutions. Similarly, Congress did in fact repay the fines that had been imposed. It is crucial that Jefferson says he exercised the pardoning power not on grounds of mercy or new evidence, but on constitutional grounds. Yet in the end he was not completely sure that even concurrent review by judges was desirable. Thus, in 1815 he observed that: "another opinion entertained by some men of such judgment and information as to lessen my confidence in my own. . . . [holds] that the legislature alone is the exclusive expounder of the sense of the Constitution, in every part of it whatever."[31]

Mr. Krislov tries to explain the absence of a "precise statement of concurrent review prior to 1801" with the assertion that "comment on construction of written, superior constitutions was academic prior to 1789 . . . ."[32] In fact there was considerable non-academic discussion of that problem. "For the period between ca. 1778 and 1789, evidence of the evolving theory or practice of reviewing legislation against a constitutional standard is available with regard, *inter alia*, to Virginia, Rhode Island, the Carolinas, New York, Connecticut, Massachusetts, and New Jersey."[33] Indeed, Jefferson's *Notes on Virginia* (1782) were in part one side of a debate on the issue of whether the Virginia constitution of 1776 was a "written, superior constitution" or merely a legislative act.[34] The other side of the debate is reflected in *Commonwealth v. Caton*,[35] in which seven of the eight judges of Virginia's highest court "were of opinion, that [they] had power to declare any resolution or act of the legislature, or of either branch of it, to be unconstitutional and void . . . ."[36] Jefferson's position, of course, was completely sympathetic in principle; his point being merely that, since the 1776 constitution was only an ordinary statute, it offered no real "legal obstacle" to legislative tyranny.

---

[30] Letter to Mrs. John Adams, Sept. 11, 1804, 11 THE WRITINGS OF THOMAS JEFFERSON 49, 50–51 (Bergh ed. 1904).

[31] Letter to Torrance, 14 *id*. at 302, 305.

[32] Krislov, *supra* note 4, at 119, 120.

[33] DOWLING, CASES ON CONSTITUTIONAL LAW 70 (5th ed. 1954). See also HAINES, THE AMERICAN DOCTRINE OF JUDICIAL SUPREMACY ch. 5 (1932).

[34] See text at notes 6 and 7 *supra*.

[35] 8 Va. (4 Call.) 5 (1782).

[36] *Id*. at 20.

Accordingly, as we have seen, he advocated a "written, superior constitution" that would remove all doubt as to whether or not there were effective limitations on legislative authority.

It was in *Commonwealth v. Caton* that Jefferson's great legal hero, Judge Wythe, proclaimed: "[I]f the whole legislature . . . should overleap the bounds prescribed to them by the people, I . . . will meet the united powers, at my seat in this tribunal; and, pointing to the Constitution, will say, to them, here is the limit of your authority; and, hither, shall you go, but no further."[37] It is difficult to believe that, if in this era the articulate Jefferson favored concurrent review, he could in view of *Caton* use the term "legal check" without explaining that he meant concurrent, rather than judicial, review. Indeed, an explanation would seem especially necessary in a letter to a fellow Virginia specialist in constitutional law. Yet this is precisely the term he used *simpliciter* in writing to Madison that "In the arguments in favor of a declaration of rights, you omit one which has great weight with me; the legal check which it puts into the hands of the judiciary."[38] The point need not be put on such narrow grounds. Is it likely that Jefferson would use in a *special, unexplained* sense a term which so naturally described a doctrine that had been spelled out in the *Federalist* and in the "evolving theory or practice" of most states—to say nothing of *Dr. Bonham's Case*,[39] colonial experience with the Privy Council,[40] Otis' famous argument against Writs of Assistance, and Jefferson's own letter of 1786 in which he seemed to consider judicial review as a generally accepted principle.[41]

Even Mr. Krislov has not been able to find any Jeffersonian enunciation of the doctrine of concurrent review to which the term "legal check" in the 1789 letter may have been a shorthand reference. Insisting that Jefferson favored concurrent review throughout his career, Mr. Krislov offers nothing but a "presage" of that doctrine prior to 1801.[42] This he purports to find in a letter of June 20, 1787, in which Jefferson urged qualified judicial, as opposed to exclusive congressional, control over state legislation in the interest of national supremacy:

> the plaintiff urges the Confederation, and the treaty made under that, as controlling the State law; the [state] judges are weak enough to decide according to the views of their legislature. An appeal to a federal court sets all to rights. It will be said, that this court may encroach on the jurisdiction of the State courts. It may. But there will be a power, to wit, Congress, to watch and restrain them.[43]

---

[37] *Id.* at 8.

[38] Letter to Madison, *supra* note 15, at 309.

[39] 8 Coke Reports 114a, 118a (1610).

[40] See, *e.g.*, HAINES, *op. cit. supra* note 33, at ch. 3.

[41] *Ibid.* See text at note 11 *supra*.

[42] Krislov, *supra* note 4, at 120, 121.

[43] Letter to Madison, June 20, 1787, 6 THE WRITINGS OF THOMAS JEFFERSON 131, 133 (Bergh ed. 1904).

I suggest that this is no evidence of even a "presage" of concurrent review. The essence of the latter is that the agency reviewed is not bound by the review, but being "truly independent ... has an equal right to decide for itself what is the meaning of the Constitution in the cases submitted to its action. ..."[44] Obviously in the letter in question Jefferson did not even vaguely contemplate any such concurrent authority for the states. Similarly the suggested relationship between Congress and the federal judiciary is a vertical or appellate, not a concurrent, relationship. It leaves no possibility of two or more competing interpretations of the same constitutional provision (which is the vice of concurrent review). As though recognizing the weakness of his own position on this point, Mr. Krislov slides away from it by concluding that in any case "the one concept [that Jefferson's proposal] ... is clearly inconsistent with is the notion of an inherent and unique power of judicial interpretation."[45] This thrust is wide of the mark; no one has claimed that Jefferson believed in an "inherent and unique power of judicial interpretation."[46] What has been suggested is that prior to 1800 Jefferson believed in judicial review. Moreover the review of *state* legislation that he here proposed is remarkably like that recognized in *Pennsylvania v. Wheeling & Belmont Bridge Co.*,[47] and more recently in *Prudential Life Ins. Co. v. Benjamin.*[48] If what these cases and Jefferson suggest constitutes a modified judicial review, it relates only to *state* measures. It has no bearing on Jefferson's conception of the "legal check" upon national acts *except to suggest that in the early period Jefferson wanted final authoritative, rather than concurrent, interpretations of the Constitution.*

The only other purported hint of concurrent review that Mr. Krislov has been able to find prior to 1801 is Jefferson's statement that: "The negative of the President is the shield provided by the Constitution to protect against the invasions of the legislature: 1. The right of the Executive. 2. Of the Judiciary. 3. Of the States . . . ."[49] Of course the presidential veto may protect the states, the executive and the judiciary. If that converts judicial review into concurrent review, we have never had judicial review in this country. "It would seem," Mr. Krislov says, "that under exclusive review the judiciary would have been well able to take care of itself in the realm of constitutional interpretation."[50] His point apparently is that Jefferson would not have men-

---

[44] Letter to Judge Roane, *supra* note 5, at 214.

[45] Krislov, *supra* note 4, at 121.

[46] If Jefferson thought any agency had an "inherent and unique power" of interpretation, presumably it would be the states. See discussion below with respect to the Virginia and Kentucky Resolution.

[47] 59 U.S. (18 How.) 421 (1856).

[48] 328 U.S. 408 (1946).

[49] Opinion Against the Constitutionality of a National Bank, 3 THE WRITINGS OF THOMAS JEFFERSON 145, 152 (Bergh ed. 1904).

[50] Krislov, *supra* note 4, at 121.

tioned presidential protection of the judiciary, if he had thought the courts had their own, more effective, power of judicial review to protect themselves. The answer is that few, if any, advocates of judicial review have ever suggested that it and the presidential veto are mutually exclusive, incompatible, or that either makes the other superfluous. One difference between them is that the veto gives its protection *ab initio;* judicial review cannot protect anything until after a case arises—and there is no guarantee that one will arise. The short of it is that the presidential veto and judicial review have existed side by side since *Marbury v. Madison.*

As suggested above, when Jefferson in the early period found legislatures and executives the chief source of danger, he would naturally seek protection in other quarters—namely, in a "legal check" and a state check. Mr. Krislov finds it "difficult to imagine why the judiciary should be granted exclusive power vis-à-vis the other two branches, yet share constitutional interpretation with the states."[51] Let Madison enlighten him:

> However true, therefore, it may be that the judicial department is, in all questions submitted to it by the forms of the Constitution, to decide in the last resort, this resort must necessarily be deemed the last in relation to the authorities of the other Departments of the [national] Government; not in relation to the rights of the parties to the constitutional compact [i.e. the states], from which the judicial as well as the other departments hold their delegated trusts.[52]

In this passage, of course, Madison was explaining the theory of the Virginia and Kentucky Resolutions; namely, that the states, *as "the sovereign parties to the Constitution,"* must have the ultimate power of interpretation as an *extraordinary* safeguard against a failure in the regular, internal check and balance system.

Finally Mr. Krislov says that my "argument boils down to the hypothesis that Jefferson concocted concurrent review in order to explain his pardoning of the victims of the Alien and Sedition Acts."[53] Apparently as Mr. Krislow indicates, Jefferson needed no excuse for the exercise of a clearly granted power in a "highly popular" cause. Why, then, did he go out of his way to give the elaborate and "unnecessary" explanation? Presumably because he was using the happy occasion as a vehicle to launch a new doctrine for future use in cases that might not be so clear, or so popular.

Mr. Krislov's original article[54] questions the evidence that Jefferson favored *judicial* review prior to 1800, and clearly established that he favored *concurrent* review thereafter. But this is no substitute for affirmative evidence of what Jefferson stood for in the earlier period. Later,[55] as though recognizing this

---

[51] *Id.* at 120.

[52] 4 ELLIOT, DEBATES ON THE FEDERAL CONSTITUTION 549–50 (1836).

[53] Krislov, *supra* note 4, at 123.

[54] Krislov, *Jefferson on Judicial Review*, 9 J. PUB. L. 374 (1960).

[55] Krislov, *The Alleged Inconsistency*, 10 J. PUB. L. 117, 120–21 (1961).

difficulty, Mr. Krislov offered the two "presages" discussed above—one of which, I suggest, entails no element of concurrency whatsoever; the other is simply a statement by Jefferson that the presidential veto is a "shield" to protect other agencies from congressional abuse (such a shield, of course, is completely compatible with judicial review; indeed, the two have lived side by side for more than a century and a half).

If my own evidence of what Jefferson thought in the early period falls short of conclusive proof, may we in the face of it *assume* that his "great silence" with respect to concurrent review prior to 1801 even presaged that doctrine? What a coincidence that, after years of constitutional discussion, Jefferson expounded concurrent review only after courts had replaced legislatures as "the great object of [his] fear. . . ."—and only after his first defenses (the "legal check" and the state check) had failed. Above all, how convenient to have thought of it (if such was the case) just as he came into control of the legislative and executive branches—when his opponents had retired into the judiciary as a battery of opposition to all that Jefferson cherished.

Addendum

The Dowling material on which this essay relies in part may overstate the case for pre-1787 judicial review at the state level, but surely Leonard Levy understates it. For a more recent and more moderate view, see J. Goebel, Jr., *History of the Supreme Court of the United States: Antecedents and Beginnings to 1801* (1971), chap. 3.

In *Commonwealth* v. *Caton,* discussed above, five (not seven) of the eight judges held "explicitly or by inference" that Virginia's highest court had the power of judicial review. Only one judge disagreed.

20 ✺ The Politics of Judicial Activism

> . . . political parties, with all their well-known human and
> structural shortcomings, are the only devices thus far invented
> by the wit of Western man which with some effectiveness can
> generate countervailing collective power on behalf of the many
> individually powerless against the relatively few who are indi-
> vidually—or organizationally—powerful.
>
> —Walter Dean Burnham

However legitimate their claims, those who cannot exercise power
effectively seem doomed to lose it. That our political party system
has weakened or worse in recent years is commonplace. This seeming degeneration coincides with the rise of Warren Court activism
or, in older terminology, judicial supremacy. In the past decade and
more the "most important decisions . . . in American politics
[have been] made essentially outside the political process proper.
They could hardly have been made within it—they concerned issues
on which no decision [was] possible within the traditional
[political party] alignments."[1] Reapportionment and a new national code of criminal case procedure, for example, were instigated

---

[1] Drucker, *New Political Alignments in the Great Society*, in B.M. GROSS, A GREAT SOCIETY 166 (1968).

by judicial fiat without any significant political discussion. An inverse relationship between Court and party power may not be a peculiarity of our day, however. It seems rather a peculiarity of our system. In fact judicial pretension appears to have thrived only in periods of unusual weakness in our political processes; at other times it has been effectively rebuffed. In short "government by judges" seems no more possible than flaws in the party system permit it to be. An exploration of these thoughts is the purpose of this essay.

The classic age of rampant judicial activism in the United States came between the 1880's and 1937. It arose with the decline of sectional politics and faded with the advent of "the new urban politics" of Franklin Roosevelt's day. In short, its first flowering came in a transitional period between two dynamic party systems. That this is not mere coincidence is suggested, as we shall see, by the fate of activist efforts by the Court before and after the era in question. Later, the decline of the New Deal political coalition invited another judicial outburst beginning in the Warren years.

The Era of Robust Sectional Politics

Frederick Turner's *The Significance of Sections in American History* concluded that, in our early days, shifting alliances between the South, successive Wests, and the Northeast—each with a distinctive economy and culture—provided the key to national politics. As he put it:

> We in America are in reality a federation of sections rather than of states. State sovereignty never was influential except as a constitutional shield for the section. In political matters the states act in groups rather than as individual members of the Union. They act in sections and are responsive to the respective interests and ideals of the sections. They have their sectional leaders, who, in Congress and party conventions, voice the attitude of the section and confer and compromise their differences, or form sectional combinations to achieve a national policy and position.[2]

Statesmanship in the old days, therefore, consisted "not only in

---

[2] F.J. TURNER, THE SIGNIFICANCE OF SECTIONS IN AMERICAN HISTORY 50 (1932).

representing the special interests of the leaders' own section, but in finding a formula that [would] bring different sections together in a common policy."[3]

Alexander Hamilton was the first great master of sectional politics. Appealing to the planter South and commercial Northeast, he achieved the political thrust that made his wide-ranging, national economic plan the law of the land. Playing favorites too plainly, however, his Federalist Party alliance was destroyed by Jefferson's "revolution at the polls" in 1800; the South had turned to the West in a sectional realignment.[4] But Hamilton's Federalist followers were entrenched in the non-elective judiciary and not by chance. John Marshall was merely the most famous of his party's lame duck and "midnight" appointees. There can be no doubt that just as the "rich and well-born" Federalists disliked democracy, they also shunned popular political parties (factions) and plainly contemplated judicial review to protect themselves from popular legislation.[5] They seem to have anticipated our thesis concerning the relationship between democracy, political parties, and judicial review. When the Federalists lost political control in 1800 and tried to make good that loss—as Jefferson charged[6]—via the judiciary, they ran into a political ambush. The Chase Impeachment, among other things, was the Jeffersonian political response to the threat implicit in *Marbury v. Madison*.[7] As John Quincy Adams observed:

> [T]he [Jeffersonian] assault upon Judge Chase, . . . was unquestionably intended to pave the way for another prosecution, which would have swept the Supreme Judicial Bench clean at a stroke.[8]

---

[3] *Id.* at 321.

[4] Massachusetts, Vermont, New Hampshire, Connecticut, Rhode Island, New Jersey, Delaware, and eastern Pennsylvania remained loyal to Hamilton's Federalist Party. The West and the South (except the eastern third of North Carolina) voted for Jefferson. Thanks to Burr (a New Yorker and Jefferson's Vice President-to-be), New York abandoned Hamilton. *See* W. CHAMBERS, POLITICAL PARTIES IN A NEW NATION: THE AMERICAN EXPERIENCE, 1776-1809 at 113-29, 150-69 (1963); V.O. KEY, POLITICS, PARTIES, AND PRESSURE GROUPS 228-53 (1964).

[5] *See* Lerner, *John Marshall and the Campaign of History, in* LEVY, AMERICAN CONSTITUTIONAL LAW: HISTORICAL ESSAYS at 49 *et seq.* (1966) [hereinafter cited as Lerner].

[6] *Id.* at 56.

[7] No one would suggest that the statute held invalid in this case embodied crucial national policy. *Marbury v. Madison*, 5 U.S. (1 Cranch) 137 (1803), however, is crucial as a ploy in the Federalist-Jeffersonian struggle for control of public policy. See Lerner, *supra* note 5, for a running account.

[8] 3 W. FORD, THE WRITINGS OF JOHN QUINCY ADAMS 106-08 (1914).

Plainly moved by this rebuff, the "great Chief Justice" wrote a telling apologia.

> I think the modern doctrine of impeachment should yield to an appellate jurisdiction in the legislature. A reversal of those legal opinions deemed unsound by the legislature would certainly better comport with the mildness of our character than [would] a removal of the Judge who has rendered them unknowing of his fault.[9]

Never thereafter, though he was on the bench for another generation, did Marshall or any member of his Court challenge an act of Congress. This was not for lack of opportunity.[10] *Marbury v. Madison* was a sport; born before its proper day, it lived in limbo until altered political conditions offered a more congenial environment. In short the Jeffersonian political combination of South and West was too effective to be defeated from the bench. Significantly, the old guard Federalists resorted after the Chase affair not to the court but to the Hartford Convention which by its resolutions confirmed John Quincy Adams' observation that "the alarm and disgust of the New England Federalists at Mr. Jefferson's anti-judiciary doctrines and measures . . . were one of the efficient causes which led to the project of separaton and a Northern Confederacy."[11] When Jefferson's West-South coalition was modernized and refurbished by the Jacksonian movement that came to power in 1828,[12] its longevity was largely assured.

To protect national and proprietary interests, the Marshall Court did, of course, strike down a significant number of *state* measures, but these were hardly activist efforts that flew in the face of popular values or ideals. The Constitution itself, after all, was a highly nationalistic response to states' rights anarchy. The Constitutional Convention was instigated by nationalists and, with one or two exceptions at most, was attended by people who insisted that state

---

[9] 3 A. BEVERIDGE, THE LIFE OF JOHN MARSHALL 177 (1916) [hereinafter cited as BEVERIDGE].

[10] *Stuart v. Laird*, 5 U.S. (1 Cranch) 299 (1803), involved a congressional measure which Marshall and his colleagues privately thought unconstitutional, "but they had not the courage [after *Marbury v. Madison* and its repercussions] to adopt the heroic course," BEVERIDGE, *supra* note 9, at 122. The validity of national legislation was questioned by counsel in Marshall's Court on at least fourteen occasions after *Marbury*.

[11] H. ADAMS, DOCUMENTS RELATING TO NEW ENGLAND FEDERALISM 162 (1877).

[12] See Map 1.

power to disturb the national welfare had to be curtailed sharply. That was precisely the goal and thesis of all nationalistic decisions of the Marshall Court.[13] As Felix Frankfurter put it: "[Marshall] was on guard against every tendency to continue treating the new Union as though it were the old Confederation."[14] Moreover, all the decisions in question came after the great wave of nationalism that followed the War of 1812. Even John C. Calhoun was then a nationalist! Finally, all these cases were decided *after* the Jefferson-Jackson coalition of South and West had filled *most* of the Supreme Court's seats. Nationalism then was not only in the Constitution, it was in the air, and judges breathed it no less than others. *The Court was not in activist defiance of the conventional wisdom of the day!*[15]

Much the same must be said of the reputed early judicial sensitivity to the claims of property. That the Founding Fathers had high respect for economic interests is no secret; Charles Beard stressed the point in his classic analysis of the Constitution.[16] Modern scholarship makes clear, however, that he was wrong in suggesting that the Fathers differed from the general community on this point.[17] In that pre-industrial, pre-Marxian day property in America was widely held, and even more widely revered and attainable. It was, after all, man's first social security system, a hedge against hazards of life, such as sickness, old age, widowhood, and orphanage.

Fletcher v. Peck[18] is the fountainhead of the Marshall Court's doctrine of property (or vested) rights. It is also the only major case of its type decided by that Court before it was dominated by Jeffersonians. If any of its members could be called the personal representative of Thomas Jefferson, it was Justice William Johnson. He wrote a concurring opinion which suggested that property once

---

[13] *See, e.g.*, Gibbons v. Ogden, 22 U.S. (9 Wheat.) 1 (1824); McCulloch v. Maryland, 17 U.S. (4 Wheat.) 316 (1819).

[14] *John Marshall and the Judicial Function in* F. FRANKFURTER, OF LAW AND MEN 8 (P. Elman ed. 1956).

[15] Arthur M. Schlesinger, Jr., writes of the "keepers of the Jeffersonian conscience," a small third-party group that remained loyal to the old ideals when so many others in both major parties had become nationalists. *See* A. SCHLESINGER, THE AGE OF JACKSON, ch. 3 (1946).

[16] C. BEARD, AN ECONOMIC INTERPRETATION OF THE CONSTITUTION OF THE UNITED STATES (1913).

[17] *See generally* R. BROWN, CHARLES BEARD AND THE CONSTITUTION (1956).

[18] 8 U.S. (6 Cranch) 490 (1810).

vested in a person "becomes intimately blended with his existence, as essentially as the blood that circulates through his system." The very "reason and nature of things" (*i.e.*, natural law) prohibits governmental interference with it. Chief Justice Marshall's opinion for the Court in *Fletcher* rested largely on the Contract Clause. Benjamin Wright has shown that, when the "great Chief Justice" took office, only three state constitutions had contract clauses similar to the one in the federal Constitution. When Chief Justice Marshall left office, nine additional states had adopted such provisions, and during the Taney era eleven more states did so. In all of these instances the contract clauses were put into the *bill of rights* sections of the state constitutions.[19] In early America the sanctity of private property was widely deemed a basic, human need! Here, too, the Court was not defying, but honoring, the generally accepted value system of its day—as reflected in the output of most American state constitutional conventions of the period.

After *Marbury v. Madison*, the Court did not again venture to assert its supremacy over the nation's political processes until the *Dred Scott*[20] decision in 1857. The repercussions of that fiasco again suggest that judicial activism cannot thrive in the face of a vigorous party system. The Democratic coalition of South and West had dominated national policy since 1800; and the slavocracy had come to dominate the Democratic party. The party's latest victories were the Fugitive Slave Law,[21] the Kansas-Nebraska Act,[22] and the tariff reform of 1857.[23] In *Dred Scott* the southern outlook overreached. Abraham Lincoln exploited that blunder in the famous debates with Douglas. At Edwardsville he attacked judicial activism:

> Familiarize yourselves with the chains of bondage and prepare your limbs to wear them. Accustomed to trample on the rights of others, you have lost the genius of your own independence and become the fit subjects of the first cunning tyrant who rises among you. And let me tell you, that all these things are prepared for you by the teaching of history, if the elections

[19] *See* B. WRIGHT, THE CONTRACT CLAUSE OF THE CONSTITUTION (1930), *summarized in* C. MAGRATH, YAZOO: LAW AND POLITICS IN THE NEW REPUBLIC 114-15 (1966).

[20] Dred Scott v. Sanford, 60 U.S. (19 Howard) 393 (1857).

[21] Act of Sept. 18, 1850, ch. 60, 9 Stat. 462.

[22] Act of May 30, 1854, ch. 59, 10 Stat. 277.

[23] Act of Mar. 3, 1857, ch. 97, 11 Stat. 192.

shall promise that the next Dred Scott decision and all future
decisions will be quietly acquiesced in by the people.[24]

At Freeport Lincoln drew from his opponent the fatal doctrine that
tore the South from the West and defeated the Democratic party.
Promptly thereafter a realignment of sectional forces brought
Northeast and West together[25] in a winning combination that put
Lincoln in the White House and overrode the *Dred Scott* decision.
Once again as in Jefferson's day a vigorous sectional politics frus-
trated judicial activism. As long as social tensions could find release
and satisfaction by prompt regrouping of geo-economic interests,
sectional politics prevailed. It was doomed when the passions of the
Civil War and Reconstruction paralyzed it.

INERT SECTIONALISM AND THE RISE OF JUDICIAL SUPREMACY

As soon as the Republican West and the Northeast had accomplished their immediate purpose (defeat of the "slave power"), their
economic incompatibility became evident. The Granger, Greenback, Alliance, Populist, and Free Silver movements were phases of
a single, persisting agrarian rebellion *within* the Republican East-
West alliance. As a matter simply of logic, the West and South
might have reunited to revive the old Democratic party; both of
them had grievances against the Eastern "money power." Those
who would lose by such a regrouping waived the "bloody shirt" to
block it. As General Sherman said, politicans were prepared to
"prolong [the hatreds of the] war ad infinitum."[26] The letters of
Blaine and Garfield, for example, reveal this to have been a calculated tactic to keep West and South apart.[27] It was not by chance
that every successful GOP candidate for the presidency from Appo-
mattox to Manila Bay was both a westerner and a "hero" of the
Union Army.

In sum, the passions of war and Reconstruction, selfishly exploited, blocked the free play of regional forces and by thus impairing its fluidity destroyed sectional politics as the arbiter of public
policy. Dixie was isolated; even the churches remained divided re-

---

[24] Quoted in 2 C. BEARD, THE RISE OF AMERICAN CIVILIZATION 16-17 (1930).

[25] See Map 2.

[26] J. & W. SHERMAN, SHERMAN LETTERS 248 (1894).

[27] *See* R. CALDWELL, JAMES A. GARFIELD: PARTY CHIEFTAIN 249 (1831); G. HAMILTON, BIOG-
RAPHY OF JAMES G. BLAINE 422 (1895).

gional bodies. The agrarian West and industrial Northeast were frozen in a union that neither could dominate by merely political processes. Their differences had to be resolved on another plane. This provided the entree for judicial "mediation" on a grand scale.

The arithmetic of the Court's efforts is revealing. From 1899 to 1937 there were 401 Supreme Court decisions invalidating state legislation—over six times more than during the entire pre-Appomattox era.[28] Most of them (224) were decided on Fourteenth Amendment grounds, yet only three afforded protection for Negroes as such, while businessmen were the major beneficiaries. National legislation suffered similarly. In contrast with the two thwarted activist efforts of the Court in the 71 years before the Civil War, the Court killed 76 congressional measures and emasculated a number of others in a like period thereafter (1866-1937). Yet cold figures hardly tell the story, for after its first coup, in *Marbury v. Madison*, the Court had not seen fit to strike again for more than half a century. Its second attempt in *Dred Scott* brought a political crisis which competent observers of that day thought the high bench could never outlive. They did not foresee what is now plain: collapse of the traditional political system and the interval before an effective new one would arise. They had no reason then to suspect that a political vacuum is a hotbed for judicial legislation.

The paralysis of the party system during Reconstruction was reflected in the parties themselves. They continued to exist, Lord Bryce said, merely "because they have existed." Drained of their dynamics, they drifted impotently. For two crucial decades after the Civil War, each was strong enough only to frustrate the other. The Democrats dominated the House in eight, their rivals held the Senate in seven, of the ten Congresses after 1873. No President from Grant to McKinley received a majority of the popular vote (two received less than a plurality), and none held office for two consecutive terms. Governor Seymour explained: "The Republicans [through corruption] have lost the confidence of the country, and the Democrats have not [re]gained it." Meanwhile, a new breed of judges went to the bench.

---

[28] The data in this paragraph are derived from B. WRIGHT, THE GROWTH OF AMERICAN CONSTITUTIONAL LAW 108-54 (1942).

In his brilliant *Reunion and Reaction*, C. Vann Woodward has shown that the "Compromise of 1877" involved far more than a withdrawal of Union troops from the South in exchange for Hayes in the White House. In its full reach it was an *extra-party* understanding between business-oriented Republicans and southern Bourbons or Redeemers. Northern businessmen had never been enthusiastic over Reconstruction—it was not good for business.[29] When the "disputed election" of 1876 compelled northern Republicanism to choose between its humane and its economic ideals, it chose the latter, abandoning the Negro to protect the tariff, hard money, a national banking system, and lush governmental subsidies. Just as GOP leaders dropped their Lincolnian (in favor of their Hamiltonian) tradition, the leaders of the New South abandoned Jefferson in favor of his arch-opponent. Many of the Redeemers were former Whigs who had never been comfortable in the Democratic Party. As harbingers of a new business-minded South, they found Republican economic ideals congenial, and they particularly resented the failure of northern Democrats to support subsidies for southern railroads. As one Washington correspondent wrote apropos the disputed election, "It is thoroughly understood here by Southern men, that Mr. Hayes means, if he should become President, to cut adrift from the carpetbaggers and make an alliance with respectable party leaders of Whig antecedents in the South."[30] In the face of the flagrant corruption of Grant's administration the southern upper crust abandoned Tilden and put another Republican in the White House—in exchange for a share of the spoils. These included the promise of a cabinet post, patronage, internal improvements (including a southern transcontinental railroad), and home rule, (*i.e.*, an end to federal protection for Blacks). In return the new southern governing class—the Bourbon Redeemers—would buttress Republican rule of the nation. By frustrating the formation of a cohesive popular majority, frozen sectionalism permitted northern and southern Bourbons to unite and conquer—with judicial help when necessary. The settlement of 1877 ushered in the Gilded Age. Ralph Gabriel describes its ethics as the Gospel of Wealth.[31]

With the decline of the party system, judges could not escape the

---

[29] *See* V. DE SANTIS, REPUBLICANS FACE THE SOUTHERN QUESTION 47-51, 125-29 (1959).

[30] 2 R. HOFSTADTER, W. MILLER & D. AARON, THE AMERICAN REPUBLIC 58-59 (1959).

[31] GABRIEL, THE COURT OF AMERICAN DEMOCRATIC THOUGHT, 151 *et seq*. (1956).

two post-bellum revolutions: emancipation and industrialization. Whether by chance or design the main grist that now came to the judicial mill were conflicts (direct or indirect) between businessmen and farmers and, later, laborers—the chief allies in the Republican combine. At first the Court refused to intervene, recognizing with Chief Justice Waite that these were essentially political issues.[32] The early Republican appointees to the bench were of the old vintage:

> Their Republicanism was that of the Civil War period—a comparatively Jeffersonian Republicanism, idealistic and humane, with faith in a democracy that involved human dignity and independence, substantiality of popular participation in the determination and control of public policy, reasonable if not equal opportunity for all to obtain as well as to pursue happiness, a considerable generality of mutual sympathy, decency, forbearance and good-will. Some of the new justices had been lawyers for great financial interests. But practice had not yet become specialized. They had been lawyers for ordinary men as well. They shared the ordinary man's anxiety as to the effect upon him of industrial expansion and the concentration of wealth. . . . [T]hey wanted the great new United States to be rather an enlargement than a subversion of the United States in which they had grown up. That United States was in danger. How could it be saved without the help of legislation? Conditions being new, legislation must be experimental. Legislative power must therefore be comparatively free.[33]

Accordingly in the *Union Pacific*,[34] and the *Legal Tender* cases,[35] *Sinking Fund Case*,[36] and Granger Cases[37] the Court—over strenuous dissent—rejected laissez faire and left policy issues for resolution by the political processes. The same Jeffersonian respect for democracy that found expression in these economic cases was reflected also in early conflicts on the status of the Negro. The classic decisions were *Strauder v. West Virginia*,[38] Ex parte *Virginia*,[39] and *Railroad v. Brown*,[40] which expressly rejected "separate but equal."

---

[32] *See, e.g.*, cases cited in notes 34-37 *infra*.
[33] W. Nelles, *Book Review*, 40 YALE L.J. 998, 999 (1931).
[34] United States v. Union Pacific R.R., 98 U.S. 569 (1879).
[35] 79 U.S. (12 Wall.) 457 (1870).
[36] 99 U.S. 700 (1878).
[37] *E.g.*, Munn v. Illinois, 97 U.S. 113 (1877).
[38] 100 U.S. 303 (1880).
[39] 100 U.S. 339 (1880).
[40] 84 U.S. (17 Wall.) 445 (1873).

The latter, like laissez faire, was still an unacceptable innovation.

Gradually the Settlement of 1877 engulfed the Court. A new generation of judges, free of blinding Jeffersonian anachronisms, saw the world as it was; America's attention had turned from slavery and emancipation to industrialization. The 1877 promise of southern autonomy vis-a-vis the Negro was constitutionalized in the *Civil Rights Cases*,[41] and *Plessy v. Ferguson*.[42] The business community got *In re Debs*,[43] *United States v. Knight*,[44] the *Income Tax*,[45] *Yellow Dog Contract*,[46] and *Child Labor Cases*[47]—as well as *Smyth v. Ames*,[48] *Lochner v. New York*,[49] and all the others. To put it in political terms, judicially enforced laissez faire checkmated the western farmer (and later the laboring man) as effectively as the "bloody shirt" neutralized the southern masses.

None of these Court decisions sprang inevitably from the "written" Constitution. They came rather from major innovating, activist doctrines: separate-but-equal, liberty-of-contract, dual federalism, substantive due process, and the fair value doctrine among others. These legalisms reflected the Spirit of '77. The price of Reunion was constitutionalized segregation and laissez faire; or rather, that was the price that could be extracted in the absence of a viable political party system. The nadir of the great American experiment in popular government had been reached.

Meanwhile, persistent agricultural depression harassed the tenuous Republican alliance. Plainly a new regional combination was struggling to be born. Hamlin Garland noted that "as ten-cent corn and ten per cent interest were troubling Kansas, so six-cent cotton was inflaming Georgia." Mrs. Lease, exhorting farmers to "raise less corn and more hell," declared that the "West and South are prostrate before the manufacturing East." In a great sectional upheaval in 1896, William Jennings Bryan tried to rally the forces of discon-

---

[41] 109 U.S. 3 (1883).
[42] 163 U.S. 537 (1896).
[43] 158 U.S. 564 (1895).
[44] 156 U.S. 1 (1895).
[45] Pollock v. Farmers Loan & Trust Co., 158 U.S. 601 (1895).
[46] Adair v. United States, 208 U.S. 161 (1908).
[47] Bailey v. Drexel Furniture Co., 259 U.S. 20 (1922); Hammer v. Dagenhart, 247 U.S. 251 (1918).
[48] 169 U.S. 466 (1898).
[49] 198 U.S. 45 (1905).

tent under the delusively simple banner of Free Silver.[50] He tried to use *Debs, Knight,* and the *Income Tax Case* as Lincoln had used *Dred Scott*—to instigate a sectional realignment, but he failed. For the first time in American history a western farm revolt suffered defeat. The core of the matter was that "reform associated with shaggy agrarianism could not carry a swiftly industrializing nation,"[51] yet the problems that Bryan raised were real and some day would have to be faced. Meanwhile, what Secretary of State Hay called "the splendid little war with Spain," Imperialism, World War I, and "back to normalcy" served, as the bloody shirt had served, to deflect attention and to keep America safe for the McKinley "modernized" Bourbon Settlement:

> The extreme sectionalism of this [new] system can be measured by virtually any yardstick. For example, excluding the special case of 1912, 84.5 per cent of the total electoral vote for Democratic presidential candidates between 1896 and 1928 was cast in the Southern and Border states.[52]

Gubernatorial contests during this period reveal a similar sectional pattern.[53]

THE NEW URBAN POLITICS AND JUDICIAL RESTRAINT

At least as early as 1933, A.N. Holcombe perceived the initial stages of a "New Party Politics."[54] It arose as urbanism discovered itself and replaced sectionalism at the heart of our party system. In 1955 Samuel Eldersveld found "quantitative evidence . . . that Professor Holcombe's observation [of a shift of the balance of power from the country-side to the cities] has been borne out. Urban presidential election tides from 1932 on . . . indicate the validity of that observation."[55] Industrial revolution had made America a nation of city dwellers and substituted labor for the farmer as the businessman's *bête noire*. Horizontal tensions became at least as

---

[50] *See, e.g.,* his famous "Cross of Gold" speech. Address by William J. Bryan, Democratic National Convention of 1896, Chicago, July 8, 1896.
[51] E. GOLDMAN, RENDEZVOUS WITH DESTINY 68 (1952).
[52] Burnham, *Party Systems and the Political Process* in W. BURNHAM & W. CHAMBERS, THE AMERICAN PARTY SYSTEMS 277-300 (1967).
[53] *Id.* See also Table 1.
[54] A. HOLCOMBE, THE NEW PARTY POLITICS (1942).
[55] Eldersveld, *The Influence of Metropolitan Party Pluralities in Presidential Elections Since 1920: A Study of Twelve Key Cities,* 43 AM. POL. SCI. REV. 1189, 1206 (1949).

crucial as those of sectionalism. In the politically potent, if economically superficial, verbiage of the 1930's, the common man was "ill-housed, ill-fed, and ill-clothed" while industry choked with "over-production."

The Great Depression, of course, was the catalyst of change in the party system. The election of 1932, however, was still essentially old fashioned, or sectional, although Roosevelt succeeded where Bryan had failed. He played upon the long obvious tension between the eastern and western wings of the Republican alliance and carried the South and West. The only states he lost (6) were in the Northeast, but despite the Great Depression, *he failed to carry a dozen major cities.*[56] This was the last election in which sectionalism played a dominant role.

As Samuel Lubell has shown, things were quite different in 1936.[57] The voters had learned what the New Deal was. Ethnic and class conscious urbanism replaced "acreage" in the alignment of political party forces. Many rural voters returned to the GOP. Most of the Midwestern Wheat Counties, for example, were on their way back. But an urban upheaval more than made up the loss: Every city with 100,000 or more inhabitants turned to the new Democratic party—and with one exception (Grand Rapids) remained there until the Eisenhower years.

> The really revolutionary surge behind the New Deal lay in this coupling of the depression with the rise of a new generation, which had been malnourished on the congestion of our cities and the abuses of industrialism. Roosevelt did not start this revolt of the city. What he did do was to awaken the climbing urban masses to a consciousness of the power in their numbers. . . . In turn, the big-city masses furnished the votes which re-elected Roosevelt again and again—and, in the process, ended the traditional Republican [sectional] majority in this country. . . . In the past American political realignments have always followed sectional lines. The Revolt of the City, however, has drawn the same class-conscious line of economic interest across the entire country, overriding not only regional distinctions but equally strong cultural differences.[58]

---

[56] S. LUBELL, THE FUTURE OF AMERICAN POLITICS, ch. 3 (1965).

[57] *Id*. at 49-63.

[58] *Id*. at 44.

The city masses had found a political tool responsive to their needs. The ragged shirt replaced the bloody shirt as a political symbol. Geographic, racial, and religious fissures no longer played so plainly into Bourbon hands. "Put crudely," Lubell said, "the hatred of bankers among native American workers had become greater than their hatred of the Pope [shades of Al Smith] or even the Negro."[59]

Like the great statesmen of sectionalism—Jefferson, Jackson,[60] and Lincoln—the new master of urban politics had his way with the Court. Roosevelt's "Packing Plan" of 1937, like the Chase Impeachment, failed only in form, for if he lost the battle, he won the war. His realignment of political forces, like those in 1800, 1828, and 1860, put the Court in its place. What the judges had achieved under a moribund sectional politics, they could not maintain in the face of a vigorous new political party system. The Bourbon Settlement of 1877 was deconstitutionalized. Returning to the *"written"* Constitution, the Supreme Court repudiated liberty-of-contract, substantive due process, dual federalism, separate-but-equal, and all the other activist creations of the old judicial regime. In sum, laissez faire and segregation lost their constitutional status. The Roosevelt Court's theme song was respect for the proposition that, except where the Constitution speaks quite clearly, basic social issues are better left to the political processes. What new doctrines the new Court devised were essentially doctrines of limitation of judicial power.[61] Policy-making reverted from judges to the people and their elected representatives—and stayed there until the New Deal coalition lost its élan.

DECLINE OF THE NEW DEAL COALITION AND RENEWED JUDICIAL ACTIVISM

Mapp v. Ohio[62] in 1961 seems an appropriate decision to mark the

---

[59] *Id.* at 59.

[60] President Jackson may, or may not, have said, "Marshall has made his decision, now let him enforce it." The fact is the decision in *Worcester v. Georgia*, 31 U.S. (6 Pet.) 515 (1832), was not enforced.

[61] *See, e.g.*, Dennis v. United States, 341 U.S. 494 (1951); Prudential Life Insurance Co. v. Benjamin, 328 U.S. 408 (1946); Graves v. New York *ex rel.* O'Keefe, 306 U.S. 466 (1939); Palko v. Connecticut, 302 U.S. 319 (1937). A good, brief account of the Roosevelt Court will be found in R. McCLOSKEY, THE AMERICAN SUPREME COURT, ch. 7 (1960).

[62] 367 U.S. 643 (1961).

beginning of a new judicial era, reflecting a new political impasse.[63] Reviewing the 1960's, Samuel Lubell's *The Hidden Crisis in American Politics* suggests we had lost our capacity for self-government.[64] Reasoned argument, compromise, and accommodation were increasingly "shoved aside" in favor of polarization, violence, and a struggle for raw power. Lubell could see *"no party coalition in command of a sufficiently stable majority to be able to advance a unifying set of policies."*[65]

Our troubles of course had been building for years; many of them had been quickened by war. President Eisenhower's well-known tranquilizer effect somehow kept the nation from responding to, or even seeing, them. A generation of exhausting crises from the Great Depression through Korea no doubt also had somethng to do with it. Meanwhile, the major political parties were disintegrating. By the time of *Mapp* the GOP had declined to abiding minority status: it had not since 1928 (and still has not) elected a President together with a majority in both houses of Congress. In fact, since 1928, it has carried the Senate only once and the House only twice. The Eisenhower victories were plainly personal; and, as the perceptive C. Vann Woodward points out, the huge Nixon-Agnew victory in 1972 can also be quite misleading:

> A sizable part of the popular vote for Nixon, perhaps a half [in the South] represented another protest against the national Democratic party rather than a real shift in party allegiance. The most recent polls on party identification [in the South] show a major disaffection with the Democratic party but no corresponding Republican gains . . . . The Democratic percentage has been dropping since 1960, but to a lesser extent so has the Republican, while the Independent percentage [34]

---

[63] Admirers of the Warren Court like to credit it with *Brown v. Board of Education*, 347 U.S. 483 (1954). That will not do. *Brown* was decided by eight members of the "old" Court plus Chief Justice Warren only a few months after he took his seat. It had been *plainly* anticipated in a unanimous opinion in *Sweatt v. Painter*, 339 U.S. 629 (1950). Obviously, much more than the Warren appointment is involved in the later sea change called the Warren Court. The decision in *Brown* was hardly an activist addition to the Constitution; it was rather a *return* to the central, *i.e.*, anti-racist, purpose of the Fourteenth Amendment as *originally recognized* in the *Slaughter House Cases*, 839 U.S. (16 Wall.) 36 (1873) and those cases cited in notes 38-40 *supra*.

[64] S. LUBELL, THE HIDDEN CRISIS IN AMERICAN POLITICS 266 (1970) [hereinafter cited as CRISIS].

[65] *Id.* at 25 (emphasis added).

has nearly doubled. The Southern shift has in some degree anticipated the more recent national inconsistency between Presidential ballots and state and local voting. Party discipline and authority are in general decline, and the two-party system is in bad health nationally.[66]

Nationwide by 1970 there were at least as many self-proclaimed Independents as Republicans.[67] Meanwhile, FDR's Democratic Coalition of Solid South, labor, farmer, Negro, and Intellectual was also deteriorating. In 1964 only six of the eleven Southern states remained Democratic; in 1968 only Texas did so; and, in 1972, no Southern state supported the Democratic national ticket. The farmer and the farm bloc, as they were known in Roosevelt's day, have all but disappeared. The tension between hardhat labor on one side and Blacks and intellectuals on the other is critical—indeed, it is a major basis of Wallace strength and Republican survival. Moreover, urbanism has assumed new dimensions: "Squeezed between the inward flow of blacks, and in some cities other minority elements, and the white movement to the suburbs, our larger cities lost those wonderful powers of social unification which they once had and which came to political fruition with the New Deal."[68] Indeed, as some see it, the political split of the future may be between the suburbs and the core cities.[69]

A crucial measure of the debility of both major parties may be the unparalleled recent rise of Independency[70] and Ticket Splitting[71]—which indicate a growing unwillingness to trust any existing party with responsibility for governing. For example, Californians elected Republican Ronald Reagan as governor at the same time in 1970 that they chose Democrat John Tunney for the federal Senate. Voters in Ohio in 1970 elected Democrat John Gilligan as governor and Republican Robert Taft as United States Senator. Earlier, Ar-

---

[66] Woodward, Book Review, 19 N.Y. Rev. of Books 39 (December 14, 1972).

[67] See Tables 2 and 3. The material in these tables comes from the Center for Political Studies, University of Michigan; Gallup Opinion Index; *Congressional Quarterly Weekly Report*; and *Newsweek*, as indicated; the tables themselves were taken from D. Palumbo, American Politics 531 (1973), and D. Nimmo & T.D. Ungs, American Political Patterns 130 (1973).

[68] Crisis, *supra* note 55, at 113.

[69] See A. Downs, Opening Up the Suburbs (1973); F. Wist, On the City's Rim (1972).

[70] See *supra* note 67; Tables 2 and 3.

[71] See Table 4. The table itself is taken from Palumbo, *supra* note 58, at 436.

kansas picked an Independent for President (George Wallace), a Republican for governor (Winthrop Rockefeller), and a Democrat for the federal Senate (J.W. Fulbright).

The flow of some recent opinion surveys (herein condensed) indicates a large and growing universe of voters who report:

(a)   It doesn't make a great deal of difference which candidate wins the election or which party runs the country;

(b)   Whether the Democrats or Republicans win will not have an important impact on the financial positions of their families;

(c)   They approve of the way the President is handling his job even though they are not members of the President's party; and

(d)   There is no difference between the parties in their capacity to handle the most important problems facing the country—for example, war, crime and lawlessness, race relations, inflation, poverty, and so on.[72]

George Wallace spoke for more than the far right when he said there is not a dime's worth of difference between the major parties. There are historic differences, of course, but for many voters they are—dreaded word—irrelevant. The nub of the matter seems plain. Republicans and Democrats alike remain largely oriented to, and structured for, the issues of the 1930's. In domestic affairs particularly they seem to have become empty shells of power largely out of touch with new realities. Masses of voters—especially the young[73] for whom the 1930's and the Depression are wearisome history—feel estranged and effectively disenfranchised. The parties seem blind to what these voters perceive as current needs. The Ripon Society put it this way:

The old economic alignments still have meaning for people in poverty, who remain attached to the Democratic Party. Con-

---

[72] W. KEEFE, PARTIES, POLITICS, AND PUBLIC POLICY IN AMERICA 148 (1972). Trend data since the 1940's on points (a) to (c) appear in Lane, *The Politics of Consensus in an Age of Affluence*, 59 AM. POL. SCI. REV. 882-85 (D. 1965). Concerning point (d), see issues of the Gallup Opinion Index (October, 1965); September, 1968; and February, 1970. Typically, between 40 and 50 percent of the respondents report that they see no difference between the parties (or have no opinion) in this respect.

[73] See Table 3.

versely, the very wealthy remain Republican. But the mass of Americans in between are no longer in economic need, and have shifted their concern to questions of status and power.[74]

As Walter Lippmann—old and conservative—saw the problem:

> To many, it does not seem right that in this time of crisis our political system should be failing to register and reflect the issues which torment our people. What has happened, it would seem, is that the American political system, which works so well in normal times, is operating regardless of and apart from the bitter war and the urban and racial crisis at home.[75]

Another index of the decline of political parties is suggested in what Frank Sorauf calls their problem of "technological unemployment." The campaign aids that candidates once got from party organizations—information, pulse-readings, man-power, political know-how—they now get from pollsters, the media, public relations experts, volunteer workers, and campaign management firms. In short, party techniques are as outmoded as party alignments. The one may be in some degree a reflection of the other.

Again, as in the late 1790's, the 1850's, and the post-bellum era, an existing and once useful party alignment appears to have lost touch with the times. Once more, as in the 1890's and thereafter, a realignment seems overdue. Again, the resulting political vacuum has invited judicial policy-making on a grand scale: the phenomenon now called Warren Court activism. As Robert M. Hutchins saw it at the close of the Warren Court era, the Supreme Court has become "the highest legislative body in the land."[76] Adolf Berle said a revolution is taking place, and "the revolutionary committee is the Supreme Court of the United States;"[77] he quoted Justice Fortas to the same effect.[78] Professor Karst has suggested that what the Warren Court did in the criminal law area "has seemed to reflect a deep distrust of the whole criminal process as a means of social control."[79]

---

[74] RIPON SOCIETY, THE LESSONS OF VICTORY 142 (1969).

[75] Brownfield, *The Irrelevance of American Politics*, in J.A. PERRY & M.S. SEIDLER, CONTEMPORARY SOCIETY 640 (1972).

[76] Center for the Study of Democratic Institutions, *The Case for Constitutional Change*, 3 CENTER REPORT 1 (Dec., 1970) (Occasional Paper).

[77] A. BERLE, POWER 342 (1969) [hereinafter cited as BERLE].

[78] *Id.*

[79] Karst, *Invidious Discrimination*, 16 U.C.L.A. L. REV. 716, 730 (1969).

All this is from *sympathetic* observers! Speaking of the earlier activism of a generation ago, Justice Cardozo is said to have put it a bit differently: "We are no longer a Court."

The two eras of "government by the judiciary" have more in common than their respective origins in political party failure. Both activist Courts rested heavily on a perversion of the Fourteenth Amendment. The one found that it incorporated segregation and laissez faire; the other that it incorporated one-man-one-vote, a national code of criminal procedure, and major elements of New Left doctrine particularly in the realm of sex and obscenity. Each in the eyes of its enemies was blindly idealistic, pushing logic beyond common sense at the expense of important public interests. Each had the support of a powerful elite: the Bourbons in one case, the Intelligentsia in the other. And each was highly unpopular with the general public.[80]

CONCLUSION

Vigorous sectional politics in early America choked off the judicial activism threatened in *Marbury* and practiced in *Dred Scott*. With the failure of the sectional system Court pretension flourished—until it was cut down by Franklin Roosevelt's new urban politics. Finally, beginning in the 1960's, after the New Deal political alignment expired and left a vacuum, judges again found room to legislate—doing so on a grand scale.

The earlier era of judicial activism began with the emasculation of the Sherman Antitrust Act and the income tax. It ended soon after the Court had destroyed most of the early New Deal's legislative efforts. Scores of state and national policies were slaughtered in the interim. Public disdain for these accomplishments is a twice-told tale. It culminated in Roosevelt's "unpacking plan" and humilitation for the "nine old men." In contrast the public has accepted the Warren Court's one-man-one-vote coup with good grace.[81] Its very name is irresistable, yet the man on the street has not yet discovered what is increasingly evident to scholars: one-man-one-

---

[80] According to a Gallup survey the Court by the time of the Warren retirement had reached bottom in public esteem. *See* New York Times, June 15, 1969, at 53, § 1. As to the old, laissez faire activists, see text *infra*.

[81] *See* New York Times, August 10, 1969, p. 80 § 1 (Gallup Survey).

vote promises much more than it delivers.[82] This in time may produce disillusionment and a "credibility gap" that activist judges perhaps can endure even less than can acknowledged politicians.

The Warren Court's rule of counsel for indigents in all felony cases[83] has been widely accepted, and, indeed, has been implemented and funded by legislation.[84] Plainly, the community is not insensitive vis-a-vis the claims of criminal justice. It is, however, obviously resentful of the sentimentality, or crime coddling, that it perceives in much of the rest of the extensive code of criminal procedure that the Warren Court imposed upon the states.[85]

That the decisions in question reflect serious problems in law enforcement, few would deny. That the Court's solutions are wise *as legislative policy* is at least arguable. It can hardly be said, however, that they were achieved with the consent of the governed. A great part of the American public is not convinced that the Warren Court's views were sound.[86] They are bound, therefore, to be difficult to enforce. Indeed, they may breed lawlessness in policemen and others who sense that the community sides with them, not with the Court. By assuming broad, criminal law-making functions while ignoring or discounting deeply felt fears of a crime ridden society, the Justices invite disrespect for themselves and the law. Surely, this is not the road to reform of criminal justice. The problem is not confined to the area of criminal law. The Warren Court's efforts with respect to the prohibition of prayers and Bible reading in the public schools are repudiated or ignored in many—perhaps most—communities.[87] Much the same must be said of the Court's attempts, during the 1960's, to define obscenity.[88]

---

[82] *See, e.g.*, Dixon, Democratic Representation: Reapportionment in Law and Politics 574 *et seq.* (1969); R. O'Rourke, Reapportionment: Law, Politics and Computers 57 *et seq.* (1972).

[83] Gideon v. Wainwright, 373 U.S. 335 (1963).

[84] *See* Criminal Justice Act of 1964, 18 U.S.C. § 3006A (1969), *as amended* (Supp. 1974).

[85] *See* Friendly, *The Bill of Rights as a Code of Criminal Procedure*, 53 Calif. L. Rev. 929 (1965); Friendly, *Is Innocence Irrelevant? Collateral Attack on Criminal Judgments*, 38 U. Chi. L. Rev. 142 (1960).

[86] *See* note 69 *supra; see also* Omnibus Crime Control and Safe Streets Act of 1968, 42 U.S.C. §§ 370 *et seq.* (1973).

[87] *See* W. Muir, Prayer in the Public Schools: Law and Attitude Change (1967); K. Dolbear & P. Hammond, Local Elites, the Impact of Judicial Decisions, and the Pressures of Change (unpublished manuscript presented at American Political Science Association Convention, 1969).

[88] *See* Ginzburg v. United States, 383 U.S. 463 (1966); Memoirs v. Massachusetts, 383

What Brandeis wrote in the context of the old activism seems equally relevant today: ". . . [A judge] may advise; he may persuade; but he may not command or coerce. He does coerce when without convincing the judgment he overcomes the will by the weight of his authority."[89] In a democracy, per our hypothesis, judicial coercion is possible only when the political processes are too weak to hold their own domain. Their seeming weakness in the recent past is reminiscent of the era of senile sectionalism. Perhaps now[90]—as then—we are in a transitional period between two dynamic polities. A generation ago, after the old judicial activists surrendered to the New Deal, an acute foreign observer—unable to believe we would ever again submit to judicial supremacy—offered this wise counsel:

> The courts are never likely again to attempt to direct the main trends of American political life, in the States or in the Union. But nature abhors a political vacuum as much as any other kind. And there is only one possible successor to the courts, and that is the body corporate, the People of the United States. . . .

> But the people of the United States will only succeed in replacing its old guardian if it emends the most famous dictum of Chief Justice Marshall. He told his brethren to remember that it was "a constitution that we are expounding." For a people, a constitution is not a legal text to be expounded but a code of political practice to be lived and the transition from the legal to the political way of life is the great immediate task of the greatest and most successful of federations.[91]

Meanwhile, the ultimate freedom—to make mistakes—has been largely taken over by judges.

U.S. 413 (1966); Jacobellis v. Ohio, 378 U.S. 184 (1964); Manual Enterprises, Inc. v. Day, 370 U.S. 478 (1962). Senatorial rancor with respect to these obscenity decisions was clear in the hearings on the nomination of Justice Fortas for the Chief Justiceship. *See* 114 Cong. Rec. 21, 168 (1968); *Hearings on the Nomination of Abe Fortas as Chief Justice Before the Committee on the Judiciary*, 90th Cong., 2d Sess. (1968). The Court perhaps responded to this political response in its recent decisions which define obscenity in terms of the local community and not the nation. Miller v. California, 413 U.S. 15 (1973).

[89] Horning v. District of Columbia, 354 U.S. 115, 139 (1920) (Brandeis, J., dissenting).

[90] *Apodaca v. Oregon*, 406 U.S. 404 (1972), *Furman v. Georgia*, 408 U.S. 238 (1972), and *Roe v. Wade*, 210 U.S. 113 (1973), suggest, *inter alia*, that activism did not die with the departure of Chief Justice Warren and three of his colleagues.

[91] D. BROGAN, THE CRISIS OF AMERICAN FEDERALISM 43 (1944).

Map 1 [From J.M. Blum, et al., *The American Experience* (1963)]. Copyright © 1973 by Harcourt Brace Jovanovich, Inc., and reproduced with their permission from THE NATIONAL EXPERIENCE, 3rd Edition, by John M. Blum et al.

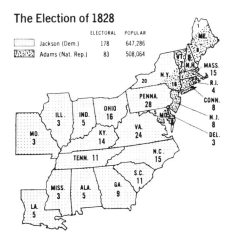

Map 2 [From J.M. Blum, et al., *The American Experience* (1963)]. Copyright © 1973 by Harcourt Brace Jovanovich, Inc., and reproduced with their permission from THE NATIONAL EXPERIENCE, 3rd Edition, by John M. Blum et al.

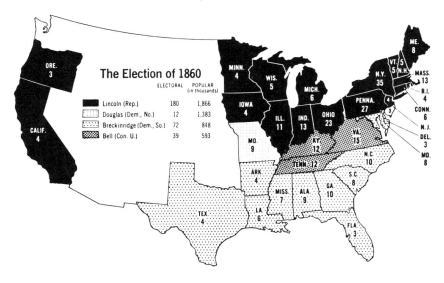

Table 1

Sectionalism and Gubernatorial Elections, 1894-1931

REGION	PERCENTAGE OF GOVERNORSHIPS WON BY:		
	DEM.	REP.	OTHER
South [a]	98.8	2.6	0.6
Border [b]	61.1	38.9	—
Midwest and West [c]	31.0	67.2	1.8
Northeast [d]	16.9	83.1	—
Total U.S.	43.0	56.0	1.0

a Eleven ex-Confederate states.

b Kentucky, Maryland, Missouri, Oklahoma, West Virginia.

c East North Central, West North Central (except for Missouri), Mountain and Pacific census regions.

d New England and Middle Atlantic census regions plus Delaware.

From W. Chambers and W. Burnham, THE AMERICAN PARTY SYSTEMS (Oxford University Press, 1967). Reprinted by permission.

Table 2

Distribution of Party Identification in the United States, 1952-1970

Question: "Generally speaking, do you usually think of yourself as a Republican, a Democrat, an Independent, or what?" (If Republican or Democrat): "Would you call yourself a strong (R) (D) or a not very strong (R) (D)?" (If Independent): "Do you think of yourself as closer to the Republican or Democratic Party?"

	Oct. 1952	Oct. 1954	Oct. 1956	Oct. 1958	Oct. 1960	Nov. 1962	Oct. 1964	Nov. 1966	Nov. 1968	Nov. 1970
Democrat										
Strong	22%	22%	21%	23%	21%	23%	26%	18%	20%	20%
Weak	25	25	23	24	25	23	25	27	25	23
Independent										
Democrat	10	9	7	7	8	8	9	9	10	10
Independent	5	7	9	8	8	8	8	12	11	13
Republican	7	6	8	4	7	6	6	7	9	8
Republican										
Weak	14	14	14	16	13	16	13	15	14	15
Strong	13	13	15	13	14	12	11	10	10	10
Apolitical, don't know	4	4	3	5	4	4	2	2	1	1
Total	100%	100%	100%	100%	100%	100%	100%	100%	100%	100%
Number of cases	1614	1139	1772	1269	3021	1289	1571	1291	1553	1802

Source: Center for Political Studies, University of Michigan.

From Dan Nimmo and Thomas D. Ungs, AMERICAN POLITICAL PATTERNS: CONFLICT AND CONSENSUS, 3rd edition, p. 130. Source: Center for Political Studies, University of Michigan. Copyright © 1967, 1969, 1973 by Little, Brown and Company (Inc.). Reprinted by permission.

Table 3

Party Identification Among the American Electorate, 1940-1971

Percentage of Voters Identifying Themselves as:

Year	Democrats	Republicans	Independents
1940	42	38	20
1950	45	33	22
1960	47	30	23
1964	53	25	22
1966	48	27	25
June 1968	46	27	27
Oct. 1971:			
Voters 21 and over	45	27	28
New voters	38	18	42

Sources: Gallup Opinion Index, *Report No. 28, October 1967, for 1940-1966 data; Congressional Quarterly,* Weekly Report *(August 23, 1968), for June 1968 data;* Newsweek *(October 25, 1971), for October 1971 data.*

Table 4

The Emergent Independent Majority, 1900-1968

Third-party candidates often inspire voters to split their tickets, but the overall trend has been for voters to ignore party labels.

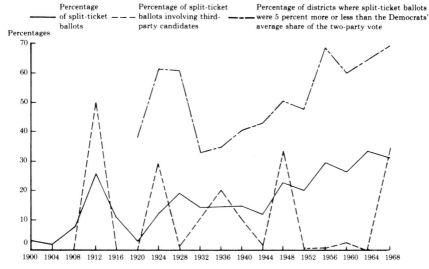

Source: Walter Dean Burnham, "The End of American Party Politics," in 7 Trans-Action 18 (1969). Published by permission of Transaction, Inc., from TRANSACTION, December 1969. Copyright © 1969 by Transaction, Inc.

21 🏵 *Dred Scott's Case — Reconsidered*

The *Dred Scott* decision[1] is not, as our folklore would have it, the classically worst, or even a typical, assertion of judicial supremacy. To be sure, earlier abolitionist-inspired interpretations have given way to a rather general acceptance of it as a "sincere" judicial effort to solve a nation-wrecking problem.[2] But even this latter view obscures the fact that the most criticized decision in American jurisprudence was undertaken only upon explicit invitation of Congress and did no more than give constitutional sanction to a position held long and persistently by most contemporary voters. This view —the present thesis—obviates an otherwise tantalizing paradox : that Chief Justice Taney should suddenly in 1857 abandon that Jacksonian respect for popular sovereignty and the democratic processes which for twenty years had been the hallmark of his philosophy upon the bench.[3]

Acquisition of the Mexican and Oregon territories during the administration of President Polk (1845-1849) revived the old problem of the extension of slavery—the problem which in the case of the Louisiana Purchase had been settled by the Missouri Compromise of 1820. After full discussion, President Polk and the members of his Cabinet unanimously agreed that the principle of the old compromise should be adapted to current needs.[4] That is, the 36° 30′ parallel should be recognized as the boundary between freedom and slavery from the Louisiana territory to the Pacific. But that simple solution was no longer acceptable in the North. The Wilmot Proviso, supported by resolutions of all but one of the Northern state legislatures, would have prohibited by act of Congress the introduction of slavery into any of the newly acquired domain.[5] After its adoption by the House of Representatives in February, 1847, Southern leaders abandoned their willingness to compromise on the old Missouri basis and took the line that Con-

---

1. Scott v. Sandford, 19 How. 393 (U.S. 1857), holding the Missouri Compromise unconstitutional on the ground, *inter alia,* that the Fifth Amendment prohibited Congress from interfering with slavery in the territories.
2. See, for example, Charles Evans Hughes, *Roger Brooke Taney,* 17 A. B. A. J. 785, 787 (1931).
3. See Mendelson, *Chief Justice Taney—Jacksonian Judge,* 12 U. of Pitt. L. Rev. 381 (1951).
4. The Diary of James K. Polk, entries for Jan. 5, 16, 1847 (Quaife ed. 1910).
5. 1 Morrison and Commager, The Growth of the American Republic 598 (1942).

gress had no power to proscribe slavery anywhere.[6] Thus in typical American fashion a vexing problem of social policy was translated into constitutional jargon and became a "legal question." Supporters of Wilmot's Proviso, of course, assumed Congressional power to outlaw slavery in the territories, while the Northern ultras held that the Constitution itself prohibited slavery in the territories. Southerners found constitutional denial of national power to interfere with their peculiar proprietary interests.[7] Upon the issue so joined Congress was unable to make a decision, for while the Northern view prevailed in the House, it was blocked in the Senate. Accordingly settlers in the new territory had to do without government because Congress could not decide whether they must do without slaves.[8]

This impasse is the background of the attempted Clayton Compromise[9] of mid-1848 whereby Congress in organizing the California and New Mexico territories was to remain silent on the subject of slavery, leaving its introduction or prohibition to rest

> ". . . on the Constitution, as the same should be expounded by the [territorial] judges, with a right to appeal to the Supreme Court of the United States."[10]

In this manner, according to Senator Clayton of Maine, Congress would "avoid the decision of this distracting question, leaving it to be settled by the silent operation of the Constitution itself. . . ."[11] After elaborate debate the Clayton Compromise was passed in the Senate and defeated in the House (the latter still intent upon the Wilmot Proviso). But the essence of Clayton's proposal lived on to be incorporated in the great Compromise of 1850[12] and the Kansas-Nebraska Act of 1854[13] and to reach fruition in the *Dred Scott* decision.

In January, 1850, Henry Clay of Kentucky introduced in the Senate the famous resolutions which were the foundation of the Compromise of 1850. His second resolution, recognizing the in-

---

6.   Id. at 599-600; McLaughlin, A Constitutional History of the United States 512-513 (1936).
7.   For a review of the opposing constitutional theories, see *id.* at 514 *et seq.*
8.   1 Morrison and Commager, *op. cit. supra* note 5, at 599.
9.   Cong. Globe, 30th Cong., 1st Sess. 950, 1002 (1848).
10.   *Ibid.*
11.   *Ibid.*
12.   Embodied in four separate measures as follows : The Texas and New Mexico Act, 9 Stat. 446 (1850) ; The Utah Act, 9 Stat. 453 (1850) ; The Fugitive Slave Act, 9 Stat. 462 (1850) ; Act Abolishing the Slave Trade in the District of Columbia, 9 Stat. 467 (1850).
13.   10 Stat. 277 (1854).

compatibility of the Northern and Southern views as to the power of Congress, proposed that

> ". . . it is inexpedient for Congress to provide by law either for its [slavery's] introduction into, or exclusion from, any part of the said territory; and that appropriate territorial governments ought to be established by Congress in all of the said territory . . . without the adoption of any restriction or condition on the subject of slavery."[14]

This was the doctrine of Congressional non-intervention with slavery in the territories which Lewis Cass, presidential candidate of the Democratic Party, had sponsored in his famous Nicholson Letter[15] of December, 1847—and which Stephen Douglas was later to adopt and make famous under the banner of "popular [read territorial] sovereignty." But it was perfectly clear that Congressional silence would leave uncertain the legal status of slavery in the new domain. To obviate this, amendments to Clay's non-intervention provisions (in the bills embodying his resolutions) were offered by both Northern and Southern ultras to embody their respective constitutional views. Thus, for example, Senator Baldwin of Connecticut, offering one such amendment, observed:

> "I agree entirely in the sentiment which was advanced the other day by the Senator from Louisiana [Mr. Soule] that we ought not to pass a law which shall be understood in a different sense by those who cooperate in its passage. . . . The people demand a law, a rule for their conduct clear and intelligible. They do not ask us to give them a Delphic response, which may be interpreted in one way or another, according to the wishes of every inquirer. . . . The object of my amendment is simply to declare what we mean."[16]

But Senator Clay knew the futility of such "clarifying" amendments. It was in exactly those rapids that settlement of the territorial problem had been floundering since 1846. Congressional avoidance of the disputed issue and reference of it, as a constitutional question, to the judiciary, was precisely the essence of his compromise. As Clay put it, in answer to Baldwin:

> "The bill leaves in full force the paramount authority of the Constitution. . . . Now what ought to be done more satisfactory to both sides of the question, to the free States and to the slaveholding States, than to apply the principle of [Congressional] non-intervention to the state of the law in New Mexico, and to

---

14. Sen. J., 31st Cong., 1st Sess. 118 (1850); Cong. Globe, 31st Cong., 1st Sess. 245 (1850).
15. McLaughlin, *op. cit. supra* note 6, at 512-513.
16. Cong. Globe, 31st Cong., 1st Sess. 1146 (1850).

leave the question of slavery or no slavery to be decided by the only competent authority that can definitely settle it forever, the authority of the Supreme Court of the United States.

"The honorable Senator from Connecticut [Mr. Baldwin] on yesterday wanted the law settled. Suppose, then, we were to make a declaration of the law pleasing to the learned Senator . . . how if we were to attempt to settle this question could it be settled? In the first place we can not settle it, because of the great diversity of opinion which exists; and yet the Senator will ask those who differ with him in opinion to surrender their opinion, and, after they have made this sacrifice of opinion, can they declare what the law is? When the question comes up before the Supreme Court of the United States, that tribunal will declare what the law is."[17]

On this basis the slavery extension aspects of the Compromise of 1850 were settled. Congress simply delegated to the territorial legislatures of Utah and New Mexico all power over slavery which Congress itself might have, the extent of that power being the subject of vigorous dispute:

". . . the legislative power of the territory shall extend to all rightful subjects of legislation consistent with the Constitution of the United States [with certain exceptions not here relevant]."[18]

Then to facilitate settlement of the constitutional question, special liberalizing provisions were made in regard to federal court jurisdiction in slavery litigation. Thus after providing that "writs of error and appeals [to the Supreme Court of the United States] from the final decisions of said [territorial] supreme court shall be allowed, and may be taken in the same manner and under the same regulations as from the circuit courts of the United States, where the value of the property or amount in controversy . . . shall exceed one thousand dollars . . . ," special exception was made "in all cases involving title to slaves" where it was provided, "the said writs of error or appeals shall be allowed . . . without regard to the value of the matter, property, or title in controversy. . . ." Similarly "a writ of error or appeal shall be allowed to the Supreme Court of the United States . . . upon any writ of habeas corpus involving the question of personal freedom. . . ."[19]

---

17. *Id.* at 1155. See the following for typical expressions of willingness to accept judicial settlement of the slavery extension problem: Yulee of Florida, Cong. Globe, 31st Cong., 1st Sess., appendix, 95-96 (1850); Phelps of Vermont, *id.* at 95; Clay of Kentucky, *id.* at 916; Davis of Mississippi, *id.* at 154; Turney of Tennessee, *id.* at 297.

18. The Texas and New Mexico Act, 9 Stat. 446 (1850); The Utah Act, 9 Stat. 453 (1850).

19. *Ibid.*

These provisions are a verbatim copy of parts of the Clayton Compromise which had been added to Senator Clayton's original bill after Senators Hamlin and Corwin had raised the point that the normal federal jurisdictional amount of one thousand dollars would prevent effective operation of Clayton's proposal to shunt the slavery extension issue over to the courts.[20] It is, of course, significant that both provisions liberalizing the right of appeal to the Supreme Court (that relating to habeas corpus as well as the eliminating the "jurisdictional amount") were new in federal law. Senator Corwin's comment on the scheme is apposite—Congress had enacted a law suit, not a law.[21]

This interpretation was adopted by Senator Stephen A. Douglas' Committee on Territories which reported out on January 4, 1854, the Dodge Bill for the organization of the Nebraska Territory:

> "In the judgment of your committee, those measures [the acts constituting the Compromise of 1850] were intended to have a far more comprehensive and enduring effect than the mere adjustment of the difficulties arising out of the recent acquisition of Mexican territory. They were designed to establish certain great principles, which would . . . in all time to come, avoid the perils of a similar agitation, by withdrawing the question of slavery from the halls of Congress and the political arena, and committing it to the arbitrament of those who were immediately interested in, and alone responsible for its consequences. [There follows recital of some of the arguments as to the constitutionality of slavery in the territories and of the power of Congress with respect to slavery.] Your committee do not feel themselves called upon to enter into the discussion of these controverted questions. They involve the same grave issues which produced the agitation, the sectional strife, and the fearful struggle of 1850. As Congress deemed it wise and prudent to refrain from deciding the matters in controversy then . . . by any act declartory of the true intent of the Constitution . . . so your committee are not now prepared to recommend a departure from the course pursued on that memorable occasion . . . by any act declaratory of the meaning of the Constitution in respect to the legal points in dispute . . . it it apparent that the compromise measures of 1850 affirm and rest upon the following propositions—First: That all questions pertaining to slavery in the territories, and in the new States to be formed therefrom, are to be left to the decision of the people residing therein. . . ."

---

20. Cong. Globe, 30th Cong., 1st Sess. 988, 989, 1002-1005 (1848). Senator Johnson of Maryland introduced the amendment (p. 1002). It will be noted that his amendment is erroneously reported to read "title to lands" instead of "title to slaves." The matter is corrected in sections 24 and 31 of the Bill as passed by the Senate (pp. 1004, 1005).

21. McLaughlin, *op. cit. supra* note 6, at 514.

"Second: That all cases involving title to slaves, and "questions of personal freedom" are referred to the adjudication of the local tribunals, with the right of appeal to the Supreme Court of the United States."[22]

The resulting legislation was the fateful Kansas-Nebraska Act of 1854.[23] In course of the Congressional debates on this Act, the familiar arguments were made in favor of the familiar "clarifying" amendments. This time we know on the authority of Senator Judah K. Benjamin of Louisiana, the problem was settled in caucus where:

"Morning after morning we met for the purpose of coming to some understanding upon that very point [slavery in the territories]; and it was finally understood by all, agreed to by all, made the basis of compromise by all the supporters of that bill, that the territories should be organized with a delegation by Congress of all the power of Congress in the Territories, and that the extent of the power of Congress should be determined by the Courts."[24]

In the course of debate on the Kansas-Nebraska Bill, Senator Brown gives what Allen Johnson calls the Southern viewpoint:

"If I thought that, in voting for the bill as it now stands, I was conceding the right of the people in the territory, during their territorial existence, to exclude slavery, I would withhold my vote. . . . It [the bill] leaves the question where I am quite willing it should be left—to the ultimate decision of the courts. It is purely a judicial question, and if Congress well refrain from intimating an opinion, I am willing that the Supreme Court shall decide it. But, Sir, I have too often seen that Court sustaining the intentions of Congress, to risk a decision in my favor, after Congress has decided against me. The alien and sedition laws, the bank law, the tariff law have all been decided constitutional. Any why? Not, in my opinion, because they were so, but because the Supreme Court, as a coordinate Department of Government, was disinclined to clash with the other Departments. If this question is allowed to go before the Supreme Court, free from the influence of a Congressional pre-judgment, I will abide the result though it be against me."[25]

---

22. Sen. Rep. No. 15, 33d Cong., 1st Sess. (1854).
23. 10 Stat. 277 (1854).
24. Cong. Globe, 36th Cong., 1st Sess. 1966 (1860). Senator Benjamin said the same thing in greater detail prior to the *Dred Scott* decision. Cong. Globe, 34th Cong., 1st Sess. 1093 (1856). For corroboration by Douglas and Hunter, see Cong. Globe, 35th Cong., 2d Sess. 1258 (1859); 33d Cong., 1st Sess., appendix, 224 (1854). See also letter of Congressman A. H. Stephens, May 9, 1860, in Cong. Globe, 36th Cong., 1st Sess., appendix, 315-316 (1860). As to the "clarifying" amendments see, for example, the efforts of Senator Chase, Cong. Globe, 33d Cong., 1st Sess. 421-423 (1854).
25. Cong. Globe, 33d Cong., 1st Sess., appendix, 232 (1854); Johnson, Stephen A. Douglas 247 (1908).

These remarks by Senator Brown may not be crucial in themselves, though Brown was one of the congressional leaders of his
day. But they become highly significant through endorsement by
the Chairman of the Senate Committee on the Judiciary, Mr. Butler,
who joined in and then supplemented Brown's remarks as follows:

"I am willing . . . to trust judges upon the bench who are sworn
to administer the law and observe the Constitution. I am therefore perfectly willing to trust this bill to fortune under the im-
pulse of justice."[26]

Accordingly what the Douglas Committee on Territories called
the "great principles" of the Compromise of 1850 were embodied
in the Kansas-Nebraska Act. After declaring the Missouri Compromise "inoperative and void" the measure in Section 14 provided
that:

"[It is] the true intent and meaning of this act not to legislate
slavery into any territory or State, nor to exclude it therefrom,
but to leave the people thereof perfectly free to form and regulate
their domestic institutions in their own way, *subject only to the
Constitution of the United States.* . . . [italics added]."[27]

The second great principle of the 1850 settlement relating to
appeals to the Supreme Court on slavery questions was reproduced
verbatim in the Kansas-Nebraska Act's Section 9.

Two years later, in July, 1856, only eight months prior to the
Dred Scott decision, Senator Lyman Trumbull of Illinois, in the
course of a debate on the admission of Kansas as a state, offered
what was probably the last "clarifying" amendment. Trumbull
wanted the above quoted "true intent and meaning" clause of the
Kansas-Nebraska Act glossed with the assertion that the latter

". . . was intended to, and does confer, upon, or leave to the
people of the Territory of Kansas full power at any time, through
its Territorial Legislature, to exclude slavery from said Territory, or to recognize and regulate it therein."[28]

This, of course, was simply the Northern view, repudiated by
the South, that Congress and hence by derivation the Territories,
had power under the Constitution to regulate territorial slavery.

Senator Cass of Michigan answered Trumbull in the following
terms:

"It is said there is a difference of construction between the North
and the South on the Kansas-Nebraska Act. . . . The difference
does not result from the words of that bill, but from the nature

---

26.   *Id.* at 240.
27.   10 Stat. 227 (1854).
28.   Cong. Globe, 34th Cong., 1st Sess., appendix, 796 (1856).

of things. The North and the South construe the Constitution differently. . . . The different constructions of . . . [the Kansas-Nebraska Act] result from no equivocations of it, but from the fact that here is an important constitutional question undetermined by the supreme judicial authority; and in the meantime individuals in different sections of the Union put their own constructions on it. . . . There is no power which the Senator from Illinois can use—no words which he can put into an Act of Congress, that will remove this constitutional doubt until it is finally settled by the proper tribunal."[29]

Senator Douglas whose genius got the Compromise of 1850 and the Kansas-Nebraska Act through Congress, suspecting that his colleague from Illinois was attempting to get commitments that would destroy Douglas at home, answered Trumbull as follows:

"My opinion [on slavery in the territories] . . . has been well known in the Senate for years. . . . I told them [in the Kansas-Nebraska debates] it was a judicial question. . . . My answer then was and now is, that if the Constitution carries slavery there [into the territories] let it go . . . but, if the Constitution does not carry it there, no power but the people can carry it there. . . . I stated I would not discuss this legal question, for by the bill we referred it to the Courts."[30]

Thereupon the Trumbull amendment was voted down.

Was reference of the slavery extension issue to the judiciary understood and acceptable outside of Congress? One month after the Trumbull amendment debate, and some seven months before the *Dred Scott* decision, which he was to condemn so bitterly, Abraham Lincoln said in a public speech at Galena, Illinois:

"Do you [Democrats] say that such restrictions of slavery [in the territories] would be unconstitutional and that some of the States would not submit to its enforcement? I grant you that an unconstitutional act is not a law; but I do not ask, and will not take your construction of the Constitution. The Supreme Court of the United States is the tribunal to decide such questions, and we [Republicans] will submit to its decisions. . . ."[31]

There had been some doubt as to whether President Pierce would sign the Kansas-Nebraska Act for he had been suspected of free-soilism. To resolve any such doubts Secretary of War Jefferson Davis arranged a conference between the President and a number of leading Senators and Congressmen where administration support

---

29. *Id.* at 797-798.
30. *Id.* at 797.
31. Speech at Galena, Illinois, July 26, 1856, II Collected Works of Abraham Lincoln 354-355 (Basler ed. 1953).

for the measure was secured.[32] Indeed as it turned out the President personally believed the Missouri Compromise unconstitutional, but rather than repeal by the Kansas-Nebraska Act he favored a "guarantee of rights of persons and property in accordance with the Constitution, and would leave it to the Supreme Court to decide what those rights were."[33] In his last message to Congress on December 22, 1856, President Pierce in effect endorsed the *Dred Scott* decision in advance:

> "All that the repeal [of the Missouri Compromise by the Kansas-Nebraska Act] did was to relieve the statute book of an objectionable enactment, unconstitutional in effect and injurious in terms to a large portion of the states."[34]

Pierce had nothing but the highest praise for the Kansas-Nebraska Act. In a historical review of the slavery controversy he condemned the Missouri settlement as conducive to sectional strife and attributed Buchanan's victory in the presidential election of the preceeding month to the desire of the people to have a termination of that difficulty.[35]

In his inaugural address two days before the *Dred Scott* decision President-elect Buchanan, referring to the problem of slavery in the territories, said:

> "[I]t is a judicial question, which legitimately belongs to the Supreme Court of the United States before whom it is now pending, and will, it is understood, be speedily and finally settled. . . . The whole Territorial question being thus settled upon the principle of popular sovereignty—a principle as ancient as free government itself—everything of a practical nature has been decided."[36]

Clearly the treatment of slavery in the territories as a judicial question by important political figures on such occasions indicates a rather general public acceptance of that mode of settlement. Similarly in his first public mention of the matter after the *Dred Scott* decision Douglas explained that by the Kansas-Nebraska Act Congressional

---

32. Simms, A Decade of Sectional Controversy 59-60 (1942).
33. *Ibid.*
34. 5 Richardson, *A Compilation of the Messages and Papers of the Presidents* 403 (1903).
35. *Ibid.*
36. *Id.* at 431. These remarks are famous in connection with evidence now available which indicates that Buchanan had advance notice of what the *Dred Scott* decision was to be. On this aspect of the matter see Swisher, Roger B. Taney, c. 24 (1935). Whether he had advance notice or not, the thoughts expressed in that public utterance make it quite plain that on the eve of the *Dred Scott* decision there was nothing unusual in the proposition that slavery in the territories was a constitutional question for the judiciary to settle.

power over slavery in the territories had been referred to the Supreme Court.[37] The latter having spoken, it was the duty of all good citizens to accept the decision. Indeed, Douglas praised the Court for having passed over mere technicalities and turned its decision upon the true merits of the issue.[38]

We must now go back to trace the history of Dred Scott's litigation.[39] Having lost a decision in the Supreme Court of Missouri,[40] Scott in late 1853 began a new action in trespass in the federal court at St. Louis against a resident of New York who claimed to be his master. Admitting that he had been a slave, the plaintiff claimed that when he was taken into territory made free by the Missouri Compromise he became free; that he had since acquired Missouri citizenship and was thus properly in a federal court on diversity grounds. Scott won on a plea in abatement which questioned his citizenship, but lost on the merits.[41] The case was argued on appeal in the Supreme Court of the United States in February, 1856.[42] At that time Mr. Greeley's New York Tribune reported that the case would probably be decided against Scott on "the pretext" that his voluntary return from free to slave territory (*i.e.*, the state of Missouri) restored his status as a slave; that the Supreme Court would thus "evade" the real issue (*i.e.*, the constitutionality of the Missouri Compromise), but that "an effort will be made to get a positive decree of some sort. . . ."[43] In April Justice Curtis wrote to a friend that the Court would "not decide the question of the Missouri Compromise line—a majority of the

---

37. Speech to the Grand Jury, Springfield, Illinois, June 12, 1857. See Milton, The Eve of Conflict 260 (1934). It will be noted, of course, that it was Douglas who won the Lincoln-Douglas debates, in the sense that it was he who won the prize at stake, a seat in the United States Senate. In that campaign the meaning and implications of the *Dred Scott* case were thoroughly canvassed by its leading critic and its leading apologist.

Of course the *Dred Scott* case did not arrive at the Supreme Court via the procedural (*i.e.*, jurisdiction-liberalizing) route provided in either the Compromise of 1850 or the Kansas-Nebraska Act, but, as Douglas recognized in the Grand Jury Speech, it did dispose of the substantive issue contemplated by that legislation. Lincoln's recognition of the latter point is implicit in his "House-divided" speech (Springfield, Illinois, June 17, 1858) where he sees a conspiracy between "Stephen [Douglas], Franklin [Pierce], Roger [Taney], and James [Buchanan]"—the main elements of their "plot" being the language of the Kansas-Nebraska Act, the *Dred Scott* decision and the *a priori* endorsements thereof by both Presidents.

38. *Id.* at 260.

39. See 2 Beveridge, Abraham Lincoln c. 7 (1928); Swisher, *op. cit. supra* note 36, c. 24; and 3 Warren, The Supreme Court in United States History c. 26, 27 (1923).

40. Scott v. Emerson, 15 Mo. 413 (1852).

41. Dred Scott Collection, Missouri Historical Society, St. Louis, Mo.

42. 3 Warren, *op. cit. supra* note 39, at 5.

43. New York Tribune, Feb. 28, 1856.

judges being of opinion that it is not necessary to do so. (This is confidential)."[44] On May 12 on the motion of Justice Nelson the case was put down for reargument. Mr. Greeley thereupon assailed the "black gowns" as "artful dodgers. The minority were prepared to meet the issue boldly and distinctly; but the controlling members were not quite ready for such an encounter of authority as could be produced; or perhaps not inclined to open the opportunity for a demolition of the fraudulent pretenses that have been set up in Congress on this question."[45]

Greeley, of course, was fishing in troubled waters and wanted at the very least what he had every reason to believe would be a strongly, pro-Republican opinion from Justice McLean for use in the presidential campaign of 1856. Justice McLean's ambitions for the presidency are, and were at the time, well known. Foiled in his apparent design to make immediate political capital via the *Dred Scott* case, McLean wrote "a long and thoroughly political letter— the letter of a candidate,"[46] publicly indicating his views on the constitutionality of the Missouri Compromise.[47] "It was because of this statement of Justice McLean and of the eagerness and expectation of the Republican press and leaders that the Supreme Court would pass upon the Missouri Compromise in its decision in the *Dred Scott* case, that Lincoln had said in the Fremont campaign [the Galena speech, quoted above] that that tribunal was the one to settle such questions, that when it did so, the Republicans would abide by what the Court held to be the law and Lincoln had challenged the Democrats to do the same. If they would not, 'who are the disunionists, you or we?' "[48]

After the presidential campaign was safely out of the way the case was reargued in December, 1856. Two months later, on February 15, Justice Nelson was directed to write the Court's opinion ignoring the constitutional issue entirely and turning the decision on the ground that regardless of Scott's status when he was in free territory he was, according to Missouri law, a slave when he voluntarily returned to Missouri and therefore could not come into a federal court on diversity of citizenship grounds.[49] But within a few days it became clear that Justices McLean and Curtis intended to give extended dissenting opinions emphasizing

44.   Curtis, The Life and Writings of Benjamin Robbins Curtis, LL.D. 180 (1879).
45.   New York Tribune, May 15, 1856.
46.   2 Beveridge, *op. cit. supra* note 39, at 461.
47.   New York Tribune, June 16, 1856.
48.   2 Beveridge, *op. cit. supra* note 39, at 461-462.
49.   3 Warren, *op. cit. supra* note 39, at 15.

the constitutionality of the Missouri Compromise.[50] According to Justice Catron, this "forced" a majority of his brethren to take up that issue, and upon the motion of Justice Wayne the Chief Justice undertook to write his fateful opinion for the Court.[51] Something of Justice Wayne's motives and the motives of those who concurred in his motion, is seen in his observation that "[t]he case involves . . . constitutional principles of the highest importance, about which there had become such a difference of opinion that the peace and harmony of the country required the settlement of them by judicial decision."[52] As ex-Justice Campbell and Mr. Justice Nelson put it almost fifteen years later "[t]he apprehension had been expressed by others of the Court [as well as Justice Wayne], that the Court would not fulfill public expectation or discharge its duties by maintaining silence upon these [constitutional] questions. . . ."[53]

In the presidential campaign of 1860 Lincoln and Douglas held the positions they had taken in their famous Illinois debates in 1858—the one bitterly rejecting the *Dred Scott* decision, the other supporting it. Breckinridge, nominee of the Southern wing of the Democratic Party, also endorsing the famous decision, demanded its implementation by a Congressional "slave code" for the territories.[54] This was the South's answer to the Douglas Freeport Doctrine. Clay and Douglas had held the nation and the Democratic Party together by a compromise that removed the most vexing problem of the day from the political to the judicial arena. This entailed an understanding that, win or lose, each claimant would accept the judicial settlement when it should finally come. But the North proved unwilling to do so. The Republicans, notwithstanding Lincoln's Galena pledge, repudiated the *Dred Scott* decision outright.[55] The Northern Democrats, following the "little giant," attempted escape by a legal quibble—the *Dred Scott* case, they held, ruled only upon the question of Congressional power over slavery. Their platform pledged them to await and accept a Supreme Court decision on the power of the territorial legislatures.[56] Upon the

50.   *Ibid.*
51.   *Id.* at 16.
52.   Scott v. Sandford, 19 How. 393, 454-455 (U.S. 1857).
53.   Quoted in Tyler, Memoir of Roger Brooke Taney, LL.D. 384-385 (1872).
54.   1 Morrison and Commager, *op. cit. supra* note 5, at 636-638.
55.   *Ibid.*
56.   Douglas spells out the constitutional theories behind this position in *The Dividing Line Between Federal and Local Authority, Popular Sovereignty in the Territories,* 19 Harper's New Monthly Magazine 519 (1859). His main point is that the territorial legislative power is not derivative but independent of, and broader than, Congressional power in respect to slavery.

issues so joined Lincoln received 1,866,452 votes, as against a combined total of 2,226,738 for Douglas and Breckinridge. Lincoln's party
obtained only a minority in each house of Congress.[57] This could
hardly be called a popular repudiation of the principle of judicial
settlement or indeed of the *Dred Scott* decision itself.

Shortly after the election, on the eve of Secession, Senator Crittin-
den, Clay's successor in the Senate as fate would have it, proposed a
settlement which would have written an extended Missouri Compromise into the Constitution. He could not even get it through a Senate
Committee![58] That approach to the slavery problem had not been
politically feasible since the impasse of 1846-1850. Resort to war between the states followed not, as some would have it, because political
settlement had been foreclosed by judicial action,[59] but more likely
because the issues cut too deeply to be solved either by courts or
legislatures. The real misfortune of the *Dred Scott* decision was that,
duly distorted, it served as a powerful weapon for the Abolitionists —
always a small, fanatical minority. The Court's fault, if it may be so
described, lay in accepting the buck which Congress and the statesmen
had passed, and in failing to anticipate the partisan, political use which
its efforts could be made to serve.

---

57. 1 Morrison and Commager, *op. cit. supra* note 5, at 637-639.
58. Hicks, A Short History of American Democracy 363 (1943).
59. See, for example, Jackson, The Struggle for Judicial Supremacy 327 (1941).

ADDENDUM

Given the breakdown of our political processes vis-a-vis slavery in the
territories, perhaps the Taney Court would *now* seem derelict had it not tried
to resolve the crisis. As Father Vincent Hopkins put it, "If there had been no
decision, men would probably ask, in the years to come, why the last
peaceful means of settling the issue that precipitated the Civil War had not
been tried." Would a Court as "activist" as that over which Chief Justice
Warren presided have hesitated? Would a decision contrary to that of the
Taney Court have resolved the problem peacefully?

 V

Jurimetrics: Decisions by the Numbers

22 🎐 The Neo-Behavioral Approach to the Judicial Process: A Critique

Leibnitz conceived a plan for an art of formal reasoning from which he hoped for a solution of all problems. . . . If controversies arose, there would be no more need of disputation between two philosophers than between two accountants, for it would suffice . . . to take their pens in hand, sit down at their tables, and say to each other, let us calculate.—Bertrand Russell

If only Leibnitz's dream could be realized in the law!—Benjamin Cardozo

A generation ago "legal realists" led by Jerome Frank and Karl Llewellyn dismissed law as a myth—a function of what judges had for breakfast. The important thing, they insisted, was what a court *did*, not what it *said*. No doubt this was good medicine for the times. Yet, however broad Frank's 1930 language,[1] later on the bench he loyally acknowledged the compulsive force of legal rules. As a lower court judge, he decided cases in accordance with what he found the law to be—and on occasion he made clear in addenda what he thought it ought to be.[2]

Llewellyn, too, changed his mind. In 1934 he had said, "The theory that rules decide cases seems for a century to have fooled, not only library-ridden recluses, but judges."[3] Seventeen years later he confessed that his earlier behavioral descriptions of law contained "unhappy words when not more fully developed, and they are plainly at best a very partial statement of the whole truth."[4]

In short, after their initial enthusiasm, these and other[5] legal realists recognized that there is and must be law in the judicial process, as well as discretion. This was inevitable, for society can no more dispense with order and coherence than it can deny the demands of changing circumstance. We must have stability, yet we cannot stand still; and so the legal system in-

evitably has both static and dynamic qualities. Holmes put it in a thimble: "The . . . law is always approaching, and never reaching, consistency. It is forever adopting new principles from life at one end, and it always retains old ones from history at the other, which have not been absorbed or sloughed off. It will become entirely consistent only when it ceases to grow."[6]

The confessed error of the legal realists was their exaggeration of the law's discretionary element, at the expense of its rule element. Today, perhaps, the neo-behavioralists are in danger of making the same mistake. For them, too, apparently, law—regarded as a body of rules—is largely a myth. Indeed, it appears that a major burden of their studies of the judicial process is to demonstrate that law is not an important element in court decisions.

Apparently disillusioned with legal rules as an explanation of judicial conduct, the new behavioralists seek understanding by mathematic analysis of judges' voting records—often regardless of judicial talk. If they succeed, it does not matter whether their disillusionment (if such it be) is justified, or merely the result of a misconception of the judicial process. They must be judged by their fruits—though techniques cannot be ignored entirely. My purpose here is to examine these matters. Only a sophisticate in mathematics could do the job full justice. My excuse for trying is that most lawyers and political scientists presumably are no more mathematical than I. Assuming then that behavioral computations are impeccable, this effort will focus mainly on the data that goes into them, and the conclusions that come out. In short, this is a "behavioral" study of some representative neo-behavioralists as they examine the "minds" or "attitudes" of Supreme Court judges. I put to one side the older behavioralism exemplified in Benjamin Wright's *The Growth of American Constitutional Law*, in the

---

[1] See Frank, *Law and the Modern Mind* (1930).

[2] See, for example, Roth v. United States, 237 F. 2d 796, 806 (1956).

[3] Llewellyn, "The Constitution as an Institution," *Columbia Law Review*, Vol. 34 (1934), pp. 1, 7.

[4] Llewellyn, *The Bramble Bush* (1951 ed.), p. 9. See also Llewellyn, "Law and the Social Sciences, Especially Sociology," *Harvard Law Review*, Vol. 62 (1949), pp. 1286, 1291.

[5] "But realism, despite its liberating virtues, is not a sustaining food for a stable civilization." Thurman Arnold in "Jerome Frank," *University of Chicago Law Review*, Vol. 24 (1957), pp. 633, 635.

[6] Holmes, *The Common Law*, (1881) p. 36

Zeisel, Kalven and Buchholz study of *Delay in the Court*, and in Robert Dahl's "Decision Making in a Democracy."[7] In short, what I mean by neo-behavioralism is the new psychometric research in judicial decision making.

I. ARTIFICIAL CATEGORIES AND MISBRANDED CASES

No matter how precise and impersonal the neo-behavioralist's mathematics, it rests like other studies on a subjective selection of cases for analysis. This raises problems of gerrymandering. Consider, for example, Professor Pritchett's statistical analysis of civil liberty issues in *The Roosevelt Court*.[8] Three of his cases concern the power of courts by injunction to protect themselves from interference by newspaper pressure.[9] Obviously such cases raise fair-trial problems as well as problems in freedom of the press. Pritchett thus had at least three choices: he could have included the three cases in a free-press category, a fair-trial category, or in both. Let us see what effect each of these choices would have had on the civil-liberties rating of Justice Black, for example:

1. If the cases are treated exclusively as free-press problems (and considered in conjunction with Pritchett's three other free-press cases[10]), Black gets a box-score rating of 50 per cent, *i.e.*, he voted anti-free press in half the six cases in this category.

2. If the three injunction cases are treated exclusively as fair-trial problems (and are thus removed from the free-press category), Black would get a pro-free press rating of zero.

3. If the three injunction cases are included in both categories, Black's low free-press rating (50 per cent) would be offset by a 100 per cent liberal rating in the appropriate fair-trial category.

In fact, Pritchett chose the first alternative—which gave Black a 50 per cent libertarian box score as to freedom of the press, with no compensating score for complete liberalism on the fair-trial problem.

So far we have been concerned primarily with the three injunction cases. The other three in Pritchett's group of six free-press cases concern

application of the Sherman Act and the Fair Labor Standards Act (FLSA) to newspapers—the defendants claiming in each case that the act in question interfered with freedom of the press.[11] In all three of these economic cases Black thought that claim was frivolous. As he put it in the Sherman Act case, "freedom to publish is guaranteed by the Constitution, but freedom to combine to keep others from publishing is not."[12] In short, Black thought there was no real utterance issue in half the six items that Pritchett treats as free-press cases. Thus it is not Black's thinking, but Pritchett's, that gives the Justice only a 50 per cent rating. Even if we accept Pritchett's choice among the categories that could have been used, there is still a serious problem in assigning cases to them. If Pritchett had not used the three cases which Black thought involved no real civil-liberty problem, the Justice's box score would have been in line with his announced absolutist position, *i.e.*, 100 per cent pro-free press.[13]

Two of these cases (those involving FLSA) are particularly interesting in this context, because only Justice Murphy thought they involved a genuine free-press problem. Pritchett "adopted" Murphy's minority-of-one position. If Murphy's views on civil liberty had been less eccentric, or if he had not participated in these cases (he had recently been Attorney General), then Pritchett could not have considered either case because his categories utilize only non-unanimous decisions. In that event Black's free-press score would have been 75 per cent.

Finally, it seems that the utterance question was so insubstantial in the three economic cases that *on this issue* none of them would ever have reached the Supreme Court. Thus, had they not presented substantial issues in other areas, they could never have plagued Black's free-press record as Pritchett computes it. In short, the Justice would again have a 100 per cent score.

To summarize this section, I suggest that Pritchett had at least three choices when he set up his free-press category—and that having made his choice there was room for rational disagreement on what cases should be included in it. This presented at least four alternatives which yield box scores ranging for Justice Black from zero to 100 per cent libertarian. One of the two zero ratings would be offset by

---

[7] *Journal of Public Law*, Vol. 6 (1958), p. 279.

[8] Table XVI, p. 131 (1948).

[9] Craig V. Harney, 331 U. S. 367 (1947); *Times-Mirror v. Superior Court of California*, 314 U.S. 252 (1941); *Nye v. United States*, 313 U. S. 33 (1941).

[10] *Mabee v. White Plains Pub. Co.*, 327 U.S. 178 (1946); *Oklahoma Press v. Walling*, 327 U.S. 186 (1946); *Associated Press v. United States*, 326 U.S. 1 (1945).

[11] See footnote 10, above.

[12] *Associated Press v. United States*, 326 U.S. 1, 20 (1945).

[13] See "Justice Black and First Amendment 'Absolutes': A Public Interview," *N.Y.U. Law Rev.*, Vol. 37 (1962), pp. 549, 557.

a perfect liberal rating in an appropriate fair-trial category. Obviously these variations, ranging from one extreme to the other, turned *not on Black's own attitudes, but upon the views or conduct of others.* Finally we saw three hypothetical situations—all plainly plausible—each of which suggests again that a behavioral score may depend largely upon matters entirely independent of the subject's own convictions, and completely beyond his control. Behind all these category problems, perhaps, lies what physicist Carroll Sparrow calls the crime of

singling out from some many-dimensional reality . . . one measurable attribute and identifying this partial aspect with the whole. . . . The result of the partial measurement is taken as an *index* of the whole. It is like measuring the length of an object and calling the result the size, only the crime is far worse when one tries to measure such attributes as beauty, excellence [or judicial behavior] in this way, for we cannot factor these as we can factor size into length, breadth and height. To [give it] a name, let me call this the crime of misplaced definiteness. The fault is logical; it cannot be attributed to any slavish imitation of physics, for the physicist makes no use of indices of this sort. It seems to me to result from the same cause as pseudo-measurement [see below], namely, an attempt to conceive all problems as problems of method. Following this conception, the offenders have concerned themselves mightily with making their numerical labels precise and objective but hardly at all with making them significant.[14]

II. UNEQUAL EQUALS

Again, no matter how precise the neo-behavioralist's mathematics, it assumes that all cases are of equal weight in determining a judge's attitude. This may not be inevitable, but it seems to be accepted practice. The resulting distortions are evident in Pritchett's free-press ratings just mentioned. In the three injunction cases,[15] Black (for example) voted consistently in favor of the press. Clearly, these cases involved substantial utterance problems. Considering the weight of the opposing fair-trial interest, the state of judicial precedent, and the power of the dissents, Black's position in these cases must have reflected a very deep concern for an unrestricted press. Yet in Pritchett's calculations they count for no more in determining Black's attitude than the three

economic cases[16] in which most judges (including Black, Douglas, and Rutledge) found no real free-press issues. It follows that in Pritchett's book Black appears to be only 50 per cent committed to freedom of the press—whereas Black himself has indicated repeatedly by word and (I suggest) by deed that he considers freedom of expression an absolute, or nearly so.

The difficulty here, perhaps, is what Sparrow calls "pseudo-measurement" which occurs where the thing measured has no autonomous existence apart from the measurement itself. Thus, when

we count the number of lawyers in a community, the number obtained is both precise and objective. But it has meaning as a datum for social science only for those relations of lawyers to society in respect of which one lawyer is indistinguishable from another lawyer. Used otherwise, it is pseudo-measurement; we count the number of coins when the question is . . . the amount of money.[17]

III. FIGURES DO LIE

Again, no matter how precise and objective the neo-behavioralist's calculating machine, it cannot rise above the errors that are fed into it. Consider, for example, the "difference" between the Brandeis opinion and the Brandeis vote in *Whitney* v. *California*.[18] The opinion is perhaps the most powerful blow for free speech in judicial history, but for jurisdictional reasons the vote led the speaker to jail. And, of course, by generally accepted behavioral technique the vote is what counts in determining the attitude of the voter. As one astute observer put it, "Neither the merits of the cases nor the reasoning of the opinions affect these statistics. In spite of the multitude of opinions, the charts record only the votes, in the manner of a voting machine. It is as if, like the courts of ancient Greece, only ballots were cast and no opinions written."[19]

The fact is that Brandeis, with Holmes concurring, gave two opinions in *Whitney*. He held first that he could not decide the clear-and-present-danger issue because it was not before the Court. That is a vital matter in the law of procedure, and it was the crucial matter on which Holmes and Brandeis voted. To count that vote as a vote for or against free speech is to pretend that red is green. The second thing that Holmes and Brandeis decided was

[14] *Voyages and Cargoes* (1947), p. 163. Quoted in L. Rogers, Book Review, *Columbia Law Rev.*, Vol. 61 (1961), pp. 308, 310.

[15] See footnote 9, above.

[16] See footnote 10, above.

[17] *Op. cit.*, footnote 14, above, at p. 163.

[18] 374 U.S. 357 (1927).

[19] Kurland, Book Review, *Yale Law Journal*, Vol. 58 (1948), pp. 206, 208.

that their colleagues and the nation needed a lecture on the meaning of freedom. This Brandeis gave in language not prone to die. Surely the lecture, rather than the vote, is the true measure of Brandeis's and Holmes's attitude on free utterance.

Here, I think, is a major weakness of neo-behavioralism as now practiced: it assumes that every vote in a case that has some connection with civil liberty, for example, is necessarily a vote for or against that liberty.[20] By similar reasoning, the John Birchers assume that every vote in a case that has something to do with communism is a vote for or against communism. A measuring system based on that kind of logic could not possibly do justice to the jurisprudence of men like Holmes and Brandeis—however accurate it may be with respect to those whom Pritchett calls "label thinkers."[21]

The difficulty is that judges who are deeply concerned for the rule of law—rather than for some proprietarian or libertarian philosophy—find that most cases involve important competing principles. Unlike academicians, a law-abiding judge is not free to concentrate on any one of them alone or in the abstract. He must weigh each in relation to others in a rude, earthly setting. Usually, indeed, he cannot vote "for" one freedom without sacrificing another. If only one principle were involved in each case, the judge's job would be as simple as the Justice Fields and Murphys pretend. Unfortunately, it is otherwise. For example, in two of the three injunction cases[22] in Pritchett's free-press category, Justice Stone is scored as having voted anti-liberally. Surely an equally valid interpretation would treat these votes in their context as votes *for* fair trials, rather than *against* free publication. Yet, as Pritchett sees it, these plus Stone's votes in the three economic cases mentioned above give the father of "footnote 4"[23] a pro-free press score of only 20 per cent. And, since Pritchett has no compensating fair-trial category, this figure contributes unduly to Stone's over-all score of only 44 per cent in civil-liberty cases.[24] In

short, Stone loses both ways.

At least in the instances so far considered, apparently either the new behavioral approach is misleading—or Stone, along with Holmes, Brandeis, and Black, is a hypocrite. Behavioralism may be caught in a dilemma. Motives are elusive and largely unmeasurable. Recorded votes are amenable to objective computation. Small wonder then that in his search for scientific objectivity the neo-behavioralist concentrates on votes. But in discounting motives he discounts a crucial, perhaps the most crucial, element in human conduct. Thus it is perfectly clear that many ballots cast for Norman Thomas were not plaudits for socialism, but protests against the lethargy of the major parties. As Holmes long ago observed, even a dog distinguishes between being kicked and being stumbled over. The behavioralist must treat the two identically, or—making allowance for motives—risk the very subjectivity that he wants to avoid.

IV. THE END PRODUCT

So far we have concentrated largely on the raw material that goes into the neo-behavioralist's calculating machine. Now the end product and something of the machinery itself. We start with Professor Ulmer's study of "Supreme Court Behavior and Civil Rights"[25] in the 1956 and 1957 Terms. By Guttman Scale Analysis of all nonunanimous civil liberty cases, Ulmer shows that in each Term Justice Douglas voted for "the" civil-liberty claim in all but one case, while Justice Clark voted *contra* in all but one. Between these two extremes each judge stood in the same relative position *vis-à-vis* his associates in both Terms. Surely this symmetry is striking. Ulmer's major conclusion was that the Court had decided civil-liberty cases not in terms of law, but in terms of one dominant variable: "deprivation of a claimed civil liberty." Thus, "the *attitude* of the judge toward civil liberty claims was the factor shaping the individual decisions."[26]

I suggest that this conclusion is vulnerable, if only because other equally plausible conclusions can be drawn from the same scalograms. For example, during the two Terms in question, 17 civil liberty cases (as defined by Ulmer)[27] were

[20] This problem is particularly striking in the dissenting position in Terminiello v. Chicago, 337 U.S. 1 (1949); Girouard v. United States, 328 U.S. 61 (1946); and West Virginia School Dist. v. Barnette, 319 U.S. 624 (1943).

[21] See Pritchett, *Civil Liberties and the Vinson Court* (1954), p. 249.

[22] Times-Mirror v. Superior Court of California, 314 U.S. 252 (1941); Nye v. United States, 313 U.S. 33 (1941).

[23] United States v. Carolene Products Co., 304 U.S. 144, 152–53 (1938).

[24] See footnote 8, above; but compare Stone's "rating" in Mason, *Harlan Fiske Stone: Pillar of the Law*, chs. 31 and 32 (1956), and Wechsler, "Stone and the Constitution," *Columbia Law Rev.*, Vol. 46 (1946), p. 764.

[25] *The Western Political Quarterly*, Vol. 13 (1960), p. 288.

[26] *Id.*, pp. 295, 311.

[27] "In this [*i.e.*, Ulmer's] paper a civil liberties

decided unanimously. Had the law been clear with respect to the non-unanimous cases, either they would not have reached the Supreme Court, or if they had, they, too, presumably would have been decided without dissent. Perhaps, then, the problem is not bias for or against personal freedom, but vagueness in the law. In this view, the symmetry of Ulmer's scalograms indicates each judge's steady conception of his duty in case of doubt—rather than his private bias for or against freedom. It also indicates two well-defined voting blocs. Thus, when the Justices could not agree as to the meaning of the law, most of them (including Clark) tended to hold off, while Douglas and three others favored intervention. This is to say, each voted in accordance with his conception of the law—not civil-liberty law, for that was wanting—but the law which should govern when the application of substantive rules is less than clear. In this view, the scalograms reflect not crude lawlessness but consistent responses to a classic problem: should judicial doubts be resolved by a presumption for, or against, the validity of challenged measures? Justice Frankfurter and those to the "right" of him favor the tradition that goes back at least to 1793;[28] those to the "left" of him prefer the view of the old activists in such cases as *Lochner* and *Adkins*.[29]

That the judges are divided can hardly be surprising. They are caught in the basic paradox of American government—majority rule versus individual liberty. Both are indispensable to political freedom, yet neither can fully prevail without destroying the other. Let those who must have labels determine whether *in case of doubt* it is more democratic, or indeed more liberal, to favor the one or the other.

The point is not that the foregoing interpretation of Ulmer's scalograms is necessarily correct, but that the same scale analysis "proves" two quite contradictory hypotheses. Another behavioralist (whose name is not to be revealed) advises that Ulmer's cases scale-out also to "prove" eight of the judges "voted not

case is one involving a claimed right of the type covered by the Bill of Rights and the Civil War Amendments. . . . On this definition it makes no difference whether the claim calls for constitutional or statutory interpretation as long as the right involved is primarily a personal rather than a property right." *Id.*, 288.
[28] See Thayer, "The Origin and Scope of the American Doctrine of Constitutional Law," *Harvard Law Rev.*, Vol. 7 (1893), p. 129.
[29] See McCloskey, *The American Supreme Court* (1960), p. 194.

for or against civil liberty, but rather for or against Justice Black's anticipated vote, or [alternatively that every judge] voted for or against what the public expects of liberals." My own efforts reveal that those of Ulmer's cases which deal with the communist problem scale-out *perfectly* to "prove" that the Court decided, not lawfully, but in terms of still another single dominant variable: tenderness toward communism. (There were no deviant votes in any of the 25 cases.) I hasten to add that the 15 homicide cases scale-out to "prove" yet another single dominant variable: tenderness toward murder and manslaughter. (Here there were a few deviant votes, but not enough to spoil a true scale pattern as defined by Guttman.) The choices apparently are numerous. Of those here mentioned, *only the one relating to uncertainty in the law avoids the implication that all of the Justices are frauds or fools.*

Could it be that scale analysis is tautological or circular, that the meaning it yields is the meaning one puts into it? In any event, the scalograms in question seem as vulnerable to misinterpretation as the bare votes on which they rest. The conclusions that Ulmer derives from his own scales seem at least as subjective as those which more orthodox scholars derive directly from the cases themselves—the *whole* cases.

Another difficulty in the scalogram technique is that it cannot handle unanimous decisions—because "the coefficient of reproducibility will be distorted by the inclusion of extreme marginals." Thus Ulmer had to omit a substantial part of the relevant data. Moreover, to omit the unanimous decisions is to treat different Justices quite differently. In the 1956 Term, for example, there were 22 divided, and 12 unanimous, opinions. All of the latter upheld libertarian claims. Thus, if only divided-opinion cases are considered, Justice Clark's libertarian rating is less than 5 per cent—whereas, if all cases are considered, it jumps to 38 per cent. Yet the corresponding gap for Justice Douglas is only two percentage points, *i.e.*, 95 *vis-à-vis* 97 per cent libertarian. Obviously, Ulmer's sample cases are far more representative of the one judge's attitude than of the other's.

In an apparent effort to avoid Pritchett's category problems, Ulmer lumps all non-unanimous "civil-liberty" cases into a single category—apples, thunderbirds and Renoirs together. But if this solves one problem, it raises another. We are asked to believe, for example, that the 74-year-old Frankfurter after 17 years on the bench suddenly in the summer of 1957 changed his basic attitude toward civil liberty, his scale score having fallen from 63.6

to only 40 per cent.[30] Surely, the change was not in the Justice's state of mind, but in the nature of the cases before the Court. Thus the proportion of federalistic problems was much higher in 1957 than 1956.[31] This difference alone accounts for much of the gap between Frankfurter's two scale scores. Further examination no doubt would reveal other differences which apparently only an activist is inclined to ignore. These might involve the distinction between constitutional and statutory construction; between *stare decisis* in relation to constitutional, as against statutory, decisions; between judicial review of procedure and judicial review of substance—to mention only the obvious. Yet Ulmer seems to brush all this aside as "semantics."[32] For me, such distinctions go to the heart of the judicial process—and ultimately of democracy itself. For they involve *in areas of doubt* experimentation by the Court versus experimentation in the insulated chambers of the states, and by the democratic process generally. What Mark DeWolfe Howe said of another behavioralist is relevant here:

He nowhere suggests that other conceptions and other standards than those of the appropriate scope of freedom have constitutional or even statistical relevance in cases concerned with civil liberties. He has prepared his tables and appraised their significance as if history has presented no problems of the role of the judiciary in a democracy, and as if the Supreme Court were not functioning in a federal society.[33]

A dedicated communist no doubt judges every work of art and science by a single standard: does it conform to the Party line? This may give an accurate picture of the victim's loyalty to communism but it gives a very inadequate account of his art or science. Neo-

behavioralism seems to suffer the same difficulty. It tends to reflect the dedicated libertarianism of most or all of its practitioners. Thus it generally applies to the judicial process an essentially political test; namely, the libertarian party line. This tendency to reduce jurisprudence to a single-value, conditioned reflex is explicit in the study just mentioned. There, Ulmer's "hypothesis assumes that [a judge] will make his decision not by asking 'What does the law require?' but by asking himself such questions as 'Shall I allow any deprivation of a claimed civil liberty?' "[34] Of course, a very high and direct correlation between the libertarian party line and a judge's voting record suggests political adjudication—as in the case of Justice Douglas. So, too, a very high inverse correlation would be suspect. But, as to a judge who falls in the middle area of Ulmer's scales, the test suggests merely that there is relatively little or no correlation; that something other than liberal-conservative considerations are crucial. At best, it reveals what a judge in the center area *does not do*. It shows nothing about the affirmative—presumably judicial—springs of his voting behavior. This may be worth something, but it is a far cry from the politically loaded meaning that Ulmer attributes to his own figures. In short, whether in communist or other hands, the party line is a poor test of art—scientific, aesthetic, or judicial.

Ulmer recognizes that there is something special about one who occupies the center positions on his scalograms. Of all the Justices, "he would appear to have the least rigid outlook."[35] This seems to be a backhanded acknowledgment of what I have just suggested: among his colleagues, such a judge must be the least prejudiced by liberal or anti-liberal bias; in this sense, then, the freest to consider each case on its own merits—our closest approximation of the non-partisan magistrate. The judge in question is Felix Frankfurter. My innocence of mathematics prevents me from measuring the width of the middle territory in the scalograms, and thus indicating what other judges occupy that select ground. It comes perhaps to this: a technique which assumes that a judge's votes are dictated by bias for or against CIVIL LIBERTY is far too naive to measure the working of a complex, judicial mind—or indeed, even of a simple mind that distinguishes between the judicial and the legislative processes. Hence Ulmer's essentially negative conclusion that Frankfurter's position was neither relatively

[30] Strictly speaking, Ulmer does not present these figures as absolute, but merely as relative to the extremist position of Douglas. Yet, the figures are, in effect, absolute, since Douglas's position is held to be "consistent and equivalent in both terms," and is all but completely libertarian. *Loc. cit.*, p. 311.

[31] *Id.*, pp. 288–89.

[32] *Id.*, p. 288. In a more perceptive scale analysis Joel Grossman shows the importance of elements that Ulmer ignores. A difficulty in Grossman's effort, I think, is that his DJR factor is too vague in expression and too narrow in application. See Grossman, "Role Playing and the Analysis of Judicial Behavior: The Case of Mr. Justice Frankfurter," *Journal of Public Law*, Vol. 11 (1962), p. 285.

[33] Howe, "Justice in a Democracy," *The Atlantic*, Vol. 185 (1949), p. 34.

[34] Ulmer, *loc. cit.*, p. 295.

[35] *Id.*, p. 296.

liberal nor the opposite. Obviously the Justice was marching to a very different tune.

Another example of the questionable tales that figures tell is Professor Spaeth's study which proves by behavioral techniques that Justice Frankfurter has a "pro-business" bias.[36] Businessmen might have difficulty swallowing this, considering that Frankfurter spent a major part of his life in a successful fight against the labor injunction—to say nothing of his landmark opinions which all but exempted unions from the anti-trust laws;[37] destroyed one of the last vestiges of the sweat shop;[38] required employers, who have refused to hire men because of their union membership, to give them not only jobs but back pay;[39] and, finally, his dissenting view that neither Congress nor Constitution bars a union from spending dues for political purposes, even though some union members object to the politics in question, yet must contribute or lose their jobs.[40] All of this would seem to strengthen the position of labor in its struggle with management.[40a]

[36] See Spaeth, "Judicial Power as a Variable Motivating Supreme Court Behavior," *Midwest Journal of Political Science*, Vol. 6 (1962), pp. 54, 55, 82.

[37] United States v. Hutcheson, 312 U.S. 219 (1941).

[38] Gemsco v. Walling, 324 U.S. 244 (1945).

[39] Phelps Dodge Corp. v. NLRB, 313 U.S. 177 (1941).

[40] International Ass'n. of Machinists v. Street, 367 U.S. 740, 797 (1961).

[40a] In a later article, Spaeth finds that Frankfurter has a *markedly* anti-union attitude. This conclusion is based on scale analysis of *non-unanimous* decisions during the 1953–1959 Terms. When all relevant (per Spaeth) decisions—unanimous and divided—are considered, it appears that Frankfurter voted "anti-union" in at most 53 per cent of the cases. This figure, however, is inaccurately high because Spaeth counts as "anti-union" the "occasional" vote (unidentified) which is in fact "pro-union" but less "pro-union" than the majority votes in the same case (p. 293). If bare numbers are to be the test, surely a voting record of 53 per cent or less either way is as close to neutrality (in 85 cases over a seven-year period) as one could hope for in this imperfect world. Surely such a record is not in itself significantly "pro" or "anti" except perhaps in relation to Douglas's more than 90 per cent "pro-union" stand. See Spaeth, "An Analysis of Judicial Attitudes in the Labor Relations Decisions of the Warren Court," *Journal of Politics*, Vol. 25 (1963), p. 290.

Considering these, among other, cases—to say nothing of Frankfurter's off-the-bench writing—the "pro-business" charge has a strange ring. To test this reaction, I put the following question to ten men who know him well:

On the basis of your personal relationships with Mr. Justice Frankfurter, have you found in him a "pro-business" attitude?

All ten responses were negative, and all expressed in one way or another surprise at the implications of the question. Here is a sample answer, from a prominent law professor:

Hell no! I think he thinks as Brandeis did, that businessmen are a bunch of inflated sillies, on the whole, who hardly know what's good for themselves, let alone the country.

If the behavioralist view and the view of these ten direct observers seem to be at odds, the discrepancy is not necessarily fatal. It can be resolved by the simple Hypocrisy Adjustment. The net result is that Frankfurter, along with Holmes, Brandeis, Stone, and Black, is a hypocrite.

The elusive meaning of numbers is suggested again in Professor Schubert's game-theory analysis of Federal Employers Liability Act (FELA) certiorari cases.[41] This technique assumes as a hypothesis that a player wants to achieve a given goal, and that *if he acts rationally* he will adopt a given strategy to do so. When as a matter of statistics the player in fact adheres to the strategy, the hypothesis (or game) is "proven." Apart from the logical difficulties in this approach, it is clear that, if the hypothesized strategy is in fact irrational (or the problem non-existent), the whole house of cards collapses; the game has in effect been rigged.

In his study, Schubert hypothesizes that the "certiorari bloc" (the activists) want to convert FELA into a workman's compensation act in defiance of Congress.[42] He further assumes that to do so its rational strategy would be: (a) to deny all railroad management petitions for certiorari; and (b) to grant worker petitions in as many cases as possible in which a pro-labor decision on the merits would not alienate professional opinion, or the uncommitted justices whose votes the activists need.[43]

[41] "Policy Without Law: An Extension of the Certiorari Game," *Stanford Law Rev.*, Vol. 14 (1962), p. 284.

[42] *Id.*, p. 288. A more technical statement of the hypothesis will be found at *id.*, p. 294.

[43] *Id.*, p. 294 *et seq.*

But in a game surely part (a) of the strategy would be irrational, indeed suicidal, because it is so obviously partisan that it would antagonize professional observers and uncommitted judges. Does it not follow then that Schubert's proof is false—that he has shown not that the certiorari bloc is playing his game, but merely that one can get as much out of a hypothesis as one puts into it?

My suggestion is not that Schubert's ultimate conclusion is erroneous, but that it is not proven by the technique employed.[44] Apparently, he arrived at it as others have[45]—by old-fashioned observation—and then forced his somewhat recalcitrant observations into a game pattern. For in fact Schubert used two different standards of rationality in the two wings of one player's assumed strategy. In part (a), he deemed it rational to ignore professional opinion and the effect upon uncommitted judges; in part (b) *of the same strategy,* he deemed it irrational to do so. The meaning of "rationality" seems to have shifted to fit the observed facts. This suggests that, if for no

[44] Of course, as Schubert shows, the bloc grants certiorari only to workmen, but *in its view* this is a matter of constitutional necessity, not of strategic choice. See, for example, *Wilkerson v. McCarthy,* 336 U.S. 53, 62 (1949), but compare *Rogers v. Missouri Pacific R.R.,* 352 U.S. 500, 509–10 (1957). For the Constitution gives the right to trial by jury, and in these cases only workmen are in a position to claim denial of it (as the result of a directed verdict or judgment notwithstanding verdict). Railroads cannot lose these cases and thus need certiorari except by jury findings. So, unlike workers, they are in no position to claim denial of the basic right. It is not clear to me whether Schubert is unaware of this distinction or merely finds it unimportant.

Of course, it is possible for the Court to grant certiorari to a railroad in one of these FELA evidentiary cases on other than constitutional grounds, but this is highly unlikely in both doctrine and practice. Indeed, Schubert's study indicates that in 24 years only two such petitions were granted, and one of them was dismissed. See New York, N. H. & H.R.R .v. Henagan, 364 U.S. 441 (1960), and McCarthy v. Bruner, 323 U.S. 673 (1944). In both cases, Schubert says, "the most reasonable assumption is that [the certiorari bloc] did not support the grant. . . . " *Loc. cit.,* 321–23.

[45] Mr. Justice Frankfurter called attention to the phenomenon at least as early as *Wilkerson v. McCarthy,* 336 U.S. 53, 67 (1949). Since then numerous studies have anticipated Schubert's conclusions.

other reason, game theory is vulnerable because the concept of rationality is so slippery.[46] It comes, perhaps, to this: the proof of the game depends upon the rationality of the players, while the meaning of rationality shifts to accommodate the observed facts of the particular "game."

A not unrelated problem is found in Pritchett's most famous study. Largely by quantitative analysis, he concludes that

there is a left wing [of the Court] which is generally favorable to all [Federal] administrative agencies except the I.C.C., and a right wing which is very enthusiastic about the I.C.C. but somewhat less so where other agencies are concerned.[47]

The I.C.C. being markedly more conservative than the others, the implication is that all or most of the Justices were in large part politically motivated. A no less plausible explanation of the same data is that one wing of the Court was consistent and law abiding, while the other danced back and forth to a political tune. On the bench, as elsewhere, movement after all is relative.

In the period covered by Pritchett's study, half the agencies in question were recently born creatures of the New Deal. Three others obviously had felt the impact of FDR's appointments. Only the old I.C.C. had somehow remained largely aloof from the spirit of the times. Unlike the others, it was not significantly moved to experiment with new procedural techniques, or to breathe new vigor into old ones. Surely then one would not expect it to have had much trouble with a judiciary which broadly speaking is charged with constitutional and statutory review of administrative procedures (as distinct from substantive policies).[48] In short, one would have expected something much like the "right wing" record from judges who in fact honored the orthodox limitations upon judicial review of administrative action—given the caution of the I.C.C. and the more experimental fervor of the younger agencies.

On the other hand, the "left wing" judges—here as elsewhere—were activists. Here as elsewhere they could tolerate much that was

[46] See P. Diesing, *Reason in Society* (1962), which suggests that there are at least five types of rationality in social action, and that the prevailing conception (the efficient achievement of predetermined ends) is unrealistically narrow.

[47] *The Roosevelt Court* (1948), p. 191. The quotation above relates to decisions during the 1941–46 Terms.

[48] Subject to what may remain of substantive due process.

liberal, and little that was conservative. Here, too, they were not apt to let "technicalities" stand in their way. No wonder then that the "left wing" accepted so much from the liberal agencies, and so little from the I.C.C.—finding in this poor old mossback the height of "procedural" promiscuity. Indeed, the danger was so great that Justice Douglas, for example, interceded (according to Pritchett) in 73 per cent of the I.C.C. cases, but in only 18 per cent of those involving the more liberal agencies.[49]

The point is not that Pritchett's interpretation of his own figures is necessarily wrong, but that another interpretation is at least as plausible—and does not require such unpleasant inferences about so many judges. A hint as to the relative accuracy of the two views may be found in Pritchett's handling of Frankfurter who, we are told, is quite inconsistent. He is said to stress "two major contentions":

The first is that the courts must leave the substance and policy of administrative regulation to the expert agencies, *limiting* the role of judicial review to insuring the "observance of those procedural safeguards . . . which are the historic foundation of due process."[50]

Frankfurter is found to have "forgotten" this rule in one I.C.C. and two S.E.C. cases.[51] Of course he did. The precept in question relates solely to review of *state* regulatory agencies.[52] No Justice, I think, has ever suggested that it applies to the I.C.C. and the S.E.C.

A page later Pritchett is on a different road. There he seems to recognize Frankfurter's orthodox view that with respect to Federal agencies, the Court is not confined to constitutional review but also has (within limits) such other reviewing authority as Congress may give. Thus Pritchett observes that Frankfurter's second major stance is a "predisposition to accept legislative limitation on judicial review."[53] Here, too, the Justice is found to be "forgetful." This is "demonstrated" by *Penfield* v. *S.E.C.*[54] But that case does not involve review of an administrative regulation. Indeed, no such regulation had been issued. What was in-

volved, as all the judges recognized, was a trial court's judicial discretion in a contempt of court proceeding. To that issue Frankfurter's "second" precept had no application. In sum, the law governing review of lower court discretion is one thing; that relating to Federal administrative orders is another; while that relating to state regulatory agencies is different from both. Perhaps the Justice is inconsistent, but surely we do not prove this by testing his conduct in one legal category against rules relevant only to another.

Let us now forget Pritchett's categories, and consider his four telltale cases in the categories to which the *Court* assigned them. This eliminates *Penfield* since in the Court's view it involved a trial judge's contempt authority, not an administrative regulation. The three remaining cases (one I.C.C. and two S.E.C.)[55] were decided on the principle that a reviewing court is entitled to an explicit statement of the considerations which guided the challenged exercise of administrative discretion. Speaking of this principle, a distinguished specialist in these matters has observed that Frankfurter "consistently applies [it] irrespective of the [Federal] agency concerned."[56]

Perhaps the most tantalizing of these number games is Fred Kort's "prediction" of Supreme Court decisions in right-to-counsel cases.[57] Arranging the relevant cases (1932–1947) in chronological order, he used the first half to derive a mathematical formula for prediction, which he then used successfully with respect to the second half of the cases. The joker is that Kort predicted decisions that had already been made. And, unfortunately, the carefully sifted data on which his predictions rested are available only when the decisions themselves are available. If he had successfully applied his formula to raw, *i.e.*, pre-decision *evidence*, his accomplishment would be stupendous. Instead he worked from the carefully prepared *statements of fact* found in Supreme Court opinions—the very opinions to which his predictions apply. Anyone familiar with the process of litigation knows there is normally quite a difference between the raw evidence that goes into the judicial machine and the pro-

[49] *Op. cit.*, p. 190.

[50] *Id.*, p. 193.

[51] New York v. United States, 331 U.S. 284 (1947); SEC v. Chenery, 318 U.S. 80 (1943), and 332 U.S. 194 (1947).

[52] See Frankfurter's opinion in Driscoll v. Edison Light and Power Co., 307 U.S. 104, 122 (1939). This is the source of the language which Pritchett quotes at note 50, above.

[53] *Op. cit.*, p. 194.

[54] 330 U.S. 585 (1947).

[55] See note 51, above.

[56] Nathanson, "Mr. Justice Frankfurter and Administrative Law," *Yale Law Journal*, Vol. 67 (1957), pp. 240, 260.

[57] "Predicting Supreme Court Decisions Mathematically: A Quantitative Analysis of the 'Right to Counsel' Cases," this REVIEW, Vol. 51 (1957), p. 1. Perhaps this should not be classified as a psychometric study.

cessed "facts" that come out in Supreme Court opinions. Plainly, then, the results in these cases are foreshadowed in the Court's handling of the factual data. What Judge Ulman—an experienced trial jurist—says of negligence cases is relevant here: "Ninety-nine times out of a hundred an appellate court disposes of a case . . . as though it [were] really quite simple. The higher court skeletonizes the facts, applies the rules of law, and files an opinion that makes its decision seem inevitable."[58] In short, it cuts away the obscuring skin and flesh, exposing the bare skeleton of decisive facts. This makes it relatively easy to see the court's theory of the case and thus to anticipate the decision. Moreover, anyone who tries to predict the outcome of decided cases has a fifty-fifty chance of success. With respect to undecided cases, the difficulty of prediction increases not only through loss of the factual clue, but also because the odds become less favorable. For some cases, which initially seem to raise right-to-counsel problems, may be decided eventually on other grounds.

It would be foolhardy to suggest that all neo-behavioral findings are misleading or unproven. Except for the dedicated, however, who has not been struck by the discrepancy between promise and product—even when presumably the latter is sound? In an article designed to "sell" the new behavioralism Professor Schubert presents a four-way "bloc analysis" of Supreme Court opinions in the 1953–1956 terms.[59] This shows that Justices Black, Douglas, and Warren constituted a bloc; Reed, Burton, and Minton another; Frankfurter and Harlan a third. The two latter groups were found to be only moderately cohesive. Schubert would hardly insist that any of this is striking news. His point apparently is that what others may know "intuitively," he knows "objectively."[60]

What Schubert finds striking in his analysis is that Justice Clark was the least bloc-inclined of the judges. He "cast dissenting votes about equally with the left and with the right wings of the Court . . . but he was definitely affiliated with the left bloc of Black-Douglas-Warren in marginal dissents. . . . "[61] This is an interesting fact, no doubt, but not in itself of great significance; and no one seems to have

found it worth further investigation. Surely we must feel let down when a show-case demonstration of a new technique yields such bland results.

In the same article Professor Schubert presents a perfect scalogram of the state "right-to-counsel" cases from 1940 through 1947. To illustrate its value, he tells us it "deflates" the Court's "official doctrine" that "the Constitution unequivocally requires representation by counsel in state criminal trials only for capital offenses."[62] Those who find this phrasing an ambiguous statement of the Court's position are bound to be less than impressed with the alleged deflation. Nevertheless, it is highly interesting to learn that the "Court has decided 66⅔ per cent of the right-to-counsel cases involving non-capital offenses, and 62½ per cent of the capital offense cases, in favor of the defendants. . . ."[63] Yet, if this is an accurate account, surely its essence was known to anyone who had read the cases. To have expressed that essence statistically (as above) would have required at most a little counting, plus some simple arithmetic—not a labored scalogram. The latter was presented as a perfect model to show the virtues of the new technique. Surely, again, we must feel disappointment when a selected example of perfection yields such commonplace results.

V. CONCLUSION

Speaking of the physical universe, Sir James Jeans observed that God must be a mathematician. He had in mind the success of modern physics in explaining material phenomena mathematically. The neo-behavioralists now propose a similar approach to the human mind, or more particularly, the judicial mind. Immediate and complete success is hardly to be expected. Such things take time. I have tried to suggest a few difficulties along the way. Perhaps at best they are mere details of no general significance. For what it may be worth, my over-all impression is that the present fault of the new behavioralism is excessive simplification—which for me is precisely the fault of judicial activism. The result is that while behavioral techniques may give an adequate picture of the extremely activist judge, they fail to depict even dimly the subtleties of the judicial process. They do not, presumably because they cannot, measure the range of values that play in the jurisprudence of a Holmes, a Brandeis, a Stone, or a Cardozo—to mention a few departed heroes.

---

[58] Quoted in Berman, *The Nature and Sources of Law* (1958), p. 274.

[59] Schubert, "The Study of Judicial Decision-Making as an Aspect of Political Behavior," this REVIEW, Vol. 52 (1958), p. 1007.

[60] *Id.*, p. 1011.

[61] *Id.*, p. 1010.

[62] *Id.*, p. 1017.

[63] *Ibid.*

To put the same point differently: I think that neo-behavioralism has been overinfluenced by the judicial activists—who are, after all, essentially behavioralists. This is to say, they are far more responsive to JUSTICE (as they see it) than to law. The trouble is their insistence that the resulting kadi-justice is not merely law, but sometimes even absolute law. Hence the well-known phenomenon of elastic, off-again-on-again rules and absolutes.[64] The resulting confusion has revived the 1930 conception of law as a myth—and again invited behavioral investigations of the judiciary. I suggest, in short, that modern behavioralism is a by-product of libertarian activism, just as legal realism was a by-product of laissez-faire activism. Both seem preoccupied with a half-truth.

If rule and order are not all there is in the judicial process, surely they are part of it. Indeed, we know on Dean Pound's authority that, "Almost all of the problems of jurisprudence come down to a fundamental one of rule and discretion, of administration of justice by law and administration of justice by the more or less trained intuition of experienced magistrates."[65] Having rediscovered the ancient truth that there is and must be pliability in the law, neo-behavioralists—like the early realists—discount the equally ancient truth that there is and must be law in the law. The difficulty of the judge's job is that he serves several masters. He must maintain at least formal symmetry while he synthesizes established rules, pragmatic needs, and moral yearnings. He must honor reasonable expectations born of the past, yet accommodate the present and the future. Thus he cannot entirely foresake either rule or discretion. The genius of the great judge is that he finds a happy blend. He knows that law is a compromise between anarchy and despotism. Above all, he recognizes that the process of legal change—the exercise of a court's inevitable discretion—must itself be principled and orderly. As Cardozo put it, a judge

is not to innovate at pleasure. He is not a knight-errant, roaming at will in pursuit of his own ideal of beauty or of goodness. He is to draw his inspiration from consecrated principles. He is not to yield to spasmodic sentiment, to vague and unregulated benevolence. He is to exercise a discretion informed by tradition, methodized by analogy, disciplined by system, and subordinated to "the primordial necessity of order in the social life."[66]

Even such a doughty old realist as Karl Llewellyn finally brought himself to recognize what he called the "law of lawful discretion" and the need for "reasonable regularity."[67] Unprincipled discretion, after all, is the essence of lawlessness; it leaves no moral basis for judicial authority. Especially is this relevant for a constitutional court of last resort, functioning as it must at the legal frontier where the law is necessarily sparse, and the area of choice correspondingly wide.

What I have been suggesting comes to this. The knight errantry of judicial activism has bred in the neo-behavioralists (among others) an iconoclasm toward law and the judicial process that goes beyond the bounds of reason. What should be charged to a few judges is chalked up against the legal system. Hypotheses tend to be self-proving, or at least to limit vision. We are apt to see what we are prepared to see—and the neo-behavioralists are prepared to see lawlessness. As a group, they have, in effect, found every member of the modern Supreme Court guilty of fraud, hypocrisy, or foolishness. Yet, is it not remarkable that in all their studies neo-behavioralists have not yet found a judge who seems to have been guided largely by law—though all profess to be? I suggest that the judge's art, when greatly practiced, is far too subtle to be measured by any existing behavioral technique. The law, said Holmes, is the painting of a picture—not the doing of a sum.[68]

[64] See Mendelson, "Mr. Justice Black and the Rule of Law," *Midwest Journal of Political Science,* Vol. 4 (1961), p. 250.

[65] Pound, *An Introduction to the Philosophy of Law* (1954 ed.), p. 54.

[66] Cardozo, *The Nature of the Judicial Process* (1921), p. 141.

[67] Llewellyn, *The Common Law Tradition* (1960), p. 217. See also Mansfield in Rex v. Wilkes, 4 Burr. 2527, 2539 (K.B. 1770).

[68] See Freund, "Mr. Justice Frankfurter," *Harvard Law Review,* Vol. 76 (1962), p. 17.

23 ❧ *The Untroubled World of Jurimetrics*

CITING STUDIES BY Professors Schubert, Ulmer and Spaeth, a leading young neo-behavioralist suggests that "the great bulk of the Supreme Court's decision-making may be reducible to a small number of attitudinal variables."[1] The Court, it would appear, is a rather simple institution; law is largely a myth; and cases are decided mainly in terms of personal predilection. These may be sound conclusions, yet their derivation leaves room for doubt.

After an elaborate quantitative analysis of Supreme Court decisions, Professor Ulmer concludes that the Court decides "civil liberty claims in terms of one dominant variable."[2] Indeed "the attitude [bias?] of the judge toward civil liberty claims was the factor shaping the individual decisions."[3] More particularly the attitude of Mr. Justice Frankfurter, for example, is found to be anti-libertarian.[4] Yet Professor Grossman's study of the same judge concludes that his votes cannot be explained accurately by a single dominant variable, and that it is "reasonable" to believe Frankfurter is "a civil libertarian."[5] *Both Ulmar and Grossman reach their contradictory conclusion via Guttman scale analysis.*

Similarly Professors Schubert and Ulmer, studying the 1960 and 1961 Terms of Court via scale analysis, reach differing conclusions as to the relative rank of the judges in their "attitudes" toward the alleged single dominant variable in civil liberty cases.[6]

---

[1]Spaeth, "Warren Court Attitudes Toward Business: The "B" Scale," in Schubert (ed), *Judicial Decision Making* 100 (1963)

[2]"Supreme Court Behavior and Civil Liberties," *The Western Political Quarterly*, Vol. 13 (1960), p. 311.

[3]*Ib.* p. 295.

[4]"The Analysis of Behavior Patterns on the United States Supreme Court," *The Journal of Politics*, Vol. 22 (1960), p. 653.

[5]"Role-Playing and the Analysis of Judicial Behavior: The Case of Mr. Justice Frankfurter," *Journal of Public Law*, Vol. II (1963), p. 308.

[6]See Schubert, "The 1960 Term of the Supreme Court: A Psychological Analysis," *The American Political Science Review*, Vol. 56 (1962), p. 98; and compare Ulmer, "A Note on Attitudinal Consistency in the United States Supreme Court," *The Indian Journal of Political Science*, Vol. 22 (1961), p. 200.

Accurate ranking, of course, is a prime purpose of scale analysis.[7]

These discrepancies are not necessarily fatal to Professor Spaeth's view of what jurimetrics may hope to accomplish.[8] But surely they are difficult to reconcile with the claim that "most important . . . is the protection against subjectivity which quantitative techniques of analysis provide."[9]

Just as Professor Ulmer finds a single dominant variable in civil liberty decisions, Professor Spaeth finds one in the labor and business regulation decisions (1953-1959).[10] Here scale analysis indicates that judges decide cases in terms of their respective "attitudes" toward "economic liberalism."[11] The result in the business regulation cases, we are told, is that the Court has an "anti-business orientation."[12] (If in this context "attitude" and "orientation" refer to something fundamentally unlike "bias" or "prejudice," would it not be well to indicate the difference?)

Professor Spaeth's interpretation of his "B Scale" finds support in his sub-scales of the cases involving federal administrative regulation of business. His Figure 6 includes such cases in which the agencies opposed business; while his Figure 7 includes those in which they favored business. Comparison of the two seems to show that the Court upheld 78 per cent of the anti-business orders, but

---

See also their respective articles on the 1961 Term in *Law and Contemporary Problems,* Vol. 28 (1963), at pp. 121, 170. The disparity, of course, is not unknown to the scholars in question (cf. *id.* 138). Entirely apart from problems in technique, the studies just mentioned suggest that these gentlemen are far from agreement as to what constitutes a civil-liberty case.

[7]With respect to the 1961 Term, for example, Professors Ulmer and Schubert agree that Mr. Justice Clark stands at one extreme in civil liberty cases, while Judges Black, Douglas, Warren and Brennan stand at the other. The relative rank of the judges in the latter category is a matter of disagreement. (The other judges apparently did not particiapte in enough decisions during the period in question to make their positions scalable.) Does this "confirmation" of the commonplace lend credence to "radical" conclusions derived from scale analysis in other areas?

[8]*Op. cit.,* note 1, above, p. 100.

[9]Spaeth, "An Approach to the Study of Attitudinal Differences as an Aspect of Judicial Behavior," *Midwest Journal of Political Science,* Vol. 5 (1961) p. 180.

[10]*Op cit.,* note 1, above

[11]Economic liberalism "is defined as pro-union [with some exceptions] pro-competition, and anti--business." *Id.* 79. This paper is not concerned with labor cases.

[12]*Ib.* 96. If for the reasons indicated below Professor Spaeth's sub-scales are vulnerable, it would seem that his major scale (from which they are derived) is also vulnerable.

only 43 per cent of those that were pro-business. "Complementing this picture is the [alleged] fact that when the Court does vote to reverse agency decision-making, it overturns pro-business agency decisions much more frequently than those which are anti-business."[13] This seems to support the conclusion that the Court is in fact anti-business.

Taken alone, the Figure 6 conclusion that 78 per cent of the anti-business orders are upheld suggests at most judicial humility. The anti-business charge rests heavily on the apparent discrepancy between Figures 6 and 7. Does Figure 7 in fact show what it purports to show; namely, that the Court upholds only 43 per cent of the pro-business administrative decisions? It included 14 cases. According to Professor Spaeth they all involve orders *favorable to business.* But do they? In the *Schaffer* case,[14] for example, the ICC denied a motor carrier permission to operate between two points previously served exclusively by rail. This order is deemed pro-business presumably because it bars competition between two carriers. Yet an ICC order in the *American Trucking* case[15] is also treated as pro-business, though it granted a railroad an unrestricted motor carrier license to compete with established truckers. Several Figure 7 cases involve this problem of extension or non-extension of competition between carriers. No doubt in some circumstances increased competition hurts enterprise; while in others it has an opposite effect. Short of a careful economic analysis of each individual situation, how can one say whether a particular order supports or opposes business?[16] Indeed what business is referred to as being supported or opposed? The applicant's business? That of the rival carriers? The affected shipper's businesses? The transportation business? Or business in general?[17]

Of course Professor Spaeth may be using something other than competition as his standard in labeling these cases. If so, he is at odds with his stated definition that "economic liberalism, is . . .

---

[13]*Ib.* 96-97.

[14]*Schaffer Transportation Company* v. *United States,* 355, U. C. 83 (1957).

[15]*American Trucking Association* v. *United States,* 355 U. S. 141 (1957).

[16]Those who find this problem simple should consult C. H. Fulda, *Competition In The Regulated Industries: Transportation* (1961).

[17]To compound the difficulty, Figure 6 (the anti-business category) also includes cases involving administrative orders granting *(Pan-Atlantic Steamship Company* v. *A.C.L.R. Company,* 353 U. S. 436 (1957), and restricting *(Nelson* v. *United States,* 355 U. S. 554 (1958), carriers permission to compete with other carriers

pro-competition. . . ."[18] Perhaps his point is that the two ICC orders in question are illiberal in that they favor "big business." Yet it is difficult to see in what sense the American Trucking Association is "small" even vis-a-vis its opponent, the Rock Island Railroad.

In the *Isbrandtsen* case[19] the Federal Maritime Board approved a carrier conference dual rate system. The effect would be to permit conference vessels to meet—and perhaps undermine or destroy —petitioner's allegedly cutthroat competition. Obviously conference rate-making is a long way from rate-making in an open competitive market. For this reason presumably Professor Spaeth treats the FMB order as pro-business and thus illiberal. Yet unqualified application of antitrust principles to American vessels—when there is no generally effective way to apply them to unregulated foreign vessels —seemed to the FMB both suicidal and contrary to long-established national policy. In short, the conference system is calculated *to permit American carriers to compete effectively* in the cartel dominated international shipping industry.

The Court held the dual rate system illegal *per se* regardless of the circumstances in any particular case (that at least was the dissenters' understanding). Then Congress—apparently in accordance with long-settled national policy—immediately suspended the sweeping decision (1958), and later after careful study modified it (1961) to permit the common conference practices in appropriate circumstances for the protection of national interests. Those who followed the Bonner and Celler investigations may find that to dismiss the FMB view out of hand as "liberal" or "illiberal" is too simple, and essentially beside the point. A better term perhaps would be "realistic"—if we must have a catchword to describe such complex phenomena. We do not live after all in an ideal laissez-faire world; and we have little or no power to impose one upon foreign governments.

In the *M & St. L.* case[20] several major railroads applied to the ICC for permission to acquire a short-line road bypassing Chicago. The commission granted one (joint) application, and denied the others—finding this would not significantly reduce competition. Again the order is deemed pro-business, as no doubt it was from the

---

[18]See note 11, above.
[19]*Federal Maritime Board* v. *Isbandtsen*, 356 U. S. 481 (1958).
[20]*Minneapolis & St. Louis Ry.* v. *United States*, 361 U. S. 173 (1959).

winner's point of view. The losers presumably had rather different opinions. If Professor Spaeth finds the order pro-business on the theory that it would in fact reduce competition, he is at odds with the ICC commissioners—whose findings were held unexceptionable by a unanimous three-judge District Court and by the Supreme Court. Indeed only one Justice dissented, but since he did so without opinion we do not know the basis of his disagreement. On what evidence then does one summarily reject the ICC finding that the acquisition would not significantly reduce competition?

Consider also, for example, the *Utah Poultry case*.[21] There the ICC issued an order limiting rail carrier liability for broken eggs. This hardly seems more pro-railroad than anti-egg-industry. No matter how a judge voted (here as in most of the other cases) he would have to support some business interests and oppose others. How would one determine whether the over-all effect of the ICC order in all its ramifications favored or opposed "business?" On Professor Spaeth's premise of "attitude" determinism, the answer is so far from clear that the two leading liberal judges, Black and Douglas, joined Frankfurter and Harlan—who are said to be highly illiberal—in overriding the commission order.

Both the farm and the railroad industries are sick, subsidized, and regulated in various degrees. Whether the cost of broken eggs is put immediately upon the one or the other, will the consumer (and perhaps the taxpayer) escape the ultimate burden? Is the egg carrier less capable than the egg shipper of passing breakage cost on to others? In this complex clash of interests surely there is no simple off-the-cuff standard for determining whether the ICC order supported or opposed "business."

Finally an FPC order licensing a private power plant on a non-navigable river in reservation territory is deemed pro-business and thus illiberal.[22] Why? The basic issue (as I see it) was whether this is a matter for state, or for federal, control. Only Mr. Jusitce Douglas voted in favor of state authority; he did not even remotely suggest the order was "soft on business." The Court—in harmony with a long standing *liberal* tenant—upheld (and perhaps extended) federal control of the nation's river resources. Ironically, Mr. Justice Frankfurter is charged with an illiberal vote, though more than a generation ago he as much as anyone instigated the then radical

---

[21]*Utah Poultry & Farmers Corp.* v. *United States*, 350 U. S. 162 (1956).
[22]*FPC* v. *Oregon*, 349 U. S. 435 (1955).

program of federal river regulation. When did it become liberal to restrict national resource control in favor of states' rights?

In my view, at least five of the 14 figure 7 cases present these or comparable problems. Since Professor Spaeth admits Guttman theory "requires a minimum of ten computable items in a scale,"[23] it would appear that Figure 7 is not an acceptable scale. Without it, we cannot make the comparison with Figure 6—the comparison on which the anti-business charge so heavily depends.

Difficulty increases via some items in Figure 6. For example, *United States* v. *Storer Broadcasting Company*[24] concerned an FCC rule against granting licenses to applicants with stakes in more than five stations. Even if we consider this as necessarily "opposed" to business in general, or indeed to the broadcasting industry, there are other problems.[25] Seven Justices on appeal voted to uphold the FCC. They are recorded in Figure 6 as having supported an anti-business administrative decision. Two dissenting judges are recorded as having voted pro-business.[26] Yet the effect of the minority vote was exactly the same as the effect of the majority vote; namely, to sustain the FCC rule. Thus one "dissenter" thought the case should not have been reviewed, but since it was, he concurred with the Court on the merits. The other minority judge simply voted against judicial review. The effect of his position was to leave the FCC order intact—which was precisely the effect of all other votes in the case. Yet seven of them are treated in Figure 6 as anti-business, and two as pro-.

On the basis of the B Scale and its Figure 6 and 7 subdivisions, Professor Spaeth derives other strange conclusions as to the "attitudes" of various judges. He finds, for example, that Mr. Justice Frankfurter is pro-business (not anti-activist as his "apologists" claim).[27] Even Professor Spaeth admits this "might be considered somewhat surprising, given [Frankfurter's] involvement with the New Deal and other earlier social and economic reforms."[28] It is

---

[23]*Op cit.,* note 1, above, p. 101, note 15.

[24]351 U. S. 192 (1956). See also note 17, above, and note 25, below.

[25]Figure 6 includes cases (Spaeth's numbers 35, 50, 66, 67, and 114) decided initially by agencies that perhaps should be considered as judicial rather than administrative. If the Tax Court, the Court of Claims, and federal District Courts, are to be treated as administrative agencies, did they not decide more than five cases relevant to Figure 6?

[26]*Storer,* the case in question, is case number 60 in Figure 6.

[27]*Op. cit.,* note 1, above, p. 98.

[28]*Ibid.* 81.

just possible that Professor Spaeth's strange treatment of *Storer*, *Isbrandtsen, Utah Poultry*, the Dam, and related cases explains his "surprising" conclusion as to Mr. Justice Frankfurter.[29]

So, too, comparing the state (Figure 4) and the federal (Figure 5) business regulatory cases, Professor Spaeth questions Frankfurter's "reputed concern" for local self-government.[30] But 11 of the 18 state regulations impinged upon federal functions or interstate commerce. Such measures involve the risk of undue local intrusion upon extra-state interests (the old problem of taxation without representation). I am not aware that any Justice has ever suggested such matters should be left to state discretion. It is one thing, as Holmes suggested, for the Court to permit "the making of social experiments . . . in the insulated chambers afforded by the several states;" it is something very different to give the state a free hand, for example, to tax or regulate interstate commerce. "For [as Holmes put it] one in my place sees how often a local policy prevails with those who are not trained to national views and how often action is taken that embodies what the Commerce Clause was meant to end."[31]

Similarly, Professor Spaeth's conclusion that Mr. Justice Black is an ardent states' righter in Figure 4 cases seems thoroughly misleading.[32] Half of the cases involve state taxation or regulation of interstate commerce. Black's repeated view has been that (discrimination aside) the Court should stay away from such problems and *leave them to Congress*.[33] On a states' rights scale this shows up as a simple states' rights "attitude." Yet in fact Black's position is not that state commerce policy should prevail over national— but that the articulation of national commerce policy is a congressional, not a judicial, function.[34]

Unlike some of his neo-behavioral colleagues who seem to hold

---

[29]The same difficulty may explain Professor Spaeth's similar conclusions in "The Judicial Restraint of Mr. Justice Frankfurter—Myth or Reality," *Midwest Journal of Political Science,* Vol. VIII, pp. 22 et seq. (1964).

[30]*Op. cit.,* note 1, above, at pp. 94-5.

[31]The quoted language is from *Truax* v. *Corrigan,* 257 U. S. 312 (1921), and *Collected Legal Papers* 295-6 (1920).

[32]*Op. cit.,* note 1, above, p. 94.

[33]See, for example, his opinions in *Southern Pacific Company* v. *Arizona,* 325 U. S. 761 (1945), and *J. D. Adams Manufacturing Company* v. *Storen,* 304 U. S. 307 (1938).

[34]*Ibid.*

that law is largely a myth,[35] Professor Kort "predicts" decisions on the premise of "rules of law" and "controlling [factual] circumstances."[36] Indeed he does so in right-to-counsel and confession cases. Yet these are included among the civil liberty cases in which Professor Ulmer finds that *every* Justice arrives at his decision "not by asking 'what does the law require?' but by asking himself such questions as 'Shall I allow a deprivation of a claimed civil liberty' "[37] If Professor Ulmer and Kort are expounding the same truth, surely they have found richly diverse ways of expressing it.

Professor Kort insists that prior to *Gideon* we could not by traditional methods know what circumstances required the appointment of a counsel[38]—and that this is "precisely the kind of problem which mathematical and statistical methods can effectively attack. . . ."[39] Suppose then an after-acquired lawyer had advised his convicted client against "appeal" because Professor Kort's 1957 (or later) mathematical studies had indicated the case was too weak to win. Unless the client had voluntarily confessed, he and his lawyer apparently would have been misled. For the fact is that, absent a voluntary pre-trial confession, the Supreme Court *after June 5, 1950 had decided every right-to-counsel case in favor of the accused.*[40] In short, the *Betts* "special-circumstances" rule had ceased to be a reality[41]—though absence of counsel at the time of

---

[35]"They . . . have debunked legal principles as factors controlling decisions . . . ." Schubert, in his work cited last in note 6, above, at p. 104.

[36]Kort, "Content Analysis of Judicial Opinions and Rules of Law" in Schubert (ed.), *Judicial Decision Making* 133-4 and 180 (1963).

[37]*Loc. cit.,* note 2, above, at pp. 295, 311. Professor Ulmer reaches essentially the same conclusion in studies relating to the 1955-1962 Terms.

[38]"To the Editor," *The American Political Science Review,* Vol. 57 (1963), p. 953. In support of this conclusion, Professor Kort cites *inter alia* an article by J. R. Green. But this and similar articles, I suggest, were briefs, i.e. arguments, written by those who favored counsel in all cases. Hence their attacks on the "vagueness" of the *Betts* rule. Whatever the faults of the latter, it was not (I think) more vague than many, perhaps most, other rules of constitutional law. Indeed I am sure that so accomplished a lawyer as Mr. Green would have known quite well—prior to *Gideon*—what evidence to use in "appealing" the case of one who had been convicted without aid of counsel. Like any competent lawyer, he would, of course, have stressed everything in the circumstances that had put his client at a disadvantage through lack of counsel.

[39]*Ibid.*

[40]In the preceding eight years since (and including) *Betts,* at least eight non-confession, right-to-counsel cases had been decided *against* the accused

[41]Or, as Mr. Justice Harlan observed in *Gideon* v. *Wainwright,* 372 U.S. 335, 351 (1963), "The Court [had] come to recognize . . . that the mere existence of a serious charge constituted in itself special circumstances requiring the services of counsel at trial. In truth the *Betts* v. *Brady* rule is no longer a reality."

an otherwise voluntary, pre-trial confession did not in itself invalidate a conviction.[42] Thus well before *Gideon*,[43] the Gideon principle (or something like it) had become in effect the law.[44] The
point is not that the elaborate neo-behavioral studies in question
failed to find significant regularities in counsel cases, but that they
missed the one controlling regularity.[45] Traditional scholarship
seems to have been more perceptive.[46]

Could it be that the Justices, the cases, and the judicial process
are more complex than neo-behavioralism contemplates?

---

[42]See *Cicenia* v. *Lagay*, 357 U.S. 504 (1958); *Crooker* v. *California*, 357
U.S. 433 (1958); *Stroble* v. *California*, 343 U.S. 181 (1953).

[43]*Gideon* v. *Wainwright*, 372 U.S. 335 (1963).

[44]"The present point relates not to prediction, but to the understanding of
past decisions. As to this, note the Kort view that, after decisions have been
made, his technique will reveal "whether or not the Court continues to apply
the rule of law consistently." *Op. cit.*, note 36, above, at pp. 179-80.

[45]One study seems to have done this as late as 1963. *Ib.* pp. 133 *et seq.*

[46]See, for example, Pollock, "Equal Justice in Practice," 45 *Minnesota
Law Review* 737, 740 (1961), and Kamisar, "Betts v. Brady Twenty Years
Later," 61 *Michigan Law Review* 219, 280-81 (1962). But see Lawlor, "What
Computers Can Do: Analysis and Prediction of Judicial Decisions," American
Bar Association Journal, Vol. 49 (1963), p. 344. Using computer technique,
Mr. Lawlor found "the odds are at least about twenty to one that [Gideon]
will prevail regardless of whether *Betts* v. *Brady* is overruled." This "prediction," of course, was empirically test-proof, for it is compatible with any
judgment that might have been given in *Gideon*. Moreover, to the extent
it rests on the premise that *Betts* was still the law, it rests on what for me is
a false assumption. Surely little can be said even for a verified conclusion based
on an erroneous premise.

24 ✺ An Open Letter to Professor Spaeth on Jurimetrics

MAY I SUGGEST that you made a revealing error when you wrote that Justices Black and Frankfurter "say the same thing" about state interference with interstate commerce?[1] Your assertion presumably springs from the behavioralist concentration upon what judges *do* as distinct from what they *say*. Yet in not knowing (or not caring) what they say, one is in a poor position to insist upon a discrepancy between their words and deeds. In short, your major thrust rests on a false premise.

You find that in state regulation cases, Mr. Justice Black is markedly "anti-business" (and correspondingly pro-states rights). Whether ultimately your conclusion is true or false, I suggest it springs from misleading data and a misconception of what the Justice says. For example, about half the cases in your Figure 4 involve state taxation or regulation of interstate commerce. Mr. Justice Black *says* that in such cases there should be *no judicial review* (whether the state act is pro- or anti-business).[2] Yet like all judges he recognizes there must be a national veto to protect interstate commerce from destruction by the states.[3] *His view is simply that the veto should be exercised by Congress rather than by the*

[1] Harold Spaeth, "Jurimetrics and Professor Mendelson: A Troubled Relationship," *Journal of Politics,* vol. 27 (November, 1965) p. 880. Mr. Spaeth's effort is a response to Wallace Mendelson, "The Troubled World of Jurimetrics," id. vol. 26 (November, 1964) pp. 914-922.

[2] See particularly his dissent in *Southern Pacific Company* v. *Arizona,* 325 U.S. 761 (1945). This position is qualified a bit in *Hood* v. *Du Mond,* 336 U.S. 525, 550-551 (1949).

courts.[4] Surely you cannot ignore the "congressional veto" cases[5] (as you do), if you want a true picture of Mr. Justice Black's *deeds* with respect to business and the states.

Rejecting Black's views, Mr. Justice Frankfurter *says* there must be judicial review in these cases.[6] He does not repudiate the congressional veto power, he insists merely that:

> To construe federal legislation so as not needlessly to forbid pre-existing State authority is to respect our federal system. Any indulgence in construction should be in favor of the States, because Congress can speak with drastic clarity whenever it chooses to assume full federal authority, completely displacing the States.[7]

Surely a comparison of the "attitudes" of the two judges with respect to business and states rights ought to consider the congressional, as well as the judicial, veto cases. It comes to this: Hugo shoots ducks with a gun; Felix shoots them with a bow and arrow. We do not get a true picture of their comparative "attitudes" toward ducks by considering only those shot down with arrows.

It seems to me that what Justices Black and Frankfurter say in these Commerce-Clause cases is an important clue to what they do—and that to ignore what they say (plus a good part of what they do) invites misunderstanding. Indeed should we not be sure a judge departs from what he says before we try to explain the "discrepancy" in terms of hidden "attitudes"?

Your "Figure 4. State Regulation of Business" is made up of 18 cases. (Three of them—Nos. 21, 38, 84—appear to be *Federal* regulation cases.) Eight are the interstate commerce cases referred to above. Six of the seven remaining cases present problems in inter-

---

[3]The unanimity on this point reflects the impact of our experience under the Articles of Confederation and the continuing short-sightedness of the states in attempting to promote local, at the expense of national, interests. Even judges who are skeptical of judicial review in general (e.g. Holmes and Frankfurter) have found it indispensable in this context. See Holmes' comments quoted in Mendelson, *loc. cit.*, note 1, above, p. 920.

[4]See cases cited in note 2, above.

[5]See the line of cases from *Cloverleaf Butter Co.* v. *Patterson,* 315 U.S. 148 (1942) to *Northern National Gas Co.* v. *State Corporation Commission,* 372 U.S. 84 (1963). I do not suggest that cases of this type are the only relevant items ignored in Mr. Spaeth's calculations.

[6]On this point Mr. Justice Frankfurter takes the traditional view which finds classic modern expression in Chief Justice Stone's majority opinion in *Southern Pacific, supra,*—Frankfurter concurring.

[7]*Bethlehem Co.* v. *State Board,* 330 U.S. 767, 780 (1947). See also the cases mentioned in note 5, above.

governmental tax immunity. It is interesting that in measuring attitudes toward state business regulation, you rely almost entirely on cases of taxes that impinge on national interests, i.e., federal functions or interstate commerce. Surely such cases involve far more than is at stake in the more typical *regulation* (substantive due process) cases. In all of the latter, both Black and Frankfurter *always* vote "anti-business." If Frankfurter votes "differently" on the Spaeth tax cases, is it because of a shifting attitude toward business—or because in the one context, but not in the other, he finds state interference with national affairs? In short, isn't Frankfurter simply recognizing Holmes' distinction (quoted in my original article) between a state measure which has only local effects, and one which has national effects?

Mr. Justice Black's so-called "anti-business" attitude in these tax cases may parallel his position in the interstate commerce cases; namely, that state impingements upon Federal interests should be left to Congress. Thus dissenting in *Kern-Limerick* (Spaeth Case No. 10) he insists: "We should hold that, until Congress says differently, the states are free to tax all sales [of materials to government contractors, even though the materials are to be used in *cost-plus* construction of a Federal military base]." Some may find in Black's "leave-it-to-Congress" gambit not an anti-business attitude, but merely a distaste for judicial review. After all, it is only in civil-liberty cases that the Justice has shown any great willingness to veto legislation. Other matters—whether "pro-" or "anti-business"—he has been much inclined to leave to the political processes.

I find other difficulties in your response, but mention only the above because it seems a major part of the "trouble" with jurimetrics.[8] The judge's art is a house of many mansions—including the irrational and the personal as well as reason and principle. In my view, neobehavioralism is so enchanted by its discovery of irrational elements in the judicial process that it *completely* discounts everything else. And so, imprisoned (like the rest of us) by a limited view, mistaking the part for the whole, it tends to measure—however accurately—the wrong things. Perhaps when a boy goes

---

[8] I have intimated elsewhere that neo-behavioralism generally takes an over-simple view of the normally complex cases that reach the Supreme Court. See *loc. cit.,* note 1, *supra,* and "The Neo-Behavioral Approach to the Judicial Process: A Critique," *The American Political Science Review,* vol. LVII (September, 1963) pp. 593-603.

with nine girls, and finally rejects all of them to marry the tenth, one might say mathematically that he has a preponderantly (nine to one) anti-girl attitude.

Can it be that the legal system to which in age after age intelligent judges, practitioners, and scholars have devoted their lives is really as shallow—as mindless—as neobehavioralism would have us believe?[9]

---

[9]The work of the neobehavioralists, we are told, "provides . . . evidence that the great bulk of the [Supreme] Court's decision-making may be reducible to a small number of attitudinal variables." Spaeth, *loc. cit.*, note 1, above, p. 100.

VI

The Path of the Law

25   Law and the Development of Nations

For centuries legal scholars have pursued the development of national law. Quite recently political scientists have begun to explore the development of nations. The literature is already massive. Yet little or none of it recognizes the place of law in national growth. My purpose here is to suggest—for those who may want to pursue it—the crucial role of law in developing nations. For in "all societies the historical function of law has been to elaborate, rationalize, and protect . . . dominant [or emerging] institutions and accredited ways of life." As Holmes put it, the law reveals "every painful step and every world-shaking contest by which mankind has worked . . . its way from savage isolation to organic social life."

I take as a model Professor Organski's view that modern nations have gone through three stages of political development: the politics of primitive unification, the politics of industrialization, and the politics of social welfare.[1] In stage one the primary problem is political integration—"the creation of national unity." Stage two is a battle for economic and political modernization. Accordingly the chief governmental function is to encourage a new elite—the industrial managers—and to promote the "accumulation of capital." Finally in stage three government's chief job is "to protect the people from the hardships of industrial life," to right by welfare programs the wrongs of the earlier stages.

Today most nations are still hovering in stages one or two. Japan, Western Europe, and the Soviet Union are somewhere— early or late—in stage three. The United States is perhaps approaching what may be a fourth stage—an age that may have greater reverence for life. Hippydom may be its harbinger.

---

[1]A. F. K. Organski, *The Stages of Political Development* (New York: Knopf, 1965), 7 ff.

For the early stages were high in human sacrifice. Yet if the cost has been great, so has been the accomplishment. Never before in human history has a people had at its fingertips the skill and wherewithal to heal, feed, clothe, and shelter adequately every one of its members. The great problem now—the stage-four problem— it would seem, is a poverty of spirit.

Let us consider first, however, the role of law—particularly judicial law—in the development of three modern nations. Stage one, the politics of primative unification, was achieved formally in the United States when we adopted the Constitution. But whether a nation on parchment would become a nation in fact was quite another matter. The centrifugal forces were great. Probably most Americans in 1789 opposed the Constitution on grounds that run the whole range of socio-economic-cultural interests. The convenient catch phrase of their opposition was "states rights." This was the background of the well-known nationalism of John Marshall's Court. Save *Marbury v. Madison*, every one of its classic decisions is a blow at parochialism. Every one of them strikes down a state claim or measure. Each repudiates a regional, political, or economic subculture. All express with compelling simplicity a vision of national unity and national supremacy. *Martin v. Hunter's Lessee, McCulloch v. Maryland, Cohens v. Virginia, Gibbons v. Ogden*, and *Brown v. Maryland* were integrating forces. They were cement for the Union, as Paul Feund put it—a cement imaginatively composed of unwritten, ie., implied, limits upon the states, and implicit grants to the nation.

The magnitude of Marshall's departure from the conventional wisdom of the day is easily demonstrated. John Taylor of Caroline, the "official" philosopher of the Jeffersonians, wrote volumes to prove that the Constitutional Convention had refused to authorize the "centralized supremacy" that Marshall's Court espoused. He urged a "return to the Constitution." Spencer Roane struck at Marshall's nationalism in a series of anonymous newspaper articles. Roane, it will be recalled, headed the highest court of Virginia. He, rather than Marshall, might well have been Chief Justice of the United States, if Ellsworth had resigned early in Jefferson's, instead of late in Adams's, administration.

By the end of the Civil War we were well into the second stage—the era of industrialization. What Walt Rostow calls the take-off had begun in the 1840s. This could easily be traced in the statistics of pig iron, railroads, capital growth, and urbanization.

A more revealing measure is Henry Adams's shock of non-recognition when he and his family returned to America in 1868 after a decade abroad. "Had they been Tyrian traders of the year B.C. 1000, landing from a [Mediterranian] galley," he said, "they could hardly have been stranger on the shore of a world so changed from what it had been ten years earlier."[2] Later he could see what had happened: the "mechanical energies—coal, iron, steam"—had attained "a distinct superiority in power over the old industrial elements—agriculture, handwork, and learning." In this new America, Adams found himself

> . . . an estray, a flotsam or jetsam of wreckage. . . . His world was dead. . . . American of Americans, with heaven knows how many Puritans and Patriots behind him [he was a stranger 'in his homeland]. He made no complaint . . . he was no worse off [he observed] than the Indians or the buffalo. . . .[3]

Obviously Adams's difficulty was that he clung to the values of the old America—values that parvenu businessmen were fast destroying in the name of progress. For him,

> it was a vulgar world that was rising and an evil day. Since 1865 [he insisted] the bankers had ruled America, and they were coming finally to cajole the American people into accepting their vulgar ideals and putting their trust in a bankers' paradise. As he watched the temples of the new society rising everywhere in the land, his gorge rose at the prospect. He had no wish to dwell in a bankers' paradise.[4]

This is to say in poetic terms, and from the point of view of the dispossessed, that we were in the throes of economic modernization, that a new elite was crowding out an old one, that familiar processes of socialization were transforming—secularizing—American culture into something new and strange. All these of course are major elements in Organski's stage-two model.

---

[2]Henry Adams, *The Education of Henry Adams* (Boston: Houghton-Mifflin, 1918), 238.

[3]*Ibid.*

[4]Vernon L. Parrington, *Main Currents in American Thought* (3 vols.; New York: Harcourt, Brace and Co., 1927), III, 216.

What was the role of judges in the brave new world that Henry Adams found so repelling? Our great problem in the nineteenth century was a scarcity of goods vis-à-vis a wealth of national resources. In that setting, as Willard Hurst has shown, the whole premise, the thrust, of the common law was to increase production by promoting economic freedom.[5] This pervasive spirit of the common law was reflected, for example, in the basic assumptions of tort, contract, and even criminal law. It found expression in the newly devised labor injunction,[6] in such specific rules as the one that protected manufacturers of defective goods from liability to third-party consumers,[7] and in those that all but freed employers from the cost of industrial accidents.[8] Toward the end of the century when legislatures tried to put some limits on entrepreneurial freedom, they encountered judicially-imposed laissez faire.

Judges, we are told, have an educational function. So be it. Mr. Justice Field was the first of a new line of professor-judges. His famous dissent in *Slaughter House* was our first formal lesson in the philosophy of what Adams called the bankers' paradise. Soon, as we all know, Field's teaching became the law of the land. Again, as in Marshall's day, the Court found new doctrines to meet the needs of the day: Dual Federalism, Substantive Due Process, and Liberty of Contract. The great bench mark decisions were the *Sugar Trust, Income Tax,* and *Child Labor* cases, *Lochner* v. *New York,* and the utility rate cases, to mention only the obvious. All of us have criticized these and the common-law decisions ad infinitum, but we may have missed their long-run significance. Decisions that block the claims of labor and consumer promote the growth of investment capital. And if a "traditional" society wants mass production, its first economic task is to accumulate capital. "The meager productive capacities of bare hands and bent backs must be supplemented by the enormous leverage of machines [and superhuman] power. . . ."

---

[5]James Willard Hurst, *Law and the Conditions of Freedom in Nineteenth Century United States* (Madison: University of Wisconsin Press, 1956).

[6]Felix Frankfurter and Nathan Greene, *The Labor Injunction* (Glouchester: P. Smith, 1930).

[7]See William L. Prosser, *Law of Torts* (St. Paul: West Publishing Co., 1964), ch. 19.

[8]*Ibid.,* ch. 15.

But how does a developing nation accumulate capital? Some it may borrow, as we did. But mainly it must save.[9] This means much more than putting money in a bank.

> It means . . . society must refrain from using all its current energies and materials to satisfy its current wants, no matter how urgent these may be. Saving is the act by which a [nation] releases some portion of its labor and material resources from the task of providing for the present so that both can be applied to building for the future.[10]

Such matters can hardly be left to individual whim. No society can hope to modernize unless it somehow begets social attitudes and institutions that induce the masses (however needy) to consume less than they produce. Without this effort there can be no tools, no factories, no roads or trains.

When the Supreme Court suppressed worker and consumer claims and taught us the blessings of laissez faire and the Gospel of Wealth, it fostered capital accumulation. Its decisions were part of a socialization process that glorified "private enterprise" and for a time at least kept the common man in his humble place. This, with the resulting stimulation of business energy and appetite, is the crux of economic modernization. To put it crudely, the Court promoted the savings and managerial effort that built our mass producing factories. The common man paid dearly in his standard of living as he has in all industrialized countries including Soviet Russia. Perhaps our judges—like the Soviet commissars— were so effective in restraining consumption because they were politically independent and not very responsive to mass hardship. Whatever the reason, capital formation rose geometrically after the Civil War. In 1850 the estimated value of our industrial and commercial plant was $3.3 billion. By 1880 it had increased to

---

[9]In advanced nations from 10 to 20 percent of national income may go into capital formation. In underdeveloped nations the rate of savings and investment may be less than 5 percent—less than enough sometimes to offset population growth. See Paul A. Samuelson, *Economics* (New York: McGraw-Hill Book Co., 1964), 768; and Colin Clark, "Population Growth and Living Standards," in *The Economics of Underdevelopment,* by Amar N. Agarwalla and S. P. Singh (New York: Oxford University Press, 1958).

[10]Robert L. Heilbroner, *The Great Ascent* (New York: Harper and Row, 1963), 92-93.

$18.6 billion. In the next 30 years it grew by almost 400 percent to $72.1 billion. By 1929 the figure was $125.7 billion in constant dollars.[11] When Henry Adams went abroad in 1859 the total value of goods manufactured in the United States was $1.8 billion. By the turn of the century forty years later, manufacturing output had increased by well over 700 percent.

Having achieved mass production, the United States entered stage three—the era of the welfare state. The problem now was not production, but distribution. Consumer goods were so potentially plentiful and so near at hand that there was less need to restrain consumption. We could afford Social Security, collective bargaining, minimum wages, the forty-hour week, Medicare, and similar measures. The common element in these programs is a "redistribution" of wealth. Income that earlier might have been channeled toward capital formation was now diverted to provide goods and services for the common man. His fathers' unwilling investment in American plant capacity began at last to pay him dividends.

In this new world judicial law was again crucial. Beginning in 1937 the Roosevelt Court cleared away Mr. Justice Field's old constitutional roadblocks. Dual Federalism, Substantive Due Process, and Liberty of Contract disappeared. Government at all levels was free to promote the interests of the weak at the expense of the strong. An elite had served its social purpose, and was now being discounted. Since 1936 no regulation of business, no social legislation—state or federal—has suffered Supreme Court veto.[12] Equally striking has been the Court's application of statutes. Never before has federal legislation been construed so lavishly to favor labor and consumer interests. The old Federal Employers' Liability Act, for example, grew by judicial construction beyond anything its congressional sponsors dreamed of. When Congress enacted F.E.L.A., it provided that workmen could have compensation for industrial

---

[11]J. Frederic Dewhurst and associates, *America's Needs and Resources* (New York: The Twentieth Century Fund, 1955), 814; Robert D. Patten and Clinton Warne, *The Development of the American Economy* (Chicago: Scott, Foresman, 1963), 243.

[12]The one exception is *Morey v. Doud*, 354 U.S. 457 (1957). Cases involving state interference with interstate commerce, i.e., with extra-state interests, are another matter.

injuries only where the company was negligent. This, of course, is hopelessly old fashioned. The new Supreme Court did not wait for Congress to adopt a more modern approach. The judges simply recast the old measure, all but eliminating the negligence requirement and substituting something very close to absolute employer liability for industrial accidents.[13]   Even in modern legislation, the Court has had little patience with the give and take of legislative compromise.   It has read the Fair Labor Standards Act, for example, almost as though the hopes of its most ardent advocates had been adopted by Congress without concession to opponents, without accommodation of rival interests.[14]   Since 1936, then, labor and consumer interests have enjoyed a preferred status in court visà-vis the businessman—an obvious reversal of roles.   Other underdogs have also risen.   The Warren Court was gracious indeed to the Negro, the criminal-case defendant, and the malapportioned voter.   The weak have inherited the judicial world just as the nationalists did in stage one, and the industrialists in stage two. Again the Court has been creative, though the precise outlines of what Mr. Justice Goldberg called the new doctrine of equality are not yet entirely clear.

ENGLAND

We turn now to the oldest western nation.   After the Conquest what we now call England was a conglomeration of Anglo-Saxon and Norman peoples.   Each had its own customs, laws, and language.   By Stephen's day (1135-54) civil war was rampant. King, barons, and clergy were at loggerheads on basic problems of constitutional authority.   Their differences spilled over into the courts, some of which derived authority from the King, some from the barons, some from the Church.   The feudalism that had promised order brought anarchy.   The Conquest—like our own written Constitution—imposed only formal unity.   By the middle of the twelfth century, England was ripe for stage one—the politics of primitive unification.   Henry II (1154-89) saw the problem and found a

---

[13]Prosser, *Torts*, 560-561; and Wallace Mendelson, *Justices Black and Frankfurter* (Chicago: University of Chicago Press, 1961), ch. 2.
    [14]*Ibid.*

remedy. First he settled what had to be settled by military means and fiscal reform. Then he turned to the legal system, recognizing apparently that no peace could last until royal, i.e., national, law replaced feudal law.

Expanding the concept of the King's Peace, he made crime an offense against the monarch—a national offense, triable only in a monarch's court. Previously crime for the most part had been merely a private wrong. In civil affairs, too, the jurisdiction of the royal courts grew. Earlier in unusual cases one could get a royal writ ordering a case to be tried in the King's Court, but Henry now expanded and regularized the writ process. Recognizing that judicial work was becoming highly specialized, he gave it only to specialists. Again drawing on sporadic precedent, he extended and regularized the use of local juries. In short he made justice more just (more rational and more acceptable) in his than in other courts. Feudal and local tribunals, for example, were still committed to trial by battle, compurgation, and ordeal.

Glanvill was the great Chief Justice—the John Marshall of that day. Because the royal, i.e., national, judges offered a better product, they gradually crowded out their rivals. In the process they developed a common law, a law common to all England and all Englishmen. What we would now call national law—developed by national courts—replaced feudal law (just as English replaced rival languages). In the process England became a nation. Here again judges and the law were crucial integrating and socializing forces.

Slow technological development presumably delayed industrialization until the eighteenth century. But when it came courts eased its way. Lord Chief Justice Mansfield (1705-93) is famous for his role in "modernizing" the common law. What he did, of course, was to weave into English jurisprudence those settled customs and understandings of the commercial world known as the law merchant.[15] This obviously promoted and encouraged business

---

[15]See William Holdsworth, *Some Makers of English Law* (Cambridge: Cambridge University Press, 1966), ch. 7. A brief account of the reign of Henry II will be found in George B. Adams, *A Constitutional History of England* (New York: Henry Holt, 1931). For more extended accounts, see Frederick Pollock and Frederick W. Maitland, *The History of English Law* (Cambridge: Cambridge University Press, 1952); William S. Holdsworth, *A History of English Law* (London: Methnen, 1936).

enterprise. Later with the factory system came decisions restricting employer liability for industrial accidents[16] and outlawing strikes as criminal conspiracies.[17] When Parliament overrode the latter, the judges responded with the doctrine of civil conspiracy.[18] A climax came in the *Taff Vale Case*[19] which made unions suable entities, liable in damages for their "conspiracies." Here again—to mention only landmark decisions—is a pattern of judicial law restricting labor's income in favor of capital formation. Charles Dickens and Karl Marx responded each in his own manner—the one with sentimentality, the other with the dialectic of surplus value (defined as the excess of what labor produced over what it was permitted to consume).

Dicey's famous lectures on *Law and Public Opinion in England* were delivered at the turn of the century. Like Henry Adams's biography, they mark a turning point in history. Lamenting the demise of the old political economy, Dicey traced in some detail what he called collectivist or socialistic developments in English law. Our cousins were entering the welfare era.[20]

JAPAN

A century ago Japan was largely a feudal realm dominated by the Tokugawa Shoguns, some 250 territorial lords (daimyo), and their retainers (the samurai). At first the peasant had been the backbone of the economy, supporting himself and the aristocracy by rice cultivation. Gradually commerce brought a merchant class, artisans, urban centers, and a money economy.

The Shogunate was not unaware of these developments. It responded mainly with policies designed to cushion their effect and to prevent excessive change. Ironically the result was

---

[16]*Priestly v. Fowler*, 150 Eng. Rep. 1030 (1837).

[17]*R. v. Rowlands*, 5 Cox at 431 (1851); *R. v. Bunn*, 12 Cox 316 (1872).

[18]*Temperton v. Russell*, (1893) Q.B. 715 (C.A.); *Quinn v. Leathem*, (1901) A.C. 495.

[19](1901) A.C. 426.

[20]Dicey, of course, was concerned primarily with statutory law. Changes in judicial law, however, were no less revealing. For excellent summaries, see Wolfgang G. Friedmann, *Law and Social Change in Contemporary Britain* (London: Stevens, 1951); Morris Ginsberg, *Law and Opinion in England in the 20th Century* (London: Stevens, 1959).

more than a trace of emerging nationhood. The Shoguns collected taxes, maintained a rudimentary peace, and used secret police (metsuke) to support the traditional morality and class structure. Most important, for our purposes, they provided courts—however reluctantly—to serve commercial needs.

Traditionally each feudal lord administered justice in his own fief (han), but had no jurisdiction over any case involving an outside party.   Commerce, however, ran throughout the land and would not conform to feudal boundaries.   To bridge this gap, to accommodate suits involving more than one fief, the Shoguns developed what we might call national courts and national law.[21]   Obviously such inter-fief jurisdiction is analogous to the diversity jurisdiction of our national, i.e., federal, courts.   So, too, as in England, this Tokugawa jurisprudence "owed a great deal . . . to the creativity of judges and much of [its] doctrine to judicial precedent."[22]   Here, then, was an emergent national or common law, judge-made, promoting social integration—the beginning of stage one: the era of primitive unification.

In the long run, the new social forces could not be contained in the old feudal forms.   Too much was required of the peasants. The aristocracy had social status, but no economic power; the merchants had wealth, but no standing.   This and foreign pressure for trade relations brought a revolution from above led by a samurai faction.

The integrating changes begun by the Shogunate attained high momentum with the Meiji Restoration of 1868.   The crumbling structure of feudalism was soon demolished—largely by buying off the old aristocracy.   Modernization was a matter of following western paths.   Indeed the new Emperor promised under oath that "intellect and learning would be sought . . . throughout the world."   Unlike the medieval English, the Japanese did not have to wait for a new technology.   "They went to England to study the navy and merchant marine, to Germany for the army and for medicine, to France for law, and to the United States for business methods."[23]   The result was rapid modernization.   By 1895

---

[21]Dan F. Henderson, *Conciliation and Japanese Law* (2 vols.; Seattle: University of Washington Press, 1965), I, 92 ff.
[22]*Ibid.*, 123.
[23]Edwin O. Reischauer, *Japan* (3rd ed.; New York: Knopf, 1964), 123.

> Japan had either established or started to develop such essential features of the modern nation-state as . . . a centralized and bureaucratic government, an army and a navy, a national system of education, newspapers, . . . a railroad [and] telegraph system, political unification, a modern system of law, and a sentiment of national unity spread widely among the people.[24]

Not the least of the imports from abroad were the Civil, Criminal, and Commercial Codes. Drawn largely from European models, these property-oriented digests were strong on protection of business interests and all but silent on labor and consumer safeguards. This left the new industrial elite (zaibatsu) free to exploit the common man. Low wages, administered prices, regressive taxation, with a strong incentive to save and invest, promoted rapid capital formation. The gross national product more than doubled in the 20 years from 1879 to 1898. In 60 years ending in 1939 it increased almost 1000 percent.[25]

Here again in a backward land law was a modernizing force. By promoting business, at the expense of other interests, it fostered capital formation without which there can be no great economic progress. In Japan, as elsewhere, modernization was expensive. The cost had to fall somewhere. In the early, critical years it fell upon the peasantry through a land tax. The rural countryside "played for Japanese capitalism the role of an internal colony." As a matter of social engineering, the leaders of the new Japan strengthened the traditional rural social structure. The "existing political, social, and economic elites of the villages were . . . confirmed in their [customary] authority; the traditional community and family systems were . . . reinforced and given new legal status and sanctions."[26] In short the rural sector was stabilized in its traditional ways to subsidize rapid modernization of the business sector.

---

[24]John M. Maki, *Government and Politics in Japan* (New York: Praeger, 1962), 16.

[25]Henry Rosovsky, *Capital Formation in Japan* (New York: Free Press, 1961); Kazushi Ohkawa and Henry Rosovsky, "A Century of Japanese Economic Growth," in *The State and Economic Enterprise in Japan*, ed. by William W. Lockwood (Princeton: Princeton University Press, 1965).

[26]Robert E. Ward, *"Modernization and Democracy in Japan,"* in *Comparative Politics*, ed. by Roy C. Macridis and Bernard E. Brown (Homewood, Illinois: Dorsey Press, 1964), 579.

By the First World War Japan had become a first-rate industrial power. The welfare state was bound to come. Indeed a substantial labor movement had developed during the war years.

> Japanese labor unions . . . were strong enough by 1919 to exert considerable pressure through strikes, and strikes became a definite part of the Japanese scene in the 1920's. . . . It seemed but a matter of time before the proletariat would join with city intellectuals and white collar workers to form a strong, possibly dominant political force in Japan.[27]

The Great Depression, the Manchurian Crisis, and the murder of Prime Minister Inukai, in 1932, however, brought the end of party government. A modern economy fell into authoritarian—largely military—hands. The labor movement and all liberal or democratic tendencies were suppressed. Then after the disaster of the war, the Occupation—by legal process—made Japan a welfare state. Not the least of the imported innovations was judicial review. Indeed it has served in Japan—as it has served here since 1936—to legitimate the welfare state.[28]

CONCLUSION

Law no doubt is a stabilizing or conserving force. It is also—simultaneously—a crucial instrument of social change. Under a facade of formal symmetry, it must honor reasonable expectations born of the past, yet allow *lebensraum* for the present and the future. As we have seen in three developing nations, it is constantly adopting new principles from current needs at one end and gradually sloughing off old ones at the other.[29] At its best, as in England, for example, it maintains that "tolerable continuity" without which society is wracked by revolution, "and men must begin again the weary path up from savagery." Law then is not, as some still insist it should be, a bucket of ready-made answers, but a reconciling process. Its role is to channel conflicting social energies

---

[27]Reischauer, *Japan,* 153.
[28]See Dan F. Henderson, ed., *The Constitution of Japan* (Seattle: University of Washington Press, 1969); and Charles L. Black, *The People and the Court* (New York: Macmillan, 1960), ch. 3.
[29]See Oliver W. Holmes, Jr., *The Common Law* (Boston: Little, Brown, 1923), 36.

into peaceful accommodations—the endless sequence of accommo-dations that we call civilization.

Surely stage three—the welfare state—cannot be the end of the line. The straws seem plain in the wind. Wordsworth saw it long ago:

> The world is too much with us: late and soon,
> Getting and spending, we lay waste our powers:
> Little we see in nature that is ours;
> We have given our hearts away, a sordid boon.

Stated in more strident language this is, of course, the New Left's basic complaint. Stage four, one may guess, must deal with that problem.

Our real dangers, I suggest, are not from the outrageous but from the conforming; not from those few who shock us with un-accustomed dress and conduct, but from the mass of us who take our virtues and our tastes—like our shirts and our shoes—from the limited patterns that the market offers. Since the world began there never have been one-tenth as many people as there are now who felt alike, thought alike, ate alike, slept alike, hated and loved alike; who went to the same games, endured the same mass media, and approved the same sentiments.[30]

For some the solution is clear: smash everything, start again, and keep it simple. But how many lives would be smashed in that process? How with a smashed economy could we maintain our 200 million people? This difficulty the would-be system smashers refuse to face. For them it is enough to kill the goose of the golden eggs. This brings us to the heart of the matter: how to use more effectively the tremendous productive capacity that has taken so long to develop and has cost so much in human sacrifice. Simple economies after all are the curse of most of the world.

It may be humiliating, but man's first needs are economic. There is no peace or dignity for those who are starving. The trouble has always been that man has had to live at the edge of famine. That has shaped all attitudes and institutions, and this is why the money changers could never be far from the temple. But,

---

[30]I have drawn here from Learned Hand, *The Spirit of Liberty* (New York: Knopf, 1952).

now at last in this country, abundance for all is possible. We are no longer doomed to fight one another for bread in a dog-eat-dog existence. Centuries of development have repealed—for a time at least —the iron law of scarcity. That is our key to the creative, the fulfilled life. And so at last stage four seems destined to recognize that men are much more than economic creatures, that we may indeed be here for something better. As our young people put it, each of us is here to do his own thing.

A great hang-up is that we haven't been able to use and enjoy adequately the wealth of goods we can produce. Distributive techniques inherited from generations of poverty seem obsolete in an era of mass production. The difficulty is not in the technology of distribution itself. It seems rather that we can't change our moral values as readily as we can alter our production techniques. When a nation suffers for lack of capital, many must sacrifice a large part of what they produce, i.e., they must submit to exploitation, if there is to be any overall improvement. In such circumstances conventional morality—in Russia, the Party Line—sanctifies and justifies the exploitation. We have had to live with all but universal poverty for so long that we accept its morality and institutions as part of the law of nature. In our hearts we feel we know that the poor are poor because of some defect of character—that to suffer in silence is a great virtue since the meek shall inherit the earth. Such a morality, calculated to make exploitation acceptable to its victims, may be highly functional in a primitive or backward economy. It may be highly dysfunctional in an Age of Affluence—particularly when it promotes racial privilege and serves no general economic need.

Not so long ago we provided free public schools for everyone. There was massive opposition. Many thought such "pandering" to the poor, as they put it, would undermine family responsibility and destroy our moral fibre. Now as affluence grows, we are asked to expand the public-school idea—to underwrite minimum health, housing, and food standards for all Americans. Again there is widespread opposition on traditional moral grounds. But are those grounds universal and eternal, or do they reflect merely the peculiar and transitory needs of an earlier, poverty-ridden economy?[31]

---

[31]It is, of course, just possible that we cannot with impunity destroy the spur of want, including hunger. Even so sanguine and hopeful an observer as Brandeis held that man (in the mass) is as lazy as he dares to be. The recent history of once Great Britain raises questions about the effect of "welfare"

If we escape the total destruction that some of our youngsters think they want, and if the developmental process of the past is a clue, stage four will not come overnight. Step by slow step we may find increasing inconvenience in traditional ideas and institutions. Responding to this, the law—legislative and judicial—may slowly bend or break old arrangements premised on scarcity and gradually devise new ones more compatible with the economics of abundance. Such changes always seem too fast for conservatives and too slow for liberals. As the level of frustration rises, radicals seek short cuts and tolerance declines.

There is an ancient Chinese curse of terrible doom: "May you live in a time of transition." We live, I suggest, in such a time. Like Henry Adams and A. V. Dicey, we feel the stress of change and know not where it leads. In such a plight we crave the safety of our cages—however narrow—and our disciplines—however archaic. These are defenses against the agony of change. The heretic makes us uneasy. Too often he is reckless, vain and shallow, strutting in the glare of the fire he kindles. But not always. Sometimes he is merely the measure of how far we have departed from our own paths. Such heresy—when true to the faith—puts its trust in life. It knows that man's upward course, from the first amoeba that felt a flicker of sentience, is mainly an effort to affirm the meaning of his own strange self, to divine his significance, and to keep a tidy soul.[32]

Such, one may hope, is the new heresy of the young. And it may be their special burden—striving unsurely and often with self-defeating tactics—to close the gap between word and deed, to drag themselves and us to a more humane stage in the developmental process called civilization.

EPILOGUE

It is of course just possible that mankind is not as pure in heart[33] as young idealists apparently assume. Even they seem hard

---

upon economic motivation, though Britain may be a special case. In any event, perduring competition of rival groups for less work and increasing shares of a relatively diminishing national product is a haunting specter—some elements of which are already apparent in the United States.

[32]See Hand, *Liberty*, 60.

[33]Those who cannot accept such an old-fashioned, non-scientific term may want to consider as a substitute the Papez-MacLean theory of schizophysi-

pressed to make silk purses from the material at hand. Witness the sad descent of SDS from its Port Huron statement to its present nadir (to say nothing of SNCC).

One of life's crucial lessons, I suggest, found expression in Gladstone's dictum: "To be engaged in opposing wrong affords . . . but a slender guarantee of being right." A corollary is that when one is sure one has the truth, it is time to look for a balancing, or countervailing, truth. Of course this is not as much fun, nor nearly as thrilling, as the thought of smashing everything in sight under the cloak, of course, of high moral principle. Nor is it as romantic as the faith that, when everything has been demolished, there will spring up spontaneously a noble world of god-like men. All this without plan or program—except destruction.

It is painful to poke even gentle fun at the dreams of the young. If I seem to do so, it is in the hope that a blending of their vision with a modicum of tolerance and humility may yet make a better world. The highest ideals may be perverted by unworthy means. Violence at home is no better than violence abroad. Disagreement is normal, even among those under thirty.

> We reach accommodations as wisdom may teach us that it does not pay to fight. And wisdom . . . comes only as false assurance goes —false assurance, that grows from pride in our power and ignorance of our ignorance. Beware then [young and old] of heathen gods; have no confidence in principles that come . . . in the trappings of [self-righteousness]. Meet them with gentle irony, friendly skepticism, and an open soul.[34]

---

ology. For a brief resume of its meaning and implications as to the nature of man, see Arthur Koestler, "Man—One of Evolution's Mistakes?", *The New York Times Magazine,* October 19, 1969, 28.

[34]Hand, *Liberty,* 101.

26 ✦ New Light on Fletcher v. Peck and Gibbons v. Ogden

In *Gibbons v. Ogden* [1] "for the one and only time in his career on the supreme bench, [Chief Justice] Marshall . . . pronounced a 'popular' opinion." [2] That opinion attained its novel distinction, of course, because it destroyed the hated steamboat monopoly on the Hudson River. Since steam navigation in 1824 was a crucial form of transportation and since the Hudson River was one of the two or three most important highways of national commerce, the unpopularity of the monopoly is easy to understand.[3] But surely the New York State legislature, which had created the monopoly (to stimulate the development of steam navigation) was not insulated from the heat of popular dissatisfaction with the situation on the Hudson. Why had it not abolished its creature—its purpose having been accomplished—years before protracted litigation came to a weary end in *Gibbons v. Ogden?*

A legislature less in harmony with "popular" social pressures than a court is a phenomenon that invites exploration. In this case, one need go no further for the explanation than John Marshall's earlier opinions in *Fletcher v. Peck* [4] and the *Dartmouth College* case,[5] where, as Professor Corwin has shown, the doctrine of vested interests was established as the first basic principle of American constitutional law. Both "natural justice" and the clause prohibiting impairment of the obligation of contract, according to Marshall, prohibit a state legislature from modifying its own acts to the detriment of interests which have vested thereunder. The important factor is the sanctity of private property. Even public property (*Fletcher v. Peck*) and the public interest in education (*Dartmouth College* case) must be subsumed to it. That sentiment, of course, came straight from Blackstone's codification—"so great . . . is the regard of the law for private property, that it will not authorize the least violation of it; no not even for the general good of the whole community." [6]

---

1. 9 Wheat. 1 (U.S. 1824).

2. 4 BEVERIDGE, THE LIFE OF JOHN MARSHALL 445 (1919). See also 2 WARREN, THE SUPREME COURT IN UNITED STATES HISTORY, 71–72 (1923).

3. The holders of the New York monopoly had similar interests on the Mississippi River which they obtained by act of the territorial legislature of Louisiana on April 19, 1811. Thus they held the key to the two most important ports in North America.

4. 6 Cranch 87 (U.S. 1810).

5. 4 Wheat. 518 (U.S. 1819).

6. 1 BL. COMM. *139. The *Commentaries* were first published in America in 1772. One of the original subscribers was John Marshall's father, "who saw to it that his son read Blackstone as carefully as circumstances permitted. He had bought the book for John's

The New York legislature was well aware of the unpopularity of the steamboat monopoly and obviously in sympathy with the desire to abolish it. Memorials and petitions for relief from the Fulton-Livingston monopoly flooded the Albany legislature between *Fletcher v. Peck* in 1810 and *Gibbons v. Ogden* in 1824. At least four select committees studied the matter and came to the same conclusion: the steamboat monopoly was a menace but the doctrine of vested interests—as yet unmitigated by the concept of the police power—prohibited direct legislative relief. The problem then became one of finding indirect methods to accomplish what could not be done directly.

In 1807, the first successful steamboat was launched on New York waters. In the following year, two years before *Fletcher v. Peck*, the legislature of New York "for the further encouragement of steamboats on the waters of this state" provided that "whenever Robert R. Livingston and Robert Fulton . . . shall establish one or more steamboats or vessels, other than that already established, they shall for each and every such additional boat, be entitled to five years prolongation of their grant or *contract* with this state [emphasis added]. Provided nevertheless, that the whole term of their exclusive privileges, shall not exceed thirty years after the passage of this act." [7] Although there had been at least five preceding acts on the subject, that of 1808 first used the word "contract" to describe the relation between the state and the steamboat proprietors. Obviously someone had anticipated *Fletcher v. Peck*.[8] Counsel for opponents of the monopoly threw some light on that point before a state court in 1812. They repudiated the idea of a contract signed, sealed, and delivered between New York and Livingston-Fulton. "The grant wanted all the essential features of a contract, inasmuch as it was gratuitous—without reciprocity or mutual obligation." In short, it was "a mere permission, and the *foisting* of the word contract, into the last act (which merely extended what prior acts had already 'granted') could not alter the nature of the grant." [9] That the word "contract" indeed had been "foisted" (by

---

use as much or more than for his own information." 1 BEVERIDGE, THE LIFE OF JOHN MARSHALL 56 (1916).

7. Act of April 9, 1811.

8. An opinion by Alexander Hamilton upon which Marshall obviously drew heavily had been widely circulated in a pamphlet by HARPER, THE CASE OF THE GEORGIA SALES ON THE MISSISSIPPI, WITH A REFERENCE TO LAW AUTHORITIES AND PUBLIC ACTS (Philadelphia, 1799).

9. *See* Livingston v. Van Ingen, 9 Johns. 507, 541 (N.Y. 1812). See also DUER, A REPLY TO MR. COLDEN'S VINDICATION OF THE STEAM-BOAT MONOPOLY 102 (Albany, 1819): "the thirty years to which the whole term of the grant appears to have been *limited* by the proviso of this clause (in the act of 1808), is computed *'from the time of the passing of the act'* of 1808, instead of from the year 1803, from which the previous term commenced,—thus in fact extending the duration of the whole grant for five years, without any pretense of *consideration*! A circumstance, which I will venture to say, was as little

representatives of Livingston and Fulton?) upon an unsuspecting legislature finds support within the act itself. For only a sentence after the
word "contract," there follows a proviso which refers to the Livingston-
Fulton interests as "exclusive privileges" rather than contractual
rights.

The unusual use of the word "contract" in the statute pointed the
line of defense which the steamboat proprietors persistently used in all
clashes with the legislature. Two prominent lawyers, Thomas A. Emmet
and Cadwallader D. Colden, represented Fulton and Livingston before
the Duer Committee (the first select committee appointed to consider a
petition for relief against the monopoly) and also before a "joint" session
of the legislature which heard the committee report and arguments
against it.[10] To Emmet and Colden, it was obvious that a contract
had been consumated:

> "That the nature of the engagement between Messrs. Livingston
> and Fulton and the state might be well understood, the legislature
> also spoke of it as a *contract*. And I ask, has it not all the features
> of a contract? It is a mutual agreement. On the one hand, Messrs.
> Livingston and Fulton, offering to spend their money, and to run
> the risk of employing their steamboats on the waters of this state,
> provided the legislature will grant them certain privileges; and on
> the other, the state accede to their propositions, and engage, that if
> they will effectively employ such boats, they shall have the con-
> sideration of an exclusive privilege for a certain time." [11]

That argument, based as it was upon *Fletcher v. Peck*, was accepted
by the Duer Committee; ". . . however inconsistent it be with the
spirit of a wise and equitable system of laws, to confer exclusive privileges . . . however contrary to the acknowledged principles of political economy, to grant a monopoly of the elements of invention in one

---

understood at the time, by those who were not in the secret, as the design by which the
word contract was *'foisted'* into the act." But, alas, *Fletcher v. Peck* itself protected
vested interests predicated in fraud. Indeed that was one of the crucial points at issue in
Fletcher v. Peck.

10. Duer, A Letter Addressed to Cadwallader D. Colden, Esquire In Answer
to the Strictures, Contained in His Life of Robert Fulton, Upon the Report of
the Select Committee, to Whom Was Referred a Memorial Relative to Steam
Navigation, Presented to the Legislature of New York, at the Session of 1814
48 (Albany, 1817). Mr. Duer later became President of Columbia College of New York.

11. A Vindication, by Cadwallader D. Colden, of the Steam-Boat Right
Granted by the State of New York in the Form of an Answer to the Letter of
Mr. Duer, Addressed to Mr. Colden 73 (New York, 1819). This position is particularly
interesting in view of the opinion dated January 19, 1811 in which Mr. Emmet advised his
clients that their monopoly was invalid since "after the adoption of the Federal Constitution no State Legislature had any authority to grant an exclusive right of making, con-
structing, or employing any machine or invention." 13 N. Y. Library Bull. 573.

whole department of discovery; yet if the legislature have fallen into this error; if they have actually vested in individuals, rights hostile in their exercise to the general interests; they cannot on that ground avoid or resume their own grant; they alone had authority to judge of the expediency of the measure, and the public faith is bound by their decision." [12]

But the Duer Committee was resourceful. An Act of 1811 "for the more effectual enforcement of" the Act of 1808 had given to Livingston and Fulton some extraordinary remedies amounting to outright confiscation of any steamboat violating their "exclusive privileges." The Duer Committee after observing in elaborate detail that the original monopoly of 1808 violated the congressional commerce and patent powers, urged that the Act of 1811 "in effect shuts the courts of justice of this state against any person who may be desirous of bringing to a legal test, the rights claimed by Livingston and Fulton, as by the provisions of that act, the defendant of any suit to be commenced by them . . . must lose his boat and his machinery even if he should eventually gain his cause . . . and as this forms no part of the *right* of Livingston and Fulton, being only a new *remedy* given them by that statute, your committee believe there can be no doubt of the right as well as the power of the legislature, so to alter or modify that remedy, as to prevent its working manifest injustice by shutting those courts which in a free country should be left open to every individual." [13]

The Committee recognized the sanctity of the "contractual right" (so far as legislative interference was concerned), but at the same time, it wrote an elaborate brief on the national commerce and patent powers for the use of any who might like to have a go in court, and then attempted to distinguish between rights and mere remedies in a way which would make litigation much easier. But as Mr. Justice Cardozo pointed out more than a century later, "In the books there is much talk about distinctions between changes of the substance of the contract and changes of the remedy. The dividing line is at times obscure." [14] Thus, Messrs. Emmet and Colden in their defense before the "joint" session of the legislature had a ready answer:

> "You insist it would be consistent with the faith of the state, to repeal the forfeiture and other remedies given by the statutes . . . you say it would not be contended in any other case that the legislature could not . . . alter, modify or take away remedies . . . for the maintenance of any right whatever. Again, you are most manifestly wrong. It would be contended *in any case* where the state had made an agreement with individuals, by which private rights

---

12.   DUER, *op. cit. supra* note 10, at 8–9.

13.   In Assembly, Tuesday, March 8th, 1814. The Committee to whom was referred the Memorial and Petition of Aaron Ogden, a Citizen of the State of New Jersey.

14.   Worthen Co. v. Kavanaugh, 295 U. S. 56, 60 (1935).

were created and vested, and where a consequent benefit was actually given the state, and where the legislature, with the concurrence of the other contracting parties, had established those remedies in order to secure and protect the rights created and vested by
the agreement. You illustrate your ideas by a very learned discussion on the remedy of distress, by the insolvent laws, and a repeal
of the laws authorizing imprisonment for debt. What they have to
do with public faith, I confess I am at a loss to comprehend. Public
faith may well be implicated and pledged to support a specific
agreement the state has made, and the terms of a particular bargain
or the incidental sanctions of that bargain, which the legislature
has advisedly assented and acceded to, at the request of the party
with whom it made its stipulations; but I see no claim upon public
faith that can be used against the modifications of general remedies,
founded on no public agreements, enacted only with a view to
general policy and expediency, and in no respect stipulated for or
entering into the bargains made between the contracting parties
themselves." [15]

The lower house of the legislature passed the Duer Committee bill
for the abolition of the extraordinary remedies by which the monopoly
rights were vindicated. But in the Senate, the bill failed of passage by
only one vote.[16] The attempt to circumvent *Fletcher v. Peck* by the
highly technical distinction between rights and remedies failed in the
New York legislature by the narrowest possible margin.

Thereafter, numerous other petitions for relief against the monopoly
were submitted and five additional select committees were appointed to
investigate. Two in 1817 [17] and a third in 1822 [18] adopted in substance
the prior views and recommendations of the Duer Committee. But no
legislation altering either the monopoly's rights or its remedies was
adopted. In 1817, however, the year in which two select committees
reported adversely to the monopoly, the legislature did enact legislation imposing a special tax upon steamboat passengers. The purpose
and effect of that tax are indicated indirectly in a petition to the legislature in 1819 in which the monopolists complained of the burden of
the tax and requested either that the state purchase the steamboat
business or relieve it of the tax burden. The petition is particularly

---

15. COLDEN, *op. cit. supra* note 11, at 78.

16. DUER, *op. cit. supra* note 10, at 80–81. See also DICKINSON, ROBERT FULTON,
ENGINEER AND ARTIST, HIS LIFE AND WORKS 252 (1913).

17. Their reports are reproduced in full in DUER, *op. cit. supra* note 10, appendix Q
and T.

18. N. Y. ASSEMBLY JOURNAL 804–806 (1822). A select committee of the Assembly
in 1820 recommended that no relief be given because the matter had been investigated
and rejected so many times previously. N. Y. ASSEMBLY JOURNAL 1014–1015 (1820). A
Senate select committee in the same year recommended that no relief be given since the
matter was then pending in the Supreme Court of the United States. N. Y. SENATE
JOURNAL 215–216 (1820).

interesting because it reveals that the monopolists were quite conscious of the unhappy position in which the legislature found itself, caught as it was between the popular demands for relief and the restrictions of *Fletcher v. Peck* (by then reinforced by the *Dartmouth College* case). Thus, "the petitioners suggest, that if the state should accept this offer, it may then throw open the navigation by steam on the Hudson River. . . ." [19] No legislative action was taken in response. Then, in the year after *Gibbons v. Ogden*, Mr. Colden advises us that "since the Supreme Court of the United States had decided that the grant to Livingston and Fulton . . . was invalid, there has been no attempt to collect the tax on steamboat passengers." [20] Obviously the legislature, despite the recommendations of four select committees, felt itself powerless under *Fletcher v. Peck* and the *Dartmouth College* case to alter either the rights or remedies connected with the steamboat monopoly. But to discourage the Livingston-Fulton interests, it did resort to the tax device and that was immediately abandoned when the monopoly was destroyed by judicial action.

Blackstone's doctrine of vested interests was indeed the first doctrine of American constitutional law. But no society, certainly no democracy, could thrive on the pristine simplicity of such a foundation. Even Marshall came by degrees to recognize that. In *Fletcher v. Peck* the public interest got rough treatment and little lip service. But eleven years later, in the *Dartmouth College* case, the idea of the Police Power is suggested:

> ". . . the framers of the constitution did not intend to restrain the states in the regulation of their civil institutions adopted for internal government." [21]

Shortly thereafter, in *Gibbons v. Ogden*, the Police Power concept becomes quite explicit:

> ". . . the acknowledged power of the state to regulate its police, its domestic trade and to govern its own citizens may enable it to legislate on this subject to a considerable extent." [22]

and the judge who earlier had subsumed public property (*Fletcher v. Peck*) and the public interest in education (*Dartmouth College* case) to private property recognized that enormously valuable business interests

---

19. See report of the select committee to whom this petition was referred which is reproduced in COLDEN, *op. cit. supra* note 11, at 93–96.

20. COLDEN, MEMOIR PREPARED AT THE REQUEST OF A COMMITTEE OF THE COMMON COUNCIL OF THE CITY OF NEW YORK AND PRESENTED TO THE MAYOR OF NEW YORK AT THE CELEBRATION OF THE COMPLETION OF THE NEW YORK CANALS 49 (N. Y. 1825).

21. 4 Wheat. 518, 629 (U.S. 1819).

22. 9 Wheat. 1, 208 (U.S. 1824).

must give way before the public stake in free steam navigation on the Hudson River.[23] In thus recognizing that private property was not the very apex in social values, and in permitting at least the judiciary to protect public, at the expense of private, interests the "great Chief Justice," as already indicated, wrote his only contemporaneously popular opinion. But *Gibbons v. Ogden* was merely the first crucial American inroad upon Blackstone's concept of the sanctity of private property. In the first term of court following Marshall's death, Chief Justice Taney—for his Court—established the Police Power concept upon a firm foundation:

> "While the rights of property are sacredly guarded, we must not forget, that the community also has rights, and that the happiness and well-being of every citizen depends on their faithful preservation. [The court could not consent to strip away] the rights reserved to the states [and by] mere technical reasoning take away from them any portion of that power over their own internal police and improvement, which is so necessary to their well-being and prosperity." [24]

---

23. In Willson v. Blackbird Marsh Creek Co., 2 Pet. 245 (U.S. 1829), Marshall goes his farthest in recognizing the Police Power and indeed virtually reverses his *Gibbons v. Ogden* position. For in the later case he permits a state by means of a dam to obstruct commerce on a *navigable* stream—even vis-a-vis a vessel operating under a federal coasting license. It was the existence of such a license which had been the crux of the decision adverse to state legislation in *Gibbons v. Ogden.*

24. In the *Charles River Bridge* case (11 Pet. 420 (U.S. 1837)), Marshall's old associate and alter-ego, Mr. Justice Story, dissented and we know on his authority that Marshall who had heard the case just before his death concurred in Story's views. For such old Federalists as Kent, Story and Webster the Police Power doctrine of the *Charles River Bridge* case "undermines the very foundations of morality, confidence and truth. . . . When we consider the revolution in opinion, in policy, and in numbers that has recently changed the character of the Supreme Court, we can scarcely avoid being reduced to a state of dispair for the commonwealth." Kent, 2 N. Y. REVIEW 387, 402 (April, 1838). For a brief account of the contest between the doctrines of Vested Interests and Police Power from Blackstone and Bentham through Marshall and Taney, see Mendelson, *Chief Justice Marshall and the Mercantile Tradition,* 29 THE SOUTHWESTERN Soc. SCI. Q. 27 (June, 1948).

Fletcher v. Peck was in effect overruled in Illinois Central Railroad Co. v. Illinois, 146 U.S. 387, 460 (1882). The facts in the two cases are strikingly similar except for the absence of any element of fraud in the later case. By 1882 the Court speaking through Mr. Justice Field, was able to hold that "any attempted cession of the ownership and control of the State in and over the submerged lands in Lake Michigan, by the act of April 6, 1869, was inoperative . . . any such attempted operation of the act was annulled by the repealing act of April 15, 1873, which to that extent was valid and effective. There can be no irrepealable contract in a conveyance of property by a grantor in disregard of a public trust. . . ."

ADDENDUM

I stand by the thesis of this essay, but not by its blind acceptance of the traditional "progressive" view of the Marshall Court's property "bias." That tradition (in which my generation was raised) is still orthodox, at least in the sense that it lives on in introductory history and political science texts. I now find it essentially false as my essays on John Marshall and on B. F. Wright suggest.

27 🪷 ERA, the Supreme Court, and Allegations of Gender Bias

Some see the proposed Equal Rights Amendment (ERA) as indispensable to womanly freedom in America. For others it is a dangerous effort by a miniscule, militant minority to use the constitution for symbolic self-assertion. Each of these views is buttressed with word-play often more ardent than accurate. A common argument, for example, holds that ERA is necessary to counteract what has been called the Supreme Court's "almost josephic aversion to women."[1] In a famous article published at the end of the Warren Era we were told the justices' approach to women's rights has been characterized, since the 1870s, by two prominent features: "a vague but strong substantive belief in women's 'separate place,' and an extraordinary methodological casualness in reviewing state legislation based on such stereotypical views of women."[2] In support of this and similar charges the following cases are commonly cited:[3] *Bradwell v. State*,[4] sustaining an Illinois rule against the practice of law by women; *Minor v. Happersett*,[5] upholding a Missouri law against female suffrage; *Muller v. Oregon*,[6] which distinguished between men and women with respect to maximum-

---

1. This terminology comes from R. HARRIS, THE QUEST FOR EQUALITY 73 (1960).
2. Brown, Emerson, Falk & Freedman, *The Equal Rights Amendment: A Constitutional Basis for Equal Rights for Women*, 80 YALE L.J. 871, 875-76 (1971).
3. *See, e.g.*, K. DAVIDSON & R. GINSBURG, SEX BASED DISCRIMINATION: TEXT, CASES, AND MATERIALS 4-25 (1974); B. BABCOCK, A. FREEDMAN, E. NORTON & S. ROSS, SEX DISCRIMINATION AND THE LAW, CAUSES AND REMEDIES 4-105 (1975); R. HARRIS, *supra* note 1, at 73, Comment, *Geduldig v. Aiello: Pregnancy Classifications and the Definition of Sex Discrimination*, 75 COLUM. L. REV. 441 (1975); Note, *Exclusion of Pregnancy from Coverage of Disability Benefits Does Not Violate Equal Protection*, 12 HOUS. L. REV. 488 (1975).
4. 83 U.S. 130 (1873).
5. 88 U.S. 162 (1875).
6. 208 U.S. 412 (1908).

hour legislation; *Goesaert v. Cleary*,[7] the restricting barmaid case; and *Geduldig v. Aiello*,[8] sustaining a California disability insurance program that excluded normal pregnancy. This article will suggest that these decisions (like a few others based thereon)[9] do not even remotely support the charge of "sexism" in the work of the high court.

Bradwell, the anti-female-lawyer case, rests with little independent discussion upon its companion decision in the *Slaughter House Cases*[10] decided one day earlier. There lies the key to much of our problem. It is crucial that *Slaughter House* was the first case in which the Court construed the fourteenth amendment — and that the justices who participated therein were not strangers to the national crises, and the discussions, that produced this and the two other Civil War amendments. It is crucial also to understand the circumstances of the case (which, one suggests, have been too often misconceived). After extensive unplanned growth, New Orleans was plagued with numerous small slaughtering establishments within its boundaries. A city effort to mitigate that noxious problem failed when several slaughterers evaded regulation by moving to a river site *above* the city, outside its jurisdiction. Dumping their waste into the river threatened the urban water supply and created the danger of an outbreak of cholera. In this impasse the state intervened. It prohibited all slaughtering in the vicinity except at a designated site on the river *below* the city. There, *following a then familiar tradition*, it induced some entrepreneurs to build *public* slaughtering facilities in exchange for exclusive toll rights for twenty-five years. These facilities were open to all who wished to slaughter for the New Orleans market, subject of course to state-prescribed tolls and health inspection. To dismiss this as a butchering monopoly (which is rather less than accurate), to dismiss it as the evil work of a carpetbag legislature, is to miss the essence of the case. The plaintiffs' position was comprehensive: by virtue of the fourteenth amendment no legislature (carpetbag, or other) could intrude upon what they called "the personal rights of men" — in this case, it seems, the right to continue slaughtering within the boundaries of New Orleans.[11] If this indeed were a fourteenth amendment right or privilege, it would be difficult to imagine what would

---

7.   335 U.S. 464 (1948).
8.   417 U.S. 484 (1974).
9.   *See, e.g.*, Hoyt v. Florida, 368 U.S. 57 (1961); Williams v. McNair, 401 U.S. 951 (1971), *aff'g* 316 F. Supp. 134 (D.S.C. 1970), referred to in Brown, Emerson, Falk & Freedman, *supra* note 2, at 881.
10.   83 U.S. 36 (1873).
11.   *Id.*, Brief for Plaintiff at 17. In their brief on reargument, at 37-38, plaintiffs recognized the state's "police power" to deal with a common law nuisance, but the law in question they argued "is a sweeping edict, that banishes from three parishes an important and necessary occupation which prevails in every community, an edict which inflicts injury upon hundreds of individuals in their property and their business . . . ." It is noteworthy that the reasonableness of the toll rates was not questioned. 83 U.S. at 65.

not be! And so, as Holmes observed later, there would be "hardly any limit but the sky" upon the meaning of the fourteenth amendment and upon the power of judges to govern thereunder.[12]

The Court met plaintiffs' expansive views head-on. It rejected substantive due process, substantive equal protection, and substantive privileges or immunities — in favor of the view that:

> No one can fail to be impressed with the one pervading purpose found in [all three Civil War amendments], lying at the foundations of each, and without which none of them would have been even suggested; we mean the freedom of the slave race, the security and firm establishment of that freedom, and the protection of the newly-made freeman. . . .[13]

In a word racism was the crux of the Civil War amendments as the Court saw them in that early day. Accordingly just a few years after *Slaughter House* the Court upheld under the fourteenth amendment perhaps the first modern business regulation in *Munn v. Illinois*[14] — but vetoed race discrimination in *Ex parte Virginia*[15] and *Strauder v. West Virginia*.[16]

John A. Campbell who argued so broadly for the butchers had been a member of the Supreme Court, and had resigned at the outbreak of the Civil War to join the Confederacy. Had he not left the bench, and had *Slaughter House* been presented as in fact it was, the four dissenters therein might have had a fifth vote — and American history might have been rather different. Senator Matt Carpenter, who had served prominently in the Congress which proposed the fourteenth amendment, was counsel in opposition to the expansive view. His argument was prophetic. Take care, Your Honors, he said in substance. Consider the consequences of the step now urged upon you. It means you will be compelled to pass upon the wisdom of a host of laws which in the public interest regulate the manner in which business is carried on, such as the licensing of public callings, the control of dangerous occupations, and "all existing laws regulating and fixing the hours of labor, and prohibiting the employment of children, women, and men in any particular occupations or places for more than a certain number of hours per day."[17] Obviously he foresaw the disaster of *Lochner v. New York*[18] *inter alia*.

---

12.   Baldwin v. Missouri, 281 U.S. 586, 595 (1930).
13.   83 U.S. at 71.
14.   94 U.S. 113 (1877).
15.   100 U.S. 339 (1880).
16.   100 U.S. 303 (1880). Mr. Justice Field who wrote the main dissent in *Slaughter House* dissented also in *Munn*, but voted to uphold race discrimination in *Strauder* and *Ex parte Virginia*, achieving thus a double perversion of the fourteenth amendment.
17.   C. FAIRMAN, MR. JUSTICE MILLER AND THE SUPREME COURT 1862-1890, at 181 (1939).
18.   198 U.S. 45 (1905).

Most of counsels' argument in *Slaughter House*, most of the Court's discussion, and most of the main dissenting opinion, rested on the privileges or immunities clause of the fourteenth amendment. *Bradwell*, which turned all but exclusively on that provision, was no more anti-female than *Slaughter House* was anti-butcher. Neither case triggered the fourteenth amendment, because neither involved a problem of race. Both rejected laissez faire — the one with respect to butchering, the other with respect to lawyering. Both entail a federalistic concern that (absent any race problem) local businesses and avocations were within the state police power after, no less than before, the fourteenth amendment. Moreover just as Bradwell lost her privileges or immunities claim, so (with one exception soon overruled) has every *man* who has ever raised the issue.[19]

A *minority* concurring opinion in *Bradwell*, it is true, was highly male-chauvinistic by today's standards — though what was said there probably reflected the general consensus of the day. How did such language get into the *minority* opinion? Those who used it had dissented in *Slaughter House* on laissez faire grounds. Logically they would have had to dissent in *Bradwell*. Lawyering after all is a "business or avocation" and these they had insisted should be substantially free of state interference. To uphold the ban on female lawyers they had to find some reason for not applying laissez faire principles in *Bradwell*. Sexism was the answer. Here is a classic example of one gross error producing another. It is a classic example also of what it would mean to have the Supreme Court abandon *Slaughter House* in favor of judicial free-wheeling as urged by the plaintiffs and dissenters therein. The fact remains, however, that the sexist views in question were minority views, completely at odds with the Court's ratio decidendi — though today's pro-ERA polemists do not always stress that point. It is worth passing notice that while *Bradwell* was pending, "the Illinois legislature . . . passed an act giving all persons, regardless of sex, freedom in selecting an occupation."[20]

What has been said above equally disposes of *Happersett* — the female-suffrage case. If it involved no problem of race, it also involved no problem of laissez faire. Still, voting — which it did involve — like local business was a matter plainly reserved for the states. This was one of the major compromises of the Constitutional Convention. Unable to agree upon voter qualifications, the Founders resolved the dispute by leaving the problem entirely to the discretion of each individual state.[21] Whatever may be the view of the man on the street, there is no constitutional connection whatsoever between suffrage and national citizenship. Nothing in the Constitution of the United States gives citizens as such the right to vote, nor does

---

19.   The exception is Colgate v. Harvey, 296 U.S. 404 (1935), *overruled*, Madden v. Kentucky, 309 U.S. 83 (1940).
20.   B. BABCOCK, A. FREEDMAN, E. NORTON & S. ROSS, *supra* note 3, at 6.
21.   U.S. CONST. art. 1, § 2.

anything therein deny it to aliens. Indeed for generations we gave the vote to some aliens; we have always denied it to some citizens — male as well as female. As the *Happersett* Court observed, the fifteenth amendment would not have been necessary if the right to vote had been deemed a privilege of federal citizenship. For the fourteenth amendment plainly gave citizenship to Blacks.

Minor, like Bradwell, based her case not on the equal protection, but on the privileges or immunities clause of the fourteenth amendment. While at first the latter was stressed in litigation, it soon passed into limbo. Both conservative and liberals came to find it had shortcomings. Conservatives, bent on promoting corporate business, soon recognized the disutility of a constitutional provision that covers only citizens. It would seem difficult to get a court to hold that corporations are citizens of the United States (and thus as it was once argued, eligible for the presidency). Liberals also became disenchanted. Citizenship after all is quite accidental. It is people, *i.e.* persons (in the language of the Constitution) who are to be protected. One of the glories of the Bill of Rights is that its shield is not confined to the happenstance of citizenship. Thus for their own separate reasons both conservative and liberals found it expedient to turn from privileges or immunities to due process and equal protection.

Many young activists today feel cheated because the privileges clause has been dismissed in effect as meaningless. Their concern arises from carelessness with respect to history. They have lost nothing. Whatever activist judges — whether on the left or the right — could have read into the intrinsically meaningless privileges or immunities clause, they have proven quite capable of reading into the due process and equal protection clauses of the same amendment. And so it was that in the 1890s and thereafter both wings of *Slaughter House* were abandoned. Laissez faire became the law of the land,[22] and so in effect did racial discrimination under the guise of "separate but equal."[23]

Then came *Muller v. Oregon*[24] which some members of the women's movement — perhaps with tongue in cheek — cite as anti-feminist. This is the case in the Court's darkest laissez faire era in which surprisingly it *upheld* a maximum hour law for women. At the time and long thereafter liberals generally — including such dedicated feminists as Florence Kelley and Jane Addams — considered *Muller* a great victory.[25] Some sophisticated women now deplore *Muller* because there the Court found it not unreasonable for legislators to believe women might be peculiarly vulnerable to long hours of employment. Surely the decision to uphold the law was not unreasonable. Are we with hindsight to fault the Court for

---

22.   *See, e.g.*, Lochner v. New York, 198 U.S. 45 (1905).
23.   Plessy v. Ferguson, 163 U.S. 537 (1896).
24.   208 U.S. 412 (1908).
25.   B. BABCOCK, A. FREEDMAN, E. NORTON & S. ROSS, *supra* note 3, at 39.

reaching the "right" result by "wrong" reasoning—when that reasoning reflected the most enlightened medical and sociological data of the day, garnered in the famous Brandeis brief from all quarters of the western world? All of us—including today's most enlightened women—run the risk that our best thinking may seem quite simple-minded in the light of future intellectual efforts! Was *Adkins v. Children's Hospital*[26] indeed a better decision? There the Court, reverting to type, invalidated a minimum-wage law for women—thus treating men and women equally.

The statute at issue in *Goesaert v. Cleary*[27] denied barmaid licenses to all women except the wives and daughters of male bar owners. Challenged by a female owner and a barmaid, the measure was upheld as within allowable legislative discretion. Standing alone, the decision may be doubtful. What its critics often fail to recognize is that it was one of a series of decisions[28] by the Roosevelt Court reacting—perhaps overreacting—to the "old Court's" substantive due process and equal protection abuses. For a period of over twenty years beginning before *Goesaert* until late in the Warren era only one measure was held invalid on substantive due process or substantive equal protection grounds. That exception, *Morey v. Doud*,[29] plainly a sport, was later overruled.[30] As late as 1961 the Warren Court without dissent used the hands-off rule of the barmaid and related cases to reject even a claim of religious freedom.[31] What all these cases mean (together with the contemporary desegregation cases[32]) is in effect a return to *Slaughter House* and the historic purpose of the fourteenth amendment. Here too, as usual, women were treated no differently from men. The only exception is *Muller* which gave females preferential treatment.

In *Geduldig v. Aiello*[33] the Court found no gender discrimination in a California employee disability insurance program which denied coverage for normal pregnancy. It did however cover abnormal pregnancies and virtually all other disabilities, including prostate problems which are as peculiarly masculine as pregnancy is feminine. This later point seems meaningless, though counsel and dissenters made something of it. The insurance program did indeed cover purely male sickness, but it also equally

---

26.   261 U.S. 525 (1923).
27.   335 U.S. 464 (1948).
28.   The leading cases are Williamson v. Lee Optical, 348 U.S. 483 (1955); Daniel v. Family Security Life Ins. Co., 336 U.S. 220 (1949); Railway Express Agency, Inc. v. New York, 336 U.S. 106 (1949); Kotch v. Board of River Pilot Comm'rs, 330 U.S. 552 (1947).
29.   354 U.S. 457 (1957).
30.   City of New Orleans v. Dukes, 427 U.S. 297 (1976).
31.   McGowan v. Maryland, 366 U.S. 420 (1961).
32.   The landmark case is Brown v. Board of Education, 347 U.S. 483 (1954).
33.   417 U.S. 484 (1974).

covered purely female *sickness*. In this respect both men and women had equal protection for their different gender ailments.

Indeed so far was the program from discrimination against women that the Supreme Court could observe:

> [T]he appellant submitted to the District Court data that indicated that both the annual claim rate and the annual claim cost are greater for women than for men. As the District Court acknowledged, "women contribute about 28 percent of the total disability insurance fund and receive back about 38 percent of the fund in benefits." Several *amici curiae* have represented to the Court that they have had a similar experience under private disability insurance programs.[34]

Now to the real point which the Supreme Court made at best only imperfectly. The challenged classification did not divide men and women into separate categories and treat them differently. For, even if we accept the view that "discrimination" against *some* women is discrimination against womankind, there is still this difficulty: a woman denied insurance is hurt no more than her mate, who after all by law is fiscally responsible for her care. The loss in question is a *joint* or *family* loss. The classification thus is gender neutral.[35] In fiscal matters too, which is all that is here involved, pregnant women do not tango alone! Or to change the figure, California's insurance sauce for the goose is sauce for the gander. If the money cost of pregnancy were not a burden on *both* males and females, *i.e.* if in fact it fell exclusively upon women, it would be unfair to ask male workers to pay insurance premiums to cover that risk. Women workers in that case ought to pay special increased premiums to cover the risk which is said to be an exclusively female matter. The point is of course pregnancy is not an exclusively female matter — fiscally or otherwise.

Finally there is no evidence of gender motivation in the California program. The concern in excluding normal pregnancy — a relatively high cost item — was to maintain the fiscal integrity of the program at premium levels affordable by all workers.[36] Yet why normal pregnancy instead of heart attack (also a relatively high cost item)? Surely it is one thing to require all workers to pay via premiums for sickness that may fall fortuitously upon any one of them; but something quite different to compel fellow workers to pay for the often *intended* results of self-serving private conduct. Sickness yes; but not healthy pregnancy that is either intentional, or

---

34.   *Id.* at 497 n.21 (citation omitted). See also the discussion *id.* at 493.

35.   The California program's distinction between normal and abnormal pregnancy reflects the difference between health and sickness. The abnormalcy coverage was added only after the program had been challenged as discriminatory against women. The addition apparently was not necessary to save the program. *See* General Electric v. Gilbert, 429 U.S. 125 (1976), where the goose-gander equation would seem dispositive as in *Geduldig*.

36.   417 U.S. at 492-95.

the result of a *calculated* effort to fool nature. In short, apart from rape, pregnancy is always willful as compared to a heart attack. Moreover, given *Roe v. Wade*,[37] which some women fought so valiantly to attain, disability due to pregnancy is now voluntary as a matter of constitutional law.[38] Whatever else one ·may think of California's classification as a policy choice, there is no evidence of anti-female bias either in motive or effect. In short there was no "showing that [the California] distinctions involving pregnancy are mere pretexts designed to effect an invidious discrimination against [females]."[39] Surely then there was no equal protection, and equally no ERA, problem.[40] The same perhaps cannot be said of California's

---

37.   410 U.S. 113 (1973).

38.   The dissenters in *Geduldig* observe that some voluntary disabilities, *e.g.*, some cosmetic surgery and sterilization, are insured. 417 U.S. at 499. These however are in toto admittedly low cost items. If their inclusion in the program amounts to constitutionally significant asymmetry, then surely the remedy is to veto them, not to compel by judicial fiat the inclusion of bankrupting normal pregnancy — simply for symmetry purposes. For, as the Court recognized, insurance for disability due to normal pregnancy is "so extraordinarily expensive that it would be impossible to maintain a program supported by employee contributions, if these disabilities are included." *Id.* at 493.

39.   Geduldig v. Aiello, 417 U.S. 484, 497 (1974).

40.   Congress indeed in proposing ERA seems to have provided in advance for the *Geduldig* decision:

> The legal principle underlying the equal rights amendment (H.J. Res. 208) is that the law must deal with the individual attributes of the particular person and not with stereotypes of over-classification based on sex. However, the original resolution does not require that women must be treated in all respects the same as men. "Equality" does not mean "sameness." As a result, the original resolution would not prohibit reasonable classifications based on characteristics that are unique to one sex.

Equal Rights for Men and Women, S. REP. NO. 92-689, 92d Cong., 2d Sess. (1972). This and much of the pro-ERA discussion in Congress rests on Brown, Emerson, Falk & Freedman, *supra* note 2, part III. *See, e.g.*, the discussion *id.* at 893:

> B.   *Laws Dealing with Physical Characteristics Unique to One Sex*
> The fundamental legal principle underlying the Equal Rights Amendment, then, is that the law must deal with particular attributes of individuals, not with a classification based on the broad and impermissible attribute of sex. This principle, however, does not preclude legislation (or other official action) which regulates, takes into account, or otherwise deals with a physical characteristic unique to one sex. In this situation it might be said that, in a certain sense, the individual obtains a benefit or is subject to a restriction because he or she belongs to one or the other sex. Thus a law relating to wet nurses would cover only women and a law regulating the donation of sperm would restrict only men. Legislation of this kind does not, however, deny equal rights to the other sex. So long as the law deals only with a characteristic found in all (or some) women but *no* men, or in all (or some) men but *no* women, it does not ignore individual characteristics found in both sexes in favor of an average based on one sex. Hence such legislation does not, without more, violate the basic principle of the Equal Rights Amendment.

premium schedule which, as noted above, seems to put an unjustified burden upon men (entirely apart from the normal pregnancy problem).[41]

The ultimate conclusion must be obvious: to the extent that ERA rests on alleged Supreme Court bias against women in these oft-cited cases it is without foundation. The matter may be put more broadly. With two innocent exceptions both since abandoned,[42] *Geduldig* is the only (allegedly anti-female) equal protection case that women have lost in the Supreme Court. Whether that decision sprang from sexism, neutral principle, or whatever, surely there is no reason to believe the result would be different under ERA.[43] The latter does not define what it prohibits any more clearly than does the equal protection clause. Both of course outlaw anti-female discrimination, but both leave the definition thereof, the application of abstract principle to concrete circumstances, as well as the problems of methodology and judicial remedy ultimately to judges. Thus *in both contexts* there is plenty of room for male chauvinism, if the Supreme Court is — as charged — so inclined. The point is: ERA no less than equal protection would allow judges a wide range of discretion in both substance and procedure — discretion that may be used to promote or frustrate the ideals of the women's movement. It will not do to argue that ERA would be helpful in cases like *Geduldig* (the female's only equal protection "defeat") on the ground that it would trigger "strict scrutiny."[44] For ERA — like equal protection in this context — could not trigger anything in a case wherein the Court finds (as in *Geduldig*) no gender classification. Nor is there any reason, one suggests, for believing that even in appropriate cases josephic judges would find ERA any more trigger-happy than the equal protection clause.

Finally it is at least arguable that the Court has begun to treat gender as a suspect classification when women are the victims[45] — and uphold "benign discrimination" in their favor.[46] On that basis it might follow that

---

41.   See text accompanying note 34 *supra*.
42.   Hoyt v. Florida, 368 U.S. 57 (1961), upheld a state law making jury service voluntary for females, though it was compulsory for males. This decision was in effect overruled in Taylor v. Louisiana, 419 U.S. 522 (1975). As to *Goesaert* — the other alleged anti-female decision — *see* text accompanying note 27 *supra*. It was disapproved in Craig v. Boren, 429 U.S. 190, 210 n.23 (1976). Those who find in Forbush v. Wallace, 405 U.S. 970 (1972), *aff'g* 341 F. Supp. 217 (M.D. Ala. 1971), an invidious anti-female decision may want to consider the comments in B. BABCOCK, A. FREEDMAN, E. NORTON & S. ROSS, *supra* note 3, at 582.
43.   See note 40 and accompanying text *supra*.
44.   See G. GUNTHER, CASES AND MATERIALS ON CONSTITUTIONAL LAW 658 (1975).
45.   Stanton v. Stanton, 421 U.S. 7 (1975); Frontiero v. Richardson, 411 U.S. 677 (1973); Reed v. Reed, 404 U.S. 71 (1971).
46.   Califano v. Webster, 430 U.S. 313, 316-17 (1977), and the cases there cited.

men would be the chief beneficiaries of ERA.[47] For benign discrimination in favor of women — like one-sided "strict scrutiny" — is after all gender discrimination against men.

---

47.   *See* Barrett, *Judicial Supervision of Legislative Classifications — A More Modest Role for Equal Protection?*, 1976 B.Y.U. L. REV. 89, 90-91 (1976).

ADDENDUM

In March 1972 ERA was submitted to the states for ratification subject to a traditional seven-year deadline. In an unprecedented move in October 1978 Congress extended the deadline to June 30, 1982. Within that period thirty-five states ratified, but five of them reconsidered and withdrew their approval. Thus ERA fell eight (or three) states short of victory.

The average ratification time for our twenty-six constitutional amendments was twenty-two months. ERA failed after more than ten years. It achieved no state endorsements in the last five years and five months of its extended deadline term. Yet, if women lost the battle, certainly they won the war by their victories in the Burger Court as well as in Congress.

28 🌼 *The Iron Ring of Discrimination*

> Every culture does at least reasonably well for those at the top of
> its social order. The crucial test is how does it treat those at the
> bottom.

Something had touched the conscience of America. Maybe it was the
shock of the Great Depression — or the rise of Hitler and Stalin. Later the
hot, and then the cold, war must have had something to do with it. Perhaps
it was all these things and more. But whatever the cause all branches of the
national government responded. In the *Gaines* case[1] (1938) the "old" Supreme
Court began the long retreat from discrimination in the schools. A few years
later President Roosevelt created the Fair Employment Practices Committee.
Presidents Truman and Eisenhower took giant steps to eliminate segregation
in the armed forces and to continue the FEPC principle in government contract, and civil service, employment. In 1947 a group of distinguished Americans
— the President's Committee on Civil Rights — issued its disturbing report.
By 1950 the "new" Supreme Court had undermined, and before the end of the
decade had outlawed, the old device of "separate-but-equal" — that had served
so long to perpetuate the discrimination it was supposed to abolish. Meanwhile,
the platforms of both major political parties struck hard at racialism. By 1957
Congress had passed the first modern Civil Rights Act; another followed in
1960.

Only a major tide of public opinion could sustain such unremitting pressure
by all three branches of government, but of course that tide did not flow uni-
formly throughout the land. This is the difficulty. For tension is inevitable
when the momentum of national opinion collides with deep-grained, local
habit — when new moral insights clash with old traditions. Extremists on both
sides respond with bitterness and brutality. Others simply close their minds
to the possibility of change, or demand perfection overnight. A more common
response is a sense of tragedy implicit in the relentless rule that every step of
progress means destruction of something that is old and dear to someone.

Discrimination against this or that minority takes many forms, but it is
essentially monolithic. The important thing is not unfair treatment in the
schools, or in employment, at the polls, in housing, or in the administration of
justice; it is the over-all effect of all these things. For each area of discrimination feeds all the others and all are directed to achieve a single end: an iron
ring of law and custom that forces *an inferior status upon its victims.* By
limiting their opportunities for self-improvement it makes and keeps them inferior. The imposed inferiority then serves to "justify" the penalizing laws and

---

1 Missouri *ex rel.* Gaines v. Canada, Registrar of University of Mo., 305 U.S. 337 (1938).

customs. In short, discrimination generates inferiority which in turn generates discrimination. And of course the suppression of a minority always gives someone an immediate advantage: a supply of cheap labor, freedom from a source of competition, a scapegoat, or a psychological punching bag.

The most difficult aspect of the extremist "Southern attitude" for outsiders to understand is its refusal to give an inch, even on seemingly unimportant points. How could Negro travelers in a "white waiting room" matter enough to anyone to provoke violence? The answer is that segregationists — and Negroes — understand the monolithic nature of discrimination. They know that a challenge at any point is a challenge to the whole system. To admit equality of opportunity anywhere is to undermine discrimination everywhere. That would mean the end of a way of life, with all its "advantages" for some and all its hardships for others.

Of course, no class or section in America ever foresaw and devised so cruel a system. Disasters of that magnitude generally spring from some accident of history, some slow and unplanned development beyond the power of human beings to foresee and block while blocking is feasible. Discrimination against our Negro citizens is a legacy of slavery that history thrust upon us long ago. Few will forget what we paid to make good the original error. But it is one thing to abolish slavery as a matter of law; it is something very different to convert a slave into a free man — or to free his master and society itself from the taint.

Slow and cruel as it may seem in retrospect, our progress has been substantial. Yet the residue of slavery is still with us in the racial prison that confines the American Negro. His freedom to vote is seriously restricted. This limits his ability to promote all his other rights and interests, including his rights in the public schools. Confined educational opportunities in turn subject him to the charge that he is not fit to vote — and drastically limit his employment opportunities. Largely restricted to menial and irregular jobs, he is apt to live in a slum. And slums have a potent tendency to produce the qualities that invite disqualification at the polls, in the better schools, and in any but the bottom levels of the economic order. Because he is confined in large measure to the very lowest strata of society, he cannot expect much help from the police or from public prosecutors in asserting his political, educational, housing and other basic rights. Indeed, in some places — especially where he is not permitted to vote — he must expect not help, but brutality, from public officials. At every point the stifling circle begins again. Each hardship leads to another. There is no saving grace by which a disability in one context is compensated by an advantage in another.

The effect upon the Negro's morale, incentives, and ambition is incalculable. Of this we may be sure: He is no stranger to Dante's insight that hell is a place in which men are condemned to live without hope. The cost in human suffering, the moral burden, the spiritual and material loss to the Nation are staggering. And in the end no man can harm another without harming himself. For conscience "doth make cowards of us all."

29 ▓ Separation, Politics, and Judicial Activism

It takes a united country to run a divided government. . . .
—Clinton Rossiter

American government was conceived in fear. Haunted by the concentrated power of kings, we fractured[1] the power of popular government. Fractured power of course means fractured responsibility—a vexing element in the American political system. To put it differently, the same Separation of Powers with its corollary "checks and balances" that was designed to impede evil government must *pari passu* impede good government (however these moralistic terms may be defined). Separation and democracy then have this in common: both are concerned with the use and misuse of power; both are precautionary. The one, however, is purely negative, overbroad, and non-selective. It blocks or hinders any use of power, however exercised, for whatever end or purpose, wise or unwise, good or bad. The other is principled and selective. It affirms and legitimizes some uses of power, repudiating others. Separation and democracy thus are mutually harmonious in some degree, beyond that they are in tension.

The parliamentary system handles the riddle of governmental power quite differently and, some insist, with more sophistication. It does not seek safety in a mechanistic clash of separated forces. Rather it concentrates power for effective action and holds that power closely and democratically accountable. This largely eliminates what for us is a perennial quandary: which of several shells hides the peas of power and responsibility? The result, one suggests, is that parliamentary electorates have more confidence in, and understanding of the governmental process than is customary in this country even in good times. Perhaps in the long view we have relied too much on self-operating, external mechanisms and too little on ourselves—enjoying as we have a wide margin for error and inefficiency thanks to great natural wealth and our protective ocean moats. Expecting the public sector to take care of itself, participating little more than nominally in the democratic process, finding our chief satisfactions in the

---

[1]Were we not here concerned only with the Separation of Powers, "splintered" would be a more accurate term. For in addition to separating, we also bicameralized and federalized. Accordingly we now have just over 200 major governmental power centers—to say nothing of thousands of "home-rule" (and other) counties, municipalities, school, and other special districts.

private sector, we are generally disappointed and cynical with respect to government. Typically we "know" there must be deceit and venality in any gap between what public men profess and what they produce. The fact is the checks and balances of Separation were designed to make professed programs difficult to implement. For to speak of checking and balancing—the terminology we learned as children to revere—is a sympathetic way of referring to frustration and deadlock. It comes perhaps to this: the Founders rejected "efficient" government with, so it seemed, a greater risk of tyranny in favor of inefficient government (checked and balanced against itself) with a better promise of safety and freedom. For the small, simple, slow-moving, agrarian society of 1789, the choice was easy. Such a society required very little government. Its needs could be served by machinery which at best worked slowly, and even then perhaps only when supported by a massive consensus of opinion so overwhelming as to neutralize the built-in impediments. Though the simple world our Fathers knew has long since passed away, their basic plan of government is still with us. We have avoided tyranny and we have prospered: we have also made some changes.

SEPARATION AND POLITICAL PARTIES

Not so long ago a scholar who would become President Woodrow Wilson warned with respect to checks and balances:

> The trouble with the theory is that government is not a machine, but a living thing. It falls, not under the theory of the universe, but under the theory of organic life. It is accountable to Darwin, not to Newton. It is modified by its environment, necessitated by its tasks, shaped to its functions by the sheer pressure of life. No living thing can have its organs offset against each other as checks, and live. On the contrary, its life is dependent upon their quick cooperation, their ready response to the commands of instinct or intelligence, their amicable community of purpose. Government is not a body of blind forces; it is a body of men, with highly differentiated functions, no doubt, in our modern day of specialization but with a common task and purpose. Their cooperation is indispensable, their warfare fatal. There can be no successful government without leadership or without the intimate, almost instinctive, coordination of the organs of life and action.[2]

The coordinating device that Wilson seems to have contemplated was a responsible party system. Early in our national history Alexander Hamilton, who thought our scheme of government far too impotent, discovered that an extra-constitutional political party superimposed upon the constitutional structure could in large measure circumvent Separation,

---

[2]W. WILSON, CONSTITUTIONAL GOVERNMENT IN THE UNITED STATES 56-57 (1911).

and thus transform what Woodrow Wilson called an unworkable New-tonian machine into an effective Darwinian organism.[3] By bridging the separated branches a strong political party, we learned, could hope to harmonize and coordinate their sundered operations.   Later we also learned, that even the dominant party is not always a reliably strong and effective coordinator.[4] When it is not, we lapse back to the frustration of checks and the deadlock of balances.   Thus it is that in the long view the history of American government seems a history of spasms.   In weak party eras (absent a crisis), *i.e.* when the Founder's Newtonian machine prevails, Congress and the President are apt to be at loggerheads.   Little then is to be expected from them.   In strong party eras (and usually in time of crisis) the built-in friction diminishes.   Then Congress and President generally respond to accumulated problems with vigorous legislative programs. There have been three such episodes in the twentieth century: the early Wilson, the F.D.R., and the L.B.J. administrations.   Wilson's bulging reform program was the fruit of the Panic of 1907 and the high tide of the Progressive Movement which, for a brief time, invigorated large segments of both major parties.   Years later the Great Depression gave Roosevelt the leverage to create a potent *new* Democratic Party dedicated to reform.   The result of course was a massive New Deal.   Yet by the 1950's F.D.R.'s party had lost its vitality, as had the Republican Party long before.[5]   A period of torpidity followed in domestic affairs.   Even the bright, new Kennedy Administration failed miserably in Congress.   Then the shock of the assassination plus the enormous congressional majorities (including many dedicated young men) that the Goldwater campaign gave the Democrats enabled L.B.J. to push a massive reform program through Congress[6]— many elements of which President Kennedy had vainly urged.   The period of harmony lasted hardly two years.   Since then it has been a matter of Separation.   As of now we have not even been able to adopt a viable response to the energy crisis, the short run interests of the consumer apparently prevailing in Congress check and balance what the White House deems to be the long run needs of the nation.

Of course the Founding Fathers are only partially responsible for the internal friction that plagues American government from time to time.   The growth of urbanism has magnified the problem.   For in large measure a modern President's constituency is urban; that of Congress is significantly more oriented toward rural and small town interests.   The reason for those "two majorities" is plain.   It begins with the unit rule that gives a state's

---

[3]*See* P. ODEGARD & E. HELMS, AMERICAN POLITICS 30-36 (1947).
[4]*See* notes 12 & 24 *infra*.
[5]*See* text accompanying notes 24-25 *infra*.
[6]The Vietnam War caused many to forget President Johnson's early legislative triumphs. *See* R. HOFSTADTER, W. MILLER & D. AARON, THE UNITED STATES 846-53 (3rd ed. 1972).

total electoral vote for president to the candidate who gets a majority of the popular votes.

> Thus the populous states with large electoral votes are particularly important. The candidate who wins most or all of them, even by a hair, will probably win the Presidency. Both parties realize this is so, and shape their strategies of nomination and electioneering accordingly. They tend to nominate men who come from the larger states, and who, in the progression of their own careers, have made alliances with urban interest groups and their representatives, such as labor unions, Negroes, and other ethnic blocs. These are, by and large, groups that in their policy preferences are conventionally described as "liberal": welfare minded, favoring civil rights legislation, and demanding of governmental services.[7]

Thus, a presidential candidate who has substantial support in some fifteen or twenty major metropolitan areas is virtually assured of victory. One who fails to carry most of them has little, if any, chance of winning.

Many men of Congress on the other hand must answer largely or exclusively to rural and small town America. But that is only the beginning of the matter. The non-urban element in Congress has been greatly magnified by congressional organization and procedure, especially the committee and seniority systems, the unique role of the House Rules Committee, and perhaps the filibuster. The leaders of Congress of course are committee chairmen who traditionally have been selected by mere seniority without regard for merit, party loyalty or concern for presidential policy. Since seniority is most readily attained by those from "safe districts," chairmanships have gone very disproportionately to Democrats from the South or Republicans from the rural Midwest.[8] So favored, non urban interests have long enjoyed a position not unlike the old English "rotten boroughs." Thus, we have long had in effect a double gerry-mander: rural interests being overrepresented in Congress; urban concerns in the White House. The tensions thus generated are increased by other phenomena. A President presumably, far more than members of Congress, is conscious of his role in history. Thus generally, it seems in "domestic affairs, he tends to take the broad and progressive . . . view; in world affairs, the adventurous and cooperative. In the former, Congress tends to be more parochial and desultory; in the latter, more cautious and nationalistic."[9] Indeed perhaps, with respect to the one we tend to vote our national ideals; with respect to the other, our more immediate and mundane needs and biases.

In any event as a matter of historical experience, the congressional-executive relationship is less than fully harmonious. A famous historian recently referred to it as "permanent guerrilla warfare" which to be sure

---

[7]N. Polsby, Congress and the Presidency 11 (1964).
[8]See note 28 infra & text accompanying.
[9]C. Rossiter, President and Congress in the 1960's, in Continuing Crisis in American Politics 105 (M.D. Irish ed. 1963).

heats and cools periodically. The result of all these constitutional and extra-constitutional stumble blocks is reminiscent of Calhoun's concurrent majority system. For almost any well led, determined and not insignificant minority *in normal times* can find one or more of many available checks and balances to kill, maim, or delay virtually anything it finds seriously objectionable.

Those who like uncluttered, logical lines of power and responsibility, and especially those who are impatient for a new social order, find all this at least close to unbearable. Their judgments typically rest, as is now fashionable, not on comparison with any system known on earth, but vis-a-vis some never-never land in an ideal world. Others, perhaps more aware of mankind's sad experience with government, find that among the world's few free nations ours does not suffer by comparison; that history gives promise of congressional and presidential cooperation often enough to meet pressing needs; that the lulls between such creative episodes are in fact healthful periods of gestation; that our tradition of government by concurrent, *i.e.* extraordinary, majorities has not prevented experimentation or discussion. It has at most only slowed the process of change in the interest of insuring a viable consensus behind public policy.[10] Or more broadly, as Robert Dahl suggests, our political.

> . . . institutions, then, offer organized minorities innumerable sites in which to fight, perhaps to defeat, at any rate to damage an opposing coalition. Consequently, the institutions place a high premium on strategies of compromise and conciliation, on a search for consensus. They inhibit and delay change until there is wide support; they render comprehensive change unlikely; they foster incremental adjustments. They generate politicians who learn how to deal gently with opponents, who struggle endlessly in building and holding coalitions together, who doubt the possibilities of great change, who seek comprosmises.[11]

THE JUDICIARY

We turn now to that other separated organ, the Supreme Court, in the context of splintered political power and responsibility. It is clear that in no other democratic system do judges play anything approaching the governing role they play in the United States. Perhaps one cannot prove, yet one surely may suspect, that this indecisive, fractured political system invites the unique role of the American judiciary. It is said that power goes to those who can use it. What follows here is a survey of some post-bellum evidence to support these thoughts.

The Civil War and the "bloody shirt" thereafter virtually eliminated the Democratic Party and the South as important forces in national

---

[10]*See* S. Bailey, *Our National Political Parties*, in POLITICAL PARTIES, U.S.A. 4 (R.A. Goldwin ed. 1964).

[11]R. DAHL, PLURALIST DEMOCRACY IN THE UNITED STATES 329 (1967).

politics. This left the Republican Party, initially a northern "anti-slavery" alliance of East and Midwest, in nominal control.   But that sectional combination was far from stable as the successive Granger, Greenback, Alliance, Free Silver and Populist movements indicated.   For these were largely Midwestern agrarian revolts against the Eastern "money power." In short East and West, at odds econcomically, were frozen in a "dominant" political alliance.   So constituted of incompatibles, the Republican Party was hardly a dynamic instrument of government.   Indeed a major part of the litigation that reached the Supreme Court in this era reflected clashes between businessmen and farmers (later labor), the chief allies in the Republican coalition.   The defeat of the great revolt that Bryan led in 1896 confirmed the inability of the Democratic Party to tear the unhappy West from its sectional accord with the East and reestablish the ante-bellum West-South Democratic coalition.[12]   It may have been this special weakness of the party system, combined with the normal contretemps of the separated political branches that invited the judicial activism, once called government by the judiciary, which began in 1890's.

The Supreme Court had resisted for a time under the leadership of Chief Justice Waite in the face of persistent dissents.[13]   Then it fell to with vigor in 1895-1896.   In a matter of months it killed the national income tax,[14] emasculated the Sherman Antitrust Act[15] as well as the Interstate Commerce Commission,[16] and it approved the labor injunction[17] as well as Separate-But-Equal.[18]   This old fashioned, largely economic activism continued through 1935-1936, when it destroyed virtually the entire early New Deal legislative program.[19]

The election of 1936, however, brought a major change in the nature of the party system.   The traditional, and long moribund, politics of sections gave way to what was then called urban politics.[20]   The election of 1932 was the last in which sectionalism played the dominant role.   By 1936 voters had learned what the New Deal was.   Ethnic and class-conscious urbanism replaced "acreage" in the alignment of political party forces. Many rural voters returned to the G.O.P.   Most of the Midwestern wheat counties, for example, were on their way back.   But urbanites more than made up the loss.   Every city of 100,000 or more inhabitants turned to the new Democratic Party, and with the sole exception of Grand Rapids,

---

[12]As to the agrarian rebellion and Bryan's efforts, *see* P. ODEGARD & E. HELMS, AMERICAN POLITICS 93-101 (1947).

[13]*See generally* C. MAGRATH, MORRISON R. WAITE: THE TRIUMPH OF CHARACTER (1963).

[14]Pollock v. Farmers' Loan & Tr. Co., 157 U.S. 429 (1895).

[15]United States v. E.C. Knight Co., 156 U.S. 1 (1895).

[16]ICC v. Alabama Midland Ry. Co., 168 U.S. 144 (1897).

[17]*In re* Debs, 158 U.S. 564 (1895).

[18]Plessy v. Ferguson, 163 U.S. 537 (1896).

[19]For a listing of the cases since those cited in notes 14-18 *supra*, see THE CONSTITUTION OF THE UNITED STATES, S. Doc. No. 82, 92d Cong., 2d Sess. 1597-1768 (1973).

[20]*See* A. HOLCOMBE, THE NEW PARTY POLITICS (1933).

remained there until the Eisenhower years.[21] The city masses had found a political tool responsive to their needs!

The blatantly activist role that the Supreme Court had achieved under moribund sectional politics apparently could not be maintained in the face of a potent new party system. The "nine old men" surrendered. And in short order the new Roosevelt Court repudiated all the activist innovations of the 1890-1936 era, including, for example, liberty-of-contract, substantive due process, the fair value doctrine, the labor injunction, dual federalism and Separate-But-Equal.[22] In a word, laissez-faire and racial segregation lost their constitutional status. What new doctrines that were devised by the Roosevelt Court were essentially doctrines of judicial restraint.[23]

Mapp v. Ohio[24], in 1961, seems appropriate to mark the advent of a new judicial era, reflecting another political party impasse. By the time *Mapp* was decided the G.O.P. had declined to abiding minority status. Since 1928 it had not, and still has not, elected a President together with a majority in both houses of Congress. By 1970 there were at least as many Independents as Republicans. Meanwhile F.D.R.'s Democratic coalition was disintegrating. The urban tension between "hard hat" labor on the one side and blacks and intellectuals on the other was crucial. Indeed it was a major source of George Wallace's strength and of G.O.P. survival. Yet these groups, the Blacks, labor, and intellecutals, had been the core of F.D.R.'s Democratic Party. Another phase of the same disintegration process was black immigration to, and white flight from, the central cities. This so polarized urban areas for a time that some suggested the major element of future politics would be a conflict between suburbs and core-cities. The South moreover was becoming less and less solidly Democratic.[25]

As of 1960 troubles had been building for years, many of them quickened by war. President Eisenhower's well know tranquilizing effect had provided a brief, much needed, respite after a generation of crises: the worst depression, the worst hot war, the worst cold war, the worst limited war in American history. But the healing era, which James Reston called the "era of prosperity and good feeling," could not last long. As Reston put it when President Eisenhower retired:

> He was popular because he was in tune with the spirit of the nation, which, during his eight years in office, was generous and optimistic, but not militant or experimental. He was criticized because he was not in tune with the world-wide spirit of the age which was convulsive and revolu-

---

[21]See S. Lubell, The Future of American Politics 49-63 (1965).

[22]See text accompanying notes 13-20 *supra*.

[23]See, e.g., Dennis v. United States, 341 U.S. 494 (1951); Prudential Life Ins. Co. v. Benjamin, 328 U.S. 408 (1946); Graves v. New York ex rel. O'Keefe, 306 U.S. 466 (1939).

[24]367 U.S. 643 (1961). See also note 34 infra & text accompanying.

[25]Much of the material in this paragraph comes from W. Keefe, Parties, Politics, and Public Policy in America 143-58 (1972).

tionary. This contrast between the spirit of the nation (which he helped to create) and the spirit of the world is the heart of the Eisenhower story.[26]

By the time of *Mapp*, America had joined the rest of the world. A mass of accumulating problems could no longer be ignored. Galbraith's exposure of poverty in *The Affluent Society* (1958) was followed by the Joint Economic Committee's report on *The Low Income Population and Economic Growth* (1959). Harrington's *The Other America* would soon appear. The year preceding *Mapp* had brought the "sit-ins" and the "freedom rides." CORE, SNICK, the White Citizens' Councils, and S.D.S. had begun to organize. The first student demonstration has just occurred, by accident, at Berkeley; the "silent generation" had passed into history. President Kennedy had just been elected. His campaign had focused on nine industrial states (New York, California, Pennsylvania, Ohio, Illinois, Michigan, Texas, Massachusetts and New Jersey) casting 237 of the 269 electoral votes necessary for election. His approach accordingly had stressed the interests of urban voters. The pattern of his electoral victory reflected the pattern of his campaign.[27] Yet the leaders of the 87th Congress with whom Kennedy had to work focused in a different direction. No Senate committee chairman came from any of the ten largest northern industrial states, though these states had more than half our total population. Nine of the sixteen chairmen came from the South. In the House, four of the twenty chairmen came from safe urban districts. Nine of the others were from the South; a tenth from the near South, Oklahoma, and others were from small, largely non-urban states such as Montana, Nevada, Arizona and New Mexico.[28] It could hardly be surprising that most of President Kennedy's program to resolve long smoldering problems of an urban-industrial nation was blocked in Congress, a humilating defeat for Camelot. It was in this era that some observers began talking about "the deadlock of democracy."[29] If for the unique circumstances already mentioned, President Johnson enjoyed a period of stunning legislative success, it did not last long. Meanwhile, the Vietnam War was bringing what eventually would be close to the full disruption of the political system. Indeed, reviewing the 1960's, Samuel Lubell suggests America had lost its capacity for self government. Reasoned argument, compromise and accomodation, he thought, were increasingly "shoved aside" in favor of polarization, confrontation, violence and a raw struggle for power. Lubbell, a careful political observer, could see "no party coalition in command of a sufficiently stable majority to advance a unifying set of policies."[30] Many on the left were convinced

[26]Quoted in 2 T. WILLIAMS, R. CURRENT & F. FRIEDEL, A. HISTORY OF THE UNITED STATES 771 (1964).
[27]L. KOENIG, CONGRESS AND THE PRESIDENT 67 (1965).
[28]F. GREENSTEIN, THE AMERICAN PARTY SYSTEM AND THE AMERICAN PEOPLE 84 (1963).
[29]*See* J. BURNS, THE DEADLOCK OF DEMOCRACY (1963).
[30]S. LUBELL, THE HIDDEN CRISIS IN AMERICAN POLITICS 25, 266 (1970).

of the "irrelevance of American politics."[31] George Wallace on the far right charged there was not a dime's worth of difference between the two major parties, meaning presumably what the left meant: the parties were not focusing on the crucial issues of the day. As Walter Lippmann, old and conservative, saw the problem:

> To many, it does not seem right that in this time of crisis our political system should be failing to register and reflect the issues which torment our people. What has happened, it would seem, is that the American political system, which works so well in normal times, is operating regardless of and apart from the bitter war and the urban and racial crises at home.[32]

How little confidence voters had in either party, *i.e.* how out of touch with reality the parties seemed, was reflected in an unprecedented increase in the number of Independent voters and in ticket splitting.[33]

And so again, by the time *Mapp* came down in the early 1960's, as in the post-bellum era, a once useful political party alignment seems to have lost touch with the times. Again we needed a restructuring of party forces. Meanwhile the Newtonian disease, as in the 1890's, seems to have invited larger scale judicial policy making: the phenomenon called Warren Court activism.[34]

ADDENDUM

Those with a taste for jurimetrics may want to consider the relative frequency of Supreme Court vetoes of both state and federal legislation in the four periods blocked out in the foregoing essay: The Waite Era, 1874-

---

[31]*See* Brownfield, *The Irrelevance of American Politics*, in CONTEMPORARY SOCIETY (J. Perry & M. Seidler eds. 1971).

[32]*Id.* at 640.

[33]W. KEEFE, PARTIES, POLITICS, AND PUBLIC POLICY IN AMERICA 143-58 (1972).

[34]The phenomenon called "Warren Court activism" did not begin in the complacent 1950's when Earl Warren became Chief Justice (1953). Rather, one suggests, it was part and parcel of the flaming 1960's. Admirers of the Warren Court like to credit it with Brown v. Board of Education, 347 U.S. 483 (1954), treating that decision as an aspect of the later activist upheaval. That will not do! *Brown* was decided by eight members of the "old" Court plus the new Chief Justice only months after he took office. It has been *plainly* foreshadowed in a unanimous opinion in Sweatt v. Painter, 339 U.S. 629 (1950). Moreover *Brown*, unlike Miranda v. Arizona, 384 U.S. 436 (1966), for example, was hardly an activist addition to the Constitution; it was rather a return to the central, anti-racist, purpose of the Fourteenth Amendment as originally recognized in the Slaughter-House Cases, 83 U.S. (16 Wall.) 36 (1873); Strauder v. West Virginia, 100 U.S. 303 (1880); and Ex parte Virginia, 100 U.S. 339 (1880). The difference between the Warren Court of the 1950's and the Warren Court of the 1960's is stupendous. See the statistics provided in the ADDENDUM, *infra*. Note also that on at least eleven occasions the later Warren Court overruled the earlier one. *See* THE CONSTITUTION OF THE UNITED STATES, S. DOC. No. 82, 92d Cong., 2d Sess. 1795-6 (1973). In this article the term "Warren Court" refers to the quintessential, "mature" Warren Court as we knew it after 1960.

1889; the Laissez-Faire Activist Era, 1890-1936; the Frankfurter Era,[55] 1937-1960; and the mature Warren Court Era,[36] 1961-1969.

Era		Acts Invalidated[37] State	Federal	Average Invalidation Per Year
Waite Restraint	(1874-1889)	61	8	4.3
Laissez-Faire Activism	(1890-1936)	359	45	8.6
Frankfurter Restraint	(1937-1960)	120	9	5.4
Mature Warren Court Activism	(1961-1969)	132	14	16.2

[55]Surely Mr. Justice Frankfurter fought harder and longer for judicial restraint than any other member of the Court at least since 1938. He was persistently opposed by a strong, activist minority which sometimes attracted enough side votes to carry the day.

[36]See note 34 supra.

[37]These figures are derived from data in THE CONSTITUTION OF THE UNITED STATES, S. Doc. No. 82, 92d Cong. 2d Sess. 1597–1768 (1963). Cases involving local measures are not included in this table.

30 ❦ B. F. Wright on the Contract Clause: A Progressive Misunderstanding of the Marshall-Taney Era

The political and social thinkers who laid the foundations of Progressivism have long enjoyed the flattery of imitation; surely they also deserve the tribute of reappraisal.

H. E. Dean (1956)

As Tocqueville remarked [1835] every poor American hoped to become rich. All Americans, rich and poor, believed that the state should protect property. Locke's doctrine of natural rights was not disputed by any American, whether aristocratic or democratic.

H. B. Parkes (1959)

THE POPULIST-PROGRESSIVE ANACHRONISM

BENJAMIN WRIGHT has been called "our foremost authority on the contract clause." For nearly half a century his book, *The Contract Clause of the Constitution* (1938), has been cited endlessly as a definitive work. No doubt in general it reflects a high order of scholarship. The present purpose, however, is to suggest it is flawed, particularly in its treatment of the Supreme Court's early contract-clause decisions. The essence of this charge is that Mr. Wright was guilty of the very thing that twenty years later he ascribed to others:[1]

A considerable amount of the historical writing of the last half century or more has been based upon a curious pair of assumptions: the men who wrote and voted for the Declaration of Independence and for the state bills of rights and the first state constitutions were great patriots, whereas the men who wrote or voted for the Constitution of 1787 were selfish, economically determined plotters. The Declaration and the state bills of rights were liberating and democratic documents, whereas the later state constitutions, with their greater emphasis upon the separation of powers, and the federal Constitution were intended "to make the country safe from democracy." This dichotomy is evidence of an unhistorical rather than a historical interpretation of our past. It is founded not so much in the history of that time as in the history of a century or more later.

The dichotomy in question sprang from Progressive muckraking of the Constitutional Convention roughly a century after the fact. The "well-to-do" Founding Fathers, it is said, produced the Constitution and foisted it upon the country as an antidote against "the evils of democracy." Their prime purpose allegedly was to protect "vested interests" via such curbs upon the masses as staggered terms of office (only Congressmen were to be directly elected), checks and balances, spurious federalism masking centralized power, a Constitution difficult to amend, and above all an oligarchic judicial veto.[2] It is hardly coincidence that this version of history developed contemporaneously with the gross judicial activism (1895–1936) that destroyed so many legislative efforts to protect worker and consumer from the "Titans of industry." Inevitably then muckrakers attacked the Marshall Court. Had it not after all perfected the judicial veto, that ultimate insult to democracy, they insisted, which even the "plotting" Founders had not "dared" to authorize explicitly?[3]

As recently as 1955 Louis Hartz (who had studied under Mr. Wright at Harvard) observed that "in American social studies we still live in the shadow of the Progressive era."[4] That the young Mr. Wright, like those he later criticized, wrote in that shadow seems clear. Surely it is significant that he produced *The Contract Clause* during the Great Depression, before the Supreme Court's massive self-reversal, when the Progressive Movement's disdain for "government by judges" was still a rampant force in liberal circles.

We should not forget that the Founding Fathers and the members of the Marshall Court struggled for freedom as they understood it, not as others in a remote future might understand it. They too were creatures of their time and place. Deeply beholden to John Locke, "godparent" of our revolt and our Constitution, they deemed liberty and property inseparable. John Adams put it succinctly: "Property must be secured, or liberty cannot exist."[5] John Taylor, the philosopher of the Jeffersonians (and Adams's political opponent), was no less emphatic: "the rights of man include life, liberty, and property. The last [mentioned] right is the chief hinge upon which social happiness depends."[6] For Thomas Jefferson, "the true foundation of republican government is the equal right of every citizen, in his person and property."[7] The Father of the Constitution argued in pure Lockean terms for the rights of property and the property in (civil) rights.[8] No wonder then that the Marshall Court in *Fletcher* v. *Peck*[9] referred to the contract clause as a bill-of-rights provision, and that in the next fifty-five years twenty-two states put contract clauses in their own bills of rights — four having done so previously.[10] Later, in a radically changed economic milieu, Populist-Progressives came to believe that in fact the property of some often hinders the liberty of others. Inevitably then, having forgotten Locke, they would "misunderstand" both the Founders and our early judges — Lockeans all. Only an anachronism makes wondrous to us the early American equation of contract, free speech, free religion, and fair trial rights! The worst that can be said of Marshall's Court is that it took an expansive view of what was then considered a basic civil liberty!

An industrial revolution produced the Populist-Progressive outburst; medieval feudalism begot our contract clauses. Those clauses reflect the drive for freedom that Sir Henry Maine would later describe as a transition from "status to contract"—from feudal obligations based on ancestry to contractual obligations *voluntarily* undertaken. This was the "new freedom." It meant in general that one's destiny on earth depended largely upon success or failure in one's covenants with respect, for example, to wages, farm and industrial goods, or artistic talent. In such a setting it is crucial that agreements be dependable—not merely to promote the individual's security and mobility but for the good of a society whose sustenance depends upon a vast network of voluntary, contractual relationships. This, not an evil conspiracy, explains why *all* of our contract clauses—those adopted before as well as those adopted after *Fletcher*—were written broadly as though to protect anyone who, for example, buys property, endows a college, loans money, or builds a bridge in reliance upon another party's formal pledge. Yet, apparently provoked by the 1895–1936 judicial activism, Mr. Wright, like liberals generally in that era, picked up the Populist-Progressive cue. However scholarly the method, the thesis seems false. John Marshall was not the ideological forerunner of the "nine old men." He was no more at odds with the men of 1787 than they were with the men of 1776. All of them, rather, were part of that Lockean liberal movement in which Mr. Wright in his later years found "consensus and continuity." As he wrote in 1958, we should not "read the point of view of the Supreme Court of the 1890s back into the attitude of the Framers of 1787"—nor, one adds, into the minds of our early judges.[11]

PUBLIC CONTRACTS

In 1938 Mr. Wright pressed hard a view that had been a Populist-Progressive assault weapon: namely, that the contract clause was not intended to apply to state contracts.[12] With respect to "the men of 1787–1789," we are told that "all of them discussed the clause only in relation to private contracts, i.e., contracts between individuals."[13] No doubt the best of us now and then resort to sweeping, undocumented and undocumentable rhetoric. The thrust of Mr. Wright's rhetoric in this instance may be sound. Yet, if "all" of "the men of 1787–1789" discussed the matter "only" in such narrow terms, why in the Constitution did they write so broadly; why did they write of "contracts" rather than "private contracts"? Given the emphasis on the unwritten-intent argument, this paradox cries out for explanation. None has been offered. In any event it does not follow that by applying the clause to state as well as to private agreements, the Marshall Court revealed an illicit proprietarian bias. Such application may offend Populist-Progressive but certainly not Lockean dogma.

If the Constitutional Convention had wanted the clause to cover only private contracts, it could easily have said so. The Continental Congress had done that in the Northwest Ordinance: "no law ought to . . . have force in the said territory that shall in any manner whatever interfere with or affect *private* contracts . . . *previously formed*" (emphasis added). Earlier in England *An Agreement of the People* (1649) had condemned acts impairing the obligation of *public* contracts.[14] On August 28, 1787, six weeks after enactment of the Northwest Ordinance, Rufus King moved to include its private contract approach in the Constitution. Following a brief discussion of possible ramifications of such a provision, it died. A few days later (September 14) at the suggestion of the Committee of Style, the Constitutional Convention adopted the contract clause without qualifying the term *contracts.* All we really know of what the Convention meant is that it was invited to adopt the private-contract approach of the Northwest Ordinance and failed to do so. Shortly thereafter it adopted a provision that refers merely to *contracts,* i.e., contracts in general, as distinct from *private* contracts according to the Ordinance (and as distinct from public contracts according to *An Agreement of the People*). Surely this suggests deliberate choice, namely, that a state too must keep its word.

Commentators repeat endlessly (as a matter of habit?) Mr. Wright's view that the only purpose of the contract clause was to protect private contract rights from debtor-relief legislation. No doubt such legislation was a major problem in early America, but as A. J. Beverige observed, "From the Nation's beginning, the States had lax notions as to the sacredness of public contracts, and often violated their obligations of them."[15] Not a word in our records of the Constitutional Convention nor in *The Federalist* even hints the Founders were concerned only with private covenants — that they thought a state should be free to violate its own agreements. Alexander Hamilton later observed, "It is . . . impossible to reconcile the idea of a [state] promise which obliges, with power to make a law which can vary the effect of it."[16] Hamilton of course had been a member of the Constitutional Convention.

Earlier in *The Federalist* (no. 44), James Madison had said of "laws impairing the obligation of contracts" (without qualifying the latter term):

[Such measures] are contrary to the first principles of the social compact, and to every principle of sound legislation. . . . Very properly, therefore, have the convention added this constitutional bulwark in favor of personal security and private rights; and I am much deceived if they have not in so doing . . . faithfully consulted the genuine sentiments . . . of their constituents.

This language, like that of the contract clause itself, literally embraces public as well as private contract violations. It is not the language of one who thought "personal security and private rights" would be served by requiring good faith in private, but not in public agreements. It is not the language of one who believed "general prudence and industry" would be promoted by allowing a state to back out of its own covenants. The crucial point is this: The "Father of the Constitution" thought laws impairing the obligation of contracts are "contrary to . . . the social compact." Thus in his view the contract clause was not just a special prescription for a peculiar malady of America's "critical period"; rather, it embodied "first principles" of natural right so basic as to be covered in the "social compact."[17] This Lockean stance inevitably implicated an axiom of the eighteenth century Enlightenment: Government must honor its contractual obligations or—for persistent lapses—suffer revolution (as in 1688, 1776, and 1789). This was the heart of Locke's compact theory of government. Behind it lay a more comprehensive moral, or natural-law, precept that was crucial in sixteenth and seventeenth century thought, namely, *pacta sunt servanda,* which bound sovereign no less than citizen and (in some minds) even deity.

Long before John Marshall became a judge, Justice Wilson asked rhetorically: "What good purpose could this constitutional provision secure if a state might pass a law impairing the obligation of its own contracts, and be amenable, for such a violation of right, to no controlling judiciary power?"[18] This from one who had been perhaps the second most prominent member of the Constitutional Convention. Justice William Paterson too had been influential at the Convention. Years before *Fletcher,* in a similar case he held a state could not impair its own contractual obligations.[19] So did the highest court of Massachusetts in *Derby* v. *Blake*[20] and in *Wales* v. *Stetson.*[21] *Fletcher* was not without significant judicial precedent.

In the face of all this we are asked to believe that "the men of 1787–1789" did not mean what they said in the Constitution: that while they wrote broadly, they thought narrowly; that they used unqualified language of principle to cover only limited, easily definable specifics; that they reflected not fears of the late eighteenth but of the late nineteenth century. *What they wrote after all is the best evidence of what they intended.* Mr. Wright's premise is that the Constitution means only what the framers supposedly had in mind. If that approach ever was viable, it is now hopelessly outmoded, especially in activist circles. On such a basis much or all modern constitutional law would be suspect, if not blatantly unconstitutional. The Marshall Court met the intent problem with a now perhaps equally old-fashioned approach: namely, that what the framers wrote is crucial:[22]

This case, being within the words of the Contract Clause, must be within its operation likewise, unless there be something in the literal construction so obviously absurd or mischievous, or repugnant to the general spirit of the instrument, as to justify those who expound the constitution in making it an exception.

No such basis for an exception having been discovered, the Supreme Court ever since has found the contract clause applicable as written to contracts generally, whether public or private.

Since *Fletcher* in 1810, the Supreme Court has blocked far more intrusions upon public than upon private agreements; the ratio is about nine to one. Could a need so persistently felt after 1789 have been unknown before? Had "the men of 1787–1789" forgotten the "cheap and easy methods of [public] debt reduction by the states" prior to the Constitutional Convention?

Another problem in *Fletcher* concerned the scope of the term *contracts* as used in the Constitution. Here again Mr. Wright sees the matter not in Lockean but in Populist-Progressive terms. The state of Georgia, pursuant to an act of its legislature, had sold and granted to speculators a vast quantity of public land. A subsequent legislature repealed the grant on the ground that it had been obtained by bribery. Meanwhile part of the property had been conveyed to the plaintiff, an innocent third-party purchaser.[23] The issue in *Fletcher* was whether the initial grant entailed obligations protected against impairment by the contract clause. The Court responded affirmatively. Of course in modern usage a grant is not a contract, but that does not solve the problem. For it is quite clear that in the late eighteenth century the term *contract* had far broader connotations than it does today. As Dean Roscoe Pound has explained:[24]

Contract was then used, and was used as late as Parsons on Contracts in 1853 to mean [what] might be called "legal transaction" . . . Not merely contract as we now understand it, but trust, will, conveyance, and grant of a franchise are included. . . . The writers on natural law considered that there was a natural legal duty not to derogate from one's grant. . . . This is the explanation of *Fletcher* . . . and no doubt is what the [contract clause] meant to those who wrote it into the Constitution.

Thus in antebellum American law a grant was understood to include an executory contractual obligation of the grantor not to violate the terms of his grant. On this point too, Mr. Wright—true to the Progressive Movement— ran afoul of an anachronism.

It is revealing that on the grant and public contract aspect of Marshall's opinions one finds no criticism or disagreement in a random selection of twelve relevant legal treatises published before 1870, including Thomas M. Cooley's famous *Constitutional Limitations* (1868). Twelve years later, however, Cooley's *General Principles of Constitutional Law* (1880) is at least mildly critical. The change apparently reflects attacks upon the Marshall Court by C. H. Hill., R. Hutchinson, and J. M. Shirley writing separately in the *American Law Review* and the *Southern Law Review* from 1874 to 1879. In due course Progressives would pick up these charges that the Marshall Court had erred and would add that "the great Chief Justice" was in fact "a stalwart . . . reactionary," a servant of property interests.[25] It seems no coincidence that the Hill-Hutchinson-Shirley attacks had germinated in an era (1865–1873) when nearly 60 percent of the laws challenged under the contract clause were held invalid—a new high. Many of those decisions upheld business claims and thus offended Populist-Progressive sensibilities. What has been variously called the Guilded Age, the Age of Cynicism, the era of the business "robber barons," was upon us. John Marshall and the Founding Fathers became suspect or worse. After all, according to the Populist-Progressive version of history, their property "bias" was responsible for what was happening to postbellum America: crude, wasteful, uniquely rapid (and thoroughly effective) industrialization that undermined old cultural traditions and left us for a time without new ones.

Does *Fletcher* indeed reveal a rude property bias? The case entailed a clash between the ownership claims of the defrauded people of Georgia and those of innocent, third-party buyers.[26] If the Court were to decide on the merits, one property interest or the other would have to be upheld. It had long been settled that while a fraudulent buyer gets a good title at *law*, that title is subject to cancellation by a court of equity. Thus in a clash between a cheating buyer and his innocent victim, the latter would prevail. But *Fletcher* involved a clash between the innocent victim and an equally innocent subsequent paying purchaser. As between the two guiltless parties, the chancellor, finding the moral claim of the one no better than that of the other, does not intervene. (The cheated seller's recourse is against those who cheated him.) Thus in holding as it did, the Marshall Court followed faithfully a then, as now, long-settled rule of Anglo-American equity jurisprudence (designed obviously to promote transactional freedom and dependability).

A few years before *Fletcher*, President Jefferson had appointed three commissioners—James Madison, Levi Lincoln, and Albert Gallatin—to explore the Georgia land-fraud problem. Those distinguished Jeffersonians reached the same conclusion on policy grounds that *Fletcher* was to reach on legal grounds, and Jefferson as well as Congress agreed.[27] If Marshall and his colleagues were property biased, so it would seem were the then leading Jeffersonians. More acutely, they were all beholden to the Lockean view that liberty and property are inseparable; that neither thrives without the other.

In *Dartmouth College* v. *Woodward*, a group of philanthropists had obtained a royal charter in 1769 to endow a school primarily for the education of Indians. Relying on the terms of the charter, they provided the necessary funds and established Dartmouth College. In 1816 New Hampshire tried by legislation to take over and govern it contrary to the charter provisions. Marshall's Court, following the thrust of *Fletcher*, held the charter was a contract that the state was not free to violate. Mr. Wright is highly critical, relying heavily on J. M. Shirley, the "father" of the late nineteenth century anti-Marshall movement.[28]

In a narrow view the college charter trustees won the case, but they had no beneficial interest in the college property. They won on behalf of the donor philanthropists (presumably deceased) and generations of future students. Was this a dangerous, proproperty, antipeople decision? The Populist-Progressive answer (to which Mr. Wright did not respond) is that the Dartmouth decision was a sly gambit purposefully designed for an ulterior purpose: protection of corporation charters from legislative interference. That it was highly successful is demonstrated, we are told, by the enormous growth of corporate enterprise thereafter. This reasoning is make-believe. Mr. Justice Story in *Dartmouth* pointed out that no state need grant irrevocable or nonamendable charters; that a state may retain power to amend or revoke. Damage resulting from failure to do so can hardly be held a fault of the judges. In fact reservation of power to alter corporate charters became widespread after *Dartmouth* and was not unknown before. The real problem moreover was not unalterable corporate charters but incorporation by special legislation (with special benefits). This gave way as part of the Jacksonian reform movement to general law, standard-provision incorporation.[29]

Fletcher and *Dartmouth* are not so much proproperty as protransaction cases. They mean that when the equities are not plainly imbalanced (there being no clearly overriding public interest as there was in *Gibbons* v. *Ogden*),[30] judges will protect the contractual arrangements, i.e., the *transactions* by which women and men conduct their affairs — be they philanthropists (*Dartmouth*) or land speculators and farmers (*Fletcher*). As Marshall put it, "the intercourse between man and man would be very seriously obstructed, if this principle be overturned." Incidentally, by killing New York's restrictive steamboat law *Gibbons* too promoted transactional freedom.[31]

While Marshall's Court found nothing in the Constitution or elsewhere that would immunize state covenants from the contract clause, it did recognize they raise special problems justifying a special rule of strict construction. In *Providence Bank* v. *Billings*,[32] Rhode Island had chartered the Providence Bank "in the usual form" with no reference or stipulation concerning taxation. Later, when the state enacted a bank tax, the Providence Bank argued that a power (taxation) that might be used to destroy its charter was foreclosed by implication. The court demurred: "as the whole community is interested in retaining [the power to tax] undiminished, that community has the right to insist that its abandonment ought not to be presumed, in a case in which the deliberate purpose to abandon it does not appear."

The Jacksonian Court under Marshall's successor, Chief Justice Taney, followed the settled path with only one (here relevant) exception: a temporary enlargement (read perversion) of the rule of strict construction. This occurred in the *Charles River Bridge* case.[33] Massachusetts had authorized private investors to build, *operate,* and *maintain* a public drawbridge in exchange for toll rights for a period of forty (later extended to seventy) years. Before that period expired the state authorized a competing, in effect toll-free, bridge only yards away from the original facility. Threatened with serious loss, the owners of the latter objected. Surely the forty-year toll, operation, and maintenance provision constituted a deliberate commitment by the state to permit unimpeded collection of tolls for the full term of the agreement. This being a business, not a charitable, venture, no one could have supposed investors would build at great expense and for many years operate and maintain a drawbridge for the convenience of the public if the state had the power *at any time* to terminate their claim to compensation and profit. Surely in these circumstances the Marshall rule of strict construction was satisfied; the state's "deliberate purpose" to permit unimpeded toll collection for the period in question seems obvious.

The Taney Court purported to follow the *Providence Bank* rule of strict construction. In fact, it simply ignored the "deliberate purpose" aspect of that rule and substituted an incompatible principle derived from English precedents that "nothing passes by implication in public grants." Justices Story and Thompson dissented on implied agreement grounds. Mr. Justice McLean agreed with them on the merits, but thought the Court lacked jurisdiction. In substance *Charles River Bridge* was a four to three decision — though five of the judges had been appointed by President Jackson and the other two by his Jeffersonian predecessors.

The majority position, exalting form over substance, would have permitted construction of an adjacent, free bridge immediately after construction of the first one. Yet surely no court would so decide. If this be true, the Taney rule against implied agreements must be untenable. The Court seems rarely to have used it, having returned long ago to the Marshall approach.[34] The principal effect of the short-lived stricter rule of construction was that thereafter those who covenanted with a state took care to secure elaborately explicit commitments.

Charles River Bridge had been argued before the Marshall Court, but the Chief Justice died prior to the decision. Otherwise, one supposes, the outcome would have been different. Taney's opinion has always had special appeal for those of liberal persuasion, stressing as it does the social interest in "progress."[35] Vested property rights, the Court intimated, must not impede developing technology. Old turnpike charters, for example, should be construed "strictly" lest they block new railroads. *But no such clash of old and new was at issue before the Court.* The real problem was that after some forty years the legislature had come to believe tolls were no longer justified — the bridge having long since paid for itself.[36] Apparently not prepared to risk direct defiance of *Fletcher,* it resorted to the competing bridge ploy.[37] So too a severely split Supreme Court, obviously unwilling to overrule *Fletcher* (or the state), decided not the real but a hypothetical case — demonstrating once again that the framing of the issue largely determines the outcome of a controversy. Surely *Charles River Bridge* deserves a more careful appraisal than Mr. Wright and the Populist-Progressives gave it.

We are told the Founders conspired to promote the interests of the prosperous few, yet intended a narrow reading of their broad language in the contract clause. At least one of those propositions must be mistaken (which suggests a false premise). H. S. Commager, a paragon of modern liberalism, reached a similar conclusion.[38] Responding to *An Economic Interpretation of the Constitution,* he found that Beard gave at most an economic interpretation of the Founders, not of the Constitution. In this view Beard did not even try to show that our basic charter is, as he charged, "an *essentially* economic document" (emphasis added). In fact, Commager wrote, the crux of the Constitution is an allocation and limitation of governmental authority. It does not, for example, deny debtors the relief of bankruptcy; it simply allocates bankruptcy power to the central government for the sake of uniformity.[39] Likewise uniformity is the aim of the other "economic" provisions in Article I, Section 10, of the Constitution (there are no corresponding limitations on the national government).

Of course the Founding Fathers were not demigods utterly unmindful of their own class interests. Yet neither apparently were they so unaware of history as to suppose they could be secure amid widespread insecurity and dissatisfaction. If they were remarkably selfish, as charged, what a monument to selfishness! Their handiwork has met the test of time. They produced what is now the world's oldest written Constitution and one of the world's two oldest and most stable governments.

Private Contracts

Hard times following the Revolutionary War brought numerous state insolvency laws that authorized, for example, delayed payment of contractual debts and payment in depreciated paper currency or even in certain commodities (at a discount). A few days after the close of the Constitutional Convention, Madison observed that these state "evils" (among others) had contributed heavily toward preparing the public for reform.[40] During the Convention he had said:[41]

> In the internal administration of the States a violation of Contracts had become familiar in the form of depreciated paper made a legal tender, of property substituted for money, of Instalment laws, and of the occlusions of the [State] Courts of Justice; although evident that all such interferences affected the rights of other States, relatively Creditor, as well as Citizens Creditors within the State.
>
> Among the defects which had been severely felt was that of a want of uniformity in cases requiring it, as laws of naturalization, bankruptcy, a Coercive authority operating on individuals and a guaranty of the internal tranquility of the State.

Initially, in *Sturges* v. *Crowninshield*,[42] the contract clause was generously construed. Later, over Marshall's objection, *Ogden* v. *Saunders*[43] read *Sturges* and the clause itself to prohibit only retroactive application of insolvency measures. Prospective application was deemed a different matter. The Court's rationale was that an act in existence when a contract was made became in effect part of that contract; thus later enforcement would not be an impairment. On this basis a retroactive measure seemingly should also be upheld, for a state's authority to adopt future insolvency acts may equally be deemed part of every contract.

Is it likely the Founders thought commodity payoff laws were objectionable only when retrospective? Are we to believe retrospectivity was their only ground for eschewing laws that made depreciated paper money legal tender for the repayment of debts? (Obviously the answer must be "no" for those who see the Constitution as a victory for the rich over the poor, for creditors over debtors.)

Had the Founders deemed retrospectivity especially noxious in insolvency cases, surely they would have outlawed it vis-à-vis the national bankruptcy power. Madison's summary of the pre-1789 "evils" did not even mention retroactivity; every one of the things he did mention (including "the occlusions" of state courts, the lack of uniformity, and discrimination against outside creditors) was as relevant to prospective as to other measures. Indeed, it is quite clear that in Madison's view a prime purpose of the contract clause was to outlaw all state insolvency laws in the interest of uniformity via the national bankruptcy power.[44]

Marshall obviously agreed with Madison's apparent view that the contract clause does not distinguish between retrospective and prospective measures. Rejecting the Court's restrictive interpretation in *Ogden,* he and two associates thought a bare majority of four had reduced a safeguard for contract obligations to no more than a ban upon retrospectivity. They also observed that the laws that had caused so much trouble before 1787 had not been merely backward-looking in operation!

The Madison-Marshall view finds support in two separate votes in the Constitutional Convention. The contract clause of the Northwest Ordinance applied only to "private contracts . . . previously formed." In "copying" it, the Founders (as we have seen) dropped the limiting word "private." *They also dropped the limiting term "previously formed."* Later (on September 15) the Convention reaffirmed this position by rejecting George Mason's motion to insert the word "previous" after the words "obligation of" in the contract clause.[45] Thus on two occasions the convention *rejected* the limitation that *Ogden* v. *Saunders* in effect read into the Constitution. The *Ogden* majority does not deny that the language of the Constitution covers postinsolvency law contracts. Rather it uses a fiction to escape that coverage.

The same fiction as we have seen would have sustained the opposite result. It is noteworthy that the decision in Ogden was reached by a four to three vote with one member of the majority observing, "I should be disingenuous were I to declare . . . that I embrace [the result] without a doubt of its correctness" (12 Wheaton at p. 254).

By the time of Marshall's dissent in *Ogden* (his only dissent on a constitutional issue), Jacksonianism was strong in the Supreme Court. *Ogden* is to private what *Charles River Bridge* is to public pledges. These two Jacksonian decisions constitute the first of a series of blows that would eventually eliminate the contract clause as a viable element in constitutional law. What C. P. Magrath wrote in 1966 had long been true: "the contract clause is [now] of negligible constitutional significance."[46] In due time even *Sturges* would be further qualified.[47] So too retrospective impairment of a public contract obligation became permissible.[48]

Some may find in these shifting progressive postures a pattern of affinity for the "common man" or underdog (debtors and those who do not have government contracts vis-à-vis creditors and those who do). If there is indeed such an affinity (read antiproperty bias), it was not plainly shared by the Founders; indeed Populist-Progressives charged them with an opposite bias. *In any event the liberal thrust has always been to restrict or abolish the contract clause by interpretation.* In this, as we have seen, it has been largely successful. Chief Justice Marshall, one suggests, merely opposed that tendency. Mr. Wright et al. consider this an "expansion of the contract clause."[49] That charge comes easily for those who accept the Populist-Progressive conspiracy view of American constitutional law. But does the contract clause reflect a plot by the rich against the poor? Or does it suggest merely that, mindful of unfortunate experience prior to 1787, the Founders opted inter alia for uniform, national treatment of the endless debtor-creditor tension via the bankruptcy power of Congress? Not the least of the old problem had been the multiplicity of state approaches; the geographic limitation upon each of them; and "the short-sighted, if not dishonorable, schemes of state legislatures to favor their debtor citizens as against [outside] creditors."[50]

Conclusion

Before 1939 Mr. Wright seems to have been a latter-day Populist-Progressive in the J. Allen Smith–Beard–Parrington tradition. A generation later, without mentioning his earlier work, he found that tradition untenable; this now seems the prevailing view.[51] Yet fighting faiths die hard. We are told that as the contract clause gradually all but withered away it was replaced by substantive due process, as though the two were essentially equivalent.[52] Surely that is a less than accurate appraisal. The contract clause is part of the Constitution's text; substantive (or economic) due process, a judicial gloss, was a crude abuse of the Constitution. The contract clause reflects the basic Lockean ideals of the Founders; substantive due process reflects a *perversion* of a much later laissez-faire ideal. Whatever one may think of some postbellum contract cases, Marshall's decisions (as suggested) are consistent with the letter and Lockean spirit of the Constitution. The substantive due process decisions are utterly at odds therewith and with democracy as well. Mr. Wright wrote *The Contract Clause and the Constitution* in the early 1930s when it was easy to be swayed by class consciousness. What he wrote in 1958 with respect to economic differences in the Constitutional Convention seems equally relevant with respect to early Supreme Court issues: "They were not [conflicts] between the burgeoisie and the proletariat but rather between rival bourgeois . . . interests."[53]

Two recent cases suggest a contract clause renaissance, a repudiation of the Populist-Progressive, in favor of the Founders' Lockean outlook.[54] Justices Brennan, White, and Marshall dissented with feeling. First in a public contract case, they quoted once again with approval Mr. Wright's undocumented view that the Founders "discussed the clause only in relation to private contracts."[55] A few months later the same dissenters condemned the Court for sustaining private contract obligations allegedly in the face of precedents "over the past 50 years."[56] Repudiating this classic Populist-Progressive fixation, the Court observed, as John Marshall might have, "The Contract Clause remains part of the Constitution. It is not a dead letter."[57]

NOTES

1. B. F. Wright, *Consensus and Continuity, 1776–1787* (1958), p. 53.
2. The classic statements of this view are found in J. Allen Smith, *The Growth and Decadence of Constitutional Government* (1907); Charles Beard, *An Economic Interpretation of the Constitution* (1913); Vernon L. Parrington, *Main Currents in American Thought* (1927).
3. See Smith.
4. Louis Hartz, *The Liberal Tradition in America* (1955), p. 27.
5. C. F. Adams, ed., *Works of John Adams*, vol. 6 (1851), p. 280.
6. John Taylor, *Construction Construed and Constitutions Vindicated* (1820), p. 67.
7. P. Ford, ed., *The Writings of Thomas Jefferson*, vol. 10 (1899), p. 39. Jefferson observed that the revolutionary mobs of Paris were composed of propertyless, and therefore insecure and dependent, "canaille." Later, despite constitutional qualms, he arranged the Louisiana Purchase to ensure inter alia that there need be no propertyless Americans. Richard Hofstadter, *The American Political Tradition* (1954), pp. 22, 31; C. and M. Beard, *The Rise of American Civilization*, vol. 1, (1927), pp. 385–86.
8. G. Hunt, ed., *Writings of James Madison*, vol. 6 (1906), p. 101.
9. 6 Cranch 87 (1810). This was the Supreme Court's first contracted clause decision.
10. B. F. Wright, *The Contract Clause and the Constitution* (1938), pp. 61, 86–87.
11. Wright, *Consensus and Continuity*, p. 41.
12. The contract clause, Article I, Section 10, of the Constitution provides: "No State shall enter into any treaty, alliance, or confederation; grant letters of marque and reprisal; coin money; emit bills of credit; make anything but gold and silver coin a tender in payment of debts; pass any bill of attainder, ex post facto law, or law impairing the obligations of contracts; or grant any title of nobility.
13. Wright, *The Contract Clause*, p. 15. Strangely, Mr. Wright makes no effort to support this assertion that is so crucial to his position. In the course of recognizing some support for a broader view he says that in two state-ratifying conventions there were "suggestions" (read "assertions") that the clause covered state agreements. In each instance he finds a brief counter-

assertion by a former member of the Constitutional Convention (one of these seems doubtful) (pp. 15–18).

14. Directors of the Old South Works, *Old South Leaflets,* vol. 2, p. 1, no. 26.

15. A. J. Beverige, *The Life of John Marshall,* vol. 3 (1919), p. 557. See also J. Madison, "Introduction to the Debates in the Federal Convention of 1787" in *The Papers of James Madison,* vol. 2 (1840), p. 712.

16. John C. Hamilton, *Works of Alexander Hamilton,* vol. 3 (1851), pp. 518–19.

17. Madison used the term *social compact* comprehensively. Following Locke, he did not distinguish sharply (if at all) between what Althusius called the social contract and the governmental contract. This usage was common in America. The Massachusetts Constitution of 1780, for example, declared itself to be "a social compact."

18. *Chisholm* v. *Georgia,* 2 Dallas 419 (1793).

19. *Van Horn's Lessee* v. *Dorrance,* 4 Dallas 14 (1800).

20. Reported in 226 Mass. 618 (1917). See also *University of North Carolina* v. *Foy,* 2 Hayw. 310 (N.C. 1804).

21. 2 Mass. 143 (1806).

22. *Dartmouth College* v. *Woodward,* 4 Wheaton 518 (1819).

23. The purchaser in *Fletcher* may not have been innocent (of knowledge of the fraud), but that matter, having been settled by demurrer, was not before the court.

24. "The Charles River Bridge Case," 27 *Massachusetts Law Quarterly,* 19–20 (1942). The writers on natural law referred to include, among others, Grotius, Vattel, Pufendorf, Vinnius, and Burlamaqui.

25. See, for example, V. L. Parrington, *Main Currents in American Literature,* vol. 2 (1927), chap. 3. (This opus is dedicated to J. Allen Smith, a leading Progressive anti-Marshall scholar. Note that those who charge the Marshall Court with illicit, proproperty bias seem to ignore the "antiproperty" elements in such cases as *Mason* v. *Haile,* 12 Wheaton 270 (1827); *Providence Bank* v. *Billings,* 4 Wheaton 514 (1830); *Barron* v. *Baltimore,* 7 Peters 243 (1833); and especially *Gibbons* v. *Ogden,* 9 Wheaton 1 (1824).

26. See note 23.

27. C. P. Magrath, *Yazoo: Law and Politics in the New Republic* (1966), chaps. 3, 6.

28. Wright, *The Contract Clause,* pp. 155–56; J. M. Shirley, *The Dartmouth College Causes and the Supreme Court of the United States* (1879).

29. A. M. Schlesinger, Jr., *The Age of Jackson* (1945), pp. 336–37.

30. Wheaton 1 (1824).

31. *Transactional freedom* as used here obviously is related to *the release of energy* principle discussed in Willard Hurst's classic, *Law and the Conditions of Freedom in Nineteenth Century America* (1956).

32. 4 Peters 514 (1830).

33. 11 Peters 420 (1837).

34. See, for example, *Northwestern Fertilizing Co.* v. *Hyde Park:* "Nothing is to be taken as conceded but which is given in unmistakable terms, *or by an implication equally clear*" (emphasis added).

35. See, for example, S. Kutler, *Privilege and Creative Destruction: The Charles River Bridge Case* (1971).

36. See *Charles River Bridge* v. *Warren Bridge,* 7 Pick. 344, 352, 379–80 (Mass. 1829).

37. See article 26, "New Light on *Fletcher* v. *Peck* and *Gibbons* v. *Ogden*."

38. J. A. Garraty, ed., "The Constitution: Was It an Economic Document?" in *Historical Viewpoints,* vol. 1 (1970), pp. 173–85.

39. In *Sturges* v. *Crowninshield,* 4 Wheaton 122 (1819), Marshall and his Court held that the national bankruptcy power does not preclude state insolvency measures.

40. Hunt, *Writings of James Madison,* vol. 5 (1906), p. 27.

41. M. Farrand, ed., *Records of the Federal Convention of 1787,* vol. 3 (1911), p. 548.

42. 4 Wheaton 122 (1819).

43. 12 Wheaton 213 (1827).

44. See notes 41 and 42 and related text.

45. Farrand, *Federal Convention,* vol. 4, p. 59.

46. Magrath, *Yazoo*, p. 109.

47. *Home Building and Loan Company* v. *Blaisdell*, 290 U.S. 398 (1934).

48. See *El Paso* v. *Simmons*, 379 U.S. 497 (1965), where Justice Black observed in dissent: "I have previously had a number of occasions to dissent from judgements of this Court balancing away the First Amendment's unequivocally guaranteed right of free speech, press, assembly and petition. In this case I am compelled to dissent from the Court's balancing away of the plain guarantee of [the Contract Clause], a balancing which results in the State of Texas taking a man's private property for public use without compensation."

49. Wright, *The Contract Clause*, chap. 2.

50. M. Isaacs, "John Marshall on Contracts: A Study in Early American Juristic Theory," 7 *Virginia Law Review* 413 (1921). See also note 15.

51. See R. Hofstadter, *The Progressive Historians* (1968), chap 12.

52. See, for example, Wright, *The Contract Clause*, p. 95.

53. Wright, *Consensus and Continuity*, p. 33.

54. See B. Schwartz, "Old Wine in New Bottles? The Renaissance of the Contract Clause," 1979 *Supreme Court Review* 95 (1980); *United States Trust Co.* v. *New Jersey*, 431 U.S. 1 (1977); and *Allied Structural Steel Co.* v. *Spannaus*, 438 U.S. 234 (1978).

55. *United States Trust Co.*, 431 U.S. at 45 n. 13 (Justice Brennan dissenting).

56. *Allied Structural Steel Co.*, 438 U.S. at 260 (Justice Brennan dissenting).

57. *Ibid*, at 241.

WALLACE MENDELSON is professor of government at the University of Texas at Austin. He has an LL.B. from Harvard (1936) and a Ph.D. from the University of Wisconsin (1940). His extra-academic work includes some four years of military service during World War II; a year with Mr. Justice Frankfurter (1953–1954); editor of the 1961 Report of the United States Civil Rights Commission; assistant to the Attorney General of the United States (1973); and at various times consultant to the National Endowment for the Humanities; regional representative, United States Civil Rights Commission; and regional representative, National Labor Relations Board. He has been president of the Southern Political Science Association and a member of the executive council of the American Political Science Association. He is author of several books and scores of articles on public law problems.